THE ART OF SIMPLE FOOD

ALICE WATERS

with

Patricia Curtan, Kelsie Kerr & Fritz Streiff

Illustrations by Patricia Curtan

Clarkson Potter / Publishers

New York

Also from Alice Waters and Chez Panisse

Chez Panisse Fruit

Chez Panisse Café Cookbook

Chez Panisse Vegetables

Fanny at Chez Panisse

Chez Panisse Cooking

Chez Panisse Desserts

Chez Panisse Pasta, Pizza, and Calzone

Chez Panisse Menu Cookbook

Copyright © 2007 by Alice Waters
Illustrations © 2007 by Patricia Curtan

All rights reserved.
Published in the United States by Clarkson Potter/Publishers,
an imprint of the Crown Publishing Group,
a division of Random House, Inc., New York.
www.crownpublishing.com
www.clarksonpotter.com

Clarkson N. Potter is a trademark and Potter and colophon
are registered trademarks of Random House, Inc.

Library of Congress Cataloging-in-Publication Data is
available upon request.

ISBN 978-0-307-33679-8

Printed in the United States of America

Design by Patricia Curtan

10 9 8 7 6 5 4 3 2 1

First Edition

For
Ella, Xavier, Fanny, Rose, and Zac
with love

CONTENTS

Part I: Starting from Scratch
Lessons & Foundation Recipes

Part II: At the Table
Recipes for Cooking Every Day

Part I:

Starting from Scratch

Lessons & Foundation Recipes

Introduction

My delicious revolution began when, young and naïve, I started a restaurant and went looking for good-tasting food to cook. I was trying to find ingredients like the ones I had loved when I was a student in France: simple things like lettuces, and green beans, and bread. I was searching for flavor, not philosophy, but what I found was that the people who were growing the tastiest food were organic farmers in my own backyard, small farmers and ranchers within a radius of a hundred miles or so of the restaurant who were planting heirloom varieties of fruits and vegetables and harvesting them at their peak. What was revolutionary about this was being able to buy directly from the source and not being limited to what I could find at the supermarket.

When you have the best and tastiest ingredients, you can cook very simply and the food will be extraordinary because it tastes like what it is. This is what we've learned at Chez Panisse after years of sourcing, preparing, and tasting food. Food tastes naturally delicious when it has been grown with care, harvested at the right moment, and brought to us immediately, direct from the producer. But food like this is not just the privilege of a restaurant like ours. The same local producers sell the same fresh food down the street, at the farmers' market. And anyone can buy it.

When I started shopping at farmers' markets, one of the best things about the experience was meeting farmers and learning from them—and influencing them, too, by asking if they could grow vegetables and fruits that had almost disappeared from commerce. After years of this weekly connection, I realized that I had become dependent on a family of friends—and they were dependent on me. By choosing to buy food grown locally and sustainably, in ways that are healthy and humane, I had woven myself into a community that cares about the same things. As a community, we share not only a commitment to protect our natural resources, but an appreciation for the value of food itself, a love for its taste and beauty and the deep pleasure it can bring by connecting us to time and place, the seasons, and the cycle of nature.

Good cooking is no mystery. You don't need years of culinary training, or rare and costly foodstuffs, or an encyclopedic knowledge of world cuisines. You need only your own five senses. You need good ingredients, too, of course, but in order to choose and prepare them, you need to experience them fully. It's the many dimensions of sensual experience that make cooking so satisfying. You never stop learning.

This book is for everyone who wants to learn to cook, or to become a better cook. The first part is a series of chapters that review the basics of simple food, beginning with how to choose fresh ingredients and stock a pantry and how to decide what to cook. The chapters that follow focus on essential cooking techniques, with detailed explanations of the whys and wherefores and simple model recipes. By cooking your way through these lessons, tasting and learning from your successes (and your mistakes), you will get to know some fundamental techniques by heart and you won't have to look them up again. This will enable you to cook with ease and confidence, inspired by recipes—rather than being ruled by them— and free to enjoy the sheer pleasure of preparing and sharing simple food with your friends and family. In the second half of the book you will find more recipes in the same format, chosen because they are easily made once you are familiar with the techniques set forth in the lessons.

I'm convinced that the underlying principles of good cooking are the same everywhere. These principles have less to do with recipes and techniques than they do with gathering good ingredients, which for me is the essence of cooking. Whenever I give cooking demonstrations, I put everything I will be cooking on display, and the audience is always wide-eyed and amazed at how beautiful it all is. They ask, "Where did you *get* that?!," and I answer, "At your farmers' market—and you can get it, too!" After all these years, I've distilled just about everything I know about cooking down to that—and a few other simple propositions. I've made a list of them here. I believe that if you follow them your cooking will be transformed. They are the principles of a delicious revolution, one that can reconnect our families and communities with the most basic human values, provide the deepest delight for all our senses, and assure our well-being for a lifetime.

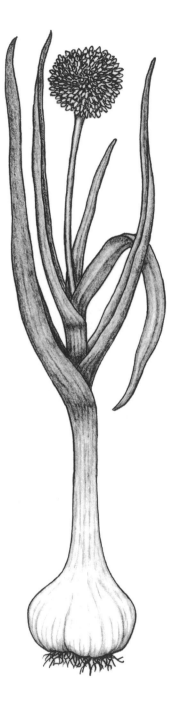

Eat locally and sustainably.

Learn where your food comes from and how it is produced. Seek out a diverse variety of vegetables and fruits from small, local producers who take care of the land. Buy eggs, meat, and fish from producers whose practices are organic, humane, and environmentally sound.

Eat seasonally.

Choose food in season. Even where the growing season is short, organic gardening and farming can extend it: greens can be grown in cold frames and greenhouses, and there are always local foods that can be stored, dried, and canned for the winter months. Eating seasonally inspires your menus, gives you a sense of time and place, and rewards you with the most flavorful food.

Shop at farmers' markets.

Farmers' markets create communities that value diversity, honesty, seasonality, locality, sustainability, and beauty. Get to know the people who grow your food. Think of yourself as a partner with the farmers, learning from them and working with them.

Plant a garden.

It is deeply satisfying to eat food you have grown yourself, in your own backyard or in a community garden. Even a pot of herbs on your windowsill can transform your cooking and connect you to the changing seasons, as can foraging for wild foods and harvesting fruit from farms that allow you to pick your own. Learn what the edible landscape has to offer.

Conserve, compost, and recycle.

Take your own basket to the market. Reuse whatever packaging you can. Keep a compost bucket nearby when you cook to recycle kitchen scraps. The more you conserve, the less you waste, the better you feel.

Cook simply, engaging all your senses.

Plan uncomplicated meals. Let things taste of what they are. Enjoy cooking as a sensory pleasure: touch, listen, watch, smell, and, above all, taste. Taste as you go. Keep tasting and keep practicing and discovering.

Cook together.

Include your family and friends, and especially children. When children grow, cook, and serve food, they want to eat it. The hands-on experience of gardening and cooking teaches children the value and pleasure of good food almost effortlessly.

Eat together.

No matter how modest the meal, create a special place to sit down together, and set the table with care and respect. Savor the ritual of the table. Mealtime is a time for empathy and generosity, a time to nourish and communicate.

Remember food is precious.

Good food can only come from good ingredients. Its proper price includes the cost of preserving the environment and paying fairly for the labor of the people who produce it. Food should never be taken for granted.

Getting Started

Ingredients and the Pantry

Equipment and Getting Organized

To become a cook you only need a few essentials: appetite, ingredients, a kitchen to work in, a few tools, and a few ideas about what to cook. But which comes first? Appetite, perhaps: the one thing that all the people I know who love to cook have in common is that they love to eat—and the desire to eat good food is what motivated them to become good cooks. They also take pleasure in thinking about food, imagining tastes and combinations of flavors, reading books and recipes, and cooking in their minds. Ideas of what to cook come from that thought process and from practice; certainly, you have to spend time in the kitchen before your own ideas come easily and before putting together a menu becomes instinctive. The way that I think about food and cooking comes from years of experience; by now, it's second nature. But how to teach how it works? I think the place to start is with ingredients: they have always been my best source of inspiration.

Ingredients

First, you have to have something to cook. The best place to look for the freshest, most seasonal ingredients, for fruits and vegetables—and for eggs and dairy products, too—is farmers' markets and markets that sell organic and locally grown foods. Go to the market with an open mind, before you decide what to cook. See what's there. Be open to what's available. The virtue of buying directly from the source is that you can learn from the producers themselves. In exchange you can influence their decisions about what to produce. Ask questions: What variety is this? How was it grown? How do you cook it? How long is it in season?

Insofar as possible, buy local food that is certified organic. But be aware that although food may be labeled organic, that does not mean it has been produced either locally or sustainably. One good way to shop for local, sustainably produced fruits and vegetables (and sometimes milk, eggs, and meat products) is to buy shares in a CSA farm. CSA stands for Community Supported Agriculture, and describes an agreement between consumers and producers in which individuals or families who make an annual commitment of support to a local farm receive a regular delivery (usually weekly) in exchange. Small family farms get cash up front to finance their operations and the consumer gets a diverse variety of fresh local food. CSA farms are growing in number all over the country.

During times of the year when there's no farmers' market, or if you are otherwise limited to a supermarket, don't hesitate to ask the management to stock healthy organic ingredients. Stick to the periphery of the store, where the fresh, unprocessed foods are usually found, and avoid the aisles upon aisles of processed food.

Certain foodstuffs I think of as essential provide my cooking with a solid foundation. These are the ingredients that I want to have available more or less all the time so that I will have lots of options for cooking the very fresh ingredients I bring home. A few are such absolute necessities to me that I sometimes travel with them, in case they are hard to find at my destination: these include olive oil and sea salt, good vinegar, garlic, and bread. (People tease me about this, but when I start unpacking these delicious things they can't wait to cook with them.) Simple and fundamental as they are, these products can be hard to find at just any market or store: depending on where you live, you may have to look in specialty stores, ethnic groceries, or health food stores. Before you resort to online resources, encourage the stores and markets in your area to stock the things you want.

The Pantry

AT HOME, my necessary foods fall into two groups that are loosely defined by how often they have to be replenished: the first group includes the longer-lasting staples such as flours and olive oil and the second consists of the relatively perishable fresh produce and dairy products that have to be refrigerated. If your pantry and refrigerator are stocked with these ingredients, you can be secure in the knowledge that no matter what time it is, and no matter who shows up hungry on your doorstep, there will always be something to eat.

Pantry Staples	Perishable Staples
olive oil	garlic
vinegars	onions
salt	shallots
black peppercorns	celery
spices	carrots
pasta	olives
polenta and cornmeal	fresh herbs
rice	eggs
dried beans	lemons
canned tomatoes	mustard
anchovies	cheese
capers	nuts
flours	chicken broth
sugar	butter
baking powder and baking soda	milk
vanilla	bread
yeast	potatoes
jam	
wine	

Pantry Staples

Olive oil

I couldn't cook without olive oil. I usually have two grades on hand: a less expensive, neutral-flavored olive oil for cooking, and a more highly flavored fruity extra-virgin olive oil to use on salads and as a sauce, for finishing dishes. Although good-quality olive oil is expensive compared to other ingredients, there's no comparing how it transforms the simplest foods. I can't count how many times I have been asked, "How did you make that?!," and my reply has been, "I just cooked it, salted it, and poured a little olive oil over it."

Extra-virgin olive oil is made simply by crushing olives, with no heating, refining, or further processing other than settling, separating out the water, and filtering. There are a number of olive varieties, each of which has its own unique flavor. Some extra-virgin olive oils have round, rich fruity flavors, and others are spicy, with green vegetal aromas and flavors. Most have a distinctive lingering peppery finish. High-quality oils are imported from Mediterranean countries, and more and more are being produced in California. Taste as many varieties as possible. Specialty stores and markets often have bottles open to taste. If you use a lot of olive oil, it is economical to buy it by the case; you can often get a discount. Look at it as a semiannual investment in some very good eating. Always store olive oil in a cool, dark place, because heat and light can harm it.

Vinegars

Good unpasteurized wine vinegar is the kind you want and it really does make a difference, whether it's made from white wine, red wine, or sherry. The good ones cost a little more, but they are well worth it. Wine vinegar you make yourself will probably be better than most vinegar you can buy. Most commercial balsamic vinegars are too sweet for me. Genuine, artisanal Italian balsamico from Modena is staggeringly expensive and is meant to be used literally by the drop. Keep a small bottle of rice wine vinegar on hand, for sushi rice and for dressing cucumbers. Tightly corked and stored out of the sun, vinegars keep almost indefinitely. Do not be put off if a cloudy mass (called a mother) begins to grow in the bottom of the bottle. This is a natural part of fermentation and is harmless to you and to the vinegar.

Salt

Learning how to salt food, when and how much, is one of the most important things you can do to make what you are cooking taste as flavorful as posssible.

Using good sea salt is one of the easiest things you can do to make your food taste better. Sea salt contains trace minerals that give it a stronger, saltier, more complex flavor than ordinary table salt, which contains chemicals to keep it from clumping that affect the flavor of everything you use it on. I keep two kinds of sea salt close by: a very coarse one sold in bulk (the gray kind, with its high mineral content, is especially good) for salting boiling water and brine, and a finer, flakier one for seasoning and finishing dishes. Perhaps the biggest "secret" to good cooking is knowing how to season with salt. Too much makes food taste salty, of course, but undersalted food tastes bland. Salt brings out the flavor of whatever is being cooked, but it also gets concentrated if you are boiling something down. Keep tasting, learn how salt works with flavor, and use it to get the most out of what you are cooking.

Black peppercorns

When pepper is ground it immediately starts losing the flavor and aroma of its volatile oils, so it should be ground just before using. Keep a pepper mill near the stove that you can reach for whenever you need it. For the freshest peppercorns, buy in small quantities from a market that sells them in bulk.

Spices

Other staple spices to keep on hand are bay leaves, cumin seed, fennel seed, aniseed, dried chiles, cayenne pepper, nutmeg, cinnamon, cloves, cardamom, and ground ginger. Whatever spices you use, they should be fresh and fragrant. Buy them in small quantities, and replenish them often. Buy from markets with a high turnover.

Pasta

Stock two or three kinds of dried pasta, in the shapes you like. My staple dried pasta choices are spaghettini, fusilli, and egg noodles. Look for pasta that is made from durum wheat or semolina, which will cook up with more texture and flavor than that made from other flours.

Polenta and cornmeal

There are more and more small mills around the country grinding local corn into fresh whole-grain polenta and cornmeal. Buy them in small amounts and store in a cool part of the house or in the refrigerator, especially in the warm months of the year.

Rice

Stock two or three kinds: short-grain varieties for risottos and sushi and a long-grain variety such as basmati. Store rice away from sunlight.

Dried beans

Keep several jars of dried beans in your cupboard. I usually have lentils, chickpeas, cannellini beans, and sometimes another kind or two. Like any product bought in bulk, beans should be labeled and dated so you remember to use them up within a year or so.

Canned tomatoes

If you don't freeze or can tomatoes yourself, buy canned whole organic tomatoes; the cans of diced, crushed, or puréed tomatoes never seem to taste as good or cook as well.

Salt-packed anchovies

Good anchovies not only pack a lot of strong flavor on their own, they enhance the flavors of other ingredients with their complex saltiness. They are indispensable in sauces such as salsa verde and bagna cauda. I think anchovies that are left on the bone and packed in salt have better flavor and texture than those that are filleted and packed in oil or brine. Look for the big imported cans that weigh over a pound. When you open the can, keep it wrapped or bagged in the refrigerator, or better, repack the anchovies in a nonmetallic container. Covered with a layer of moist salt, the fish should keep up to a year. To use, soak them for up to 10 minutes or so in a little cold water to soften; then gently pull the two fillets off the bones. Remove any clinging scales, the fins, and the tail, and rinse the fillets clean.

Capers

Buy good-size capers that are salt-packed, if possible; they have more flavor. Store in the refrigerator. To use, rinse off the salt, soak them for a while, drain, and squeeze dry. Capers packed in brine should also be soaked, rinsed, and squeezed. Capers are good in salsa verde and other sauces, and they add pizzazz and punch to egg salad.

Flours

Fresh, unbleached, all-purpose flour is far superior in flavor and performance to bleached flour. Cake flour is useful to have on hand if you bake cakes often. I recommend buying flours in bulk. To monitor their freshness: sniff when you open the bin. They should smell fresh, with no sign of rancidity or staleness. Replenish your flour every few months. All flours go stale faster when exposed to direct sunlight. Whole-grain flours should be stored in the refrigerator.

Sugar

Organic sugar—granulated, brown, or powdered—is less refined than conventional white sugar. It retains more flavor and nutrients, but it burns more quickly. Desserts that depend on caramelization, such as flans and tartes Tatins, are a little harder to make with organic granulated sugar, because it caramelizes less evenly than refined granulated sugar.

Baking powder and baking soda

Baking powder and baking soda are both chemical leavening agents. Depending on the brand, baking powder may contain sodium aluminum sulfate, which I find gives food an unpleasant metallic taste. Look for a brand without it. Baking powder has a relatively short shelf life; replace it after about a year.

Vanilla bean and vanilla extract

Vanilla beans are wonderful for flavoring custards and ice cream. Keep them tightly wrapped and store them out of direct light. When you buy vanilla extract make sure it contains only pure vanilla bean extract and not synthetic vanillin, an artificial flavoring, which is quite bitter. Organic vanilla is widely available.

Yeast

The yeast called for in this book is active dry yeast, which will keep for months stored in the refrigerator in a tightly closed container.

Jam

I like to have some jam on hand to glaze fruit tarts as well as for spreading on breakfast toast or for topping pancakes. Apricot is a favorite, and so are orange and lemon marmalades.

Wine

Wine is useful for some sauces, for risottos, and for moistening braises. Except for desserts, I prefer to cook with wines that are simple and dry, without any pronounced oaky flavors. Such wines compete less with the flavors of what is being cooked. Keep any unused wine tightly corked and refrigerated.

Perishable Staples

THE ESSENTIAL PERISHABLES are the fresh ingredients that you need on hand for a wide variety of dishes: simple salads and dressings, soups and stews, quick meals of pasta or eggs, and so on. They are the things you automatically check on before you go to the market, and they are all available just about year round.

Garlic

Garlic is at the top of the list for things I need in my pantry. It is a rare day that I don't use it for something: to flavor a vinaigrette, a pasta sauce, a marinade, or just to rub on a piece of toast. Store garlic in a dark, ventilated place to discourage it from sprouting. The only garlic that should be refrigerated is spring or green garlic, which should be kept in a plastic bag to keep it from drying out.

Onions

Onions are indispensable for countless dishes—broths, soups, braises, stews—and as a base to many pasta sauces and vegetable dishes. Look for all the different varieties of onions that are available throughout the year. Spring onions and green onions should be stored in the refrigerator. Onions with dry, papery skin should be kept in a dark, well-ventilated place.

Shallots

The shallot is a small-bulbed variety of onion with a distinctive character of its own, both less hot and more intense than that of other onions. I keep them on hand mostly for salads (diced very fine, macerated in a little vinegar, and made into a vinaigrette sauce) and for a few classic sauces. Store them like other onions, in a cool, dark, airy place.

Celery

Along with carrots and onions, celery is one of the so-called aromatic vegetables that provide indispensable background flavor to all sorts of classic stocks, stews, braises, and sautés. When the aromatics are chopped uniformly, combined, and gently sautéed, they constitute what is called a *mirepoix*.

Carrots

Choose carrots that are loose or bunched, not bagged, with fresh-looking tops (if they still have them). Carrot peel has a bitter taste, so carrots should be peeled, with the exception of the tiniest new ones you sometimes get at farmers' markets. Cut off the tops before refrigerating the carrots, and peel them just before using.

Olives

Taste olives to see which kinds you like, and taste them again whenever you buy: they vary a great deal. I prefer the flavor of whole unpitted olives. The ones I use most are black niçoises, Nyon, and Kalamatas, and green Picholines and Lucques. Niçoises are especially good for cooking. Olives are an instant hors d'oeuvre, the perfect thing to have with a glass of wine if someone drops by.

Fresh herbs

Fresh herbs are vital to my cooking. Parsley, thyme, rosemary, sage, basil, mint, marjoram, oregano, winter and summer savory, chives, tarragon, chervil—I use them constantly. Branches and bouquets of herbs flavor stocks, soups, roasts, and stews; the leaves of tender herbs are tossed into salads; chopped herbs are scattered over any number of dishes to add a final burst of freshness. An easy way to keep fresh herbs on hand is to grow them. Many herbs are amazingly hardy and will grow almost anywhere. Even if you don't have a garden, grow a pot or two of herbs in a sunny window. When buying herbs look for lively, perky bunches.

Eggs

If you have eggs, you can always make something to eat. Pay close attention to how they were produced. Organic eggs from a nearby farm that treats its chickens well will be fresher, healthier, and easier to separate; they will rise higher; and they will taste remarkably better than factory-produced eggs.

Lemons

A squeeze of lemon juice can brighten a dish at the last minute. Lemons are also used for sauces, in baking, with fish, and for the occasional glass of lemonade. The peel—more precisely, the yellow part of the peel, the zest—is used for flavoring, too, either grated or peeled off in paper-thin slices with a vegetable peeler and chopped. I also candy lemon peel and offer it with dessert—or as a dessert all by itseslf. Lemons keep best in the refrigerator.

Mustard

Prepared mustard, with its combination of heat (from the mustard seed) and acid (from vinegar), is another ingredient that adds lots of flavor. I prefer Dijon-style mustards because they are rarely sweetened and their pungency is unadulterated by turmeric and other spices. Keep some on hand to stir into salad dressings and sauces and to serve as a condiment with sausages or a boiled dinner.

Cheese

When possible, shop where you can taste the cheese for freshness or at a busy market with a high turnover of cheese. Always check the date on the wrapper. For best flavor, grate or slice cheeses at the last minute. Keep a few kinds on hand, including a hard grating cheese such as Parmesan or grana padana. (Italian Parmigiano-Reggiano is the original Parmesan cheese; it is expensive, but it makes a remarkable difference in your cooking.) A softer melting cheese such as Monterey Jack is good for making quesadillas or grilled cheese sandwiches. Gruyère is excellent in sandwiches, omelets, gratins, and soufflés—and just by itself, too. Look at farmers' markets for handmade, locally produced cheeses such as soft fresh goat cheeses.

Nuts

Keep nuts on hand to use in salads and baking and to be roasted at a moment's notice for a tasty little something to offer unexpected visitors. Nuts are harvested in the fall, and they have exceptional flavor at that time of the year. Keep them in the refrigerator; they will stay fresh for only a few months. Never store nuts in direct light. They can go rancid quite easily, and they will taste terrible. A sniff will tell you all you need to know. Buy nuts in bulk: they are more likely to be fresh when sold that way.

Chicken broth

Chicken broth is a wonderful ingredient to keep on hand as a staple. It is easy to make in large amounts and freeze in small quantities. Soups, stews, risottos, and sauces always taste better made with good home-made broth than with stock from a can or a box. You can freeze the bones and carcasses from roasted chickens and use them to make a stock later (with the addition of either a whole uncooked chicken or chicken pieces), a couple of gallons at a time.

Butter

Butter is used for sauces, frying, finishing vegetables, baking—and sometimes just to spread on a piece of bread. It freezes very well. If you don't use butter very often, keep one stick in the refrigerator at a time and store the rest in the freezer, sealed tightly. Butter absorbs unwelcome flavors and rapidly deteriorates. Whether it is salted or not is a matter of personal preference (although salted butter seems to keep better). When you use salted butter in baking, remember to adjust the salt accordingly: a stick of salted butter contains about ¼ teaspoon of salt.

Milk

Read the label. Support local, organic dairy farming, and buy milk and cream that is hormone- and additive-free. Avoid ultra-pasteurized milk and cream (sometimes labeled UHT, for the ultra-high temperature at which it is sterilized); health issues aside, UHT cream and milk perform poorly in the kitchen.

Bread

One of the lessons that follows deals entirely with bread, which I serve in one form or another at nearly every meal. I find the most versatile everyday bread to be whole crusty country-style loaves, the kind that are naturally leavened and slow-rising. Properly stored, it keeps for days. Bread need never be wasted. You can turn it into breadcrumbs to sprinkle over a gratin or into dried-out slices to ladle your soup over; and it freezes well.

Potatoes

Depending on the time of year and the local crop, it should be possible to keep a few different kinds of potatoes on hand: for example, the small fingerling types for roasting whole, larger Yellow Finns for gratins and mashing, russets for pan-frying, and, in season, the true new potatoes with their fragile papery skins. Except for new potatoes, which should be refrigerated and eaten quickly, most potatoes will keep for weeks in a dark place with a cool temperature and good air circulation. Any sign of green skin on potatoes indicates the presence of a toxin and is a sign not to buy them—or to throw them away.

Cooking from the Pantry

If you have a pantry stocked with only the staples and ingredients listed on pages 11–20 you can make a surprising number of dishes.

Soups	Rice
Chicken broth	Plain rice
Garlic soup	Red rice pilaf
Carrot soup	Risotto
Minestrone	
Chicken noodle soup	Pasta and Polenta
Chicken rice soup	Spaghettini with oil and garlic
Onion soup	Pasta with anchovy and parsley
Panade	Egg noodles, butter, and
Bean soup	Parmesan
Bean and pasta soup	Fusilli and cheese gratin
Tomato soup	Pasta with white beans
Potato soup	Fusilli and tomato sauce
Polentina	Spaghettini alla puttanesca

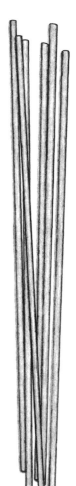

Polenta
Polenta torta

Cheese and Eggs
Grilled cheese sandwich
Cheese soufflé
Cheese and herb omelet
Hard-cooked eggs
Stuffed eggs
Egg salad
Eggs any style

Croutons
Bean purée
Garlic and oil
Tapenade
Anchovy
Cheese

Vegetables
Fried potatoes
Mashed potatoes
Potato salad
Potato cakes
Roasted potatoes
Baked spicy onions
Roast garlic
Roast shallots
Potato and garlic purée
Grilled onions
Onion tart
Braised celery
Bagna cauda
Glazed carrots
Grated carrot salad
Carrot purée
Marinated olives and toasted nuts

Sauces
Vinaigrette
Salsa verde
Mayonnaise
  (mustard, lemon, herb, aïoli)
Herb butter
  (anchovy butter, garlic butter)
Béarnaise sauce
Hollandaise sauce

Breads and Pancakes
Pizza
Herb bread
Cornbread
Biscuits
Soda bread
Pancakes
Waffles
Blini

Desserts
Pouring custard
Flan
Crème caramel
Bread pudding
Lemon curd
Lemon tart
Lemon sherbet
Tart dough
Sweet tart dough
Butter cookies
1-2-3-4 cake

Equipment

I AM A MINIMALIST in the equipment department. I don't like a lot of gadgets and I don't like cluttering up the kitchen with things I rarely use. My friends tease me and call me a Luddite because I don't particularly like even small electrical appliances. Instead, I love to use a mortar and pestle and have hands-on contact with the food. That may be unusual these days, but I've found you don't really need that much equipment. I tend to use the same few knives and pots and pans over and over again. What matters is, they're comfortable, well made, hard-wearing, and long-lasting.

The list of equipment given here contains everything you might need to make all the recipes in this book, but if you're starting from scratch and outfitting a kitchen on a limited budget, spend your money on two or three very good knives and a few pieces of good, heavy heat-conductive cookware. These are truly lifetime investments. Acquire other equipment piecemeal, when you can afford it, at your own pace. Don't overlook garage sales and thrift stores for such equipment as cast-iron skillets, pasta machines, baking pans and dishes, and small tools.

Knives

Knives should be comfortable to hold, they should be well balanced, and they should fit your hand. They don't have to be heavy, and you don't need as many of them as you think you do. Start with one paring knife, with a three- to four-inch-long blade; one chef's knife, with an eight-inch blade; and a long serrated knife for cutting bread. The best kitchen knives have a relatively high carbon-steel content, which makes them softer and easier to keep sharp; when harder stainless-steel knives lose their edge they are difficult to sharpen at home. Find knives that you like and then take care of them: wash and dry the blade after every use, don't leave knives in the sink or put them in the dishwasher, and keep them sharp! It's a good idea to hone a knife regularly by stroking it a few times on a sharpening steel (a very hard steel rod with a handle), at a twenty-degree angle. When a knife has lost its edge, sharpen it on a whetstone or take it to a professional knife-sharpener.

Cutting board

Your cutting board should be big enough to work on, with a surface area of at least a couple of square feet. I prefer wooden cutting boards; they are more beautiful than plastic ones and are easier on knives. To maintain, keep them clean and dry and out of the dishwasher. Wash a cutting board with soap and water and scrape it dry with a bench scraper. Oil it with mineral oil or olive oil every once in a while when the wood looks dry.

Heavy-bottomed pots and pans

Your pots and pans should be heavy-duty and solid with thick, heavy bottoms and sides that disperse the heat evenly, not just on the bottom of the pan, but up the sides as well. Pans like this will stay flat without warping when they are placed over direct heat. Cookware that meets these standards may be made out of copper, cast iron, or aluminum clad with stainless steel.

Recipes often call for nonreactive pots and pans, because some metals react chemically with acidic foods, causing metallic flavors and discoloration of both food and cooking vessel. Nonreactive pots and pans either are made of stainless steel, earthenware, or enameled cast iron, or else are lined with nonreactive stainless steel. Cast-iron pans are virtually nonreactive if they are well seasoned (heated and reheated with a film of oil, which gradually forms a nonstick surface).

This is the core group of pots and pans that I use most often:

10-inch cast-iron skillet, well seasoned
12-inch stainless-steel–lined sauté pan
2- to 3-quart stainless-steel–lined saucepan with lid
3- to 4-gallon stockpot
4- to 6-quart ovenproof pot with lid
3-quart shallow saucepan, or saucier
1-quart saucepan

Earthenware

Earthenware, glazed on the inside and sometimes the outside, is particularly good for slow, even cooking. Earthenware pots should be seasoned before their first use: after being soaked in water overnight, then filled with water and simmered for a few hours, they can be used in the oven and on the stovetop, over low to medium heat. It's a good idea to protect them from a direct flame with a flame-taming insulating pad.

Most versatile are gratin dishes of various sizes (these are shallow, low-sided baking dishes, 2 to 3 inches deep, with a large surface area), and a bean pot or soup pot with a capacity of at least 4 to 6 quarts and a lid.

Bowls

A set of relatively lightweight nesting mixing bowls is always useful; they don't have to be fancy.

Colanders and sieves

I routinely use two colanders, for draining and transferring washed salad greens and the like. It also helps to have a couple of sieves or strainers of different sizes, at least one of which should have a fine-mesh stainless-steel screen.

Salad spinner

A salad spinner is very useful for drying greens. Look for sturdy ones, either the hand-crank type or the pump type, which has the advantage of a nonskid bottom.

Food mill

For certain preparations, a food mill is preferable to a food processor or a blender because it will purée food without aerating it.

Pasta machine

Pasta can be rolled and cut by hand, but the Italian hand-crank machines are great for kneading and rolling, and for making long sheets of pasta for lasagna and ravioli.

Mortars and pestles

A large mortar with a capacity of two cups or more is most versatile, but a smaller one is fine for many pounding chores, such as pulverizing spices, seeds, garlic, and ginger, for example. The Japanese suribachi consists of an earthenware bowl with a pattern of striated sharp ridges on its unglazed inside surface and a wooden pestle.

Baking sheets

Standard home baking sheets are about 12 by 18 inches and flat, with just one edge turned up as a lip for easier handling. When they have sides, these are called jelly-roll pans or half-sheet pans. (Sheet pans are about 18 by 24 inches, too big for most home ovens.) It is worth your while to go to a cooking equipment store or a restaurant supply store and buy two professional-weight half-sheet pans: at best, the thin light-weight kind will never brown cookies evenly and, at worst, it will warp and burn.

Pan liners

Used to line baking sheets and cake pans, parchment paper prevents food from sticking and makes cleanup easier. The nonstick liners made of woven glass and silicone called Silpat mats are equally effective, and are reusable.

Baking pans

I own a 9½-inch springform cake pan, two 9 by 2-inch round cake pans, one 9 by 3-inch round cake pan, an angel food cake pan, and a muffin tin, as well as several pie pans. Look for pie pans that are relatively deep. You may also want to acquire both a 9-inch round tart pan with a removable bottom and several more pans: such as 4-inch round pans with removable bottoms and little mini-tartlet pans, which come in several shapes.

Food processor or blender

I am not one for food processors in general, but it is very difficult to make fresh breadcrumbs of the right texture without either a food processor or a blender. And a blender is very good for puréeing soups.

Stand mixer
A sturdy mixer with a strong motor is best, especially for making bread dough, but they are not inexpensive. Although mixers are labor saving, you can make the recipes included here by hand without one.

Ice cream maker
There are many products to choose from, and most will do the job. Choose one that suits your budget and storage capacity.

Toaster oven
My favorite appliance is a small toaster oven, especially for making croutons and toasting nuts.

Small Tools

Tongs
Look for tongs that are spring-loaded, lightweight, and about 10 inches long. Restaurant supply houses are good sources. Avoid the kind of tongs that lock shut with a sliding metal band: they pinch!

Spider
A spider is a big wire skimming spoon for lifting solids out of liquid (imagine a spider's web at the end of a rigid handle). The Chinese ones with bamboo handles are very inexpensive and widely available.

Metal spatulas
A large one for turning pancakes and such, and a small trowel-shaped offset one for frosting and smoothing.

Pepper grinder
Rubber spatula
Wooden spoons
Large metal spoon and slotted spoon
Ladle
Whisk
Vegetable peeler
Can opener
Instant-read thermometer
Oven thermometer
Steamer basket
Oyster knife

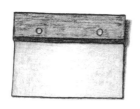

Zester

The type that has a ½-inch metal row of small sharp holes does a delicate and excellent job of cutting fine, thin strips of peel.

Graters

Box graters are a little easier to use than flat ones for cheese, but the flat ones manufactured by Microplane are usually sharper. It's useful to have two: one for zest and nutmeg and the like and a coarser one for cheese.

Measuring cups and spoons

You will need a marked spouted measuring cup for liquids that holds at least two cups and a set of nesting measuring cups for dry ingredients.

Bowl scraper

A flexible oval plastic disc used for folding and scraping.

Bench scraper

These are blunt rectangular metal blades with a plastic or wood handle. They are used for working and cutting dough and for cleaning up a sticky, doughy work surface. They are very useful for scooping up chopped onions and such or for doing very rough chopping.

Rolling pin
Pastry brush(es)
Pastry bag and tips
Juicer
Kitchen towels
Cotton string
Corkscrew

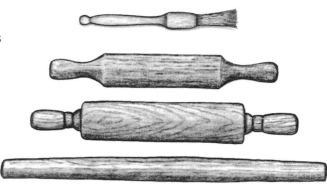

Getting Organized

A RECIPE IS A GUIDE to cooking a specific dish, but preparing it should not be a rote exercise. Even a well-written recipe, with accurate measurements and correct proportions, cannot be made successfully without your active engagement. This starts well before the cooking begins. Your first step is to read the recipe all the way through, developing a vivid mental picture of what it is you are going to cook, complete with aromas and tastes. Then read the recipe again, but this time take notes—mental or on paper—of the ingredients used and the amounts needed, the techniques employed, the order of events, and the timing. After this you should have a pretty good idea of what the final outcome will look and taste like and how to get there. If any parts of the recipe are hazy or confusing, take the time to research or review them until you feel comfortable. You will have the most success if you understand the entire process before you begin. When I try a new recipe I often write out a shorthand version of it in my own words, sort of a personalized map of the process. When you are well prepared, the cooking will flow along without your having to stop and look something up while the pots and pans sizzle away.

After reading the recipe through and familiarizing yourself with the techniques and ingredients needed, the next thing to do is organize your ingredients and equipment. This is a crucial part of cooking. Take things out of the refrigerator that need to be at room temperature. Wash, peel, chop, and measure the ingredients as directed in the recipe. Put them in bowls or colanders or on plates, in order to transport them easily when they are needed. Gather the equipment that you will need to execute the recipe. Have at your fingertips all the small tools, bowls, pots, and pans that you will need. Preheat the oven and rearrange the racks if necessary. All this preparation is referred to as your *mise en place*, a French phrase that means "put in place." When everything is in its place, you can cook without any mad rushes to prepare something you've overlooked while something else is threatening to burn or otherwise fall apart. The mise en place is also a source of aesthetic pleasure: laying out the prepared ingredients and arranging them in the order in which they will be used, in bowls that please you, can be enormously satisfying.

Cutting Techniques

Cutting and preparing vegetables and other foods becomes second nature once you acquire a few basic knife skills and techniques. Sharp knives that have a comfortable weight and balance in the hand are essential. The rest depends on practice—and on a familiarity with the vocabulary of recipes.

Chop means to cut into pieces, cutting smaller and smaller until you achieve the desired size. Chopping is most appropriate for ingredients such as herbs, greens, zest, olives, and capers.

To chop herbs, make a pile of leaves and cut them into small pieces. Use the fingers of your free hand to press down lightly on the end of the knife to steady and guide the blade as you rock it up and down and back and forth through the herbs. Hold the knife handle lightly with your fingertips: a light touch allows more control and efficient movement. Continue chopping the herbs, sweeping the pile together again occasionally, until they are chopped as fine as you want them.

Dice means to cut into cubes. In general, I find it faster and easier to dice rather than chop most vegetables. Sometimes an even dice is desirable, but for the most part, when a recipe says to dice, I do a quick, informal dice and don't worry about making precise cubes. Think of what you are cutting as a grid. Cut even slices in one direction, then cut the slices (in a stack or not) into even-sized baton or matchstick shapes, then cut across the matchsticks into cubes. The thinner the slice, the finer the dice.

To dice onions and other round vegetables such as shallots or fennel bulbs, trim the stem and root ends, leaving most of the root end. Cut in half lengthwise and peel off the outer layers from each half. Put the halves on a cutting board, cut sides down; rest but don't press your open palm on an onion half to steady it, and, with the knife parallel to the cutting board, make a few cuts horizontally, starting at the stem end and cutting to, but not through, the root end. Then use the tip of the knife to make several vertical cuts straight down, again cutting just to the root end but not through it. Slice crosswise into dice and discard the root end. Chop further for a finer texture. The size of dice is determined by the number of vertical and horizontal (if any) cuts initially made.

It is even easier to cut garlic cloves this way into a fine dice, one clove at a time, than to chop a number of whole cloves, repeatedly chopping

them down to a fine texture. Dicing also has the advantage of cutting cleanly through a vegetable, especially for shallots, garlic, and onions, where chopping sometimes smashes as much as cuts the food.

Mince means to chop very fine. First dice the food—garlic, for example—very fine and then chop it even finer.

Julienne is the technique of cutting food into thin matchstick shapes, requiring only the first two steps of the dicing technique. A classic julienne is 2 inches by ⅛ inch by ⅛ inch. First cut the vegetable into 2-inch lengths, cut the lengths into ⅛-inch slices, and then cut the slices into ⅛-inch matchsticks. For vegetables such as carrots, cut off a thin lengthwise slice and rest the vegetable on this flat surface to keep it from rolling while you are cutting it. For a smaller, finer julienne, very thin and even slices can be cut with a mandoline, stacked a few layers high (or overlapped), and cut into matchsticks with a knife. These matchsticks can be turned into a beautiful, fine dice.

Chiffonade means a preparation of leafy herbs, lettuces, or greens cut into thin strips or ribbons. To make a chiffonade, neatly pile the leaves one on top of another and then roll the pile up lengthwise into a neat cigar. Slice the roll of leaves crosswise, cutting it into very thin ribbons. This works especially well for basil, which oxidizes when cut. Chopped, it turns black, but when cut in chiffonade, only the edges discolor and the rest stays bright green.

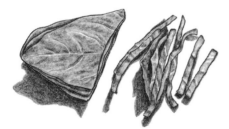

What to Cook?

Planning Menus

Everyday Meals and Friends for Dinner

Picnics and Packing a Lunch

A T SOME POINT IN EVERY DAY, the question arises, "What's for dinner?" That is when I try to collect my thoughts and decide what to cook. I embark on an internal dialog that's different every time: What do I feel like having? Who else is eating? What's the weather like? How much time do I have? How much energy do I want to put into it? What's in the fridge? What's at the market? What's my budget? As you answer these questions, different solutions will suggest themselves and you'll go back and forth, weighing the alternatives. The process has a rhythm of its own, whether you're deciding on a menu for a simple family meal at home or for a gathering of friends celebrating a special occasion.

Planning Menus

WHEN PLANNING MENUS, I try to think fluidly and consider the possibilities for more than one day at a time. When you cook regularly, you fall naturally into a routine of planning ahead a little. I find that the key is to shop well so that I have a good selection of ingredients on hand: some meats and poultry perhaps, a variety of vegetables, salad, and fruit. After shopping, I come home and make a few preparations: season the chicken, marinate pork chops with herbs and seasoning, soak some beans. Having these things in the refrigerator, ready to cook, is a comforting start: I don't have to worry at the last minute, or at the end of a tiring day, about what I can possibly make for dinner. Instead I can consider which of those things I want to cook and what to combine with them. Usually I will begin with a primary ingredient such as a chicken. I may decide to roast it, and then I choose a vegetable or a combination of vegetables, or rice or salad and so on, mentally reviewing the contents of the refrigerator and the pantry. In the process, the ingredients I don't choose become the basis of the next night's dinner.

This process is typical for me because I like to shop without a detailed plan, feeling open to whatever looks best at the market and is particularly fresh and of the season. I then make menus around what I find. Another approach is to plan some menu ideas and a shopping list before going to the market, and that can be a stimulating way to think through ideas and be organized and efficient. However, it is good to be able to alter the plan and the list on the fly to accommodate the discoveries at the market. If you have really good ingredients you can always make something delicious with them.

When making a simple family meal around something like a roast chicken, I tend to think in pairs of accompanying dishes that achieve a balance of flavor, color, and texture. I also consider how much time and energy is available. After settling on the main dish, I may add a salad (or not) and some fresh fruit or a fruit dessert.

Here are some sample menu ideas:

Roast Chicken and . . .

Roasted potatoes, and garden salad with garlic vinaigrette
Steamed turnips and turnip greens with basmati rice
Wilted greens with garlic, and potato and celery root purée
Roasted winter squash with sage, and polenta
Roasted eggplant and baked tomatoes with salsa verde
Steamed cauliflower with lemon and capers and aïoli
Green bean and cherry tomato salad
Glazed carrots and sautéed mushrooms
Asparagus with olive oil, lemon, and Parmesan

To develop your menu ideas, start with a simple repertoire of your favorite dishes. Then look for other sources and recipes. Talk to your friends to find out what they're cooking. Make mental notes about what you like to eat and what sounds good. Interview those that share your table and kitchen. Use this information to slowly expand your repertoire, revisiting old favorites with different flavors or refined techniques. Capitalize on the seasons, experimenting with various ways to cook and eat the same vegetables.

Many times the best dish is the simplest: vegetables steamed or sautéed and finished with a bit of olive oil or butter and lemon; or a steak, a chop, or a chicken seasoned with salt, fresh-ground black pepper, and herbs and quickly grilled, fried, or roasted. These fast, easy dishes require minimal time and experience but offer maximum flavor.

Some days you may feel like spending a little more time and energy in the kitchen, making a stew or braise, a vegetable gratin or ragout, or a fruit tart or a crisp. The stew or braise can be made in quantity for another meal later in the week, while a complex vegetable dish can be the center of a gratifying meal that satisfies nutritionally and sensually.

Experiment with different ways to make shopping and cooking fit into your schedule. Have your family help with planning the menus. Spend a day cooking together; this can be a nice way to spend time together and cook several things to last through the week. Have friends over to cook together, sharing the work and the table and making enough so that everyone has a portion to take home.

Everyday Meals

People always ask me for ideas for everyday meals—not restaurant food or special-occasion dinners, but just regular dinners at home. ("Please, just tell me what to cook. I can't think of anything.") What makes a good meal is not how fancy it is or how difficult and complicated the preparations are, but how satisfying it is. I'm satisfied when a meal balances flavor, color, and texture, when I've enjoyed cooking it, and when it is presented with care. An all-white meal, or one that is all soft, is not nearly as agreeable as one that has a variety of colors and textures. Flavors should complement each other and meld into a whole, not rival one another for dominance. A dinner that has left me stressed after cooking it is not a dinner I want to serve to my family and friends. Presenting food so that it looks appetizing and pretty makes it taste better, and it is fulfilling for both the cook and the diners. A well-set table (and this can be as humble a setting as a folded napkin and a fork) is the crowning touch to a satisfying meal, one that feeds all the senses and nourishes the body.

The following are some seasonal menu ideas. I rarely make dessert for family meals, but I love to end a meal with ripe fresh fruit.

FALL

Onion and anchovy tart
Rocket salad
Fruit: Honeydew melon

Persimmon salad
Braised chicken legs with fennel and egg noodles

Chicory salad
Braised pork shoulder and shell bean gratin
Fruit: Apples

Lentil soup and cornbread
Flan

Chopped salad
Pappardelle with Bolognese sauce
Pear sherbet

WINTER

Winter squash soup
Braised duck legs with wilted greens
Fruit: Pears

Romaine salad
Linguine with clams
Winter fruit compote

Shaved fennel salad
Fish fried in breadcrumbs with wilted spinach
Fruit: Tangerines

Curly endive salad
Boiled dinner with salsa verde
Apple tart

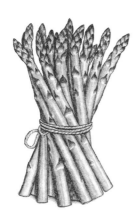

SPRING

Shallow-poached salmon with herb butter
Steamed asparagus and roasted new potatoes
Fruit: Strawberries

Artichoke salad
Roast leg of lamb with tapenade and steamed turnips
Fruit: Cherries

Avocado and grapefruit salad
Grilled pork chops and spring onions
with herb butter and polenta

Linguine with pesto and green beans
Baked stuffed apricots

Grilled chicken breast
Spring vegetable ragout
Cherry pie

SUMMER

Sliced tomatoes with basil
Cold roast pork with potato salad
Fruit: Summer berries

Herb and radish salad
Summer minestrone with garlic croutons
Fruit: Nectarines

Sweet corn soup
Grilled fish and summer squash with salsa verde
Strawberries in red wine

Tomato croutons
Steak with herbs, roasted potatoes, and salad
Biscotti and grapes

Green bean and roasted pepper salad
Baked halibut and roasted eggplant with aïoli
Fruit: Raspberries and peaches

Penne rigate with fresh tomato sauce
Garden salad
Goat cheese and figs

Cheese soufflé
Green salad
Fruit: Santa Rosa plums

Friends for Dinner

*Write out the menu,
then make
a shopping list,
a prep list,
and a timetable.*

I LOVE COOKING and eating with friends; I think that's why I started a restaurant. I give more thought and consideration to the menu and the evening when I'm cooking for guests, whether it is a special occasion such as a birthday party or holiday feast or just a casual gathering of close friends. I try to plan a menu that I think will please and is fitting to the occasion, but, just as important, one that is not too complicated and difficult to prepare. I want to enjoy myself and I want my guests to feel relaxed, knowing that things are under control.

Here are a few practices I employ to help me plan a menu, think it through, and cook it. These are critical for large gatherings and complex events, but they are useful for simple dinners, too. Once you have decided on the menu, make a game plan. First write out the menu and draft a shopping list. If, when you make the shopping list, you discover that the shopping, not to mention the cooking, is too complicated, go back and revise the menu—or see if anyone can help. Shop far enough in advance that you don't arrive at home laden with shopping bags without enough time to cook—a recipe for a very frazzled cook.

From the menu and shopping list, you can devise a prep list (a list of all the different preparations that need to be done to cook and serve the meal) and a timetable. I like to deconstruct each course into its elements. Take a green salad, for example: the greens need to be washed and dried, the radishes washed and trimmed, the vinaigrette prepared, and finally, the salad dressed and served. The timetable is the plan of when to do each of those steps. The lettuces and radishes can be prepared early in the day, the vinaigrette made an hour or two ahead, the bowl that the salad will be served in selected and put aside, but the salad won't be tossed until right before serving. To figure out the timing for longer cooking items such as a roast, count backward from the time dinner is to be served. For example, if dinner is to be served at seven o'clock and the roast is going to take around an hour and a half to cook and a half hour to rest before serving, it should go into a preheated oven around five o'clock.

When the menu consists of several courses, it is helpful to have one or two that are ready in advance, needing only reheating or finishing with a sauce. This allows you to concentrate on the one dish that occupies your full last-minute attention. If planning allows, make something like a braise or a soup the day before, which will only need reheating and will taste better for having been made a day ahead. Depending on what it is, I like to make dessert early in the day or even the day before. For example, if dessert is to be apple tart, I make the tart dough the day before or pull it out of the freezer. The day of the dinner, I roll out the dough in the afternoon and have it ready in the refrigerator. When company arrives I have one of my willing guests peel and slice the apples and arrange them on the dough while I do something else. The tart can go into the oven when we sit down to eat and it will be baked and still warm at dessert time. People love to join in the cooking and if you have thought through a timetable, you will know how to direct them.

Choosing the serving dishes and setting the table is part of the timetable, too. Ever since I was a little girl, I've loved setting the table, and I still do. I always get the table ready long before the guests arrive, because once I get involved with cooking I won't want to be bothered, and also because I want people to arrive and see the table ready and think, "They were expecting me!" It also gives me a moment to imagine the meal and how it will be served. I serve just about everything family-style—the food passed around the table on platters or in big bowls or in the dishes it was cooked in. There are a few exceptions—most pasta dishes, for example—that are better dished up in the kitchen. I also like to have a little something ready to nibble on when the guests arrive. This can be as simple as a bowl of warm olives or roasted nuts. I often make croutons topped with a little tasty tidbit (see page 58). Another of my favorite little somethings is a plate or bowl of freshly cut seasonal vegetables (carrots, fennel, radishes, celery, sweet peppers) served with nothing more than a sprinkle of salt and a squeeze of lemon. I serve this in the kitchen so the guests can mingle, nibble, and visit with me while I am finishing up the last steps of the dinner.

I can't stress enough the importance of keeping the menu simple, inviting, and doable. It is much better to cook something you know how to do confidently than to attempt an ambitious menu that leaves you feeling exhausted and frustrated. With good organization and planning you can have fabulous dinner parties and enjoy every moment of them.

These are a few ideas for special-occasion dinner-party menus.

FESTIVE MENUS

Halibut tartare with frisée salad
Roast leg of lamb with potato and green garlic gratin
Buttered peas
Strawberries in red wine

Garlic soup
Baked whole fish and saffron rice with chermoula and harissa
Steamed turnips and carrots
Apricot soufflé and lemon verbena tisane

Anchovy and tapenade croutons
Grand aïoli with grilled fish, green beans, cauliflower, potatoes,
fennel, and carrots
Garden salad
Nectarine tart and mint tisane

Artichoke, fennel, and Parmesan salad
Braised beef with egg noodles and gremolata
Orange sherbet and cat's-tongue cookies

Raw oysters and rye bread toasts
Leeks vinaigrette with chopped egg
Roast pork loin with braised cabbage
Steamed potatoes
Tarte Tatin

Picnics

A PICNIC is a great way to change the routine and get outdoors to your neighborhood park, or the woods, or the beach. It's true that appetites are sharpened and tastes are enlivened in the open air, and the setting adds extra flavor to even very simple picnic fare. One thing that transforms the experience is to put the food on real dishes. Nothing too fragile or irreplaceable, to be sure, but most plates and bowls will survive a picnic. It makes all the difference to see, instead of storage containers, an array of lovely bowls and plates with food nicely arranged on them and spread out on a big colorful cloth. I like to pack actual reusable tableware (not paper or plastic): tin plates and cups, for example, which are fun and practical, or chipped and mismatched china, and small glass tumblers that are equally good for wine, water, lemonade, or tea. A wide basket or two can accommodate dishes and food; they may be a bit heavy to carry, but it is so worth the extra effort. In warm weather, bring a small cooler for ice (to chill beverages and fruit and to keep aïoli cold and fresh greens from wilting). On cold days a tall thermos is handy for hot tea or soup.

Some of my favorite foods for picnics are bread and croutons; olives and radishes; cured meats such as prosciutto, salami, and ham; pâté, pickles, and mustard; cheese; cherry tomatoes and other raw vegetables such as carrots, fennel, and celery; rocket and watercress; chicken salad, egg salad, potato salad, lentil salad, green bean and tomato salad, aïoli and vegetables; hard-cooked eggs with anchovies or deviled eggs; frittatas; cold roasted meats or chicken; tabbouleh; fava bean purée; and sandwiches of all kinds, of course. Fresh fruits, almond tarts, lemon tartlets, biscotti, cookies. Elaborate or not, plain or fancy—just about anything portable.

Packing a Lunch

As ANY PARENT KNOWS, packing a school lunch that is nutritious and tasty—and one your child will eat—can be a challenge. One of my goals is to revolutionize school lunch programs so that schoolchildren nationwide can eat healthy, delicious food that they have participated in growing, cooking, and serving themselves. The best way for children to learn how to take care of themselves, how to eat well, and how to sustain our natural resources is to learn where food comes from. This is a long-term effort and the subject for another book. Meanwhile, there are bag lunches.

When my daughter was young, I realized that if I thought of the bagged lunch not as the sandwich-chips-juice formula, but more like something we would eat at home at the table, I could come up with much better ideas. She loves vinaigrette (which I have found to be true of most children) and will eat almost anything dressed with it. So one thing I did for years, with many variations, was to make some vinaigrette, put it in a small container, and prepare a selection of things to dip into it: romaine lettuce leaves, carrot sticks or shaved carrot curls, green beans, slices of fennel, radishes, cucumbers, steamed broccoli and cauliflower florets, raw and cooked vegetables of all kinds, a little leftover chicken or fish, croutons. Many of the foods that are good for picnics are good for lunches as well. Rice salads with bits of vegetables and meat or fruit and nuts; lentil, farro, and tabbouleh salads; potato, egg, and vegetable salads made with oil instead of mayonnaise—these are all good choices for kids who don't like sandwiches. A small thermos is wonderful for soups or a warm stew. And instead of sweets, I would send along fresh fruit, ripe and irresistible. Delicate pears, tender berries, and other fragile foods should be packed in containers so that they do not get crushed. Insulated bags offer another layer of protection and help things stay cool.

I always tried to include my daughter when I was deciding what to pack for lunch. This was not successful in the morning; getting ready for school was frantic enough already. But frequently after dinner we would take a moment to consider if there were leftovers that might be an appealing part of the next day's lunch. Preparing some part of lunch the night before makes the morning much easier and it is more likely that you will come up with a balanced combination. Another thing I would do to keep her interested in lunch was try to surprise her, to put in something unexpected. I wanted her to look forward to what she would find in her lunch bag and not assume it would be the same old thing.

Packing a lunch for work can be less expensive, healthier, and tastier than buying lunch out. If you cook enough dinner and plan for leftovers, there will always be something for lunch the next day.

Four Essential Sauces

Vinaigrette

Salsa Verde

Aïoli

Herb Butter

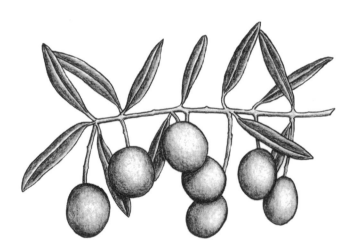

These four sauces, though basic, add so much flavor, dimension, and color to meals that I can't imagine cooking without them. Any one of them can pull a meal together and turn a simple plate of meat and vegetables into a finished dish; and they're so easy to prepare that once you've made them a few times, you'll never have to look up these recipes again. The only catch: because they're so simple, there's no hiding what these sauces are made of. You've got to start with ingredients that taste good by themselves: fruity olive oil, wine vinegar with character and flavor, lively garden herbs, and good fresh butter.

Vinaigrette

MAKES ABOUT ¼ CUP

RULE OF THUMB
1 : 4
1 part vinegar :
3 to 4 parts oil

THIS IS THE SAUCE I make most often, and if it's made out of good olive oil and good wine vinegar, it's the best salad dressing I can imagine. At its simplest, vinaigrette is a mixture of vinegar and oil in a ratio of 1 part vinegar to about 3 or 4 parts oil. Start by estimating roughly how much vinaigrette you will need. This depends on what you're using it for; a quarter cup is more than enough for four servings of green salad, for example, but you really never need to measure out exact amounts. Start by pouring the vinegar into a bowl. Dissolve a pinch of salt in it and taste for balance. The salt has a real relationship with the vinegar. When you add just enough salt, it subdues the acid of the vinegar and brings it into a wonderful balance. Try adding salt bit by bit and tasting to see what happens. How much salt is too much? How much is too little? What tastes best? If you add too much salt, just add a touch more vinegar.

Grind in some black pepper and whisk in the oil. The vinaigrette should taste brightly balanced, neither too oily nor overly acidic. Adjust the sauce, adding more vinegar if you've added too much oil, and more salt, if it needs it.

Pour into a small bowl:
   1 tablespoon red wine vinegar
Add:
   Salt
   Fresh-ground black pepper
Stir to dissolve the salt, taste, and adjust if needed. Use a fork or small whisk to beat in, a little at a time:
   3 to 4 tablespoons extra-virgin olive oil
Taste as you go and stop when it tastes right.

VARIATIONS
◆ Add a little puréed garlic or diced shallot, or both, to the vinegar.
◆ White wine vinegar, sherry vinegar, or lemon juice can replace some or all of the red wine vinegar.
◆ Beat in a little mustard before you start adding the oil.
◆ For part of the olive oil, substitute a very fresh nut oil, such as walnut or hazelnut.
◆ Heavy cream or crème fraîche can replace some or all the olive oil.
◆ Chop some fresh herbs and stir them into the finished vinaigrette.

Salsa Verde

MAKES ⅔ CUP

HERBS OF CHOICE

parsley

basil

chives

chervil

tarragon

cilantro

sorrel

marjoram

savory

thyme

mint

rosemary

SALSA VERDE, the classic green sauce of Italy, is a sauce of olive oil and chopped parsley flavored with lemon zest, garlic, and capers. It adds lively freshness to almost any simple dish. Flat-leaved Italian parsley is preferable, but curly parsley is good, too. Fresh parsley—the fresher the better—is the majority herb, but almost any other fresh, tender herb can enhance a salsa verde: tarragon, chervil, and chives are good choices.

Use a sharp knife when you chop parsley (and other herbs). A sharp knife slices cleanly through the leaves, preserving both flavor and color, while a dull knife mashes and bruises them.

The zest is the thin yellow outer layer of the lemon's skin; avoid grating any of the bitter white part (called the pith) beneath. The zest brightens the flavor of the sauce, so don't be shy with it; you may need more than one lemon's worth.

Don't hesitate to experiment. I make salsa verde more or less thick depending on what I am using it for. I tend to use less oil when it's for roasted meats and grilled vegetables and more for fish.

Combine in a small bowl:

⅓ cup coarsely chopped parsley (leaves and thin stems only)
Grated zest of 1 lemon
1 small garlic clove, chopped very fine or pounded into a purée
1 tablespoon capers, rinsed, drained, and coarsely chopped
½ teaspoon salt
Fresh-ground black pepper to taste
½ cup olive oil

Mix well and taste for salt. Let the sauce sit for a while to develop the flavors.

VARIATIONS

• Other herbs, or combinations of herbs, can replace part or all of the parsley.
• Add a little chopped salt-packed anchovy fillet, or chopped shallot, or chopped hard-cooked egg—or all three.
• Lemon juice or vinegar makes the sauce zestier, but add them just before serving, as the acid will cause the herbs to discolor. (You can macerate a little chopped shallot in the vinegar or lemon, if you wish.)

Making Mayonnaise

Velvety, luscious, garlicky mayonnaise—what the French call *aïoli* (pronounced *eye-oh-lee*)—is another sauce I use all the time: on sandwiches; with vegetables, both raw and cooked; with meat and fish; as the binder for chicken salad and egg salad; and as a base for sauces such as tartar sauce. Most children, even very young ones, love aïoli and will happily use it as a dip for bite after bite of bread, carrots, potatoes, and even vegetables they might otherwise refuse.

Two or three small cloves of garlic per egg yolk, pounded with a mortar and pestle, make a fairly pungent garlic mayonnaise—depending on the garlic. The strength of garlic's flavor can vary a lot, depending on freshness, season, and variety. I always pound the garlic in a mortar and pestle and reserve half of it, so I can add it later if the aïoli needs it. (You can always add more garlic, but you can't subtract it.) It's important to pound the garlic to a very smooth purée so the sauce will be garlicky through and through, not just a mayonnaise with bits of garlic in it.

One egg yolk will absorb up to one cup of oil, but you can add less if you don't need that much mayonnaise. Whisk the oil in drop by drop at first, adding more as you go. It is much easier to whisk when the bowl is steadied. To help hold it still, set it on top of a coiled dish towel.

Adding a small amount of water to the egg yolk before you incorporate the oil helps prevent the sauce from separating or "breaking." If mayonnaise does separate, stop adding oil, but don't despair. Just crack a fresh egg, separate the yolk into a new bowl, add a little water as before, and slowly whisk in first the broken sauce and then the rest of the oil.

Make aïoli half an hour ahead of time, to give the flavors a chance to marry. As with anything made with raw eggs, if you're not going to serve mayonnaise within an hour, refrigerate it. Aïoli tastes best the day it's made.

Aïoli (Garlic Mayonnaise)

MAKES ABOUT 1 CUP

RULE OF THUMB
1 egg yolk :
1 cup olive oil

Peel:

2 or 3 small garlic cloves

Pound until smooth with a mortar and pestle, along with:

A pinch of salt

Separate into a mixing bowl:

1 egg yolk

Add about half the garlic and:

½ teaspoon water

Mix well with a whisk. Into a cup with a pour spout, measure about:

1 cup olive oil

Slowly dribble the oil into the egg yolk mixture, whisking constantly. As the egg yolk absorbs the oil, the sauce will thicken, lighten in color, and become opaque. This will happen rather quickly. Then you can add the oil a little faster, whisking all the while.

If the sauce is thicker than you like, thin it with a few drops of water. Taste and add more salt and garlic, as desired.

VARIATIONS

* When I serve a roast, I love to add some of the roasting juices to the finished aïoli.
* A boiled crab with aïoli is even more delicious when a little crab butter is added to the aïoli. (Crab butter, or tomalley, is the soft yellow matter inside the shell of a cooked crab.)
* For an intense aïoli, add lots of chopped capers and anchovy.

Plain mayonnaise—made the same way as aïoli, but without garlic, and finished with a touch of vinegar or lemon juice—can be varied in many different ways:

* Mustard or horseradish mayonnaise is wonderful for sandwiches.
* An herb mayonnaise with chopped herbs such as parsley, chives, tarragon, and chervil and a little lemon juice goes extremely well with fish and shellfish.
* To make tartar sauce, add chopped pickles, pickle juice, grated onion, capers, parsley, and a pinch of cayenne.
* To make a beautiful green mayonnaise, pound watercress or basil in the mortar and pestle and add to the mayonnaise.

Herb Butter

MAKES ABOUT ¾ CUP

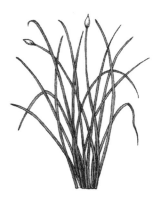

OTHER BUTTERS
parsley butter
anchovy butter
black pepper butter
sage butter
basil butter
chipotle butter
nasturtium butter

HERB BUTTER is softened butter that has been flavored with herbs. It makes a great sauce for meat, fish, or vegetables, providing lots of flavor for next to no effort. I like it to be really green, full of lots and lots of herbs, with just enough butter to bind them together. Poached fish served with an herb butter made with the classic fines herbes of French cuisine (parsley, chives, tarragon, and chervil) is sublime.

Either salted or unsalted butter will do for an herb butter. Just remember to season accordingly when you start adding salt.

Lemon juice brings out the flavor of the herbs. The cayenne adds a little zing. Almost any fresh herb can be used. The more tender-leafed herbs, such as parsley, basil, chives, or chervil, should be very fresh and chopped at the last minute. More pungent herbs such as sage or rosemary are tastier when they are chopped and gently heated on the stove in a little melted butter. (Allow to cool to room temperature before adding to the softened butter.) Or, with or without herbs, make a butter flavored with one or two salt-packed anchovies (rinsed, filleted, and chopped), lemon zest, and black pepper, or, for an unusual twist and color, with some chopped nasturtium flowers or hot spicy peppers.

Serve the butter as is, soft and spreadable; or put it in a piece of plastic wrap or waxed paper, roll it into a log, chill until hard, and cut it into coin-shaped pieces to put on top of hot food. Any extra herb butter can be frozen and used later.

Stir together in a small bowl, mixing well:
> **8 tablespoons (1 stick) butter, softened**
> **½ cup chopped herbs (such as parsley, chervil, and chives)**
> **1 garlic clove, finely chopped**
> **Squeeze of lemon juice**
> **Salt and fresh-ground black pepper**
> **A pinch of cayenne**

Taste and adjust the salt and lemon as needed.

VARIATIONS
◆ Chopped shallots and pounded garlic are delicious additions.
◆ For a more lemony flavor, add some finely grated lemon zest.
◆ For a more pungent butter that is perfect with corn on the cob, flavor with dried chile peppers, soaked, drained, and pounded to a paste.

Salads

Garden Lettuce Salad

Greek Salad

Orange and Olive Salad

I LOVE SALAD: I love to wash it, I love to eat it. As far as I am concerned, a meal without one is incomplete. The salads I crave are combinations of lettuces, vegetables, and fruits prepared very simply and tossed, typically, with a lively vinaigrette. It's the immediacy that makes a salad so compelling and seductive, so use ingredients that are fresh and radiant and in season, be they lettuces, tomatoes, carrots, radishes, potatoes, persimmons, or pecans. Almost anything good can be turned into a delicious salad—even the leaves plucked off a bunch of fresh parsley, tossed with lemon juice and olive oil and a little salt.

Garden Lettuce

FOR ME, making a garden lettuce salad—washing beautiful fresh-picked lettuces and tossing them together with a scattering of herbs and a vinaigrette—is as much of a joy as eating one. I love the colorful variety of lettuces, bitter and sweet; the flavor and complexity of herbs such as chervil and chives; and the brightness of a simple vinaigrette made with red wine vinegar, olive oil, and a whisper of garlic, which highlights the lettuces and herbs without overwhelming them.

For a salad to have flavor and life, you have to start with fresh, just-picked lettuces. I'm fortunate to have a small kitchen garden in my backyard where I grow various lettuces and herbs for salad, but if you don't have such a garden it can take some real dedication to find good greens. Farmers' markets are the best places to start. When my garden is not producing, or when I'm away from home, I shop for head lettuces and try to create my own combinations of lettuces, arugula, chicories, and whatever tender herbs I can find. I generally avoid the salad mixes, especially the pre-bagged ones, which usually seem to include one or two kinds of greens that don't belong with the others. If there is a lovely mixture from a local salad grower, fine, but otherwise try to buy the best head lettuces you can find and make your own mix.

Wash the lettuce, gently but thoroughly, in a basin or bowl of cold water. First cull through the lettuces, pulling off and throwing into the compost bin any outer leaves that are tough, yellowed, or damaged. Then cut out the stem end, separating the rest of the leaves into the water. Gently swish the leaves in the water with your open hands and lift the lettuce out of the water and into a colander. If the lettuces are very dirty, change the water, and wash again.

Dry the lettuces in a salad spinner, but don't overfill it. It's much more effective to spin-dry a few small batches than one or two large ones. Empty the water from the spinner after each batch. Any water clinging to the leaves will dilute the vinaigrette, so check the leaves and spin them again if they're still a little wet. I spread out each batch of leaves in a single layer on a dish towel as I go. Then I gently roll up the towel and put it in the refrigerator until it's time to serve the salad. You can do this a few hours ahead.

When the time comes, put the lettuce in a bowl big enough to allow you to toss the salad. If you have some, add a small handful of chives or chervil, or both, either chopped quickly or snipped with scissors.

Toss everything with the vinaigrette, using just enough sauce to coat the leaves lightly, so they glisten. Beware of overdressing small, tender lettuces: they will wilt and turn soggy. I usually toss salads with my hands. (I eat salads with my hands, too.) That way I can be gentle and precise and make sure that each leaf is evenly dressed. Taste, and if needed, finish the salad with a sprinkling of salt or brighten it with a splash of vinegar or a squeeze of lemon juice. Taste again and see what you think, then toss one last time and serve the salad right away.

One of my favorite tools is a small Japanese ceramic mortar called a suribachi. It has grooved ridges that are perfect for making a quick purée or for pounding a few herbs. I purée a clove of garlic and then make a vinaigrette right in the suribachi.

Garden Lettuce Salad

4 SERVINGS

Carefully wash and dry:

4 generous handfuls of lettuce

Mix together:

1 garlic clove, pounded to a fine purée

1 tablespoon red wine vinegar

Salt

Fresh-ground black pepper

Stir to dissolve the salt, taste, and adjust if needed. Whisk in:

3 to 4 tablespoons olive oil

Use a lettuce leaf to taste the vinaigrette as you add the oil. Put the lettuce in a large bowl, add about three quarters of the vinaigrette, toss, and taste. Add more dressing as needed. Serve immediately.

VARIATIONS

◆ Lettuces vary in availability according to season. Romaine lettuce is usually best in the summertime. Fall and winter bring heartier lettuces such as the chicories (radicchio, escarole, Belgian endive, and frisée or curly endive).

Putting a Salad Together

A SALAD OF many ingredients, either all tossed together or dressed separately and arranged on a plate, is called a "composed" salad. A composed salad such as the Greek salad that follows is a hearty dish; with some crusty bread, it could be the main event of a dinner on a warm night. Or, a composed salad might be a delicate arrangement of, say, a few pieces of crabmeat, some grapefruit sections, and a little curly endive in a creamy dressing, served as an elegant first course. Almost anything can be an element in a composed salad: all the various lettuces and salad greens, of course, but also raw or cooked vegetables, chopped, diced, or cut into thin shavings; roasted meats cut into cubes or thin slices; tuna and other fish or shellfish; and hard-cooked eggs, quartered or chopped.

Tasty leftovers can be delicious in a composed salad. Don't combine too many ingredients into a single salad or it will have too many conflicting flavors. The components should be chosen thoughtfully with regard to the tastes and textures they contribute, and the dressing must complement them all. Sometimes a vinaigrette works best, when a tangy sauce is needed; sometimes mayonnaise, for mellow richness; at other times, a creamy sauce. A potato salad, for example, can be made with any of these dressings, and each will yield a distinctly different salad.

When dressing a composed salad that includes both tender lettuces and heavier ingredients such as artichoke hearts or pieces of fruit, dress all the heavier elements separately and arrange them around the tossed lettuces on a platter. Otherwise the salad is hard to serve because everything ends up at the bottom and the leaves get crushed. Even salads that have no lettuce should be assembled carefully. What's most important is that each ingredient be tasty on its own. Taste everything and season each element with a little salt or dressing as needed before adding it to the whole. When things are tossed together, don't overmix, or the parts will start to lose their distinctiveness, muddying the flavors and spoiling the look of the salad. (You can always arrange a salad and drizzle vinaigrette over it, or even pass the vinaigrette in a pitcher.)

As for what to include in such a salad and how to dress it, taste each ingredient before you decide. That is really the only rule you must follow, and while it may sound frustratingly vague, as you acquire a little salad-making experience, you'll begin to recognize and remember the flavors you like and the ones that you like together.

When I serve a composed salad, I arrange the lettuces on a platter and scatter over them the other ingredients, dressed separately.

Greek Salad

4 SERVINGS

Cut out the stem end and cut into wedges:

2 small ripe tomatoes

Season with:

Salt

Peel, cut in half lengthwise, and thickly slice:

1 medium cucumber

(If the seeds are large, remove them by scraping a spoon down the center of the halved cucumber.)

Peel and thinly slice:

½ small red onion or 5 green onions

Cut in half, core and seed, and slice thin:

1 small sweet red pepper

Rinse (and if you prefer, pit):

About ¼ cup black olives

(2 or 3 olives per person)

Break up or cut into small pieces:

4 ounces feta cheese

Make a vinaigrette. Mix:

2 teaspoons red wine vinegar

1 teaspoon lemon juice (optional)

2 teaspoons fresh oregano, chopped

Salt and fresh-ground black pepper

Whisk in:

6 tablespoons extra-virgin olive oil

Season the cucumbers and onions with salt. Taste the tomatoes and season again if they need it. Gently toss the vegetables with about three quarters of the vinaigrette. Taste and add more salt or vinegar as needed. The salad can sit for a few minutes to let the flavors blend together. Just before serving, gently toss the salad again and garnish with the cheese and olives. Spoon over the remaining vinaigrette.

VARIATIONS

◆ Serve the salad over a few leaves of romaine or other lettuce.

◆ A few salt-packed anchovies, rinsed and filleted, make a nice garnish.

◆ Dried oregano may be substituted for fresh, but use only 1 teaspoon.

Making Salads from Fruit

Crisp and sweet fuyu persimmons make lovely fall salads, especially in combination with walnuts and other fruits such as pears and pomegranates.

I WANTED TO BE SURE to include a few words about fruit salads—not sweet fruit cocktails in heavy syrup, but savory salads made like other composed salads. These may consist of fresh fruit alone, or fresh fruit combined with lettuces or other salad greens, with nuts and cheese often added for richness and texture. When there are no greens available and I desperately want something fresh, fruit salads are refreshing alternatives, either at the beginning or the end of a meal. Figs, apples, pears, pomegranates, persimmons, and almost all of the citrus fruits make good salads, with or without greens. All these fruits of fall and winter have an affinity for hearty chicories such as escarole, radicchio, and curly endive. Among my favorite fruit salads are an orange salad with black olives; avocado slices and grapefruit sections; persimmons or Asian pears with nuts and balsamic vinegar; and orange slices with marinated beets.

Oranges and other citrus fruits need to be peeled and sectioned for a salad. When skinning the fruit, you want to remove all the outer peel and the membranes that enclose the sections, exposing the juicy fruit inside. You will need a small, sharp knife to do this. First, slice off the top and bottom of each fruit, slicing deeply enough to expose the inner flesh. Then, position your knife blade at the top where the fruit and peel meet, and carefully cut down following the contours of the fruit. Continue around the fruit, cutting from top to bottom, rotating the orange, until all the peel and membrane is removed. Trim away any remaining white bits of membrane. You can then slice the orange crosswise or cut between the membranes to free the individual sections.

Apples and pears can be peeled or not, but to avoid oxidation, which turns the cut surfaces brown, they should be prepared just before serving. Persimmons must be peeled; this can be done in advance, but keep them covered so they don't dry out.

Fruit salads are usually dressed very simply, sometimes with nothing more than a drizzle of olive oil or vinegar, or with a vinaigrette made of some citrus juice and a touch of vinegar, a little chopped shallot, salt, pepper, and olive oil.

Orange and Olive Salad

4 SERVINGS

Blood oranges are gorgeous, with gem-like shades of ruby and amber. They're in season for only a few months in midwinter.

Remove the peel and membrane, exposing the juicy flesh, of:

4 small or 3 medium oranges

Slice into ¼-inch-thick round pinwheels and arrange them on a plate.

Cut in half lengthwise, peel, and slice thin:

1 small red onion

Onion slices cut horizontally are prettier than slices cut lengthwise. If the onions are particularly strong, soak them in ice water for 5 to 10 minutes. Drain them well before adding to the salad.

Make a vinaigrette. Mix together:

2 tablespoons orange juice

1 teaspoon red wine vinegar

Salt and fresh-ground black pepper

Whisk in:

2 tablespoons olive oil

Taste and adjust with more salt and vinegar as needed. Scatter the onion slices over the oranges and spoon the vinaigrette over.

Garnish with:

Small black olives (4 or 5 per person)

I prefer to serve the olives unpitted to preserve their integrity and beauty, but be sure to tell your friends so they know the pits are there. Use niçoise olives if you can find them, but any briny black olive will do (large ones can be coarsely chopped, if you like).

Bread

Croutons

Herb Bread or Pizza Dough

Breadcrumbs

THERE IS SOMETHING MAGICAL about mixing flour, yeast, salt, and water together and having it turn into a loaf of bread. Although I am not a baker and have a wonderful bakery in my neighborhood, I sometimes bake bread or pizza at home for the sheer pleasure of handling the dough, seeing it rise, and smelling the irresistible warm yeasty aroma that fills the whole house. Furthermore, *everyone* loves homemade bread: I've never seen a homemade loaf of bread linger uneaten, even an imperfect one that didn't rise high enough or that baked a little too long or not quite long enough.

Croutons

TOP CROUTONS
WITH
garlic and oil
tapenade (olive paste)
bean purée
radish and butter
avocado
sautéed chicken liver
ripe tomatoes
crab salad
egg salad
smoked fish
sautéed greens
eggplant caviar
anchovies
cheese
cured meats

For a quick bite to eat, or when a few guests are about to arrive and I want to have a little something ready, a crouton is the first thing I think of. Croutons, croutes, crostini, toast, and bruschetta are all names for variously sized pieces of bread, usually toasted or grilled, sometimes dried out in the oven, sometimes fried. A bruschetta is a thick piece of bread that is grilled over an open fire, or toasted, and rubbed with garlic and drizzled with olive oil, to be served either as is or piled high with juicy tomatoes and basil. Croutons, crostini, and toasts usually refer to thin slices of bread, but croutons can also be small pieces of bread cut into cubes or torn in irregular pieces and either toasted or fried in butter or olive oil and used to garnish a soup or a salad.

Any good-quality bread will make a good crouton. A thick slice of a big round, country-style loaf grilled and drizzled with green olive oil makes a distinctly different crouton than a thin triangular toasted slice of dense white bread with its crusts cut off, brushed with melted butter, and one point dipped in chopped parsley before serving. The croutons I make most often are sliced from a big round loaf of levain bread. They're usually not uniform sizes and I always oil them *after* toasting, just after I've rubbed some garlic on them.

Roughly torn pieces of bread (what's sometimes called pulled bread), toasted in the oven and tossed in oil, make good croutons for a salad.

Baguettes are handy for croutons because they can be easily sliced into regular rounds or cut on the diagonal into long ovals, which are good for dipping into fava bean purée or tapenade.

For croutons that are more evenly browned and crunchier and that have a more fried taste, oil or butter the bread slices before you cook them. Small croutons can be tossed in a bowl with oil or melted butter before going into the oven. Place larger, flat croutons in a single layer on a baking sheet, brush with oil or butter, and bake at 350°F until they just start to turn golden at the edges. Keep an eye on them; the timing will vary greatly, depending on the kind of bread used, how dry it is, and how thick it's cut. For a tasty garnish to a soup or salad, toss croutons hot out of the oven with chopped garlic and herbs.

Fry little cubed croutons in butter to strew atop a delicate puréed soup. Use enough butter to coat the pan generously, adding more as it is absorbed by the croutons, stirring or tossing frequently over medium heat until the croutons are golden brown.

To grill slices of bread, place them on the grill rack over a bed of medium-hot coals for a minute or two on each side. The bread should have nice charred marks from the grill and be golden brown here and there. I rub the slices with a clove of garlic and drizzle olive oil over the bread after it's grilled.

Croutons taste best when they are made fresh, but the bread can be cut in advance. Wrap the bread slices in a kitchen towel to keep them from drying out (croutons tend to warp and curl up if left uncovered). When ready to serve, the bread can be quickly laid out and toasted.

Making Bread

A dough scraper (bench scraper) is a very useful tool for cutting dough, for working a soft dough on a work surface, and for cleaning the work surface.

WHEN IT COMES to making bread, many things affect the outcome, some more obvious than others. Most important is the flour. You cannot make good bread from mediocre flour. Choose flour that is unbleached, untreated, and free of additives. All flours, and especially whole-grain flours, will eventually spoil and taste and smell rancid. Try to buy flour that's relatively fresh; your best bet is to look for a local organic food retailer with a rapid turnover who sells in bulk.

The water makes a difference, too; both its temperature and its quantity influence texture. The type of leavening agent and the length of time bread is allowed to sit and rise will both affect the outcome enormously: quickbreads made with baking soda or powder are tender and almost cakelike, while breads leavened with wild yeast and given repeated slow risings will be the chewiest and crustiest, with the most complex flavors. Weather also affects bread: humidity, heat, and cold each exert their influence. All this makes baking ever-changing and forever fascinating.

There is a world of breads: quickbreads such as cornbread and Irish soda bread that are easy to put on the table on relatively short notice; wonderful flatbreads such as tortillas fresh off the griddle or whole-wheat-flour puris that puff up when they're fried or pita bread grilled over a fire; and the classic yeasted breads of France and Italy—including my everyday favorite, levain bread. Levain bread is leavened with a natural starter of wild yeast and allowed a long, slow fermentation and rising period in canvas-lined baskets. Traditionally, before each batch is baked, some of the starter is held back to leaven the next batch. Rather than give a recipe for a levain-type bread (which is a little complicated to make at home), I offer instead a recipe for a dough that's versatile enough to be formed and baked as a flat crusty focaccia or a traditional pizza. (Kids love to stretch out the dough and make their own pizzas.)

Herb Bread or Pizza Dough

MAKES ONE FOCACCIA
OR TWO 10-INCH PIZZAS

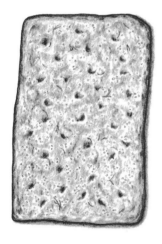

A little rye or other whole-grain flour adds more flavor to the dough.

Stir together:

2 teaspoons dry yeast

½ cup lukewarm water

Add and mix well:

¼ cup unbleached white flour

¼ cup rye flour

Allow this mixture to sit until quite bubbly, about 30 minutes.

Mix together in another bowl:

3¼ cups unbleached white flour

1 teaspoon salt

Stir this into the yeast and flour mixture with:

¾ cup cold water

¼ cup olive oil

Mix thoroughly by hand or in an electric stand mixer. If working by hand, turn the dough out onto a lightly floured board and knead until the dough is soft and elastic, about 5 minutes. If the dough is too wet and sticky, add more flour, but only enough to form a soft, slightly sticky dough. Or use the mixer, fitted with the dough hook, and knead for about 5 minutes. The dough is the right texture when it pulls away from the sides of the bowl of the mixer, but still adheres to the bottom. A very soft, slightly moist dough will make the best focaccia.

Put the dough in a large bowl, cover, and let rise in a warm place until doubled in size, about 2 hours. For an even better-tasting and more supple dough, let the dough rise slowly overnight in the refrigerator. (Remove from the refrigerator 2 hours before shaping.)

Generously oil a 10-inch by 15½-inch rimmed baking or sheet pan. Gently remove the dough from the bowl and flatten it on the baking pan, shaping it to fit the pan by gently pressing down from the center out towards the edges. If the dough starts to resist and spring back, let it rest for 10 minutes, then continue shaping. Try not to deflate or smash all of the air out of the dough as you are shaping it. Dimple the surface of the dough by lightly poking it with your fingertips.

Drizzle with:

2 tablespoons olive oil

Cover and let rise until doubled in height, about 2 hours.

While the dough is rising, preheat the oven to 450°F. If you have one, place a baking stone on the lower rack and let it heat for 30 minutes before baking the bread. Sprinkle the dough with:

1 teaspoon coarse sea salt

and put the baking pan directly on the stone. Bake the focaccia until golden and crisp on the top and bottom, about 20 to 25 minutes. Invert the pan to remove the bread and place on a rack to cool.

VARIATIONS

• Sprinkle 1 tablespoon chopped fresh rosemary or sage leaves over the dough before baking.

• Chop about 1 tablespoon fresh tender herbs and add to the dough with the oil.

• Divide the dough in two before shaping and press into two ½-inch-thick disks. Put the disks into oiled 8-inch pie plates. Dimple, oil, let rise as above, and bake, checking after 10 minutes.

• Top with sautéed onions, cheese, tomato slices, or sautéed greens before baking.

Making Pizza

To MAKE PIZZAS, instead of shaping the dough into a rectangle, divide the dough in two and form each piece into a nice, smooth ball. Allow the dough balls to rest at room temperature, wrapped loosely in plastic, for an hour or so. Flatten each ball into a disk about 5 or 6 inches in diameter, flour lightly, cover, and let rest for another 15 minutes. Place a baking stone on the lowest rack in the oven (remove the other racks for easy access). Preheat the oven to 500°F.

Gently stretch one of the disks into a round roughly 10 inches in diameter and put on a floured peel or an inverted baking sheet. Brush the dough with olive oil and, leaving a ½-inch border uncovered, top with your choice of ingredients such as chopped garlic, fresh tomato sauce, and mozzarella cheese; long-cooked onions, herbs, and anchovies; sautéed greens and sausage; and on and on. Slide the pizza onto the baking stone and bake until the crust is browned, about 10 minutes.

Breadcrumbs

Fʀᴇsʜ-ᴍᴀᴅᴇ, homemade breadcrumbs have some obvious uses: sprinkled over a gratin to form a crust; as a coating for about-to-be-fried meats, fish, and vegetables; and to give a lighter texture to stuffings and meatballs. But in my kitchen they also have a major role as a sort of endlessly versatile crunchy sauce: golden, fresh-toasted breadcrumbs, tossed with almost any chopped fresh tender herb or combination of herbs (parsley, marjoram, thyme) and perhaps a little fine-chopped garlic, and then strewn over almost anything—pasta, vegetables, roasts, salads—as a finishing touch. Recently I've started to embellish toasted breadcrumbs with fried herbs. I fry the leaves of herbs such as rosemary, sage, and winter savory in olive oil for a minute (or less), just until crisp and then toss them with the crumbs.

Not all breads make good fresh breadcrumbs. Most bagged, sliced, commercial breads—the kinds with preservatives and added sweeteners—simply won't work: the additives reduce bread's natural crumbiness and the sweeteners add the wrong flavor and cause overrapid browning. Breadcrumbs are best made from bread that has had a day or two to dry out just a little. Fresh bread has too much internal moisture to make good crumbs. Instead it clumps, forming moist wads of bread instead of integral crumbs. For breading and frying, loaves of fine-textured white bread such as *pain de mie* or pullman bread make the best crumbs. For toasted breadcrumbs, however, I prefer to use levain bread or another coarse-textured, country-style bread.

These kinds of breadcrumbs are different from breadcrumbs made from completely dried out bread, and are totally different from the crumbs sold in boxes at the grocery, which are too fine, don't taste good, and just won't work for the recipes in this book.

The easiest way to turn bread into breadcrumbs is with a blender or food processor. First remove the crust; it's too tough and crumbs with crust in them brown unevenly. Cut the crustless bread into cubes and process them in batches. The bread should be thoroughly ground up so the crumbs are more or less the same size; this will ensure even browning while cooking. Crumbs to be used for breading need to be ground very fine, so they will stick to and evenly coat whatever is being breaded. Crumbs to be toasted can be coarse or fine, depending on the end use.

When toasting crumbs, toss them first with olive oil (or melted butter or duck fat) and spread them evenly on a baking sheet. Every few minutes or so, stir them with a metal spatula. The crumbs along the edges of the pan always brown first, so mix these in well, moving them into the center away from the outer edges. The crumbs brown slowly at first, because they must dry before they brown, but they finish quickly during the last minute or two of toasting. Keep a close eye on them towards the end of their cooking time to prevent overbrowning.

If you find you have more old bread than you can use, turn it into crumbs and freeze them for future use. When there is no dried-out bread and you need to make crumbs, cut thick slices of fresh bread and put them on a baking sheet in a warm oven to dry out slightly before processing.

Toasted Breadcrumbs

Preheat the oven to 350°F. Pare away all the crust from:

Levain or other country-style bread

Cut the bread into cubes and process in a blender or food processor until the crumbs reach the fineness you want.

Toss with:

A pinch of salt

1 tablespoon olive oil for every cup of breadcrumbs

Spread the crumbs on a baking sheet in a thin layer. Bake until golden brown, stirring the crumbs every few minutes for even browning.

VARIATIONS

• Fry a handful of herbs in hot olive oil over medium heat until crisp. Drain well and toss together with the toasted crumbs and a pinch of salt, if needed.

• A few dried chile flakes can be mixed into the crumbs for spice.

Broth and Soup

Chicken Broth

Carrot Soup

Minestrone

WHEN I FIRST started cooking, I never liked soup—because I didn't know how to make it! I was naïve; I thought the process was nothing more than putting leftovers in a pot, heating them with stock or water, and—*voilà*! Soup. Eventually I realized that it's necessary to learn some simple techniques for maximizing flavor: how to make a good broth; how to begin a soup with a base of softened vegetables and herbs; and how to add either a single vegetable, for a pure and simple soup, or a combination of many vegetables (as well as pasta, meat, or fish), for a more complicated soup. The variations are endless.

Making a Broth

STEPS
bring to a boil
skim
add vegetables
simmer
strain

THE BASIS of many soups is a broth (or stock) of meat and vegetables (or vegetables alone), which provides a foundation of body and flavor. A sufficiently rich and fragrant broth makes a wonderful soup all by itself. I love a bowl of chicken broth garnished with a bit of pasta and parsley or a poached egg. Broth is not only easy to make, it's one of the few things I freeze so as to have the makings of a soup or a risotto always at hand.

I use a whole chicken to make broth, which may seem extravagant, but it produces lots of sweet, fragrant, and full-bodied broth. (After an hour of cooking you can lift the chicken out of the pot, remove the breasts, and then return the rest to the pot. The poached breasts make a great meal, especially with a little salsa verde.) It is the meat that makes the difference in the broth. If you use bones, choose meaty ones, such as necks, backs, and wings. Meatless bones yield a thin broth. The leftover carcass of a roast chicken can also be added to the broth. The roasted meat adds depth of flavor. (Leftover grilled chicken bones are not recommended; they make an acrid, smoky-tasting broth.)

When making broth from a whole chicken, include the neck from inside the cavity. Also, remove and unwrap the giblets (usually the heart, gizzard, and liver). Put the gizzard and heart in the broth, but save the liver for some other purpose. Always start the broth with cold water; the flavor is drawn out of the meat and bones as it heats up to a boil. The amount of water you use will determine the intensity of your broth. A chicken barely submerged in water will produce a very rich, fragrant soup. Adding more water will make a lighter, more delicate broth.

Bring the broth to a full rolling boil and then turn it down right away. The boil causes all the blood and extra proteins to coagulate into a foam that rises and collects at the top where you can skim it off, ensuring a clearer broth. If the broth is allowed to boil for long it will turn cloudy and the fat may emulsify, bonding with the water and making the stock murky and greasy.

When skimming the broth, use a ladle and remove only the foam, not the fat. The fat contributes lots of flavor as the broth cooks and it can all be removed at the end. Add the vegetables after you have skimmed off the foam; that way they don't get in the way. Add the vegetables either whole or in large pieces so they don't fall apart and cloud the broth.

Salt helps develop the flavor as the broth cooks and makes a much more flavorful stock than if you were to add all the salt at the end. Don't add too much, though. The stock will lose volume to evaporation as it cooks, so it should start out under-seasoned.

Cook the broth at a simmer, which means at a very gentle boil with bubbles just breaking the surface of the liquid at irregular intervals. If by accident the broth is cooking too quickly and has reduced, add some more water and return to a simmer.

When I want a light and delicate stock I will only cook it for 3 hours or so; otherwise I allow at least 4 to 5 hours.

Broth should cook long enough to extract all the flavor from the meat and bones, but not so long that it starts to lose its delicacy and freshness. For chicken broth allow 4 to 5 hours. Taste the stock often as it cooks and turn it off when it is full of flavor. When you taste, spoon out a little and salt it to get a better idea of how it will taste when it is fully seasoned. Try this at different times throughout the cooking process to discover how the flavors develop.

Strain the broth when it is finished cooking. Ladle it out of the pot and pass it through a strainer into a nonreactive container. For a very clear broth, strain it again through a clean wet cotton towel or cheesecloth.

If you plan to use the broth right away, skim the fat. I only do this if I am using the broth right away. Otherwise, allow the broth to cool and refrigerate it with its fat, which solidifies on top, helping to preserve the broth and its flavor. The cold, hard fat is easy to lift off. Do not cover the broth until it's cool or it may not cool down fast enough in the refrigerator and will ferment and turn sour. (This has happened to me. You will know right away that it has spoiled.) The broth will keep for one week in the refrigerator or for three months in the freezer. It's handy to freeze the broth in one- or two-pint containers so you won't have to thaw out more than you'll need. It is always safest to bring refrigerated or frozen stock back to a full boil before using.

Chicken Broth

MAKES ABOUT 5 QUARTS

Put in a large pot:

1 whole chicken, 3½ to 4 pounds

Pour in:

1½ gallons cold water

Place over high heat, bring to a boil, then turn the heat to low. Skim the broth. Add:

1 carrot, peeled

1 onion, peeled and halved

1 head of garlic, cut in half

1 celery stalk

Salt

½ teaspoon black peppercorns

1 bouquet garni of parsley and thyme sprigs and a large bay leaf

Simmer the broth for about 4 to 5 hours. Strain. If using immediately, skim the fat and season with salt to taste. Serve hot, or allow to cool and then refrigerate or freeze.

A Simple Vegetable Soup

THE SIMPLE SOUP I make most often starts with a base of softened onions to which one or two vegetables are added. The soup is moistened with broth or water and simmered until the vegetables are tender.

First, onions are gently cooked in butter or oil until soft and flavorful. A heavy-bottomed pot makes all the difference for this: it disperses the heat evenly, making it easier to cook vegetables slowly without browning. The amount of fat is important, too. You want enough butter or oil to really coat the onions. After 15 minutes or so of slow cooking, the onions will be transformed into a very soft, translucent, sweet base for the soup.

Next, add a vegetable, such as carrots, sliced uniformly for even cooking. (Otherwise you will have underdone and overdone vegetables in your soup.) Salt generously (enough for the vegetables to taste good on their own) and continue cooking for a few minutes. This preliminary seasoning and cooking infuses the fat with the perfume and flavor of the vegetables. (The fat disperses the flavor throughout the soup.) This is an important technique, not just for soup but for cooking in general: building and developing flavor at each step before moving on.

Now add broth or water, bring to a boil, and reduce to a simmer. Cook until the vegetables are tender but not falling apart. The soup will not taste finished until the vegetables have cooked through and given their flavor to the broth. Keep tasting. It is wonderful to discover how the flavors change and develop as the soup cooks. Does it need more salt? If you're unsure, season a small spoonful and see if it tastes better with more. This is the only way you can find out.

Many, many vegetables will make great soup when you follow this formula. The only variable is the length of time they take to cook. The best way to keep track is to keep tasting as you go. Some favorite vegetable soups that jump to mind are: turnip and turnip greens, corn, potato and leek, butternut squash, and onion.

A vegetable soup made this way, with a flavorful stock rather than water, and served as a rustic "brothy" soup, will be delicious. (In fact, if the broth is rich enough, I sometimes skip any precooking in butter and add both onions and vegetables directly to the simmering broth.) If the soup is made with water instead of broth, and puréed to a uniform texture, the result will be a more delicate soup dominated by the pure flavor of the vegetables themselves. This is especially desirable for soups made from such sweet, tender vegetables as fava beans, peas, or corn. I purée such soups through a food mill, but you can also use a blender, which generates finer purées. Do be careful when using a blender to purée hot soup: always make sure the lid has an open vent hole to let the steam escape so that the whole lot doesn't explode.

When a vegetable is especially fresh and wonderful, make the soup with water alone for the purest, most delicate flavor.

Various garnishes and enrichments can be added when you serve the soup. Many cooks finish a puréed soup by spooning in a dollop of cream or stirring in a lump of butter, and a last-minute addition of herbs and spices or a squeeze of lemon can be enlivening. But use discretion; a garnish can overcomplicate or overpower the flavor of the soup itself.

Carrot Soup

8 SERVINGS

Melt in a heavy-bottomed pot:

4 tablespoons (½ stick) butter

Add:

2 onions, sliced

1 thyme sprig

Cook over medium-low heat until tender, about 10 minutes. Add:

2½ pounds carrots, peeled and sliced (about 6 cups)

Season with:

Salt

Cook for 5 minutes. Cooking the carrots with the onions for a while builds flavor. Add:

6 cups broth

Bring to a boil, lower the heat, and simmer until the carrots are tender, about 30 minutes. When done, season with salt to taste, and purée if desired.

VARIATIONS

• For a lighter, simpler version, use broth, but skip the preliminary cooking of the onions. Instead add them directly to the broth with the carrots and simmer until tender.

• Garnish with a bit of whipped cream or crème fraîche seasoned with salt and pepper and chopped herbs. Chervil, chives, or tarragon are all good choices.

• Add ¼ cup basmati rice with the carrots, use water instead of broth, add 1 cup of plain yogurt just before puréeing, and garnish with mint.

• Cook a jalapeño pepper with the onions, add some cilantro before puréeing, and garnish with chopped cilantro.

• Heat some clarified butter or olive oil, sizzle a spoonful of cumin seeds in it, and spoon this over the soup as a garnish.

A Soup of Many Vegetables

A hearty soup like minestrone is a deeply satisfying meal in itself. You can serve this soup throughout the year, changing the vegetables to reflect the seasons.

MINESTRONE MEANS "big soup" in Italian: a big soup of many vegetables. In order for them all to be cooked through at the same time, they're added in stages. First a tasty *soffritto* (a base of aromatic vegetables) is made, long-cooking vegetables are added and moistened with water or broth, and the soup is brought to a boil, at which point the more tender vegetables are added. Dried beans and pasta are cooked separately and added at the end. The recipe below is for a classic summertime minestrone, followed by seasonal variations.

The soffritto can be made of onions only but often includes carrots and celery. Fennel can be substituted for the celery when a more delicate flavor is wanted. Garlic is always added at the end of the cooking to ensure that it does not burn. Be sure to use a heavy-bottomed pot and lots of olive oil. For a more hearty soup, let the soffritto cook to a golden hue; for a less robust version, don't let the vegetables color at all. Either way, the vegetables should be cooked through to give the soup the full benefit of their flavors; this will take 10 minutes or more. They're done when they look and taste good enough to eat on their own.

The vegetables added after the soffritto—such as squash and green beans—are cut into pieces small enough to ensure that each spoonful of soup will contain a mixture. They're added sequentially, according to the length of time they take to cook through without getting mushy. Greens need to be cut into bite-size pieces, too; if they're cut in strips they can hang down and dribble hot soup on your chin or your clothes. Winter greens such as kale or chard take longer to cook and should go in with the first group of vegetables. Tender greens such as spinach will cook in just a few minutes and should be added towards the end of cooking. Salt the soup as it cooks; this will intensify and improve the flavor as a last-minute salting cannot.

Dried beans—and pasta, if you're using it—should be cooked separately before being added to the soup. Save the bean cooking liquid; it adds flavor and body to the soup. The cooked beans should be added during the last 10 minutes so they have a chance to absorb flavor, but not overcook. The pasta should be added at the very end so it doesn't overcook and get bloated and flabby.

To preserve its fresh flavor, the garnish of olive oil and cheese should be added to the bowls of soup, not to the pot. I always pass a bowl of grated cheese and a bottle of olive oil at the table.

Minestrone

8 SERVINGS

Cut all the vegetables into bite-size pieces so that each spoonful will have a variety of tastes and textures.

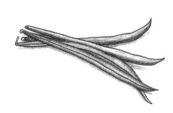

Pesto is another excellent garnish for the soup.

Prepare:

1 cup dried cannellini or borlotti beans (see page 78)

This will yield 2½ to 3 cups of cooked beans. Reserve the cooking liquid.

Heat in a heavy-bottomed pan over medium heat:

¼ cup olive oil

Add:

1 large onion, finely chopped

2 carrots, peeled and finely chopped

Cook for 15 minutes, or until tender. Add:

4 garlic cloves, coarsely chopped

5 thyme sprigs

1 bay leaf

2 teaspoons salt

Cook for 5 minutes longer. Add, and bring to a boil:

3 cups water

When boiling, add:

1 small leek, diced

½ pound green beans, cut into 1-inch lengths

Cook for 5 minutes, then add:

2 medium zucchini, cut into small dice

2 medium tomatoes, peeled, seeded, and chopped

Cook for 15 minutes. Taste for salt and adjust as necessary.

Add the cooked beans, along with:

1 cup bean cooking liquid

2 cups spinach leaves, coarsely chopped (about 1 pound)

Cook for 5 minutes. If the soup is too thick, add more bean cooking liquid. Remove the bay leaf.

Serve in bowls, each one garnished with:

2 teaspoons extra-virgin olive oil

1 tablespoon or more grated Parmesan cheese

◆ Fall Minestrone with Kale and Butternut Squash: Follow the recipe, but add 2 finely chopped celery stalks to the soffritto and cook to a rich golden brown. Instead of thyme, add about ½ teaspoon chopped rosemary and 1 teaspoon chopped sage with the garlic. Borlotti or cranberry beans can be substituted for the cannellini beans. Omit the green beans, zucchini, fresh tomatoes, and spinach, and use instead 1 bunch kale, stemmed, washed, and chopped; 1 small can of tomatoes, drained and chopped; and ½ butternut squash, peeled and cut into ¼-inch cubes (about 2 cups). Cook the tomatoes and kale with the soffritto for 5 minutes, add the water, and cook for 15 minutes. Add the squash and continue cooking until tender, about 10 to 15 minutes, before adding the cooked beans.

◆ Winter Minestrone with Turnips, Potatoes, and Cabbage: Follow the recipe, but to the soffritto add 2 celery stalks, chopped fine, and cook to a rich golden brown. Cut up ½ head cabbage into bite-size pieces and cook until tender in salted boiling water. For the green beans, zucchini, and tomatoes, substitute 1 pound turnips and ½ pound yellow potatoes, peeled and cut into bite-size pieces. If the turnips have fresh greens attached, stem, wash, and chop them and add them to the soup with the turnips and potatoes. Towards the end of the cooking, add the beans and, instead of the spinach, the cooked cabbage.

◆ Spring Minestrone with Peas and Asparagus: Instead of carrot in the soffritto, use 1 fennel bulb, trimmed and cut into bite-size pieces. Do not let it brown. If green garlic is available, use 2 or 3 stalks, trimmed and chopped, instead of garlic cloves. Use 2 leeks instead of one. Add the liquid (half water, half broth, if possible), bring to a boil, and simmer for 10 minutes. Omit the green beans, zucchini, and tomatoes. Substitute 1 cup shelled peas (from 1 pound in the pod) and ½ pound asparagus, trimmed and sliced on the diagonal into ½-inch-thick pieces. Add with the beans and cook for 5 minutes before adding the spinach. If not serving this soup right away, cool it down quickly in an ice bath so the asparagus does not lose its bright green color.

Beans, Dried and Fresh

White Beans with Rosemary and Garlic

Cranberry Bean Gratin

Fava Bean Purée

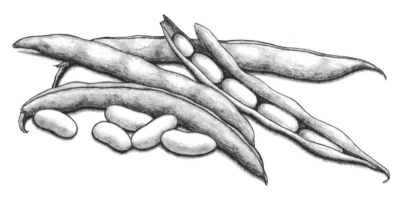

BEANS BELONG to a huge botanical family that includes all the flowering plants whose fertilized flowers form pods, or shells, with seeds inside. These are the legumes; beans, peas, soybeans, and lentils all fall into this family. After these plants bloom in spring, their pods grow and swell; and the seeds within ripen until, for a brief moment in time—no more than a few weeks—they reach full maturity and deliciousness before beginning to dry on the vine. The shells become dry and papery and the beans are ready to harvest. Green beans, of course, are consumed pod and all, although some green bean varieties such as romano mature into very good shell beans when left on the vine to ripen. The recipes in this section, however, are about the so-called shell beans, or shelling beans: the dryable kinds that are removed from their shells and either cooked and eaten fresh, right at harvest; or else dried and stored, to be soaked and cooked later on.

Shell Beans

I COOK SHELL BEANS in different ways: sometimes plain, with rosemary, garlic, and olive oil; sometimes in soup, alone or with other vegetables, puréed or not; other times in gratins, under crunchy breadcrumbs. Beans can be cooked in advance, and they keep well for a day or two, refrigerated in their cooking liquid, to be reheated and served plain or incorporated into any number of dishes. What's more, beans are extremely nutritious and affordable compared to other sources of protein; and, perhaps best of all, little kids love them.

Today it's easy to find many different fresh and dried beans in farmers' markets and good grocery stores. Spring is the season for fresh fava beans. (Dried fava beans are widely available, but I usually stick to the fresh ones.) In late summer, from August through September, I look for the many varieties of fresh ripe shell beans that may be fleetingly available. They are a real treasure of the late summer and early fall. Unlike their dried counterparts, fresh shell beans do not need to be soaked and they cook quite quickly. And all winter long there are the many, many dried bean varieties to bring variety and color to winter menus.

As time passes, beans continue to dry out. When soaked, a bean from a recent harvest will plump quickly and cook quickly, too. I find that dried beans are best bought in bulk; that way it's more likely they'll be from a recent harvest. Older beans take a lot longer to soak and cook and won't taste nearly as good. They often cook unevenly, with some turning to mush while others remain hard. If you can't find good organic beans in your area, talk to the produce manager at your grocery store. Talk to the farmers at your farmers' market. Let them know you're looking for beans. Meanwhile, you can order organic beans by mail or on the Internet.

Bean Varieties

HERE IS A SHORT LIST of varieties from among the astonishing array of available dried beans, lentils, and peas. In my experience, old-fashioned bean varieties—those sold as heirloom varieties—are usually tastier than many of the more common varieties. Keep trying different ones in pursuit of your own personal favorites.

Cannellini beans are the white beans I use the most. Mild-flavored, with a creamy texture, they are good for many Italian and French dishes. Other white beans include: haricots blancs, white runner beans, European soldiers, Great Northerns, navys, and tiny rice beans.

Cranberry beans are light reddish brown with dark brown speckles. Plump and full-flavored, they are the typical beans for *pasta e fagioli*, *ribollita*, and other hearty Italian fare. They are found fresh in the late summer and fall and dried year-round. There are many similar bean varieties, with beautiful names: borlotti, eye of the goat, and tongue of fire, for examples.

Flageolet beans are diminutive, light green beans with a distinctive vegetable flavor and a relatively firm texture. These are commonly paired with lamb and duck in French cuisine.

Lima beans are exquisite when fresh. Among the varieties I especially like, fresh and dried, is the huge brown-and-pink-speckled Christmas lima, which has a unique nutty flavor.

Pinto beans are a staple of Mexican and Tex-Mex cuisine. They're tasty either whole or fried in lard and crushed up. Many varieties have exceptional flavor, including flor de mayo, flor de junio, and rattlesnake beans.

Black beans are the mainstay of many Latin American cuisines. They have a wonderful earthy flavor that makes tasty soup, among other things, but they often take longer to cook than other beans.

Lentils are not true beans, exactly; they are tiny, lens-shaped pulses that belong to another species of dried legume, and come in many colors. They cook quickly and don't need to be soaked. There are many varieties, but the ones I use the most are small French green lentils and tiny black beluga lentils, which both hold their shape when cooked. I also love the yellow and red-orange lentils used in Indian cooking for soups and purées.

Black-eyed peas (and their cousins crowder peas) are ingredients in some classic Southern dishes. Although hard to shell, they are well worth trying fresh. I love them in ragouts with green beans and herbs.

Chickpeas or garbanzo beans are hard and dense when dried and take a little longer to cook than other beans. In the late summer, you may be lucky enough to find fresh chickpeas, which are green and delicate. (The flour made from dried chickpeas makes many interesting dishes.)

Soybeans I cook fresh, in boiling salted water, and serve in their shells with sea salt sprinkled over (*edamame* in Japan). Eat them plain, popping the beans out of the pods into your mouth. They make a healthy and well-received snack for kids.

Soaking and Cooking Beans

RULE OF THUMB
1 pound dried beans =
2 cups dried beans =
6 cups cooked beans

Dried beans cook best when soaked for a number of hours. Overnight is best. Cover the beans with plenty of water to keep them from poking up above the surface when they have absorbed water and swelled. I cover them with at least three times as much water as beans. If all the beans were not completely submerged overnight some will cook at a different rate than others and you'll end up with overdone and underdone beans in the same pot. Drain after soaking and use fresh water for cooking them.

All over the world, beans are traditionally cooked in earthenware pots (and for some reason they seem to taste better when they are), but any heavy nonreactive pot will do. Try to choose a wide pot so the layer of beans isn't too deep; otherwise the beans are hard to stir and the ones on the bottom of the pot get crushed. Be sure to use enough water that stirring them is easy: the water level should always be an inch or so above the level of the beans. If the water is too low, the beans will be crowded and will tend to fall apart when they are stirred. Worst of all they might start to stick and burn on the bottom of the pot. Salt is best added towards the end of the cooking to keep the beans tender.

When done, the beans should be tender but not falling apart, though it is better to overcook them than undercook them! You don't want them to be the least bit al dente, or crunchy. The best way to test them is to bite one. Start testing after an hour. When they are fully cooked, let the beans cool in their liquid before you drain them. If they're drained right away, the skins will crack and they'll look shaggy.

When cooking fresh shell beans there is no need to soak them. Just pop them out of their shells and put them in a pot. Cover with water by no more than about 1½ inches: the beans will not absorb much water. Add the salt at the beginning and begin testing for doneness after about 10 minutes. Depending on the variety, the beans may take as long as an hour to cook, but usually they are done in much less time.

Beans can be flavored at the end of their cooking and served right away; or once cooked, they can be cooled, flavored or not, refrigerated (or frozen) in their liquid, and used later.

RULE OF THUMB
1 pound fresh beans =
1 cup shelled beans =
1 cup cooked beans

White Beans with Rosemary and Garlic

MAKES 3 CUPS BEANS

Soak overnight in 4 cups water:

1 cup dried white beans (cannellini, white runner, Great Northern, navy, and so on)

Drain and transfer to a heavy pot. Add water to cover by 2 inches. Bring to a boil. Lower the heat and skim off any foam. Simmer gently for 2 hours or so, until the beans are tender. Add more water if necessary during the cooking.

Season to taste with:

Salt

In a heavy-bottomed saucepan or skillet, warm over low heat:

¼ cup extra-virgin olive oil

Add:

4 garlic cloves, coarsely chopped
1 teaspoon coarsely chopped rosemary leaves

Cook just until the garlic is soft, about 2 minutes. Stir into the beans, taste for salt, and adjust as needed. Let the dish sit for a few minutes before serving to allow the flavors to marry.

VARIATION

◆ Leaves of either sage or winter or summer savory are delicious substitutes for rosemary.

Flavoring Beans

The key to flavorful beans is to cook them tender first, then add fresh flavorings such as garlic and herbs.

Beans cooked and served simply seasoned—like the cannellini beans in the previous recipe with garlic and rosemary—is only one of a great many bean dishes—soups, gratins, purées, and more—that are tastier when their primary flavoring comes after an initial cooking. I sometimes add garlic or herbs or even a bit of onion while the beans are cooking the first time, but I find that good flavor is most prominent when it's added after the primary cooking. Added flavor can mean anything from a dash of olive oil to a complex tomato sauce, depending on the dish. For example, in the classic Italian dish called *fagioli all'uccelletto* (which means beans seasoned like a small bird), the cooked beans are simmered in a garlicky tomato sauce with plenty of sage. An example from Mexican cuisine is *frijoles refritos*, beans which, after an initial cooking, are fried in lard with garlic and sautéed onions, and then mashed. (There are exceptions to every rule, and one that comes immediately to mind is that when something like a ham hock or a prosciutto bone is used to flavor beans, it can be added at the beginning to cook slowly with the beans throughout their cooking.)

The beans should be drained of most of their liquid before final flavorings are added. (Save the bean water to make a tasty soup base or to moisten a gratin as it cooks.) Once the beans are ready, stir in the flavorings. Continue to cook them together for at least 10 minutes or so, to allow the flavors to infuse the beans.

To make gratins like the one that follows, first sauté onions, carrots, and celery together. To make sure they contribute their full flavor, season the vegetables to taste before adding them to the beans. Beans are very lean and the addition of a flavorful oil or fat makes them taste even better.

Cranberry Bean Gratin
6 SERVINGS

Soak overnight in 4 cups water:
   1¼ cups cranberry or borlotti beans
Drain and cover with fresh water by 2 inches in a saucepan. Bring to a boil. Lower the heat and skim off any foam. Simmer gently for 2 hours or so until the beans are tender. Add more water if necessary during the cooking.

Season to taste with:

Salt

Set the beans aside to cool in their liquid. Meanwhile finely dice:

½ onion (about ¼ cup diced)

1 small peeled carrot (about ¼ cup diced)

1 small celery stalk (about ¼ cup diced)

Heat in a heavy-bottomed pan:

¼ cup olive oil

Add the diced vegetables and cook until tender, about 10 minutes. Add:

4 garlic cloves, thinly sliced

6 fresh sage leaves, chopped

Salt

Cook for 5 minutes and then stir in:

½ cup chopped tomatoes, fresh or canned organic

Cook for 5 minutes. Taste and add salt if necessary.

Drain the beans, reserving the liquid. Mix the beans with the vegetables and put into a medium-size gratin or baking dish. Taste for salt. Add enough bean liquid to almost cover. Drizzle with:

¼ cup extra-virgin olive oil

Cover with:

½ cup Toasted Breadcrumbs (page 63)

Bake for 40 minutes in a preheated 350°F oven, checking occasionally. If the gratin is drying out, carefully spoon in a little bean liquid (pouring at the sides of the gratin dish to avoid getting the crumbs wet).

The oil and breadcrumbs on top bake to a delicious and crunchy crust.

VARIATIONS

◆ Fresh shell beans make an even tastier gratin. Shell 3 pounds fresh cranberry beans. Cover them with water to a depth of about an inch, bring to a boil, reduce to a simmer, and start checking for doneness after about 20 minutes.

◆ You don't have to turn the beans into a gratin. Simply cook the beans together with the tomatoes and vegetables for 10 minutes before serving.

◆ Other herbs can be substituted for sage: try about ½ tablespoon of the finely chopped leaves of rosemary, thyme, summer or winter savory, marjoram, parsley, or oregano.

Fresh Fava Beans

Fᴀᴠᴀ ʙᴇᴀɴs are a harbinger of spring. Like other kinds of beans, they form in pods, but they are also covered in a tough, rather bitter skin. The earliest harvests offer beans that are tiny, brilliant green, and so tender they don't need to be peeled. When not eaten raw, straight from the pod, these are best cooked briefly with a little water and oil or butter. As the season progresses, the beans continue to mature, and they become larger and starchier. At this point they can be popped out of their pods, skinned, and cooked into a luscious, bright green purée that I adore slathering on crisp croutons or serving alongside roasted meats. Still later in the season the beans turn yellow and dry out and are too mature to use this way.

Fava beans do require a bit of preparation, but their delicate taste and splash of color are well worth the effort. Popping the beans from their thick soft pods is an enjoyable group project that even little children can join. An easy way to pop the beans out of the pod is to grasp one with both hands; bend the pod back against your thumbs and press out, snapping the beans out of the pod. After the beans are shelled the opaque outer skin of the bean needs to be removed. (Although in Mediterranean cooking the skins are sometimes left on, this increases the cooking time and results in a different taste.) To do so, plunge the beans into boiling water and leave them until the skin is easy to remove. This will take less than a minute, so check one right away. (If you cook the beans too long they will get mashed when you try to slip them out of their skins.) Drain the beans and put them in a bowl of icy cold water. When they are cool, drain them, and pop out the beans, using a fingernail to slit the skin and squeezing the bean out with the fingers of the other hand.

Don't cook the skinned beans too quickly; medium-low heat is best. Stir them occasionally as they are cooking, and, if you notice that they are drying out, add a bit of water. They are done when they can be crushed into a smooth paste when pressed with a spoon.

All kinds of beans, fresh or dried, can be flavored and made into tasty purées. I love cannellini bean purée, fresh cranberry bean purée, and refried pinto beans, too. Another favorite hors d'oeuvre is chickpeas with olive oil and hot pepper puréed and served with flatbread or crackers.

Fava Bean Purée

MAKES ABOUT 3 CUPS

Fresh favas that are more mature, with a higher starch content than very young beans, make the best-tasting purée.

Bring a pot of water to a boil as you shell the beans from:

4 pounds fava beans

Blanch quickly in the boiling water and then cool in ice water. Drain and pop the beans out of their skins.

Heat in a heavy-bottomed saucepan:

½ cup olive oil

Add the fava beans with:

4 garlic cloves, sliced

1 branch rosemary

Salt

½ cup water

Cook until the fava beans are very tender, stirring occasionally, and adding more water as necessary. The beans are done when they can be crushed easily with the back of a spoon, about 15 minutes. Mash with a spoon or pass them through a food mill.

Stir in:

¼ cup extra-virgin olive oil

Taste and season with salt as needed. Thin with water if necessary. Serve right away or at room temperature.

Pasta and Polenta

Fresh Pasta

Spaghettini with Oil and Garlic

Polenta and Polenta Torta

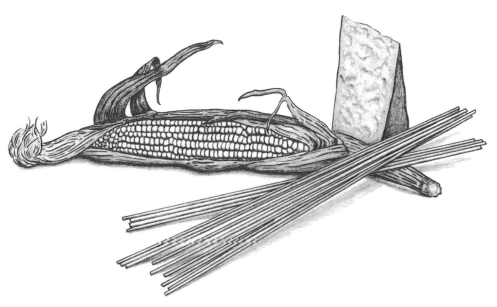

Pasta and polenta are two of the great standbys of the pantry and two of the great mainstays of the Italian table. A box of dried pasta and a few other staples can always be turned into a quick meal without much planning; and polenta, which is simply corn ground into cornmeal, is also remarkably versatile and exceptionally tasty. Pasta and polenta are prepared similarly, in salted boiling water; and at their simplest, both can be served with little more than butter or oil and some cheese. I like to make fresh pasta, too, because its texture is particularly well suited to certain dishes such as baked lasagna and hand-cut fresh noodles with a savory meat sauce or stew, and it is essential for homemade ravioli and cannelloni.

Making Fresh Pasta

Pasta dough can be made many hours ahead and refrigerated until ready to roll out.

Fʀᴇsʜ ᴘᴀsᴛᴀ, at least the version I make most often, is nothing more than flour and eggs. The prospect of making pasta may seem intimidating, but I assure you, it is surprisingly easy. The most time-consuming part is rolling it out, but a hand-cranked machine makes this job quick and easy. (Thrift stores and yard sales are great places to look for pasta machines.)

The main ingredient of pasta is flour. The flour I use most often is unbleached, organic, and all-purpose. (Bleached flour, besides having added chemicals, has very little flavor and makes a sticky dough.) For different flavors and textures, whole-grain flours such as whole wheat, buckwheat, farro, and others can be substituted for up to half the amount of flour; more than that and the dough becomes friable or crumbly and can't be rolled as thin as needed for some recipes. Durum flour makes great pasta with a good bite but unfortunately it is hard to find; if you do come across it, substitute it for up to half of the total flour. Semolina is ground from durum wheat, but it is very coarse and hard to turn into egg pasta. Experiment to see what your favorite flours and ratios are.

To make the dough by hand, measure the flour into a bowl, one that easily holds the flour with plenty of extra room for stirring. Break the eggs into another bowl or cup and beat them slightly to mix the yolks and whites. Make a well in the flour (use a spoon or your hand to make a depression) and pour in the beaten eggs. Use a fork to stir as though scrambling the eggs, scraping in flour from the sides bit by bit. When the egg and flour mixture gets too stiff to stir with a fork, continue mixing with your hands. When the flour is mostly absorbed, turn the dough out onto a lightly floured surface and knead lightly until the dough comes together. It won't be perfectly smooth. Wrap it in a plastic bag or plastic wrap and let sit for an hour at room temperature (or longer, refrigerated). The dough needs to rest to allow the gluten that has been activated by the stirring and kneading to relax, making the dough easier to roll out.

To make the dough with a stand mixer, put the flour in the bowl, attach the paddle, and slowly pour in the eggs while mixing at low speed. Mix until the dough begins to come together in small, moist clumps. Turn out onto a lightly floured surface and knead together. Cover and let rest as above.

Through trial and error I have discovered that a wetter dough is much easier to work with, especially when rolling out by hand (it does not spring back as quickly as a dry dough). The ideal texture for pasta is a dough that comes together easily but is not sticky. If, after mixing, the dough is crumbly and dry, moisten with a sprinkling of water. Add more as needed, a little at a time, but avoid making it *too* wet. If the dough is too wet and sticky, you can knead in more flour, but let it rest at least an hour to come together. Flour will vary from batch to batch, so what seemed like the perfect amount of liquid one time may be too much or too little another.

Pasta can be rolled by hand or with a machine. The rollers of the machine create perfectly smooth noodles, while hand-rolling results in interesting surface irregularities for the sauce to cling to, adding nuance and flavor. It's worth rolling the dough by hand once to taste and feel the difference.

Knead the dough in the machine by repeatedly rolling the dough, folding it in thirds, and rolling again.

When rolling pasta with a machine, first flatten the ball of dough with your hands, then open the machine up to its fullest setting, and, while cranking slowly but steadily, pass the dough through the rollers of the machine. (If you are making a large amount of dough, divide it into smaller balls to avoid overloading the machine.) Fold the rolled dough over itself into thirds, as though folding a letter, and put it through the machine again. This process kneads the dough. If the dough is sticking, sprinkle it lightly with flour. Smooth out the flour with your hand before rolling again. Fold and roll two more times; the dough should be soft and silky. If not, repeat the kneading one more time.

Once kneaded, the dough is ready to be stretched. Put it through the widest setting one more time, then lower the setting each time you put the dough through. As the dough begins to lengthen and thin, put your hand (the one that is not turning the crank) very, very lightly on top of the dough as it goes through the machine; this helps it to stay on course and not veer off and crumple up under the rollers. Keep track of the surface of the pasta; if it gets sticky, sprinkle lightly with flour again, smoothing the flour with your hand. (Any lumps of flour will make pits in the dough.) To deal with the pasta between rollings, fold the lengthening sheet of dough as it comes out of the machine, back and forth over itself, like ribbon candy. Then feed one end of the folded pasta through the rollers on the next thinnest setting and it will unfold as it is drawn through the machine.

Once the dough has reached the desired thickness, it's time to cut it. Bear in mind that pasta expands quite a bit as it cooks, so if you're unsure how thin to roll the dough, cut and cook a couple of trial noodles. If the noodles are just a bit too thick and only need a slight adjustment, run the pasta through the same setting again. Most pasta makers come with cutting attachments, but noodles are easy to cut by hand; they look charmingly handmade and have a pleasing irregular texture. Cut the dough into 12- to 16-inch-long sheets and stack these on top of each other, flouring generously between sheets. Fold the stack in half, lengthwise, and then in half again. Cut across the stack to make noodles of the desired width. Toss with a bit of extra flour to unfold them (I love the way the noodles feel falling through my fingers), and spread on a plate or sheet pan. Cover with parchment paper or a light towel and refrigerate if not cooking right away. For lasagne, cannelloni, ravioli, and other stuffed pasta, the sheets of pasta are cut into larger squares or left in long sheets to be stuffed.

Fresh pasta absorbs a lot of water, so it needs to be cooked in a generous amount of salted, rapidly boiling water. Stir to ensure that the noodles don't stick together. The pasta is done when the noodles are cooked through, but still have a good bite (in Italian, *al dente*, "to the tooth"). Fresh pasta cooks very quickly, in 3 to 6 minutes, depending on the thickness of the noodles.

Wide hand-cut egg noodles, such as pappardelle, are perfect to serve with a stew or a Bolognese sauce.

Fresh Pasta

4 SERVINGS

WITH FRESH PASTA
YOU CAN MAKE

linguine

fettuccine

pappardelle

lasagne

cannelloni

fazzoletti

cappelletti

agnolotti

ravioli

tortellini

*Fresh hand-cut noodles,
such as fettuccine
and linguine, are well
matched with creamy
or buttery sauces and
delicate vegetables, such
as peas and prosciutto.*

Measure and put into a bowl:

2 cups flour

Mix together in another bowl:

2 eggs

2 egg yolks

Make a well in the flour and pour in the eggs. Mix with a fork, as though scrambling the eggs, incorporating the flour bit by bit. When the flour is too stiff to mix with a fork, finish the mixing by hand. Turn the dough out onto a floured surface and knead lightly. Or put the flour in a stand mixer fitted with the paddle attachment and pour in the eggs while mixing at low speed. Mix until the dough just starts to come together, adding a few drops of water if the dough is dry and crumbly. Turn out and knead as above. Shape the dough into a disk and wrap in plastic. Let rest at least an hour before rolling.

Roll out by hand on a lightly floured board or using a machine. When using a machine, roll the pasta through the widest setting, fold into thirds, and pass through the machine again. Repeat two more times. Then roll, decreasing the setting on the machine one notch at a time, until the pasta is the desired thickness. Cut into noodles.

VARIATIONS

◆ For herb noodles, before adding the eggs mix into the flour ¼ cup chopped parsley, marjoram, or thyme, or 2 tablespoons chopped rosemary or sage.

◆ To make spinach noodles, gently sauté in a little butter ¼ pound spinach leaves until tender. Cool and squeeze dry, and blend until smooth with 1 egg and 1 egg yolk; use this purée in place of the eggs.

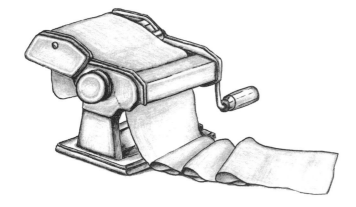

Making Cannelloni and Ravioli

FOR CANNELLONI roll out the pasta and cut the sheets into rectangles about 4 by 3 inches. Cook in salted boiling water until done. Cool in a large bowl of cold water and lay the rectangles out on a cloth. Avoid stacking them; they will stick to each other unless you brush them first with olive oil or melted butter.

Pipe or spoon a bit of filling along one third of the length of a piece of pasta. Gently roll the pasta to form a large straw. Place the cannelloni seam side down in a buttered ovenproof pan. Bake them with sauce, stock, or melted butter and cheese for 20 minutes at 400°F.

To make ravioli, roll out the pasta fairly thin and cut into sheets about 14 inches long. Keep the stack of well-floured pasta sheets under a towel to keep them from drying as you work with one sheet at a time. Pipe or spoon 1 tablespoon of filling along the lower third of a sheet of pasta. Keep about 1½ inches between each blob of filling. Spray very lightly with a fine mist of water. Fold the upper half of the pasta over the lower half; then, starting at the fold, gently coax all the air out of the ravioli, pressing the two layers of pasta together with your fingertips. When the sheet of ravioli has been formed and pressed, use a zigzag rolling cutter to cut off the bottom edge and to cut between each pocket of filling. Separate the ravioli and lay them out on a sheet pan sprinkled with flour; make sure they aren't touching each other or they will stick together. Cover with a towel or parchment paper and refrigerate until ready to cook. Keep refrigerated right up to the time of cooking to prevent the filling from seeping through the pasta, which can cause the ravioli to stick to the pan.

Cook the ravioli in salted boiling water for 5 to 6 minutes or until the pasta is done. Drain and place on a platter or in individual bowls. Sauce and garnish as desired.

Cooking Dry Pasta

ALTHOUGH SPAGHETTI is a perennial favorite, there are lots of different noodle shapes and many different grain varieties that merit equal attention. Whichever you choose, proper cooking and saucing make all the difference. Here are a few bits of advice to follow for a really great plate of pasta.

Water plays an important role in cooking and dressing pasta. Cook pasta in a large quantity of salted boiling water. As it cooks it absorbs

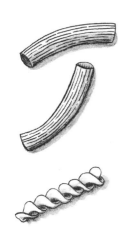

The secret of many an Italian grandmother is saving some of the pasta cooking water to add to the sauce.

the water and it will stick together if the noodles are crowded too tightly. Bring the water to a rolling boil before adding the noodles; this helps keep them moving instead of settling to the bottom of the pan. Stir them once or twice in the beginning to keep them from sticking to one another or to the pan. Salting the water seasons the noodles before they are sauced, making for a tastier dish. It is not necessary to put oil in the water. Doing so may help keep the noodles from sticking (which they won't anyway if there is enough boiling water in the pot), but the oily coating they receive while cooking prevents the sauce from adhering to the noodles in the bowl. And unless you are making a pasta salad, don't rinse the noodles after they are cooked: this takes away all the outer starch, which adds texture and flavor to the sauce.

Cook the pasta al dente: there should be no white core left in it but it should be still firm to the bite. Taste a noodle now and then to gauge the doneness; the white core is very apparent in a bitten piece of undercooked pasta. Dry egg noodles will cook fairly quickly (5 to 6 minutes) while more rustic noodles will take a lot longer (10 to 13 minutes). When the pasta is cooked, drain it right away to keep it from cooking further. Always save a little of the cooking water before draining; it can come in very handy when saucing the pasta.

There are a few different strategies for combining pasta with sauce. One is to put the drained pasta directly into the sauce and toss. (It is a good idea to season the noodles directly with a bit of salt before tossing them; this is especially true when a very simple sauce is being used.) Another is to toss the noodles with oil or butter and cheese and a little sauce, plate them, and then top with more sauce—a good way to serve pasta with meat sauce. Yet another is to drain the pasta when it is a touch underdone and finish cooking it in the sauce for a few minutes. This only works with sauces that are juicy, as the pasta will continue to absorb liquid as it cooks. The pasta water that was saved before draining the noodles is very helpful for loosening thick sauces or stodgy noodles; it is full of flavor and texture from the salt and starch of the noodles and makes for a much lighter dish than adding more oil, butter, or sauce.

Different noodles are better suited for certain sauces. Large chunky noodles go well with chunky sauces, egg noodles are good with buttery sauces or meat ragùs, and thin long noodles are complemented by simple tomato-based sauces as well as olive oil sauces like the one that follows.

Spaghettini with Oil and Garlic

4 SERVINGS

This is a pasta that can be made even when the pantry is nearly bare and in as little as 15 minutes.

Bring a large pot of salted water to a boil and cook until al dente:

1 pound spaghettini

Meanwhile, heat in a heavy-bottomed pan over medium-low heat:

⅓ cup extra-virgin olive oil

When the oil is just warm, add:

4 garlic cloves, chopped fine

3 parsley branches, stems removed, leaves chopped

A pinch of hot pepper flakes

Salt

Cook until the garlic is soft, turning off the heat just as the garlic starts to sizzle. Don't let it brown or burn.

Drain the pasta when cooked, reserving some of the cooking water. Add the noodles to the sauce in the pan with a pinch of salt and toss. Taste for seasoning and loosen with some of the cooking water if needed. Serve immediately.

VARIATIONS

• Double the amount of parsley, or add other chopped tender herbs, such as basil, marjoram, or summer savory.

• Add ⅔ cup washed and halved cherry tomatoes to the oil a minute after adding the garlic.

• Garnish with grated Parmesan cheese.

• Add a few chopped black olives and/or chopped anchovies with the garlic and parsley.

• Substitute egg fettuccine for the spaghettini, and butter for the oil.

Making Polenta

POLENTA IS A VERY SIMPLE DISH of ground corn cooked in water. It is exceptionally tasty and, like pasta, remarkably versatile. When first cooked, polenta is soft; as it cools, it becomes firm and can then be fried, grilled, or baked. Soft or firm, polenta is great next to roasted or braised meats, or sauced with a spoonful of tomato, meat, or mushroom sauce. For variety, fresh corn or fava beans can be stirred into soft polenta. Polenta can be turned into a luscious torta by layering it with cooked vegetables, cheese, and sauce. Whether ground from yellow or white corn, polenta is ground coarser than cornmeal but finer than grits. When fresh it smells sweet and looks bright yellow. Like all grains, it should be stored in a cool, dark place and replaced when old.

Cook polenta in boiling water. The approximate ratio of water to grain is four to one. This will vary depending on the variety of corn, how coarse it is ground, and how fresh it is; each batch you buy may be slightly different. Choose a heavy-bottomed pot when cooking polenta to avoid sticking and burning; use a flame tamer if a heavy pot is not available. Bring the water to a rolling boil and add the polenta in a slow, steady stream while stirring constantly with a whisk. Turn the heat down and continue whisking for 2 or 3 minutes, until the polenta is suspended in the water and no longer settles to the bottom of the pot. (This helps keep it from sticking to the bottom of the pan.) Season with salt and cook the polenta at a bare simmer, stirring occasionally, for about an hour. The polenta will be fully cooked and softened after 20 to 30 minutes, but the longer cooking time allows its full flavor to develop. Be warned that the thick polenta is very hot, so be careful when stirring and tasting. I spoon a bit onto a small plate to cool before tasting.

Cooking the polenta long and slow for as much as an hour develops a deep corn flavor and light texture.

Polenta should have a pourable, creamy consistency. If the polenta becomes thick or stiff while cooking, add water as needed to maintain the proper consistency. If too much water is added by accident, and the polenta becomes thin and soupy, just keep cooking it to evaporate the water. Polenta will set up quickly if not kept warm, so turn off the heat and cover the pot to keep it soft and hot for 20 minutes or so, or hold it for a longer time in a double boiler or by setting the pot in a larger pot of hot water. Polenta can be finished with butter or olive oil and cheese to enrich it and add flavor. Parmesan is the classic cheese to stir in, but try others; fontina, cheddar, or pecorino for example. Mascarpone or blue cheese is a luxurious garnish to top a bowl of soft polenta.

To make firm polenta, spread hot soft polenta evenly onto a rimmed baking sheet (it is not necessary to oil the pan). A depth of about one inch works well for most purposes. Let the polenta sit at room temperature or refrigerate until set. Don't cover until it has cooled. The firm polenta can be cut into shapes to bake, grill, or fry. To bake, brush with oil and bake at 350°F for 20 minutes or until crisp. To grill polenta, brush it with oil and place on a grill over hot coals; to prevent it from sticking, make sure the grill is hot. To fry, use shallow or deep fat. Polenta will always set up when cooled, but both very thin polenta and polenta that has been finished with a lot of butter or oil can fall apart when grilled or fried.

A polenta torta is made of alternate layers of polenta—either freshly made soft polenta or polenta that has already cooled and set—and sauce, such as tomato sauce, meat sauce, or pesto; cooked greens or other vegetables; and cheese. A polenta torta is a great make-ahead dish, ready to heat up any time.

Polenta

4 SERVINGS

RULE OF THUMB
1 : 4
1 part polenta
4 parts water

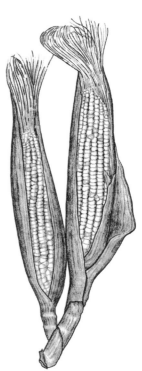

Boil, in a heavy-bottomed pot:

4 cups water

When boiling, whisk in:

1 cup polenta

1 teaspoon salt

Turn down the heat and stir constantly until the polenta is suspended in the water and no longer settles to the bottom of the pot. Cook for 1 hour, stirring occasionally, at a bare simmer. Add water if the polenta gets too thick. Stir in:

3 tablespoons butter or olive oil

½ cup grated Parmesan cheese

Taste and add more salt if needed. (Be careful when tasting the polenta; it is very hot.) Keep warm until ready to serve or spread it out on a rimmed baking sheet and let cool.

VARIATIONS

◆ Sauté 1 cup fresh corn kernels for 4 minutes, season with salt, and stir into the finished polenta.

◆ Stir 1 cup shelled and peeled fava beans into the finished polenta.

◆ Replace the Parmesan cheese with fontina, pecorino, or cheddar cheese.

Polenta Torta

6 SERVINGS

Prepare:

4 cups soft polenta (see page 92)

Prepare:

2 cups Simple Tomato Sauce (page 264)

Grate:

1 cup Parmesan cheese

Slice about ¼-inch thick:

½ pound fresh mozzarella (about 2 medium balls)

Oil an earthenware or other low-sided baking dish. Ladle in 1⅓ cups soft polenta. Spread 1 cup of tomato sauce over the polenta. On top of the tomato sauce, arrange half of the mozzarella slices. Sprinkle with half the grated Parmesan cheese. Ladle over another 1⅓ cups polenta, spread on the rest of the tomato sauce, layer on the rest of the mozzarella, then sprinkle with the rest of the Parmesan cheese. Ladle over the remaining 1⅓ cups of polenta and allow the torta to sit for at least 30 minutes before baking to allow the polenta to set. Fifteen minutes before baking, preheat the oven to 350°F. Bake until hot and bubbling, about 30 minutes.

VARIATIONS

◆ Prepare 1 recipe Wilted Chard with Onion (page 309), and layer half the cooked chard over each layer of grated Parmesan cheese.

◆ Make the torta with firm polenta, cutting pieces to fit the pan and layering as above.

◆ Stir 2 cups cooked vegetables (greens, dried beans, or corn, for example) into the polenta itself and layer as above with sauce and cheese.

◆ Use 1 cup Pesto (page 230) instead of, or in addition to, the tomato sauce.

◆ Use 1 cup grated fontina cheese instead of mozzarella.

◆ Use 2 cups Bolognese Sauce (page 227) or Mushroom Ragù (page 228) instead of tomato sauce.

Rice

Plain Rice

Red Rice Pilaf

Risotto Bianco

A BOWL OF RICE is as basic, as comforting, and as adaptable to everyday eating as bread. There are more than 40,000 varieties of rice, all stemming from a single species, *Oryza sativa*, but they all fall, more or less, into one of two categories: short-grain or long-grain. The varieties with short, fat, starchy grains have traditionally been grown and eaten in Japan, Korea, parts of China, and parts of Europe (the varieties grown for paella in Spain and for risotto in Italy are short-grain). The many long-grain varieties, which are relatively less sticky and have longer, thinner grains, include fragrant basmati rice from India, jasmine rice from Thailand, and Carolina rice from our own country.

Cooking
Plain Rice

For those who cook rice regularly or every day, a rice cooker is convenient and nearly foolproof. It works best for short-grain varieties and sushi rice.

If you have cooked too much rice (and it is easier to cook too much rather than too little), use it the next day. Reheat it with a little water in a covered pan, or make fried rice.

WHEN HARVESTED, every grain of rice, whether short or long, is surrounded by a layer of bran and encased within a husk, or hull. Rice with just the husks removed is called brown rice. When the bran layer of brown rice is milled and polished away, the result is white rice, which cooks more quickly, is less nutty-tasting, and is much less chewy than brown rice. (What is known as wild rice is the nearly black seed kernel of another plant entirely, a wild North American aquatic grass.) Plain rice can be central to many a quick meal: a make-your-own-sushi dinner, for example, with a big bowl of warm short-grain Japanese sticky rice and a plate of sliced fish, thinly sliced carrots and cucumbers, and sheets of crisp seaweed; or a thoroughly satisfying lunch of golden lentil soup flavored with cumin and garlic and accompanied by delicate basmati rice.

Cooking plain rice used to seem mysteriously difficult to me, even though I knew objectively that it involves nothing more than cooking the dried grains of rice in liquid, covered or uncovered, until they are done. And, in fact, you can boil rice in a generous quantity of water and drain it when it's done, or you can use no more water than will both evaporate and be absorbed by the rice in the time it takes the rice to cook perfectly. Or you can use a combination of these methods. The trick is learning the correct ratios of water to rice.

When rice is cooked it can end up unpleasantly sticky, which is why certain varieties benefit from a preliminary washing to remove excess surface starch. (The kinds of rice used for risotto and paella are never washed, however; the extra starch is an essential ingredient in these dishes.) To wash rice, put it in a large bowl, add cold water to cover, and swish the rice around, rubbing it between your hands now and then. When the water looks cloudy, pour it off (a strainer can be helpful here), and repeat the process until the rinsing water is clear or almost clear. Drain the rice well. If the recipe calls for soaking, this is the time to do it. Cover with water by at least one inch (or with the amount of water specified in a recipe) and soak for the required time.

To cook rice by the simplest absorption method, measure rice and water into a pot, bring to a boil, immediately turn down to a simmer, cover the pot tightly, and cook the rice until all the water is absorbed, about 15 to 20 minutes for white rice—and about 40 minutes for brown. Different kinds of rice absorb different quantities of liquid: 1 cup of brown rice absorbs 2 cups of water; 1 cup of long-grain white rice absorbs about 1½ cups; and 1 cup of short-grain white rice absorbs only 1 cup and 2 tablespoons of water. As in the second absorption method given here, many cooks add a pinch of salt and a teaspoon of butter or olive oil to each cup of rice, both for flavor and to help keep the grains from sticking together. Whichever method you use, when the rice is cooked, let it rest, covered, for 5 to 10 minutes before fluffing and serving it. It will be easier to fluff because the grains separate a bit when they have cooled down slightly.

How do you know if all the water has been absorbed? Although some people say this will ruin the rice, you can take off the lid and stir the rice to get a peek at the bottom of the pot. I assure you, you will not ruin the rice! If it is still wet, it probably needs to cook longer. If the bottom of the pot is dry, the rice is probably done. Taste a grain: if it is still too hard, and there's no more water in the pan, sprinkle a few tablespoons of warm water over the rice and keep cooking. If, on the other hand, the rice seems done but is still wet, take off the lid and cook until the water has evaporated.

To cook rice by boiling, for each cup of rice bring about a quart of salted water to a boil. Add the rice and cook at a rapid boil until the rice is tender but not mushy. If soaked first, white rice cooks in 6 to 7 minutes; unsoaked it takes 10 to 12. Brown rice takes much longer, at least 30 minutes. When cooked, drain the rice well and toss with salt, if needed, and a bit of butter or olive oil.

Yet another way to cook rice is a combination of the absorption and the boiling methods: Boil rice in a generous amount of water for 6 or 7 minutes, until almost tender; drain and return to the pot with butter or oil; cover tightly, and bake in a hot oven for an additional 15 to 20 minutes. This makes relatively dry, fluffy rice that can be kept nicely warm.

Basmati is a long-grain rice common to northern India. It is aged for a year or more, which concentrates its flavor and aroma and allows it to expand into light fluffy grains when cooked.

Plain Rice: Absorption Method One

3 TO 4 SERVINGS

This is the method I prefer for cooking short-grain rice such as Japanese-style rice for sushi.

Rinse or wash:

1 cup short-grain rice

Drain well and put into a heavy saucepan with:

1 cup plus 2 tablespoons cold water

Cover and bring to a boil over medium-high heat. Immediately turn the heat down to low and cook until all the water is absorbed, about 15 minutes. Turn off the heat and let rest, still covered, for another 10 minutes. Fluff and serve.

VARIATIONS

• Add a pinch of salt and 1 teaspoon butter or olive oil to the pot before cooking.

• For long-grain rice, wash well, and increase the water to 1½ cups.

• For brown rice, increase the water to 2 cups and the cooking time to 40 minutes.

Absorption Method Two

3 TO 4 SERVINGS

Basmati rice is my everyday favorite; I love the toasty aroma and delicate texture.

Wash well in a few changes of water:

1 cup basmati or other long-grain rice

Put into a heavy saucepan with:

A pinch of salt

2 cups water

Set aside to soak for 30 minutes. When ready to cook, add:

1 tablespoon butter

Bring to a boil and cook, uncovered, until the water is absorbed and the surface of the rice is covered with steam holes. Turn the heat to low and cover tightly. Cook for 7 minutes. Turn off the heat and let sit for 10 minutes. Stir gently to fluff and serve.

VARIATION

Add ⅛ teaspoon saffron with the butter.

Boiled and Baked Long-Grain Rice

3 TO 4 SERVINGS

This is a good way to cook a large quantity of rice in advance to be kept warm, which allows you to avoid the stress of last-minute timing.

Wash well in a few changes of water:

1 cup basmati or other long-grain rice

Cover with water by 1 inch, and soak for about 20 minutes. In a heavy-bottomed pot, bring to a boil:

1 quart salted water

Drain the rice, add it to the boiling water, and cook for 6 to 7 minutes. Test for doneness. The grains should be slightly al dente, or hard in the center. Drain well and mound back into the pot. Heat until just melted:

2 tablespoons butter

1½ tablespoons milk or water

Pour the butter mixture over the rice and cover the pot tightly with foil or a tight-fitting lid. Bake in a 350°F oven for 15 minutes until dry and fluffy.

Making Pilaf

A PILAF IS A SAVORY DISH of rice that has first been sautéed in fat and then cooked in a seasoned liquid. (It differs from a risotto in that the liquid is entirely absorbed.) Depending on the recipe, a pilaf may also include nuts, spices, a few vegetables, or even a complex meat stew. I make mostly simple pilafs, such as the red rice pilaf that follows, to go with quesadillas and black beans, or a basmati rice pilaf with saffron and onions to eat with a vegetable ragout. Long-grain rice is usually used in pilafs, although some cuisines use short-grain rice.

Sautéing the rice before adding the liquid enriches the flavor of the dish and coats each grain in fat. This, along with thorough washing, keeps the rice from sticking together or clumping. Olive oil and butter are the most commonly used fats. To avoid burning the butter while sautéing the rice, add a little oil to it, or use clarified butter (see page 125).

Onion is usually sautéed for a few minutes in the fat before the rice is added. After the rice is sautéed, a flavorful liquid is poured over it and brought to a boil. The pilaf is simmered, covered, until all the liquid has been absorbed, about 15 minutes. Depending on their cooking times, vegetables and meats are added sometimes with the liquid, sometimes after the rice has been cooking for a while. The tomato in the red rice pilaf here is added at the beginning to color the rice evenly. When done, pilafs should be allowed to rest for about 10 minutes before serving.

Red Rice Pilaf

3 TO 4 SERVINGS

Sauté the rice to a light brown color for a nuttier-tasting pilaf.

In a heavy-bottomed pot, heat:
>   **1½ tablespoons olive oil**

Add and cook over medium heat until translucent, about 5 minutes:
>   **1 small onion, diced fine**

Stir in and cook for 5 minutes:
>   **1 cup long-grain rice, rinsed and drained**

Add:
>   **2 garlic cloves, chopped fine**
>   **1 small tomato, peeled, seeded, and chopped fine**
>   **(or 2 plum tomatoes, canned or fresh)**
>   **½ teaspoon salt (less, if using seasoned broth)**
>   **2 tablespoons coarsely chopped cilantro**

Stir and cook for 1 or 2 minutes. Pour in:
>   **1½ cups chicken broth or water**

Bring to a boil, turn the heat down to low, and cover tightly. Cook until all the liquid is absorbed and the rice is tender, about 15 minutes. Turn off the heat and let rest, covered, for 10 minutes before serving.

VARIATIONS

• After the rice has been cooking, covered, for about 7 minutes, strew over the top of the rice vegetables such as green peas, cut green beans, or small florets of cauliflower or broccoli. Cover and continue cooking until the rice is done. Let rest for 10 minutes. Right before serving, stir together the rice and vegetables.

• Add pieces of boned leftover roast chicken or roast or braised pork before covering and cooking the rice for the last 15 minutes.

• Omit the tomatoes and increase the cilantro to ¼ cup.

• Use basmati rice; soak in water for 20 minutes and drain. Sauté diced onion and add to the rice with a generous pinch of saffron threads. Cook for a few minutes more and add the broth or water and salt, and cook, covered, until done.

Making Risotto

For 1½ cups of rice, I use a 3-quart saucepan that is wider than it is tall.

Listen to the sounds the risotto makes as it cooks. The crackling sizzle of the rice tells you it's time to add the wine, which makes a gratifying whoosh; and the bloop-bloop of the bubbles popping signals that it's time to add more broth.

Risotto is Italian comfort food, a luscious dish of tender rice in its own creamy sauce. Considered by many to be labor-intensive restaurant fare, risotto is actually a basic one-pot dinner that pleases everyone. Risotto is made from starchy short-grain rice, which, when moistened with successive additions of stock, gains concentrated flavor and a distinctive saucy texture.

Of the special short-grain varieties that have been developed in northern Italy specifically for risotto the best known is Arborio; others are Vialone Nano (an extra-short-grain rice), Baldo, and my favorite, Carnaroli. All these varieties have short, plump grains that can absorb a lot of liquid while retaining some textural integrity (the grains are said to have a good bite), with abundant superficial starch to make the risotto creamy.

Because the rice for a risotto is cooked in fat before any broth is added, use a heavy pot, preferably stainless steel or enameled cast iron, or the rice will scorch too easily. Pick a pot with relatively high sides (but not so high that stirring is difficult and evaporation is inhibited) and a diameter that is wide enough so that when the raw rice is added it's between one-quarter and one-half inch deep in the pot.

The first step is to make a flavorful base of sautéed diced onions. The onion is cooked until soft in a generous amount of fat (usually butter, but olive oil, beef marrow, and even bacon fat are sometimes used). Once the onions are soft the rice is added and sautéed for a few minutes. In Italian this is called the *tostatura*, or "roasting." The idea is to coat and seal each grain of rice. The rice will begin to sizzle and turn translucent, but it should not color or brown. At this point, some wine is added, for fruit and acidity. For 1½ cups of rice, I use about ½ cup of wine, but I never bother to measure it exactly; I simply pour in enough wine to reach the top of the rice, without covering it. This works for any quantity of rice and is much easier than trying to make a calculation. Adding the wine before the broth gives it time to reduce and lose its raw alcohol flavor. Red wine or even beer can be substituted. When you are caught without a bottle of wine, a teaspoon or so of tasty wine vinegar added to the first addition of broth will approximate the acidity of wine.

After the wine is absorbed, broth is added. I use light chicken broth most often, but vegetable, mushroom, and shellfish broths also make

Threads of saffron, classically used to flavor and color risotto, are the stamens of a crocus flower, which are painstakingly gathered by hand. A little goes a long way; too much can be overpowering.

lovely risottos. Keep in mind that your risotto will only be as good as the broth you use to make it. Unseasoned or lightly seasoned broths are best. Many recipes say to keep the broth simmering (in its separate pan) the whole time the risotto is cooking. This isn't necessary; in fact, I prefer not to. The longer the broth simmers, the more it reduces, and its flavor can become too strongly concentrated. I bring the broth to a boil while the onions are cooking and then turn it off. The broth stays plenty warm.

The first addition of broth should just cover the rice. Adjust the heat to maintain a constant, fairly vigorous simmer. It is not necessary to stir constantly, but the risotto needs to be tended to frequently, and it certainly cannot be left on its own. When the level of liquid has dropped low enough that the rice is exposed, add more broth to cover. The broth should never be allowed to evaporate completely; the starch will coagulate and burn. Keep adding the broth in small increments; the rice should neither be flooded nor be allowed to dry out.

Season the rice with salt early on. My personal rule is to salt the risotto when I make the second addition of broth. This allows the salt to penetrate the grains of rice while they are cooking. The amount of salt needed will depend on the saltiness of the broth you're using.

From the time the rice is added to the onion, a risotto takes 20 to 30 minutes to cook. Taste it often to keep track of the seasoning and the state of the rice as it cooks. The final addition of broth is the deciding factor of the consistency of the risotto. Too much liquid, and the risotto will be soupy and overdone; too little, and it will be stodgy and underdone. It is easy to add more broth but difficult to take it out.

When the rice is nearly done and ready for its last addition of broth, stir in at the same time a pat of butter and a handful of grated Parmesan cheese. Give the pot a good stir, turn off the heat, and let it sit for a couple of minutes—this procedure, called the *mantecatura*, is the grand finale that develops the starch into wonderful creaminess. The risotto should be perfectly cooked, the rice tender with the suggestion of a bite (but not white at the core), and the sauce around it loose, but not too soupy. Serve it right away and leave it uncovered, as the rice will otherwise continue to absorb liquid and cook, even with the heat off.

Risotto bianco, or plain white risotto, delicious on its own, is also a blank canvas onto which almost anything can be painted in the foreground: meats, vegetables, seafood, other cheeses, and more. A good rule of thumb to follow when adding raw ingredients is to add them at twice the normal cooking time. For example, peas or shrimp, which take 4 to 5 minutes to cook in boiling water, should be added to risotto 10 minutes before it is done, when the rice is a little more than half-cooked. Long-cooking vegetables such as carrots can be sautéed with the onions. Vegetable purées and vegetables and meats that have been cooked apart can be stirred in at the end. Mushrooms can be sautéed and added in two stages: early on, to flavor the broth, and at the end, to provide bites of contrasting flavor and texture. Add saffron and the stronger herbs with the onions, but stir in tender herbs right before serving. Citrus zest can be added in two stages, like mushrooms; when added in quantity, it should be blanched ahead. Some risottos, especially those made with shellfish, do not require cheese at the end.

Risotto Bianco

4 SERVINGS

If you are running out of broth towards the end of the cooking, thin out the stock with some hot water.

Melt in a heavy-bottomed 2½- to 3-quart saucepan over medium heat:

2 tablespoons butter

Add:

1 small onion, diced fine

Cook until the onion is soft and translucent, about 10 minutes.

Add:

1½ cups risotto rice (Arborio, Carnaroli, Baldo, or Vialone Nano)

Cook the rice, stirring now and then, until translucent, about 4 minutes. Do not let it brown.

Meanwhile, in a separate pan, bring to a boil and then turn off:

5 cups chicken broth

Pour over the sautéed rice:

½ cup dry white wine

Cook, stirring fairly often, until all the wine is absorbed. Add 1 cup of the warm chicken broth and cook at a vigorous simmer, stirring occasionally. When the rice starts to get thick, pour in another ½ cup of the broth and add some salt (how much depends on the saltiness of the broth). Keep adding broth, ½ cup at a time, every time the rice thickens. Do not let the rice dry out. After 12 minutes, start tasting the rice, for doneness as well as for seasoning. Cook until the rice is tender but still has a firm core, 20 to 30 minutes in all. The final addition of broth is the most important: add just enough to finish cooking the rice without leaving it soupy. When the rice is just about done stir in:

1 tablespoon butter

⅓ cup grated Parmesan cheese

Stir vigorously to develop the creamy starch. Turn off the heat, let sit for 2 minutes, and serve. Add a splash of broth if the rice is too thick.

VARIATIONS

• Red wine or beer may be substituted for the white wine.

• If there is no wine available, add 1 teaspoon vinegar with the first addition of broth.

• Rosemary or sage can be added to the onions as they are sautéing.

• A pinch of saffron can be added to the cooking onions.

Into the Oven

Roast Chicken

Roast Leg of Lamb

Roasted Root Vegetables

A PLUMP BIRD or a large piece of meat, burnished by heat, and served forth whole: traditionally, holidays have been honored, and extended families fed, by such roasted offerings, and it still feels fitting to entertain our families and friends with this sort of fare. Joints of meat were once turned on spits in front of the glowing coals of wood fires; today they are usually cooked in the enclosed heat of a conventional oven. Either way, with careful roasting, meat will develop both a browned surface with concentrated flavors and a moist, tender interior; after resting, it can be carved into juicy slices. Loins and legs and ribs—such cuts as prime rib, leg of lamb, and loin of pork—and whole birds, such as chickens and turkeys, are all eminently roastable. And remember that vegetables also benefit from the browning and flavor-boosting effects of oven-roasting.

Roasting a Chicken

I love to roast a chicken with lots of whole unpeeled garlic cloves. They cook to a soft purée that you can squeeze out of the papery skins to mingle with the juices and the chicken.

ROAST CHICKEN, plump, golden, and juicy, is perfect for anything from a feast to a weekday family dinner. Happily, it is an easy dish to prepare, especially if you follow these few tips.

First and foremost: find a good chicken, one that has been raised with care. Because chickens are so widely available and inexpensive, we don't often think about where they come from and how they are raised. Unfortunately, these days most chickens are produced under factory conditions, cooped up in tiny overcrowded cages, de-beaked, and fed a diet that is heavily laced with antibiotics and frequently includes animal by-products. These conditions are unhealthy and stressful for the birds (and the workers as well) and produce chickens of compromised integrity and flavor. Organic free-range chickens are raised on organic grain, without antibiotics or hormones, in less confined and more humane conditions, resulting in healthier, tastier birds. Starting with such a bird is what makes a really delicious roast chicken. Organic, free-range chickens can be found at some farmers' markets. These are usually pasture-raised in small flocks and are the tastiest of all. If your butcher or market doesn't carry organic chicken, you can help create demand by asking them to do so.

If possible, season the chicken with salt a day or even two days before you roast it. If you roast it the day you buy it, season it as soon as you bring the bird home. The seasoning will penetrate the bird, making the meat more tender, juicy, and tasty. Make a mixture of about 1½ teaspoons salt and a scant ¼ teaspoon of fresh-ground black pepper. Unwrap the chicken. If it is wrapped in paper keep it right on the paper. Swivel the wing tips and tuck them underneath the bird; this keeps them from burning while roasting. Sprinkle the salt and pepper all over the bird, inside and out, wrap it right back up, and put it in the refrigerator. If you want to, this is the time to put herbs and garlic under the skin. Gently loosen the skin and slide thick slices of peeled garlic cloves and tender sprigs of fresh herbs underneath, working them under the skin until they are situated over the breasts and thighs.

Take the chicken out of the refrigerator at least an hour before cooking. A cold bird straight from the fridge won't roast evenly; the outside will cook but the interior will be underdone. Preheat the oven to 400°F. Roast the chicken in an ovenproof dish or pan that's about the same size as the chicken. If a too-large pan is used, the juices that accumulate while the chicken is roasting will start to burn and smoke. An earthenware dish or small roasting pan will do, and so will an ovenproof skillet or a pie pan. Lightly oil the dish; put the chicken in it, breast side up; and roast for 20 minutes, then turn the chicken breast side down. Turning the chicken helps it cook evenly by circulating the juices and fat throughout the bird and allows the skin to brown and crisp all over. After another 20 minutes turn the chicken breast side up again and roast until done.

A 3½- to 4-pound chicken takes about an hour or so to cook. Start checking after about 50 minutes. The bird is ready when the legs and thighs are no longer pink and the breast is still juicy and tender. With experience you will be able to judge the doneness of a roast bird by sight, but at first you have to do a little investigating. Don't be afraid to cut into it. The thighs are the last parts to finish cooking, so cut into the bird near the joint between the drumstick and the thigh. The meat should be hot and no longer red. After having roasted countless chickens, I rely on visual cues: I know that when the skin has started to separate from the meat on the drumsticks the bird is done. I also give the leg a little wiggle; if it moves freely, without bouncing back, this confirms what the skin has already told me. It's important that the chicken be cooked through—but it's equally important that it not be overdone. A dried-out, overcooked chicken is a waste.

Let the chicken rest in a warm place for a minimum of 10 to 15 minutes before serving. The juices will settle, the internal temperature will stabilize, and the chicken will be much more succulent than if you carve it immediately. Remove the chicken to a warm platter. Skim the fat from the juices left in the pan and turn them into a sauce or a little gravy or pour into a pitcher to pass at the table.

To cut up the roasted chicken, slice through the skin between the thigh and breast. Put the bird back in the roasting pan to do this because this will release a lot of juices. Tip the bird forward to drain the juices and then remove it from the pan. Bend or pull the leg out from the body and locate the hip joint with your knife, slicing down firmly through the joint to remove the leg. To remove the drumstick, hold the knob of the drumstick and cut through the joint from the inside. To carve the breast, start at the wishbone at the top of the breast: slide the point of your knife down each side of the breastbone. Then cut down

The pan juices produced by a roasting chicken are really delicious. After skimming, I like to add some chicken stock to the pan, scrape loose all the browned bits, and let it cook down to thicken and concentrate. A treat for the cook after serving the chicken is to mop up the juicy remains with a crust of bread—my favorite bite!

along the wishbone towards the wings. Slide your knife under the meat, lifting it off the rib cage. Last, holding the meat away from the bird cut down through the wing joint removing the breast and wing in one piece. Either carve the breast into slices or cut it in half diagonally, making the half with the wing attached slightly smaller. Save the carcass; it makes a lovely stock.

Roast Chicken

4 SERVINGS

RULE OF THUMB
20 minutes up
20 minutes down
20 minutes up

Remove the giblets from the cavity of:
1 chicken weighing 3½ to 4 pounds
Inside the cavity there are frequently large pads of fat. Pull these out and discard them. Tuck the wing tips up and under to keep them from burning. Season, 1 or 2 days in advance, if possible.
Sprinkle, inside and out, with:
Salt and fresh-ground black pepper
Cover loosely and refrigerate. At least 1 hour before cooking, remove and place in a lightly oiled pan, breast side up. Preheat the oven to 400°F. Roast for 20 minutes, turn the bird breast side down, and cook for another 20 minutes. Then turn breast side up again and roast until done, another 10 to 20 minutes. Let rest for 10 to 15 minutes before carving.

VARIATIONS
◆ Put a few tender sprigs of thyme, savory, or rosemary under the skin of the breast and thighs before roasting.
◆ Put a few thick slices of garlic clove under the skin, with or without herbs.
◆ Stuff the cavity of the bird with herbs; they will perfume the meat as the chicken roasts. Don't hold back: fill the whole cavity.

Roasting Meat

Olive oil and sprigs of fresh herbs strewn over a roast make a quick and delicious marinade.

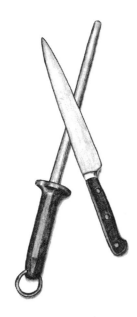

A long, thin-bladed and sharp (!) knife is very helpful for carving good-looking slices from a roast. A few strokes on a sharpening steel helps maintain the edge.

A PROPERLY SEASONED and cooked roast is an elegant and simple dish to prepare, and something very valuable to know how to do confidently for feeding a large gathering of family or friends. With insufficient know-how, roasting meat can be an intimidating prospect, so here are a few basic ground rules to equip you for cooking a superb roast.

I know I'm repeating myself here, but the best meat comes from animals that are locally produced, pasture-raised, and organically fed. Factory farms may produce a lot of inexpensive meat, but it is at great cost to the health of the land, the animals, and both the people who eat them and those involved in their production. Not only is the meat from humanely raised animals the tastiest, but your purchase supports those in your community who are tending the land, creating a very rewarding reciprocal relationship. It is really important to seek out markets and butchers who carry this type of meat.

Some cuts of meat can be bought with or without the bone. Roasting meat on the bone will produce a better roast; it helps the meat to retain its juices and adds flavor as the roast cooks. Leg of lamb, lamb shoulder roast, rack of lamb, saddle of lamb, bone-in pork loin, pork shoulder roast, and prime rib are some examples of cuts that can be roasted on the bone. For easier carving, the bone may be removed before the meat is taken to the table to be cut. Or slice it in the kitchen and arrange it on a warm platter to pass; that is what I do most often.

Seasoning the meat in advance makes a roast more juicy, tender, and tasty. Applying the salt one day ahead of cooking will do, but two or three days ahead is not too far in advance, especially for a large roast. A fresh herb marinade or dry rub is good to put on a few hours ahead or even the night before.

It is important to bring the meat to room temperature before you cook it. Meat put to roast when still cold will cook very unevenly. The exterior will be fully cooked before the interior has even had a chance to warm up. Take the meat from the refrigerator at least 1 hour before roasting, or 2 hours for a bone-in roast.

A good temperature for roasting is 375°F. Choose a pan just slightly larger than the roast. A rack is not necessary; instead, turn the meat twice while it is cooking. First, after the meat has browned, after 20 to 30 minutes; then, after another 20 minutes, when the underside has browned, turn it again and finish cooking. This allows for even browning and distributes the juices and fat all through the meat as it is cooking. (If the roast is small, brown it in a pan with a little olive oil over high heat before putting it into the oven to roast. It does not need to be turned then, unless it is browning too much on the top.) If you are roasting a rack of lamb, a bone-in pork loin, or a prime rib, lay the meat in the pan, bones down, for a natural rack. These roasts do not need to be turned.

An instant-read thermometer is very handy for keeping track of the internal temperature of a roast.

RULE OF THUMB
Internal temperatures for roasted meat:

Lamb, medium rare
128° F

Beef, medium rare
120 to 125°F

Pork, medium to medium rare
135°F

How do you know when it is done? I will poke and prod a roast to see if it is done, but I always take the internal temperature to confirm my judgment. An instant-read thermometer can be inserted anywhere in the roast and will immediately reveal the interior temperature. For the most accurate temperature reading, insert the thermometer lengthwise into the thickest part of the roast, parallel to the bone (but not touching it). You want to take the reading at the coldest part of the roast, as that will tell you where it is least done. For lamb I take the meat out at 128°F, for beef at 120 to 125°F, and for pork loin at 135°F. These temperatures are for medium-rare lamb and beef and medium-rare to medium pork. At these temperatures, the meat is still tender, juicy, and full of flavor. If you prefer your meat cooked more, for each increasing level of doneness, take the temperature up ten degrees—138°F for a medium leg of lamb, for example.

It is very important to let roasted meat rest before cutting and serving. This allows the internal temperature to stabilize and the juices to settle. Twenty minutes is the minimum time recommended for a roast (it can sit much longer with no ill effects, if you keep it in a warm place so it does not get too cool). The meat doesn't stop cooking when it is pulled out of the oven; as it rests the internal temperature continues to rise for a while. If you cut into the meat right away, the inside will be underdone and the juices will run more quickly, creating unevenly cooked, dry slices.

The resting juices that accumulate and the crispy brown bits in the bottom of the roasting pan will make a great sauce or gravy. Pour off or skim the fat from the juices and scrape up the crispy bits from the pan, adding a splash of wine if you want. Spoon it over the sliced meat or pour it into a pitcher to pass at the table.

Roast Leg of Lamb

10 SERVINGS

A wonderful way to flavor and perfume a leg of lamb is to roast it on a thick bed of thyme or rosemary branches.

To keep the roast warm while resting, fold a piece of foil over it like a tent, shiny side down. Don't seal it shut or the meat will continue to cook.

One or two days before roasting, trim all but a thin layer of fat from:

1 leg of lamb, bone-in, around 7 pounds

Season all over with:

Salt and fresh-ground black pepper

If the leg is boned, or partially boned, tie with cotton string as necessary for even cooking. Cover and refrigerate. At least 2 hours before cooking, take the roast out of the refrigerator and place in a roasting pan just slightly larger than the roast. Preheat the oven to 375°F. Roast the leg of lamb for 30 minutes, or until it has browned on top, then turn it over and cook for another 20 minutes, or until the underside has browned. Turn again and finish cooking until the internal temperature registers 128°F on an instant-read thermometer. Start checking after 45 minutes; the leg will probably take about 1 hour and 20 minutes total cooking time. Let it rest for 20 minutes in a warm place.

To carve a leg of lamb with the bone in, hold onto the shank bone with a napkin or towel and cut thin slices from the large round muscle at the butt end, sliding your knife (always away from yourself) almost parallel to the bone. Turn the leg and slice some from the thinner side. The shank can be sliced perpendicular to the bone. A thin-bladed sharp knife makes the slicing a lot easier. Alternatively, cut the major muscle groups off the bone whole, and slice them in the kitchen.

VARIATIONS

◆ Rub dried thyme into the fat with the salt and pepper.

◆ When you take the leg out of the refrigerator to come to room temperature, drizzle it with olive oil and pat coarsely chopped rosemary over the surface.

◆ Pound fennel seeds and add to the salt and pepper when seasoning the lamb.

◆ Cook the lamb on a grill over a low even fire. Baste it with olive oil, using a branch of rosemary for a brush.

Roasted Vegetables

ROASTABLE
VEGETABLES

Brussels sprouts

asparagus

carrots

turnips

celery root

rutabagas

parsnips

kohlrabi

potatoes

squash

garlic

broccoli

eggplant

fennel

artichokes

onions

W‌HEN I serve roasted vegetables, my guests often ask me, "How did you cook these vegetables? They are so delicious!" I tossed them with a bit of oil and salt and threw them in the oven, is my answer. Eyebrows rise in disbelief, but it's true: roasting vegetables is that easy and that delicious. As vegetables roast, their flavors intensify and the brown caramelized edges they get add sweetness and texture. Very little oil is used during the cooking so they are quite light as well. Most any vegetable can be roasted, either simply with salt and olive oil or with garlic, herbs, and spices for added flavor. The critical points for roasting vegetables are: the shape in which they are cut; the seasoning and oiling; and the temperature at which they are cooked.

Winter root vegetables should be peeled and cut up into smaller pieces, though the very tiny ones can be left whole. Carrots, turnips, celery root, rutabagas, parsnips, and kohlrabi are all excellent roasted. Cut the vegetables into pieces more or less the same size so they will cook evenly and be done at the same time. Avoid shapes that have thin edges, as they tend to burn before the centers are done; and don't cut the vegetables too small or they will be mostly browned bits with very little soft flavorful vegetable left to eat.

Toss the cut vegetables in a large bowl, using your hands or a spoon to coat them evenly with salt and olive oil. They only need a light coating of oil; if oil is accumulating on the bottom of the bowl you've used too much. Taste a piece to see if they are seasoned correctly and keep adding salt until it tastes right. Lay the vegetables out in a single layer on a baking sheet that has low sides. The sides make it much easier to stir the vegetables while they are cooking and keep them from drying out.

Cook the vegetables in a hot oven preheated to 400°F. A lower temperature will dry out the vegetables while they cook, making them leathery before they are done; a higher temperature will burn them before they are cooked all the way through. Stir the vegetables a few times while they are cooking, turning those along the edges into the center. Cook them until they are tender and nicely browned here and there. Probe a piece with the tip of a knife to test for doneness, or better still, taste one (be sure to let it cool first). Don't let them go too far: a little browning makes them sweeter, but if you let them get too dark they will taste bitter.

Potatoes can be roasted whole. Use small new potatoes (fingerlings or creamer-size potatoes work really well). Wash the potatoes and peel them or not, as you prefer. Put them into a baking dish with sides as high as or slightly higher than the potatoes themselves. Sprinkle with salt and drizzle with olive oil. Add a head or more of garlic cloves, separated but not peeled, and a few sprigs of fresh herbs. Shake the pan now and then while the potatoes are cooking; turn them if they are browning too much on the top or bottom.

Smaller winter squash, such as Delicata and acorn varieties, can be roasted in halves to serve right in the shell. Halve the squash and scoop out the seeds, place the halves cut side up on an oiled baking sheet, drizzle lightly with oil and sprinkle with salt, turn cut side down, and roast until soft. Unpeeled butternut or Delicata squash, once halved and seeded, can be cut into slices and laid on an oiled baking sheet to roast. The skin is so tender after roasting that it is fine to eat. Squash can be cut into cubes and roasted as well; it is wonderful with lots of fresh sage leaves tossed in before cooking.

Fat asparagus—the butt ends snapped off, the spears peeled and tossed with oil and salt—roasts very well. Lemon thyme is an intriguing herb to use with asparagus. Stick to larger spears when roasting; the smaller spears tend to shrivel and dry. To roast broccoli, peel and cut the stems into thick slices and break the head into florets. Oil and season. Eggplant can be cut into large wedges or slices and placed on an oiled baking sheet. Drizzle the tops with olive oil and sprinkle with salt. The eggplant pieces may stick at first, but once they caramelize and brown they are easily lifted off the pan. These are delicious sprinkled with vinegar and chopped herbs (basil, for example) and served at room temperature as an appetizer.

Lining the roasting pan with parchment paper helps keep the vegetables from sticking and makes cleanup easier.

Roasted Root Vegetables

4 SERVINGS

Cut the vegetables into pieces that are roughly the same size and shape so they will cook evenly.

In a large bowl toss together:

3 medium carrots, peeled and cut into ½-inch slices
1 small celery root, peeled, quartered, and cut into ½-inch slices
2 medium parsnips, peeled and cut into ½-inch slices

With:

Salt to taste
Olive oil, just enough to coat the vegetables

Spread out on a low-sided baking sheet. Roast, stirring occasionally, in a 400°F to 425°F oven until tender, about 25 minutes.

VARIATIONS

◆ Cut the vegetables into different shapes, such as ½-inch cubes or 2-inch-long batons.
◆ Use other vegetables, such as rutabagas, kohlrabi, fennel, or turnips.
◆ Toss the vegetables with leaves of fresh marjoram, thyme, or savory along with the salt and oil.
◆ Along with the salt and oil, toss the vegetables with ¼ teaspoon cumin or fennel seed, lightly crushed in a mortar and pestle.
◆ While still hot from the oven, toss the vegetables with 2 garlic cloves, peeled and chopped fine, or 1 tablespoon chopped parsley, or both.

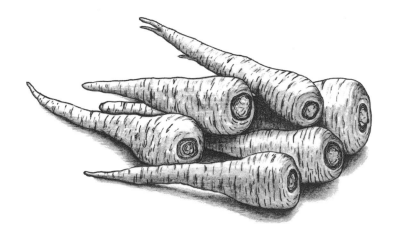

Out of the Frying Pan

Sautéed Cauliflower

Pan-Fried Pork Chops

Fish in Breadcrumbs

A FRYING PAN is the workhorse of the kitchen. Sautéed vegetables and shrimp; pan-fried pork chops and steaks; sole in breadcrumbs and crispy potatoes—all these are cooked rapidly, over direct heat, in the same type of pan. Sautéing (from the French *sauter*, which means "to jump or leap") is a very fast way of cooking over high heat, in just a little oil or fat: food is cut in small pieces and quickly tossed or stirred in the pan until done. Food that is pan-fried is left in larger pieces and turned only once or twice. Shallow-frying requires more fat, but not so much that the food is submerged, as it is when deep-fried. Food to be shallow-fried is usually coated with flour or breadcrumbs; the extra fat is needed to crisp the coating and protect it from direct contact with the pan. Frying is the kind of cooking that requires your active attention. Set the table before you start, because the food should go right out of the frying pan, onto the plate, and straight to the table, still juicy and sizzling.

Sautéing

I almost always use olive oil, especially to sauté vegetables, but I keep my eye on the heat of the pan so the oil doesn't get too hot.

Sautéing is an exciting cooking experience. All your senses are engaged with the high heat, the loud sizzle of the pan, the active stirring and tossing, and the delightful smells of browning food and the perfumes of aromatics added at the end.

Sautéing is best suited to small pieces of meat, fish, shellfish, and vegetables. The pieces are tossed or stirred in a hot pan with a small amount of oil. This cooks them quickly; meat stays succulent and vegetables fresh and juicy. A sauté pan has rounded sides, which makes it easier to toss the food than if you use a classic frying pan or skillet—although in a pinch, a frying pan will do a fine job.

When sautéing, ingredients are added in quantity—though not in quantities that can't be easily tossed or stirred—and need to be moved about quickly so that all sides of all the pieces make contact with the hot pan right away. The pan must be quite hot and the heat turned up before the cooking begins to ensure that the food is seared immediately. Otherwise it will start to sweat, lowering the chances of browning and raising the chances of sticking. There should be a gratifying sizzle when the food hits the pan. To check if the pan is hot enough, add a drop or two of water beforehand.

Use an oil with a high smoking point to sauté. Clarified butter also works well, but whole butter will eventually burn, even when mixed with oil. Only a small amount of fat is needed, just enough to coat the pan and keep the food from sticking. Occasionally, some ingredients absorb all the oil and threaten to stick; add more oil right away, pouring it down the side of the pan so it has a chance to heat up on its way in.

Meat and vegetables are seasoned with salt and pepper either in advance or right at the start of the cooking; most other seasonings are added towards the end to keep them from burning. In some recipes, garlic or ginger is cooked briefly in hot oil for flavor and removed before the main ingredients are added to the pan. Have all your ingredients ready to go before you start cooking, as there will be no time to gather them once you start to sauté.

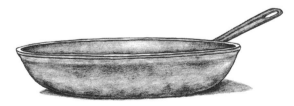

Sautéed Cauliflower

4 SERVINGS

This is tasty as a side vegetable or served as a pasta sauce, tossed with large noodles.

Clean the leaves from:

1 large head or 2 small heads cauliflower

Remove the base of the stem with a small, sharp knife. From the top down, cut the cauliflower into ¼-inch slices. (If the cauliflower is large, cut in half for easier slicing.)

Heat in a heavy-bottomed pan over medium-high heat:

2 tablespoons olive oil

Once the oil is hot, but not smoking, add the cauliflower with:

Salt

Let the cauliflower sit until it starts to brown a bit before stirring or tossing. Cook, continuing to stir or toss until the cauliflower is tender, about 7 minutes total. Don't worry if the cauliflower starts to break up; that is part of the charm of the dish. Taste for salt and add more if needed. Finish with a drizzle of:

Extra-virgin olive oil

VARIATIONS

• When the cauliflower is a minute or so from being done, add a couple of chopped garlic cloves and 1 tablespoon chopped parsley.

• Garnish with a handful of Toasted Breadcrumbs (page 63).

• A classic Italian dish adds the parsley and garlic along with chopped salt-cured anchovies and capers, hot chile flakes, and coarsely chopped olives. This is delicious on pasta.

• Sprinkle with fresh-ground cumin, chopped garlic, turmeric, and chopped cilantro during the last few minutes of cooking.

Pan-Frying

The first minute of frying is the most critical, especially when browning meat. It is essential to use a heavy pan and preheat it before you add fat and begin to fry.

TENDER CUTS of meat—chicken breasts, steaks, and chops, for example—are prime candidates for pan-frying, and when properly cooked have a mouthwateringly crisp, browned exterior and a tender, juicy interior. Pan-frying makes dinner a breeze; there is practically no preparation involved and the meat is cooked quickly and sent straight to the table. The fundamentals for achieving good results are a heavy pan, high heat, and a fairly thin piece of meat.

Why does a heavy pan matter? Have you ever cooked something in a thin pan and had it burn, with the burn exactly the same shape as the electrical element below? This shows how a thin pan transmits heat directly from the burner to what is cooking instead of diffusing the heat across the pan's surface. A heavy pan can distribute heat—and a lot of it—from the burner to the bottom of the pan. This is key in pan-frying and sautéing, because the pan needs to be quite hot to sear and caramelize or brown, but not burn, the surface of what is being cooked.

If I could have only one pan, it would be a cast-iron skillet. The heavy iron heats evenly, making it a wonderful vehicle for browning and frying. An added bonus is that a seasoned cast-iron pan is virtually nonstick. The next-best thing after a cast-iron skillet is a stainless-steel-lined heavy aluminum or aluminum-core frying pan. The aluminum is an excellent heat conductor, while the stainless steel offers a good nonreactive surface to cook on. Besides being heavy, the pan should have low sides so the meat won't steam as it cooks.

Because pan-frying requires high heat, the meat you choose should be fairly thin. Chops should be ½ to ¾ inch thick and steaks 1 inch thick or less. Over high heat, thicker cuts will get crusty and dry on the outside before the inside is done. (A good method for cooking thicker chops and steaks is to brown them, by cooking them briefly on both sides at high heat, and pop them, skillet and all, into a 375°F oven to finish cooking. Alternatively, after browning, finish cooking over lowered heat, with the pan covered.) For even cooking, the thickness should be uniform. Chicken breasts can be lightly pounded at the thicker end to even them out so they will cook consistently.

It is wise to have all your ingredients ready to go before you start cooking: the oil should be handy, the meat should be seasoned, and, if you are going to make a pan sauce, those ingredients should be on hand as well. Heat the pan first: a hot pan in combination with oil will sear the meat and keep it from sticking. Otherwise, the meat will sweat and its leaking juices will cause the meat to adhere to the bottom of the pan. Once the pan is hot, add a little bit of oil, or oil and butter (butter alone burns too quickly at high temperatures). Add the oil after the pan has heated so that it does not start to smoke and burn before you are ready to start cooking. For pan-frying only a little oil is needed, just enough to generously coat the bottom of the pan. After a few seconds, when the oil is shimmering, put the meat in the pan.

I always salt meat— and usually season with chopped fresh herbs, too—well before I begin to cook.

Meat at room temperature will cook more quickly and evenly than meat straight out of the refrigerator.

The meat should fit in the pan in a single layer with a little space between each piece. If the pieces are crowded or overlapping, the liquid they release will keep the meat from browning; if there are large areas of the pan left exposed, the oil in these areas will burn and smoke. If necessary, fry in batches or in two pans simultaneously. Cook the meat on one side until it is nicely browned. Peek underneath after 2 or 3 minutes to monitor the browning; lower the heat if it is browning too quickly, or, if nothing is happening, turn it up. To brown the other side, turn the meat with tongs or a long, sharp-tined fork. In general, most cuts of meat need to cook for 4 to 5 minutes on each side. Chicken breasts can cook for a longer time on the skin side, 8 minutes or so, leaving the tender meaty side to cook only a few minutes. I am an advocate for leaving the skin on, the advantage being that it protects the meat from drying out and bathes the breast with flavor while it is cooking. If you don't want to eat the skin, simply peel it off after cooking.

Check the doneness of the meat by pushing on it with your finger. It will feel soft when rare. As it cooks and sets it will start to feel a bit springy. Don't hesitate to cut into it to see how done it is. Chicken breasts and pork chops are juiciest when they are a tiny bit pink at the bone or in the center. Take the meat from the pan and let it rest for about 5 minutes before serving to let the residual heat finish the cooking, and to allow the juices to stabilize. This is essential.

A quick sauce can be made right in the hot pan. Pour in some water, wine, or stock, and cook the liquid down by half, scraping up the brown bits stuck to the bottom of the pan. Swirl in a bit of butter at the end if you want and finish by adding any resting juices from the meat. I almost always sprinkle pan-fried meats with some chopped garlic and parsley.

Pan-Fried Pork Chops

4 SERVINGS

There are exceptional heritage breeds of pork available; ask your butcher.

Season:

4 pork chops, ½ inch thick

with

Salt and fresh-ground black pepper

Heat a heavy frying pan over medium-high heat. Pour in:

Olive oil to coat the pan

Add the pork chops and cook until brown on one side, about 5 minutes. Turn them over and cook until done, turning again if necessary for even cooking. Let the chops rest for 4 minutes before serving, to tenderize them.

VARIATIONS

• Garnish with chopped parsley, garlic, or lemon zest. (Chopped together this mixture is called gremolata; see page 231.)

• Serve with sage butter, chile butter, fennel butter, rosemary butter, or another herb butter (see page 48).

• Press herb leaves onto the chops before frying them. Sage, rosemary, marjoram, or savory are good choices.

• Make a quick pan sauce with ½ cup stock or water, cooked down by half, and 2 teaspoons Dijon mustard and 1 tablespoon butter whisked in. Taste for salt and stir in any resting juices before serving.

Shallow-Frying

As THE NAME IMPLIES, shallow-frying requires more fat than pan-frying or sautéing but not as much as deep-frying. When they are to be shallow-fried, most foods are first coated with breadcrumbs or covered (or dredged) in flour. This coating turns golden brown and seals in juices resulting in such crisp, succulent dishes as fried chicken, breaded pork cutlets, fried zucchini, and sole in breadcrumbs.

The goal is a light, even, unbroken coating. To dredge, first season the food with salt and pepper, and drag it or toss it in flour, shaking off any excess. Some foods, such as thin fillets of fish, are then fried directly. Other foods, particularly those that take longer to cook, such as pieces of chicken on the bone or a whole fish, benefit from resting an hour or so after dredging to allow the floured surface to dry and firm up. Don't let the pieces touch one another or the coating will stick and tear when it is time to cook. (An easy way to flour chicken is to put the flour in a strong paper bag, add the chicken and shake.)

Breadcrumbs burn more easily than flour and are best applied to meat and vegetables that have been cut thin enough that the interior will be cooked by the time the crumbs have browned. Season the meat or vegetables with salt, pepper, and any herbs or spices, as desired. For breadcrumbs to stick, the food needs to be evenly moist. First dredge it in flour, dip it in egg beaten with a little water, and then roll it (or pat it) in dry fresh breadcrumbs. (Coarse cornmeal can be substituted for breadcrumbs.) To keep your fingers from getting breaded along the way, use one hand to roll the food in the flour and crumbs and the other to dip it in the egg mixture. A breadcrumb coating will be crisper if allowed to rest an hour or so before cooking. Once again, be sure that the breaded pieces are not touching one another while they rest.

Food fried in fresh breadcrumbs you make yourself is a revelation of flavor.

For shallow-frying, choose oils with a high smoking temperature, such as pure olive oil or peanut oil, or clarified butter, which adds rich flavor. Or use a combination of oil and clarified butter. Lard, suet, duck fat, and schmaltz (chicken fat) are all distinctively flavorful frying fats. Potatoes, one of the few foods that don't need to be floured or breaded before being shallow-fried, are especially tasty when cooked in a combination of clarified butter and duck fat.

A heavy pan heats the fat evenly, and it should have low sides, for easy turning and to prevent steaming. The pan must be filled with enough fat to come halfway up the sides of what you are cooking. For most shallow-frying, that will be ¼ to ½ inch deep. Otherwise the coating will get soggy and not cook along the edges where the oil didn't reach. Heat the oil until it is hot but not smoking and gently add the food. Don't crowd the pan; fry in batches if necessary. Cook until brown and crisp, then turn and cook until crisp on the other side. Monitor the heat, turning it down if the food is browning too quickly and turning it up if there is no browning after a minute or two. If fat is absorbed during the cooking, add more as necessary to maintain the proper level. Food that takes a while to cook, such as chicken, may need to be turned a few times. Remove from the pan when cooked and drain well on paper or an absorbent towel before serving.

Fish in Breadcrumbs

4 SERVINGS

BREADING STEPS

flour

egg

breadcrumbs

Season with salt and pepper:

4 fillets of sole, about 5 ounces each

Beat together:

1 egg

1 tablespoon water

Spread on a plate or in a shallow bowl:

2 cups fresh breadcrumbs, processed fine

Dredge the fillets in:

Flour

Shake off the excess flour, then dip in the egg mixture and finally roll or pat in the breadcrumbs. (Use one hand for the dry ingredients and one hand for the eggs.) Refrigerate the breaded fillets for 1 hour to dry. (Don't let the fillets touch each other or the crumbs will not dry properly.)

Heat in a heavy low-sided pan:

Clarified butter, or oil and butter, ½ inch deep

When hot but not smoking, add the fish fillets and cook until brown and crisp, about 3 minutes. Turn and cook until the other side is brown and crisp. Remove from the pan and drain on an absorbent towel or paper. Serve immediately.

VARIATIONS

◆ Before breading, sprinkle the fillets with chopped tender herbs such as chervil, chives, parsley, or tarragon, alone or in combination.

◆ Put a pinch of cayenne or paprika in the flour.

◆ Sprinkle the fillets with finely grated lemon zest when seasoning with salt and pepper.

◆ Use coarse cornmeal in place of the breadcrumbs.

◆ For fried oysters in breadcrumbs use 12 shucked oysters in place of the fish. These are delicious, as is the fish, with Tartar Sauce (page 225).

Clarified Butter

CLARIFIED BUTTER is butter that has had all of the milk solids and water removed. The milk solids brown and burn at a low temperature; when the solids are separated out, the clear fat that remains is delicious and excellent for frying and sautéing.

To make clarified butter: Melt butter in a small heavy pan over medium heat. Cook the butter until it has separated and the milk solids are just turning a light golden brown, about 10 to 15 minutes. Pour it through a strainer to remove the solids, leaving clear golden clarified butter. It will keep for months in the refrigerator, so it is worthwhile to make a pound or so at a time.

In a pinch, you can make a quick semi-clarified butter. Gently melt butter and when the solids first foam to the top, skim them off the surface and discard. There will still be some solids remaining but you can remove most of them this way. Then add a bit of oil to the butter and fry. This works well for foods coated in breadcrumbs that cook quickly.

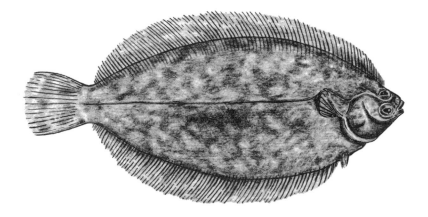

Slow Cooking

Braised Chicken Legs

Beef Stew

Pork Shoulder Braised with Dried Chiles

Nothing creates a sense of well-being like a barely simmering braise or stew cooking quietly on the stove or in the oven. The warm aromas wafting in the air are deeply comforting. Dinner is cooking. A simple and economical cut of meat is slowly altering in moist heat, gradually reaching a state of falling-off-the-bone tenderness, surrounded by a rich and tasty sauce. I love the ease and economy of cooking this way, which involves neither the ostentation of an expensive roast nor the flash-in-the-pan excitement of a last-minute sauté. Once assembled, a stew or braise cooks in a single pot, largely unwatched. It can be made ahead and reheated the next day, without a worry, and it will be even tastier.

Braising and Stewing Meat

Grass-fed beef has very good flavor and it tends to be lean; it becomes luscious and tender in a braise.

A simple bouquet garni might include sprigs of parsley, thyme, and bay leaves.

Braising and stewing meat is a long, slow, gentle process of cooking with moist heat in a small amount of liquid in a covered pot. A braise is typically made from larger pieces of meat, frequently still on the bone, while a stew is made from smaller pieces of meat cut into even-size chunks and cooked in a bit more liquid than a braise, almost enough to cover. (Fish and vegetables may be cooked in a similar manner, but being more delicate they do not cook for nearly as long.) The basic components of a braise or stew are meat, aromatic vegetables, flavorings such as herbs and spices, and liquid.

Inexpensive cuts of meat are best for slow cooking as their tough connective tissues melt while cooking, producing a silky texture with lots of flavor. Lean meat, or meat that is mostly muscle, contracts and squeezes out all its moisture as it cooks, leaving it dry like a wrung-out towel. Tougher cuts such as shoulders, shanks, legs, and tails (the parts that do the most work) are full of tendons and ligaments made of collagen; that collagen turns to gelatin when cooked in liquid over time. The surrounding lean, dry muscle fibers absorb this flavorful gelatinous liquid and become deliciously tender. The gelatin enriches and adds body to the sauce as well.

Onions, celery, carrots, fennel, and leeks are called aromatic vegetables. They can withstand long cooking and add flavor and texture to a braise or stew. The vegetables can be removed at the end of cooking or left in the dish. Add them raw, slightly cooked, or even cooked until brown. Raw or lightly cooked vegetables make a lighter, fresher sauce. In general, the more color on the vegetables, the deeper the flavor and color of the sauce. If they are too browned, however, they will become bitter.

Add branches and sprigs of fresh herbs either loose or bundled together into a bouquet tied with cotton string. A bouquet is easier to remove, but if the sauce is going to be strained or if the dish is quite rustic, I usually don't bother to tie the herbs together. When removing a bouquet from the pot, press it well to extract all the tasty juices it holds. Dried herbs are very pungent and can easily take over a dish, so add them judiciously, taste the sauce after 30 minutes of cooking, and add more if necessary. Spices are better added whole, particularly black pepper. Wrap them in a piece of cheesecloth if you don't want them floating around in the sauce.

Wine for cooking doesn't need to be the best, but it should be good enough to drink on its own: dry and fruity, without strong tannins or an oaky flavor.

Wine, stock, and water are the liquids most commonly used in a braise or stew. Wine contributes both acidity and fruit. Before being added it is sometimes reduced (boiled down) to concentrate its flavors. Tomatoes, or a splash of vinegar, can be used instead. Stock will add a depth of flavor and richness that water cannot. Chicken stock works well with any meat and even with some fish. Otherwise, use beef stock with beef, lamb stock with lamb, and so forth.

Whether they are made of earthenware, enameled cast iron, or metal, the best pots to use for braising and stewing are heavy, because they allow for slow, even cooking. Choose a pot just big enough to comfortably hold the meat you are cooking. A larger pot requires more liquid, diluting the flavors of the sauce; a smaller one may crowd the meat too tightly for proper cooking and there may not be enough sauce for all the meat. A comfortable but close environment is best for keeping the liquid at a steady low simmer. A tight-fitting lid is desirable; but a loose one can be augmented, or a missing one replaced, by foil. The pot should be deep enough to accommodate the meat and its liquid, but not so deep that there's a lot of airspace between the underside of the lid and the meat, in which case too much liquid may evaporate and the meat may dry out. If you have to use a pot that's too deep, cut a piece of parchment paper to fit the pot's inside dimensions and lay it over the meat before covering.

To prepare a braise or stew, first season the meat with salt and pepper. For better flavor, do this a day in advance. The meat is usually seared or browned before it is added to the pot, which makes it look more appetizing and adds flavor and color to the sauce. Use the pot the dish will be cooked in if it's suitable for browning meat; otherwise use a heavy pan such as cast iron. Heat the pan well, then add the fat and then the meat, as for sautéing. Don't crowd the pieces or they will start to sweat and will color only with difficulty. Take time to brown them well on all sides, in as many batches as it takes. Remove the meat, turn off the heat, pour off the fat, and while the pan is still quite hot, add the wine or some other liquid. As the liquid bubbles, scrape up all the crusty brown bits stuck to the bottom of the pan; they add loads of flavor. This step is called deglazing the pan. Really scrape up these bits; they won't add much flavor to the sauce if they are left stuck to the bottom of the pan, even if the dish cooks for hours.

If the vegetables are to be cooked, pour the deglazing juices over the browned meat and wipe out the pan. Heat a bit of oil in it and add the vegetables, cooking them as directed. Transfer the vegetables, the meat, and its deglazing juices into the pot they will cook in and pour in the stock or water. For a braise the liquid should come about halfway up the meat; for a stew it should almost cover the meat, but not completely submerge it. Bring the liquid to a boil, reduce the heat, and cook at the gentlest simmer until tender, either on top of the stove or in a 300°F oven. Check occasionally to make sure that it is not cooking too fast and that the level of liquid has not fallen. Top it up if it has.

If you have a fireplace and a Dutch oven, try cooking the braise over the coals. The flavor of the wood permeates the dish in an extraordinary way.

Some recipes call for various additional elements, such as vegetables and pieces of bacon, to be cooked apart in different ways and added to the finished braise or stew. This preserves the freshness and integrity of the vegetables. For example, roasted small potatoes and steamed turnips can add complexity to a beef stew; or first-of-the-season peas and fava beans can enliven a braise of spring lamb. Glazed little onions, sautéed mushrooms, and browned bacon are always added to coq au vin, the classic French dish of chicken braised in red wine. Scattering chopped tender herbs over any finished stew or braise gives a bright fresh touch, as does a zingy confetti of chopped parsley mixed with finely chopped garlic (and possibly grated lemon zest) sprinkled over at the last minute.

To soak up all the tasty juices, serve a braise or stew with fresh pasta or egg noodles, mashed or steamed potatoes, rice pilaf, polenta, or a grilled or toasted piece of bread rubbed with garlic.

Braised Chicken Legs

Duck legs can be braised in the same way as chicken legs, but they take a little longer to cook.

ONCE THE DISH is assembled, braised chicken legs take less than an hour to cook, and they can be combined with almost any herbs, spices, and vegetables. Their meat is tender and succulent, their sauce concentrated and tasty. Legs are the best choice for a braise, but breasts may be included for those who prefer white meat. Just keep in mind that in order to remain tender and juicy, breasts need to cook for a much shorter time.

Start by seasoning the legs with salt and pepper. If time allows, do this a day ahead. Leave the legs whole, or cut them through the joint to separate them into thighs and drumsticks. Brown them in a cast-iron or other heavy pan over medium heat, in a generous amount of oil, skin side down. Or for more flavor, use a mixture of oil and butter. It takes about 12 minutes to get the skin really crisp and golden brown. Take the time to do this or you will be disappointed in the end, because if there is only superficial color on the skin it will wash off in the braise, leaving the skin pale and unappetizing. Once the skin is browned, turn the pieces and cook briefly on the other side, about 4 minutes (there is no skin to crisp on this side and the meat will brown quickly).

Remove the chicken legs from the pan and pour off the fat. Add wine, tomatoes, broth, or water to deglaze the pan, scraping up any brown bits stuck to the bottom of the pan. Cook the aromatic vegetables in a bit of oil as directed or add them raw to the pan. Arrange the chicken legs, skin side up, on the vegetables, and pour in the deglazing juices and broth or water to come halfway up the sides of the legs. Bring to a boil, turn down to a simmer, cover the pan, and cook for 45 minutes. Or bake in a 325° F oven.

When the chicken legs are cooked, remove them from the pan and discard any loose herb stems or bay leaves or bouquet garni (squeezing it first to extract any juices). Strain the juices into a small pan or bowl and skim off all the fat. Taste the sauce and add salt if needed. Reunite all the parts, plus any vegetables that have been cooked separately, and serve at once or reheat later. If there is too much sauce, reduce it to concentrate the flavors. The salt will concentrate, too, so don't add any more until the sauce has finished reducing.

When braising chicken breasts, do not remove the skin or the bones; they both contribute flavor and help keep the meat moist and tender. Remove the first two joints of the wing by cutting through the joint.

Leave the breasts whole or cut them in two so that the thicker wing portion is slightly smaller. Season and brown the breast pieces with the legs. Add the browned breasts with their resting juices to the pan after the legs have been cooking for 30 minutes.

There is another method for braising chicken legs. The legs are cooked in the oven, covered, until tender and uncovered and browned at the end. This works especially well when cooking for a crowd, but is not suitable for breasts. Nestle the seasoned legs, skin side down, into the aromatic vegetables (cooked or not, as required by the recipe) with the herbs and spices. Pour in enough wine and stock or water to reach halfway up the legs. To save time, bring the stock to a boil before adding. Cover the dish tightly and bake in a 350°F oven for 40 minutes, or until the legs are tender. Uncover the dish and turn the legs over. If the liquid is so deep it covers the legs, pour enough off to fully expose the skin and reserve it for later. Return the legs to the oven, uncovered, and cook until they are golden brown on top, about 20 minutes. Skim the sauce and serve as above.

Chicken Legs Braised with Tomatoes, Onions, and Garlic

4 SERVINGS

Leftover braised chicken can be chopped and made into a tasty chicken salad sandwich (very good for a bag lunch).

Season, the day before if possible:

4 chicken legs

with:

Salt and fresh-ground black pepper

Heat a heavy-bottomed pan over medium heat. Add:

2 tablespoons olive oil

Place the chicken legs into the pan skin side down and cook until crisp and brown, about 12 minutes. Turn and cook for another 4 minutes. Remove the chicken and add:

2 onions, sliced thick (or diced large)

Cook until translucent, about 5 minutes. Add and cook for 2 minutes:

4 garlic cloves, sliced thin

1 bay leaf

1 small rosemary sprig

Add and cook for 5 minutes, scraping up any brown bits from the bottom of the pan:

4 tomatoes, diced coarse, or 1 small (12-ounce) can organic whole tomatoes, diced (including juice)

Arrange the chicken in the pan, skin side up, and pour in any juices that have collected. Pour in:

1 cup chicken broth

The liquid should reach halfway up the chicken; add more if needed. Bring to a boil and then turn down to a simmer. Cover and cook at a bare simmer or in a 325°F oven for 45 minutes. When done, pour the braising liquid into a small bowl and skim the fat. Discard the bay leaf and rosemary. Taste for salt and adjust as needed. Return to the pan and serve.

VARIATIONS

◆ Before adding the tomatoes to the onions add ⅓ cup dry white wine and reduce by half.

◆ Garnish with 1 tablespoon chopped parsley mixed with 1 garlic clove chopped fine.

◆ Substitute 2 breasts for 2 of the legs. Brown them, but do not add them to the braise until the legs have been cooking for 30 minutes.

◆ Use basil, oregano, or marjoram instead of rosemary.

Making Stew

When stewing bone-in cuts of meat, allow about 1 pound per person; for boneless stew meat, figure about ¾ pound.

Good choices for stew meat are oxtails, shanks, beef chuck, short ribs, pork shoulder, beef cheeks, lamb shoulder, and lamb neck. These cuts all have lots of connective tissue and fat to make them tender and full of flavor. For stew, the meat is cut into smaller pieces. Have your butcher cut bony cuts such as short ribs and lamb shanks into 2-inch lengths. Cut boneless meat such as chuck or shoulder into 1½-inch cubes. The pieces may be cut larger for a more rustic stew, but cut any smaller they tend to fall apart when cooked. If you are buying beef that has already been cut up for stew, ask what cut it is from. Most meat counters use top and bottom round, which I find too lean to make a good stew; they cook up dry. Ask the butcher to cut some chuck into stew meat for you instead, or buy a large piece and cut it at home.

Season the meat with salt and pepper. If you have the time, season it a day ahead. If you make a marinade, stir the meat now and then while it is marinating; this will help the marinade flavor the meat evenly. Any vegetables in the marinade I first cook slightly in a bit of oil, for more flavor. Let them cool before adding to the meat.

Brown the meat well in a fair amount of oil, lard, or fat. Don't crowd the pieces; brown them in as many batches as necessary. You can use the same oil for each batch as long as the pan does not burn. If it does, wipe out the pan and continue with fresh oil. When the meat is browned, drain the fat from the pan and deglaze the pan with wine, tomatoes, broth, or water. Short ribs and oxtails are some of my favorite stewing cuts, because they make such a flavorful sauce. These cuts can be browned in the oven: Preheat the oven to 450°F; lay the meat out on a rack in a shallow pan; and cook until the meat is brown and the fat is rendered. With this method there is no pan to deglaze, but it is quicker and easier than browning on the stovetop.

If the aromatic vegetables are to be left in the stew, cut them into even, medium-size pieces. If they are to be discarded at the end, leave them in large chunks, for easy removal. Put the vegetables, meat, and deglazing liquid into a pot. Choose a pot large enough to accommodate the meat in two, or possibly three, layers. If the meat is piled higher than this, the bottom layer will cook and fall apart before the upper layers are done. Stirring doesn't really help this much, and the chance of sticking and burning is much greater. Add broth or water, as the recipe asks, almost to the top of the meat, but do not submerge it. When I am using a marinade that is mostly wine, I like to reduce it (boil it down) by half or more before adding it to the pot. This removes the raw taste of the wine and allows room for more broth, which makes a richer sauce.

Bring the liquid to a boil, then turn the heat down to a bare simmer, and cover the pot. Use a flame tamer if necessary to keep the stew from boiling. Or cook the stew in a preheated 325°F oven. If the stew boils hard there's a good chance the meat will fall apart and the sauce emulsify (the fat and the liquid bind together, which makes the sauce murky). Check the pot now and then to monitor the cooking and the level of the liquid; add more broth or water if needed.

Check the braise several times towards the end of the cooking. The best way to make sure the meat has cooked long enough to be tender is to taste a little piece.

Cook until the meat is very tender. This will take anywhere from 2 to 4 hours depending on what cut is being used. There should be very little or no resistance when the meat is poked with a small knife or skewer. When the meat is done, skim the sauce well, removing as much of the fat as you can. This is much easier to do after the simmering has stopped and the liquid has had a chance to settle. The sauce may be strained, but do so carefully: the meat is very delicate now and can fall apart. If the stew is being served another day, the fat can be simply lifted off after chilling in the refrigerator.

Thicken a thin or watery sauce with a mixture of one part flour stirred together with one part soft butter. Whisk this into the boiling sauce bit by bit, cooking each addition into the sauce for a minute before going on to the next; you want just enough to give the sauce a little body. I prefer this method to sprinkling flour over the meat as it is browning.

Heat the stew, taste it for salt, and add any vegetables that were cooked separately. The stew is ready! Serve sprinkled with herbs (or not), and be sure to serve something to soak up all the great sauce.

Beef Stew

4 SERVINGS

Fragrant whole cloves subtly enhance the other flavors in the stew.

It's easy to cut paper-thin strips of orange zest with a swivel-bladed vegetable peeler.

Season generously, a day ahead if possible:

3 pounds grass-fed beef chuck, cut into 1½-inch cubes

with

Salt and fresh-ground black pepper

Heat, in a heavy-bottomed pan over medium-high heat:

2 tablespoons oil

Add:

3 slices bacon, cut into ½-inch pieces

Cook until rendered and lightly brown but not crisp. Remove the bacon and add the meat, browning well on all sides, in as many batches as necessary. Put the browned meat into a heavy pot or braising dish. Pour off most of the fat, lower the heat, and add:

2 onions, peeled and cut into quarters

2 cloves (stick them into onion quarters)

2 carrots, peeled and cut into 2-inch chunks

2 sprigs each of thyme, savory, and parsley

1 bay leaf

A few peppercorns

Cook until slightly browned and add to the beef in the pot. Return the pan to the stove and raise the heat. Pour in:

3 tablespoons brandy (optional)

This may flame up, so be careful. Then add:

1¾ cups red wine

Cook until reduced by two thirds, scraping up all the brown bits from the bottom of the pan. Pour this over the beef and vegetables. Add:

3 diced tomatoes, fresh or canned

1 small head of garlic, separated into cloves, peeled, and coarsely chopped

1 thin strip of orange zest

2 cups beef stock (or chicken broth)

Check the level of the liquid; it should be at least three-quarters of the way up the cubes of beef. Add more if needed. Cover the pot tightly and cook at a bare simmer on the stovetop, or in a 325°F oven, for 2 to 3 hours. Check the stew occasionally to be sure that it is not boiling and that there is enough liquid. When the meat is tender, turn off the heat, and let the stew settle for a few minutes. Skim off all the fat. Discard the bay leaf, cloves, and peppercorns. Taste for salt and adjust as needed.

Serve sprinkled with a mixture of:
1 tablespoon chopped parsley
1 or 2 garlic cloves, chopped fine

VARIATIONS

◆ Stir in ½ cup small black olives with their pits 30 minutes before the stew is finished cooking. If using pitted olives, add them after the stew has finished cooking.

◆ Use ¾ cup white wine instead of red wine. Only reduce by half.

◆ To make pot roast, keep the meat whole instead of cutting it into cubes. Bottom round or brisket can be used as well as chuck. The liquid should come only halfway up the roast. Increase the cooking time by 1 hour.

◆ Soak ¼ cup dried porcini mushrooms in ½ cup hot water for 10 minutes. Drain, chop coarse, and add to the stew along with 2½ tablespoons tomato paste instead of tomatoes. If the mushroom liquid is not too sandy, substitute it for some of the broth. Omit the orange zest.

Braising a Shoulder Roast

THIS IS AN EXCELLENT WAY to cook a shoulder roast, whether pork, lamb, or beef; it combines the best of roasting and braising into one method to produce a meltingly tender, mouthwatering golden roast with a rich, deeply flavorful sauce. The meat is cooked in the oven, uncovered, with a small amount of liquid, which allows a large part of the roast to brown and render its fat in the dry heat of the oven while the underside is simmering in flavorful juices. After about an hour the roast is turned, submerging the browned meat in the juices to absorb moisture and flavor, while exposing the underside to the browning heat of the oven. From then on, the roast is turned in and out of the liquid to alternately brown and braise. While the meat is in the liquid it is bathed with sugars from the vegetables and wine; these sugars caramelize when exposed to the dry heat, making a fabulous golden crust that is protected from burning each time it is turned back into the sauce.

Any shoulder cut will do—for more flavor, when possible choose a roast that has the bone in (called blade-in for beef chuck). The meat will be tender after it is cooked and will easily separate from the bone. If the butcher has not already done so, trim the majority of the fat from the outside of the roast and season well with salt and pepper. For added flavor use a dry rub: herbs, ground spices, and chiles mixed with the salt and pepper. Or make a paste with pounded garlic, herbs, spices, and a bit of olive oil to rub into the meat after it is seasoned. Do this in advance—overnight if there's time—to allow the flavors to penetrate the meat.

Shredded tender braised meat is very good as a filling for sandwiches, a sauce for egg noodles, or a filling for ravioli or tortellini.

Cut the aromatic vegetables into large pieces. Place them in a heavy baking dish just a bit larger than the roast. Add any herbs and spices and set the seasoned meat on top of the vegetables, fat side up. Pour in liquid (wine, stock, or water) about a quarter of the way up the sides of the roast. Cook, uncovered, in a 375°F oven for an hour or so. Turn the roast over and cook for 30 minutes, then turn it again and cook for another 30 minutes. At this point check the meat to see if it is done. It should offer little or no resistance to the probing of a sharp knife or skewer. If it needs more time, turn and cook until done, turning the roast every half hour. The total cooking time may be as much as 3½ hours depending on the size of the roast.

While the meat is cooking, keep an eye on the liquid and add more as needed. This can be deceptive at times, since rendered fat can make it look as though there is more liquid than there really is. Check with a spoon to gauge the level of the actual liquid and add more as needed. If all the liquid were to evaporate, the vegetables and meat would stick and burn, and there would be no sauce to serve with the meat.

When done, remove the meat from the pan. Skim the sauce well and either discard the vegetables if they've lost all their flavor and you don't want to serve them, or else push them through a food mill or coarse strainer and add them to the skimmed sauce. Reheat the sauce, slice the meat, and serve it with the sauce poured over or passed around in a pitcher or sauceboat.

Pork Shoulder Braised with Dried Chiles

4 SERVINGS

Ancho chiles have a deep, sweet flavor and are not very hot; chipotle chiles have a smoky flavor and are quite spicy.

The pork is also delicious braised without the chiles.

Make a dry rub by mixing together:

1 tablespoon salt

¼ teaspoon fresh-ground black pepper

1 tablespoon chopped fresh marjoram or oregano

1 teaspoon ground ancho chile

Use the dry rub to season, the day before if possible:

One 4-pound, bone-in pork shoulder roast, trimmed of excess fat

Cover and refrigerate until 1 hour before cooking.

Put in a heavy baking dish or roasting pan that just fits the roast:

2 onions, peeled and coarsely chopped

1 carrot, peeled and coarsely chopped

3 dried ancho chiles, split and seeds removed

1 dried chipotle chile, split and seeds removed

1 large head of garlic, peeled and coarsely chopped

A few black peppercorns

A few fresh marjoram or oregano sprigs

Preheat the oven to 375°F. Place the seasoned meat on top of the vegetables and pour in:

2 cups chicken broth (or water)

Check the level of the liquid; it should reach about one quarter of the way up the roast. Add more if needed. Cook in the oven for 1 hour and 15 minutes. Turn the roast over and cook for 30 minutes, then turn again. Check the level of liquid every once in a while, adding more broth or water if it gets too low. Cook for another 30 minutes and test the meat for doneness, continuing to turn and cook until done. Remove the meat from the pan. Strain the sauce and skim well. Pass the vegetables through a food mill and return to the skimmed sauce. Remove the bones, slice the meat, and arrange on a warm platter. Serve with the sauce poured over or pass it around in a pitcher or sauceboat.

VARIATIONS

◆ Use any combination of dried chile varieties.

◆ Sprinkle with chopped fresh marjoram or oregano before serving.

◆ Pound 4 garlic cloves and stir into the dry rub with 2 teaspoons olive oil. Rub this on the roast to season.

Simmering

Poached Egg
with Curly Endive Salad

Shallow-Poached Salmon

Boiled Dinner

Simmering and poaching are methods of cooking in liquid over low heat. When food is poached, it cooks delicately over the gentlest heat; not a bubble breaks the surface of the liquid in the pan. An egg is sublime cooked this way; so is a piece of salmon. When food is simmering, the heat has been turned up slightly, and the liquid has bubbles breaking across its surface now and then. A pot of barely simmering broth is a fine place in which to cook together a chicken, a well-marbled piece of beef, a sausage or two, and a few flavorful vegetables. This sort of meal may sound more romantic when called a *pot-au-feu* or a *bollito misto* instead of its ancestral American name, a boiled dinner. But regardless of where such a dinner is eaten or what it is called, the deep-flavored broth and lusciously tender meats from a simmering pot should not be missed.

Poached Egg

A POACHED EGG is easily cooked, incredibly nutritious, economical, and easily served at any meal. Poached eggs perched on a buttered toasted slice of tender bread is a perfect breakfast; a shimmering bowl of chicken broth served with an egg poached in it is a nourishing lunch that can generate a warm sense of well-being; and curly endive tossed in a warm vinaigrette with bacon and topped with a poached egg is a favorite dinner salad of mine—the egg enriching the vinaigrette as it coats the leaves.

A poached egg is cracked from its shell and cooked in water, stock, or, sometimes, wine until the white has just solidified and the yolk has heated through. The poaching liquid should be very hot, but without any bubbles breaking the surface. This gentle still heat keeps the white tender and helps the egg keep its shape while cooking. Fresh eggs are best. A fresh egg cracked onto a plate has a thick, jellylike white that clings to the deep orange yolk, which stands up plump and high. As eggs age, their flavor dissipates and their whites thin out to the point of being watery at the edges, making it difficult to poach one with any success.

Use a heavy pan for even heat dispersal, which helps keep the eggs from sticking to the bottom. If a heavy pan is not available, use a flame tamer. A relatively shallow pan will make it easier to remove the eggs from the hot water. I use a low-sided saucepan. Fill the pan with water 2 to 3 inches deep, add a large splash of vinegar, and put the pan over a medium fire. The vinegar speeds the coagulation of the whites, keeping them from billowing out into the water. Use good-tasting vinegar, as you will be able to taste it slightly. I add about 1 tablespoon to 4 cups of water, but if you particularly like the flavor of vinegar on your eggs (and it is delicious), add more. When poaching eggs in soup or broth don't use the vinegar.

Carefully, without breaking the yolks, crack the eggs into individual cups or small bowls. This way you can easily remove any fragments of eggshell and it will be easier to slip each egg gently into the water; and if you do break a yolk, you can set it aside for another use. When the water is very hot, but not bubbling, hold the cup right at the level of the water and carefully slide the egg in. This gentle entry into the water will help the egg keep its shape. After a minute you can gently stir the water a while to discourage the eggs from sticking to the bottom of the pan.

Use care, though; the eggs are very delicate until the whites are set. Lower the heat if the water begins to simmer.

The cooking time will vary depending on the number of eggs, their size, and the temperature they were when they went into the water. On average, a single large egg straight from the refrigerator will take about 3 minutes to cook. The white will be set but the yolk will still be soft; for a firmer yolk allow up to 5 minutes. Test for doneness by gently lifting the egg with a slotted spoon and pressing it gently with your finger to feel how set the white and yolk are. Carefully remove the cooked eggs and drain for a moment on a towel, blotting the top very gently to dry. When cooking for a crowd, freshly poached eggs can be kept for a few minutes in a bowl of warm water or stock while another batch is being cooked.

Poached Egg with Curly Endive Salad

4 SERVINGS

Remove the dark green outer leaves from:

2 large heads of curly endive (frisée)

Separate into individual leaves and wash and dry well.

Cut into ⅓-inch pieces:

2 bacon slices

Warm in a small heavy pan, over medium heat:

2 teaspoons olive oil

Add the bacon pieces and cook until brown and rendered, but not crisp. Remove from the pan. Pour off the fat from the pan and reserve.

To make the dressing, mix together:

1 tablespoon red wine vinegar

1 tablespoon Dijon mustard

Salt

Fresh-ground black pepper

1 garlic clove, crushed

Whisk in:

2½ tablespoons olive oil

1½ tablespoons bacon fat

Taste for salt and acid and adjust as needed.

Fill a heavy saucepan with 4 cups of water and add:

1½ tablespoons red wine vinegar

Heat to just below a simmer and slide in:

4 eggs, cracked from their shells

Poach for 3½ to 4 minutes. Use a slotted spoon to remove them from the water and keep warm. Put the vinaigrette into a large bowl (remove the crushed garlic clove), add the bacon, and put the bowl over the pan of hot water to warm. Add the greens and toss well. Divide the greens among 4 warm plates. Gently blot the eggs dry, and put 1 egg on top of each salad. Grind a little black pepper over the top and serve immediately.

VARIATIONS

◆ Other greens work well in this salad: try spinach, escarole, dandelion greens, or tender radicchio varieties such as Castelfranco or Sugar Loaf.

◆ The warm salad can be served without poached eggs.

◆ Omit the bacon, increasing the amount of olive oil in the dressing to make up for the loss of bacon fat.

◆ Make some rustic croutons and toss them while still hot with fine-chopped garlic. Dress the croutons with a little vinaigrette and toss with the greens.

Poaching Fish

FISH IS PARTICULARLY GOOD when poached; its fine flavor and texture are preserved in the gentle heat of the liquid. Submerged until done in hot, but not boiling, liquid, the flesh remains moist, tender, and light. Salmon, halibut, cod, sole, and trout are a few examples of fish that are well suited to poaching, whole or in steaks or fillets. Anything from plain salted water to a flavorful vegetable stock with wine (called a Court Bouillon; see page 335) can be used for the liquid. Because of its delicate flavors, poached fish is best served with a simple sauce such as a butter sauce, a mayonnaise, or a variation of salsa verde.

Another way to poach fish, especially for a casual meal, is slightly different from the classic method of completely submerging the fish in the poaching liquid. I call it shallow poaching. There's no special stock to make, the fish is in and out of the pan and onto the table in a matter of minutes, and a quick delicious sauce can be made from the liquid. Fill a low-sided heavy pan with an inch or two of water, or enough to come about halfway up the sides of the fish. Add a good splash of white wine (or a smaller one of wine vinegar); a sprig or two of parsley, fennel, or thyme—or a combination; and a large pinch of salt. Sometimes I float a slice or two of lemon in the water. Bring this to a boil and immediately turn it down to a barely perceptible simmer. Put in the fish, having seasoned it first with salt. Cook the fish for a few minutes on one side, carefully turn it over, and continue cooking until done. Be sure the water does not come back to a boil during the cooking. A thin fillet about ½ inch thick will cook in 5 to 7 minutes; a thick steak may take up to 12 minutes. Probe the fish to monitor the doneness.

When done, remove the fish with a slotted spatula to a warm plate. To make a quick pan sauce, raise the heat and reduce the liquid by half. Have ready two generous pats of butter cut into small pieces. Whisk or swirl in the butter, bit by bit. Turn off the heat and remove the pan from the burner when the last bit of butter is added, and finish incorporating it off the heat. Taste the sauce and add, as needed, a squeeze of lemon or a pinch of salt or both. Pour the sauce over the warm fish and serve.

Very thin fillets such as sole can be cooked in even less water, with butter already added. Pour ¼ inch of water into a heavy pan, season with salt, and add a sprig or two of fresh herbs. Pour in a splash of wine or wine vinegar and about 2 tablespoons of butter. Put the pan over medium heat and when the liquid is just below a simmer, add the seasoned fillets and cover the pan. Cook until done, for 4 to 5 minutes, checking occasionally to monitor the heat. Remove the fish, raise the heat, and bring the sauce to a boil to thicken it. Taste and adjust the seasoning as needed. Pour the sauce over the fish and serve.

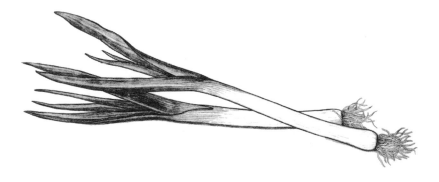

Shallow–Poached Salmon

4 SERVINGS

Season:

Four 5-ounce salmon fillets or

    2 large (12- to 14-ounce) salmon steaks

with:

Salt

Fill a heavy pan with enough water to come halfway up the sides of the fish. Add:

¼ cup dry white wine

2 parsley sprigs

2 thyme sprigs

A large pinch of salt

Bring to a boil and immediately lower the heat to a bare simmer. Add the fish and cook for 3½ minutes (1 or 2 minutes longer for steaks), turn the fish, and cook until done, about 3 minutes more. Keep the heat adjusted so that the water is very hot but never boils. Remove the fish to a warm plate and serve. For a quick sauce, boil down the liquid by half, and whisk or swirl in:

4 tablespoons (½ stick) butter, cut in pieces

Taste, and, if needed, add:

Salt

Lemon juice

Pour the sauce over the warm fish.

VARIATIONS

• Use 1½ tablespoons white wine vinegar instead of wine.

• Add 2 thin slices of lemon to the water.

• Vary the herbs: fennel, basil, tarragon, chervil, and marjoram are all delicious.

Simmering Meats and Vegetables

A boiled dinner is not just a wintertime meal. I like to make it at different times of the year with different combinations of vegetables, depending on the season.

A BOILED DINNER, which to be more precise might be called a simmered dinner, is an assortment of meats and vegetables simmered slowly and gently until tender. The resulting broth is clear and full of flavor and the meat is fork-tender and moist, comfort food at its best, restorative to body and soul. A variety of meats can be put into the pot; among them is usually a gelatinous cut to add a bit of body to the broth and a bony one to enrich the flavor. Some favorites are short ribs, brisket, beef cheeks, shanks, oxtail, chuck, beef tongue, chicken (either legs or a whole chicken), and sausage, or sausage-stuffed cabbage leaves. A boiled dinner is often served with the broth as a first course followed by the meats and vegetables, but I prefer to serve it all at once, with the meat and vegetables arranged in deep soup plates, moistened with a generous ladle of broth. Typical accompaniments for the meat are coarse sea salt, pickles, and a piquant sauce such as salsa verde, Dijon mustard, horseradish cream (grated horseradish, heavy cream, a pinch of salt, and a splash of white wine vinegar), or a tomato sauce spiked with capers.

It is worthwhile to get the meat a couple of days ahead and to season it generously with salt and pepper. This will make it even more succulent and tasty. When a beef tongue is included (and I am quite partial to tongue in a boiled dinner), it should be soaked in salted water for at least eight hours to purge and season it. When deciding how much meat to buy, plan for ample leftovers. The broth makes fabulous soups and risottos and the meat is great sliced and served hot or cold with salsa verde, or in sandwiches, or chopped for hash.

Classically, a boiled dinner is made with water. For a richer, sweeter broth, I like to use chicken broth instead, or half chicken broth and half water. This dish is easy to make, but it does take a while to cook, so plan for a few hours of simmering. Keep the pot at a bare simmer, with bubbles breaking the surface only now and then. Cooking meat at a boil will make it dry and stringy. Because their flavors can dominate the broth's, beef tongue, sausage, and cabbage should be cooked separately from the beef and chicken. As an option to cabbage and sausage, or as a lovely further addition, consider preparing stuffed cabbage leaves. Add vegetables to be served with the meats towards the end of the cooking so that they leave a fresh, sweet taste in the broth.

Boiled Dinner

8 TO 10 SERVINGS

HERE IS A RECIPE for a complete boiled dinner—a classic Italian *bollito misto*—that includes different cuts of beef, a beef tongue, chicken legs, sausage, and stuffed cabbage. This is a bountiful dish that can easily be pared back all the way to the simplicity of boiled beef with carrots alone. Although this is a long recipe, some parts can be prepared in advance. The meats and tongue can be cooked ahead and stored in their broth. The sausage, stuffed cabbage, and vegetables are best prepared and cooked close to serving time. Timing is not critical; once everything is cooked and ready to eat, all the meats and vegetables can be reheated together in the broth and served.

A day or two before cooking, season:

3 pounds grass-fed beef short ribs, beef brisket, or chuck
4 chicken legs

with:

Salt
Fresh-ground black pepper

Mix together to make a brine:

4 tablespoons salt
2 quarts water

Add to the brine and soak overnight:

1 grass-fed beef tongue, about 2 pounds

To cook the tongue, remove it from the brine and put it in a heavy pot with water to cover by 2 inches. Bring to a boil, then turn down to a bare simmer, skim well, and add:

1 onion, sliced thick
1 carrot, peeled
¼ teaspoon black peppercorns
3 allspice berries
4 thyme sprigs
1 bay leaf
½ cup white wine or 3 tablespoons white wine vinegar
A large pinch of salt

Cook until tender, which can take up to 5 hours. Add water as needed to keep the tongue submerged in simmering liquid. When done, allow to cool, and peel off the thick outer layer of skin. Discard cooking liquid.

Meanwhile, put the seasoned beef into a 3-gallon stock pot with:

2 quarts chicken broth

2 quarts water

The level of the liquid should be 2 inches above the meat. Add more if necessary. Bring to a boil, turn down to a bare simmer, and skim. Add:

1 onion

2 cloves, stuck into the onion

1 carrot, peeled

1 bay leaf

Cook, barely simmering, for 2 hours. Skim every now and then.

Meanwhile prepare the stuffed cabbage. Carefully separate 10 whole leaves from:

1 head of savoy cabbage

Cook the leaves in boiling salted water until tender, about 4 minutes. Drain and cool. Mix together and leave to soak for 10 minutes:

½ cup fresh breadcrumbs (see page 62)

⅓ cup cream

Meanwhile, in another bowl, gently mix together:

¾ pound ground pork or chicken

2 chicken livers, cleaned and chopped

1 egg

1 teaspoon salt

¼ teaspoon fresh-ground black pepper

1 teaspoon chopped fresh thyme

Stir into the breadcrumb and cream mixture. Test by frying a little patty of stuffing in a small pan; taste for salt and adjust as needed.

Trim away the thick hard rib from each cabbage leaf, lay them out flat, and spoon a generous bit of stuffing onto the lower third of each leaf. Roll up each leaf, folding in the sides over the stuffing on the way up. Tie loosely with cotton string.

After the beef has cooked for 2 hours, add the chicken legs and cook for 30 minutes more. Remove the onion and carrot added at the beginning of the cooking.

Add:

8 small carrots, peeled, or 4 large carrots, peeled and cut in half

4 large or 8 small leeks, trimmed and cleaned

Red, yellow, and white heritage varieties of carrots enliven the presentation in the winter months.

4 medium onions, peeled and cut in half, or 24 small boiling onions, peeled

Simmer until the vegetables are quite tender but not mushy, about 30 minutes, removing them as they are cooked.

Ladle some of the broth from the poaching meat and vegetables into a smaller saucepan. Heat to a bare simmer and add the stuffed cabbage leaves along with:

4 or 5 garlic sausages

Simmer for 20 minutes or until done. Remove and keep warm. If you like, save this broth for another use.

When everything is cooked, strain the meat broth through a fine sieve and skim thoroughly. When it's time to serve, slice the meats and sausage and warm them with the vegetables and stuffed cabbage, moistened with some of the broth. Arrange on a deep platter or in individual soup plates and ladle the warm broth over. Pass coarse salt, Salsa Verde (page 45), and mustard, as desired.

VARIATIONS

• Use only beef. Use 8 pounds of bony cuts, such as oxtail or short ribs, or 6 pounds of boneless meat such as brisket, beef cheeks, or chuck. When using boneless meat, if they're available, add a couple of marrow bones to the pot.

• Use a whole chicken instead of the chicken legs and omit the tongue. Simmer the chicken for 45 minutes and then cool. Remove the legs and, if they are still rare, cook them a few minutes longer in the broth. When ready to serve, slice the chicken breast and divide the legs in two at the joint. Reheat in a bit of broth.

• If not making stuffed cabbage leaves, cut a small head of cabbage into wedges, simmer in broth or water separately until done, remove, and serve reheated with the meat and other vegetables.

• Root vegetables other than carrots are delicious simmered and served with the meats—parsnips, rutabagas, or turnips, for example.

• Serve the broth hot, as a first course, garnished with cooked pasta or a toasted crouton and some grated Parmesan cheese, and serve the meats and vegetables as a second course.

Over the Coals

Grilled Sirloin Steak with Herbs

Grilled Whole Fish

Ratatouille of Grilled Vegetables

To GRILL OVER AN OPEN FIRE is to cook at the most primal level. There is a universal magic in fire that transforms food as it grills. For me and many other cooks, grilling is our favorite way to cook. Grilling is nothing like cooking on a stovetop or in a gas or electric oven: there's an unpredictability to it, a wild side, an immediacy that sets it apart. The elements must be taken into account, the fire carefully tended. Cooks who love to grill have an instinctive attraction to the fire, where it's warm and sociable and where we can smell the food cooking; we have a built-in need to poke at coals and take in the perfume of smoke and the visual sizzle of the action on the grill.

Learning to Grill

A chimney starter makes starting the fire very easy, without the need for lighter fluids.

If you have access to grapevine cuttings—or fig or other fruitwoods— they lend exceptionally delicious flavors to meat, poultry, and fish on the grill.

I LOVE THE WHOLE PROCESS of grilling—lighting the fire, tending the coals, and cooking the food. Preparing a good bed of coals is vital. It is the radiant heat from these glowing embers that cooks the food, and they perform best when the heat is constant, sustaining the proper cooking temperature for the length of time needed. For me it is of the utmost importance that the fire be accessible while the food is cooking; I need to be able to manipulate the bed of coals under the grill to control the heat and cook with finesse, which is why I am frustrated by any type of grill with an unreachable firebox.

I recommend a grill with a heavy grate to grill on, one that can be raised and lowered over the fire and that allows access to the coals below. Such a device can be as simple as two stacks of bricks supporting a grill, with room between them to build a fire. I use a Tuscan grill, a simple forged iron apparatus that straddles the fire and has three different heights at which its movable grill can be supported. It fits in almost any indoor fireplace and it can be easily used outdoors. I set mine up in my backyard in a little area paved with bricks. A heavy grill like this performs much the same way as a cast-iron pan does, retaining high heat across its surface and cooking food evenly, and it makes beautiful grill marks, too.

For fuel I use lump charcoal, hardwood, or a combination of the two. Lump charcoal is pure carbonized wood with no chemical additives. It burns hot and fast, taking about 20 minutes to produce useable embers. Hardwood alone takes about 40 to 50 minutes to make coals suitable for grilling. To start the fire with charcoal, I always use a chimney starter, filling the upper compartment starter with charcoal and igniting it by setting fire to some sheets of newspaper wadded up in the compartment below. (Lighter fluid imparts an unpleasant petroleum flavor to the food.) The embers are ready when they have gone from bright glowing red to ashy gray. Once they are ready, the embers will last about 30 minutes. Depending on what I'm cooking and for how long, I like to keep a reserve of burning coals to rake under the grill to replenish the fire as the other coals burn out. Either keep adding a few new pieces of charcoal on the periphery of the main bed of coals once it has been spread out, or use two chimney lighters, and light the second one 15 or 20 minutes after the first. A good bed of coals is about 2 inches deep and extends 1 or 2 inches beyond the edges of what is being grilled.

Once the coals have been spread out, put the grill in place to get hot. While it is heating, clean it well with a wire brush. Just before placing food on it, oil it generously to prevent sticking. This is especially helpful when grilling fish. Use some paper towels or a clean rag, moisten with oil, and rub over the surface of the grill; you can use a pair of tongs to do this. Before starting to grill check the temperature of the fire. Different foods require different cooking temperatures. A steak is best seared over a hot fire. Fish fillets need a fairly hot fire, too, but chicken, sausages, hamburgers, vegetables, and slices of bread cook best over medium-hot coals. If the fire is too hot, food will burn before it cooks through. Hold your hand an inch over the grill: if you can only keep it there for 2 seconds, the fire is hot; if you can hold it there for 4 seconds, it's medium-hot. Adjust the fire by moving the coals: spread them out to cool; pile them together or rake more in to raise the temperature. Raising and lowering the grill will control the heat as well; the closer the food is to the coals the higher the cooking temperature will be.

Grilled Steak

A STEAK IS PERFECT for the grill; tender, well marbled, cut thin and flat, it is tailor-made for searing over a bed of hot coals. A properly grilled steak is mouthwatering: brown and crisp on the outside, pink and juicy on the inside. Is there an easier, less complicated dinner than a grilled steak with a green salad? And, agreeably, the cleanup is practically effortless.

Most any cut of steak will do. The classics are rib eye, New York, filet or tenderloin, and porterhouse. There are others that are more economical, but every bit as tasty. Flatiron from the chuck, skirt steak, hangar steak, and bavette are all flavorful cuts, as are flank, top sirloin, and tri-tip. Steaks can be grilled as single portions, or larger steaks can be grilled whole and sliced for more than one. When bound for the grill, a steak is best cut 1 to 2 inches thick. Any thinner and the inside will be overdone before the outside is properly seared; any thicker, the outside starts to char before the inside is ready. Trim off all but a ¼-inch layer of fat; the less dripping fat, the fewer flare-ups.

While seasoning a steak simply, with only salt and fresh-ground black pepper, is enough, I especially like an herb crust. I chop lots of fresh herbs together—thyme, oregano, and marjoram, in any combination, but always with rosemary—and mix them with coarse salt and fresh-ground black pepper. This is rubbed onto the steak with a bit of olive oil an hour or so before grilling. For even cooking, steak should be taken out of the refrigerator and allowed to come to room temperature, which takes 30 minutes to an hour.

TESTING THE HEAT

2 seconds = hot

4 seconds = medium-hot

6 seconds = medium

The ideal steak for me is very browned and herbaceous on the outside and rare on the inside; for that you need a good hot fire.

Prepare a hot fire and preheat and clean the grill with a wire brush. You should not be able to tolerate the heat for more than 2 seconds when you hold your hand over the grill. Oil the grill and put on the steak. Cook for 2 to 3 minutes and if you want to make nice cross-hatched grill marks, rotate the steak a little over 90 degrees. Cook for another 2 to 3 minutes and then turn the steak over. (If the steak has a border of fat, turn this onto the grill, holding the steak up with tongs, to sear the fat for a minute or two before grilling the other side.) Cook the other side for 2 to 3 minutes and rotate a little over 90 degrees. Start checking for doneness after another 2 minutes, pressing your index finger or the back of the tongs into the meat. It will still be soft when rare, a bit springy when medium-rare, and quite resilient when well-done. You can verify this by cutting into the steak, but keep testing by pressure—after a few steaks, you will be able to judge without cutting. Take the steak off the grill when it is a little less done than you want; residual heat will continue to cook the meat while it rests. A 1-inch steak will be grilled rare in about 8 minutes, and grilled medium in about 10 to 12 minutes.

Monitor your fire while the steak is cooking, moving the coals to make the fire hotter or cooler as needed. If the fire flares up, move the meat out of the flames right away or the fire will burn the meat, forming an acrid, black crust. After you take a steak off the grill, let it rest a few minutes before serving to stabilize the internal juices so that they don't run out excessively when the steak is cut into. If it's not to be served right away, cover it loosely with foil to help keep it warm; but don't seal it tightly or it will continue to cook.

Grilled Sirloin Steak with Herbs

4 SERVINGS

My favorite tool for turning food on the grill is a pair of tongs. Tongs are lightweight, they won't pierce the meat, and they are very easy to use.

Trim off and discard all but ¼ inch of the fat from:

One 20-ounce grass-fed sirloin steak, cut 1½ inches thick

Mix together and rub into the steak:

3 tablespoons mixed chopped herbs (rosemary, thyme, oregano, or marjoram)

1½ teaspoons coarse salt

1 teaspoon fresh-ground black pepper

Drizzle with:

1 tablespoon olive oil

Let the steak sit for 1 hour at room temperature.

Prepare a hot fire. Preheat, clean, and oil the grill. Put the steak on the grill and cook for 3 minutes, rotate 110 degrees to make crosshatching grill marks, if desired, and cook for another 2 to 3 minutes. Turn the steak over and repeat. Check for doneness after 8 to 10 minutes total cooking time. If not done, turn and continue cooking. A steak grilled rare takes about 8 to 10 minutes in all, medium-rare takes 10 to 12 minutes, and so forth. Remove from the grill and let rest for 5 minutes before serving.

Grilled Fish and Shellfish

Fɪsʜ ᴀɴᴅ sʜᴇʟʟғɪsʜ are superb grilled. The searing heat quickly seals in juices and delicately perfumes the flesh with smoke. Fish can be grilled as fillets, as steaks, or whole. Shellfish such as scallops and oysters can be grilled in the shell or shucked. Shrimp can be grilled peeled or unpeeled. All these are delicious seasoned with nothing more than salt and pepper and a squeeze of lemon, but advance marinades of olive oil and herbs, tangy salsas such as the peach (page 231) or tomato (page 231), and Herb Butter (page 48), Béarnaise (page 229), or warm butter sauce (page 228) are also possibilities.

A hot fire is best for everything except large whole fish. Use the hand test: you should be able to hold your hand an inch or two over the grill for no more than 2 seconds. The grill should be preheated, cleaned, and, most importantly, oiled, just before putting on the fish, to help keep it from sticking. Season fish fillets and steaks with salt and pepper and brush them with oil before putting to grill. Or marinate them with a combination of herbs, spices, citrus zest, and olive oil. Let fish sit in a marinade for at least an hour to allow the flavors to penetrate. An

A long, slightly flexible metal spatula is best for turning delicate fish.

Don't hesitate to cut into the fish to check for doneness and to see if it is cooked the way you like it.

average fillet about an inch thick will take 6 to 8 minutes to cook. If the skin has been left on (it gets crispy and delicious cooked on a grill), place the fillet skin side down and cook it mostly on the skin side. Check for doneness after about 6 minutes, and turn at the last minute to sear the other side. A fillet without the skin should be cooked 3 to 4 minutes on each side. Rotate after about 2 minutes to make cross-hatched grill marks. Check for doneness after about 6 minutes, and turn at the last minute to sear the other side. To test, press on the flesh with your finger or a spatula, or probe the flesh with a knife. The fish is done when the meat is just set and slightly firm to the touch but still moist. Fish such as salmon and tuna are delicious seared on the outside and very rare inside, still shiny and translucent. Remember that the fish will continue to cook after it is taken off the grill. If cooked for too long, fish can become quite dry.

A fish steak is a cross-section at least 1 inch thick that contains some backbone and is surrounded by the skin. Grill the same way as a skinless fillet, but turn it after 5 minutes and check for doneness after 8. Check by feel or by cutting into the flesh near the backbone to see inside. The flesh should separate easily from the bones but still be quite moist.

A whole fish should be scaled and gutted; any fishmonger will do this. Cook the fish whole and unboned, with its head on, if possible; the fish will be more succulent. Season well with salt and pepper or marinate as described above, turning the fish now and then in the marinade. Cook smaller fish like anchovies and sardines over a hot fire, threaded on skewers for easy turning. (I love fresh anchovies marinated with a little chopped mint and grilled over a searing hot fire.) Trim off the fins and the tail-ends of larger fish (kitchen shears make short work of this chore). The belly cavity can be stuffed with lemon slices and herbs. Because they take much longer to cook, big fish need a medium-hot fire. To turn over a big fish on the grill, gently roll it as often as necessary to keep the skin from burning. Measure the fish at its thickest point and allow about 10 minutes per inch. A good friend of mine catches big fish, cleans and scales them, and grills them wrapped entirely in fennel fronds or herb branches, or sometimes in tender leafing branches from his lemon tree, tied in place with wet string. This overcoat of greenery steams and perfumes the fish and they taste divine. Whole fish are done when the flesh easily separates from the bone. If tied up in greenery, unwrap it, and gently separate the fillets from the central backbone, picking out any rib bones that come off with the fillets.

Shucked scallops, oysters, squid, and shrimp (peeled or not) are easiest cooked on skewers. Season the skewered seafood and marinate as desired. A hot fire and quick cooking will preserve the juicy tenderness of the flesh. Once again, a preheated, clean, well-oiled grill will keep sticking to a minimum. After being washed clean of loose sand and grit, whole bivalves such as clams, mussels, and oysters can be placed right on the grill. The shells of most bivalves have one flatter half-shell and one that's more rounded or cupped. Place the cupped side down on the grill to catch the liquor of the shellfish as it cooks. The shellfish are done as soon as the shells steam open.

Grilled Whole Fish

4 SERVINGS

The yield in edible fillets of a whole fish is about 40 to 45 percent of its weight.

Buy the very freshest fish you can. Ask your fishmonger which fish came in that day.

Have your fishmonger scale, gut, and trim the tail and fins from:
  1 whole 3-pound fish, or two 1½-pound fishes (such as rockfish, red snapper, bluefish, or striped bass)
Season generously, inside and out, with:
  Salt
  Fresh-ground black pepper
Stuff the cavity with:
  Lemon slices
  1 large handful of fennel fronds (the feathery leaves of wild or cultivated fennel) or other herb branches
Scatter a few of the fronds or herb branches around the outside of the fish as well.
Rub with:
  Olive oil
Let the fish sit for an hour or so.

Prepare a medium fire. Preheat and clean the grill well. When ready to cook the fish, oil the grill with an oiled towel, and put the fish on the grill. Cook until done, turning the fish as often as needed to keep the skin from burning. Plan on about 10 minutes of cooking per inch of thickness at the thickest part of the fish. The fish is done when the flesh separates easily from the bones but is still moist. Test by inserting a skewer; it should meet little resistance. Remove from the grill and present whole at the table or fillet first in the kitchen. Serve with:

Lemon wedges

A pitcher of extra-virgin olive oil

VARIATIONS

• Serve the fish with a salsa verde (see page 45) made with the same herb the fish is stuffed with.

• Before grilling, wrap the fish entirely in fennel fronds or herb branches and secure them with wet string wrapped and tied around.

Grilling Vegetables

Fire temperature is very important for grilling vegetables. If the fire is too hot, the vegetables will char on the outside and be underdone on the inside.

No less than meat and fish, vegetables are enhanced by the smoky perfume and radiant heat of the grill, whether served plain with a simple salsa verde or vinaigrette, stirred into a risotto, or combined into a grilled version of a vegetable stew such as ratatouille or peperonata. Grilled potatoes can be made into an intriguing potato salad that is even tastier when it includes a few grilled scallions.

Different vegetables require different grilling approaches, and some vegetables can be grilled in more than one way. In general, grill vegetables over a medium to medium-hot bed of coals; a hotter fire will scorch the vegetables before they cook through. Conveniently, the fire is often at the perfect temperature for vegetables after the meat or fish has been grilled. You can also distribute the coals to create areas with different temperatures, so that one area burns hot while the other is medium-hot, allowing you to grill vegetables at the same time as a steak, for example. Use the hand test. If the fire is medium-hot, you should be able to hold your hand over the grill for about 4 seconds. Clean the grill well and oil it after it has heated up, before putting the vegetables on.

Summer squash, eggplant, potatoes, and onions should be sliced ¼ inch to ½ inch thick, as uniform as possible. Cut peppers in half or in quarters and clean out the ribs and seeds. Onion slices can be skewered flat, which makes them easier to turn. (Soak skewers in water for a few minutes to keep them from igniting.) Salt the vegetables. This can be done ahead of time, but note that salting accelerates moisture loss, so don't be alarmed by liquid around them when you're ready to grill.

Brush olive oil generously over the vegetables before grilling. They can also be tossed with chopped herbs. After the vegetable slices have been on the grill for a few minutes, rotate them a little over 90 degrees to make a nice crosshatch of grill marks. After a couple more minutes turn the vegetables and finish cooking, rotating them once more to make grill marks, and turning them again, if necessary. Take the slices off the grill as soon as they are tender. Check for doneness at the stem end, which always takes the longest to cook. (Again, tongs are my favorite grilling tool; they make turning the vegetables a breeze.)

Leafy vegetables such as scallions, small leeks, and wedges of radicchio benefit from an initial moistening before they go on the grill. Oil them, and then sprinkle them with water or mist them with a spray bottle. Turn them often as they grill to prevent scorching, and keep sprinkling or misting them to keep them moist. To accelerate their cooking, invert a metal bowl over them, to steam them while they grill.

Some vegetables are better when cooked until tender in boiling water before being finished on the grill: asparagus, for example, and leeks that are larger than scallions, and small artichokes and potatoes, whole or halved. For easy turning on the grill, skewer potatoes and artichokes, taking care that all the cut faces are on the same plane when skewered to ensure equal contact with the grill.

Tomatoes can be grilled, but they need a hot fire. Cut them in half and slide them onto the grill, cut side down. Let them grill for 3 minutes to seal the flesh before trying to rotate them. Be sure to clean the grill before you grill anything else, as tomatoes are a bit messy.

Vegetables such as eggplants, summer squashes, and peppers can be cooked whole, but because they will take longer to cook through, the fire should be medium rather than medium-hot. Make a couple of deep incisions in their sides to speed up the cooking and to keep them from bursting from a buildup of steam. Corn can be grilled with great success after a little preparation. Peel back the husks, leaving them connected at the base of the ear, and remove all the silk. Season the corn with salt and pepper and a little chile or herbs, if you want; brush with some butter or oil; and sprinkle with a little water. Rewrap the ears in their husks to protect them and grill over a medium to medium-hot fire, turning now and then, for about 10 minutes. Very large mushrooms can be sliced thick and grilled; smaller ones can be skewered

Grilled bread is delicious still hot from the fire, drizzled with olive oil and rubbed with a clove of garlic.

and grilled whole or halved. Before putting them on the grill, brush them with oil, and season them with salt and pepper. Wild mushrooms grilled over a campfire are unforgettable.

Like vegetables, bread is best grilled over a medium to medium-hot fire. When it is sliced thick, oil it after it has been grilled, but thin slices are better brushed with oil beforehand. Bread to be grilled can be sliced and even oiled a few hours in advance as long as the bread is kept tightly wrapped in a towel to prevent the slices from drying out and warping.

Ratatouille of Grilled Vegetables
4 SERVINGS

A RATATOUILLE is a colorful garlicky stew of summer vegetables cooked together in olive oil and their own juices and finished with basil. This recipe deviates from tradition: the same summer vegetables are first grilled until done, and only then cut in bite-size pieces, and combined with garlic, basil, and olive oil.

Prepare all the vegetables, seasoning them with salt as you go.
Trim the ends from:

1 medium eggplant
2 medium summer squash

Cut into ¼-inch slices.
Peel and cut crosswise into ¼-inch-thick slices:

1 large onion

Cut in half lengthwise and remove the stem and seeds from:

2 sweet peppers

Remove the core from:

3 ripe tomatoes

Cut off the ends and then cut in half crosswise.

Prepare a medium-hot fire and place a grill over it to preheat. When the fire is ready, clean the grill well and oil it using a cloth or paper towels. Pile up a few coals under part of the grill to make the fire hotter there.
Brush all the vegetables with:

Olive oil

Put the tomatoes cut side down on the grill over the hottest area of the fire. Leave them for 3 to 4 minutes, turn them, cook them another 4 minutes, and remove them from the grill. At the same time arrange the other vegetables over the medium-hot fire and grill them about 4 minutes on each side. Keep turning as needed to keep them from burning, checking for doneness at the stem ends. Remove when tender and set aside to cool down. When all the vegetables are grilled and cool enough to handle, cut them into ½-inch squares. Combine in a bowl with:

> **2 to 3 garlic cloves, chopped fine**
> **Salt**
> **10 basil leaves, chopped or cut into thin strips**
> **3 tablespoons extra-virgin olive oil**

Taste and adjust the seasoning as needed with more oil, salt, basil, or garlic. Serve warm or at room temperature.

Omelets and Soufflés

Cheese Omelet

Chard Frittata

Goat Cheese Soufflé

THE MANY VARIETIES of omelets and frittatas are all appealing variations on a simple theme: fresh eggs beaten together and cooked quickly in butter or oil. Omelets are basically a layer of scrambled eggs wrapped around a meat or vegetable or cheese filling, while a frittata is more of an egg cake in which beaten egg acts as a binder for a cooked savory vegetable, as in a Spanish (not a Mexican) *tortilla*. Soufflés are the dramatic result of separating eggs into yolks and whites: the yolks are first made into a rich base and then lightened by whites whipped into airy peaks and folded in. The mixture bakes and expands into a magnificent, ethereal tower. I love the theater of a puffy soufflé, whether it's sweet or savory. Sweet soufflés are among my favorite desserts, warm and light, but full of flavor.

Omelets

I particularly enjoy an omelet accompanied by a toasted slice of levain bread rubbed with garlic, and a green salad that contrasts refreshingly with the rich flavor of eggs.

AN OMELET makes a light, quick, nutritious, and economical breakfast, lunch, or dinner. It is a comforting dish, thanks to its tenderness and the simplicity of its flavors: fresh eggs, a touch of butter, and a little cheese or other filling to add flavor and nuance. For the omelet I make most often, I stir fresh herbs (parsley, chive, sorrel, tarragon, or chervil) into the eggs before they are cooked and fill the omelet with a bit of Gruyère or soft ricotta. There are countless other possible fillings for omelets: the leftover spoonful of last night's sautéed greens or roasted peppers, for example, or a morsel of braised lamb or sautéed ham.

It should go without saying that very fresh eggs from hens fed organic feed and allowed to forage freely outdoors make the tastiest omelets. Farmers' markets often sell such eggs. At grocery stores, look for eggs that are local, free-range, and, if possible, certified organic. Count 2 to 3 eggs per person. I prefer omelets that are not too thick, are delicately puffed and folded, and are still moist on the inside. To achieve this, I use this rule of thumb for the size of pan: 2 eggs in a 6-inch pan, 3 eggs in an 8-inch pan, 6 in a 10-inch pan, and no more than 12 in a 12-inch pan. The beaten eggs should be no more than ¼ inch deep. The pan itself should be heavy and smooth-surfaced or nonstick. Preheat the pan over medium-low heat for 3 to 5 minutes before adding the eggs. This is the most important step for quick, consistent, and nonstick cooking. Crack your eggs into a bowl and, right before they are to be cooked, add a pinch of salt per egg (they turn watery when salted ahead), and beat them lightly with a fork or a whisk. The omelet will be more fluffy and tender if the eggs are well combined, but not beaten into a completely homogenous mixture.

Put a knob of butter in the hot pan; it will melt and foam up. Swirl it around and, as the foam subsides and the butter starts to give off its distinctive nut-like aroma, but before it starts to brown, pour in the eggs. If you are making a large omelet, turn the heat up at this time to medium (this is not necessary with a small omelet). There should be a satisfying sizzle as the eggs enter the pan. The edges of the omelet will begin to set almost immediately (if they don't, turn up the heat). Pull the edges towards the center with a fork or spatula, allowing uncooked egg to flow over the exposed bottom of the hot pan. Do this until the bottom of the omelet is set, lifting the edges and tilting the pan to let liquid egg flow underneath. When the eggs are mostly set, sprinkle on the cheese or other fillings. Cook a moment longer, fold the omelet in half over itself, and slide it onto a plate. To make a rolled omelet, tilt the pan down and away from you, shaking the pan to scoot the omelet towards the far edge of the pan and folding the near edge of the omelet over onto itself. Continue to tilt the pan, rolling the omelet towards the downward side. Then fold the far edge over the top and roll the omelet out of the pan onto a warm plate, seam side down. The whole process will have taken less than a minute. Drag a piece of butter over the top to make the omelet shine.

Cheese Omelet

4 SERVINGS

Crack into a large bowl:

8 to 12 eggs

Add:

2 tablespoons chopped parsley

2 tablespoons mixed chopped herbs (chives, chervil, tarragon, or marjoram)

A few grinds of black pepper

and beat lightly, until just combined. When ready to cook, season the eggs with:

Salt

Preheat a large (12-inch) heavy or nonstick pan for 3 to 5 minutes over medium-low heat. When the pan is completely heated, put in:

1 tablespoon butter

When the foaming butter begins to subside, pour in the eggs. Turn the heat up to medium. Pull the sides towards the center, letting uncooked egg flow onto the exposed pan. When the eggs have set on the bottom, continue lifting the edges and tilting the pan to allow uncooked egg to flow under to cook. When most of the egg is set, sprinkle over the top:

4 ounces Gruyère or cheddar cheese, grated

Cook for a moment to heat the cheese. Fold the omelet in half over itself and slide onto a large plate. Rub the top with a bit of butter and serve.

VARIATIONS

◆ Substitute 4 ounces ricotta cheese for the Gruyère or cheddar.

◆ Omit the herbs.

◆ Make 4 individual omelets with 2 or 3 eggs each.

Frittata

A FRITTATA IS a flat round omelet with its filling stirred into the eggs before cooking. I like my frittatas dense in vegetables, almost like pies without crusts. Many things can be stirred into frittatas: sautéed onions, wilted greens, roasted peppers, sliced potatoes, mushrooms, even pasta. Frittatas can be served warm or at room temperature, plain or with a sauce, as a first course or as dinner. And they are great for sandwiches and as picnic food.

Any filling should be cooked before being added to the eggs. For more flavor, vegetables can be browned or seasoned with herbs and spices. Although some recipes say to pour beaten eggs into the pan over vegetables after they have been cooked, I have better luck turning the frittata later when I beat the eggs with a little oil and salt, stir in the vegetables and any other ingredients such as herbs or cheese, and cook the frittata in a clean preheated pan.

Cook frittatas over medium to medium-high heat. Any higher and the eggs will burn on the bottom. As the edges set, lift them away from the side of the pan and tilt the pan to let uncooked egg flow underneath. When the frittata is mostly set, place an inverted plate the same size or a little larger over the pan, hold them firmly together, and turn the pan upside down on top of the plate. (Protect the hand holding the plate with a towel or potholder.) Add a bit more oil to the pan and slide the frittata back in. Cook for another 2 or 3 minutes and then slide onto a plate. The frittata should be cooked through but still moist inside.

Another way to cook a frittata is in the oven, as long as the pan you use is ovenproof. Preheat the oven to 350°F. Start the frittata on top of the stove, as above. After a couple of minutes, put the pan in the oven and cook until the frittata is set on top, about 7 to 10 minutes.

Chard Frittata

4 SERVINGS

Wash and separate the stems from:
> **1 bunch of chard**

Cut the stems into ¼-inch slices. Coarsely chop the leaves.

Heat in a heavy pan, over medium heat:
> **1 tablespoon olive oil**

Add:
> **1 medium onion, peeled and sliced thin**

Cook for 5 minutes and add the chard stems. Season with:

Salt

Cook for 4 minutes and add the leaves. Cook until the leaves are tender, adding a splash of water if the pan dries out. Turn out of the pan onto a plate.

Crack into a large bowl:

6 eggs

Add:

Salt

2 teaspoons olive oil

Fresh-ground black pepper

A pinch of cayenne

4 garlic cloves, chopped

Beat lightly. Gently squeeze the chard with your hands, wringing out most, but not all, of the liquid. Stir the chard into the beaten eggs. Thoroughly preheat a 10-inch heavy or nonstick pan over medium-low heat. Pour in:

2 tablespoons olive oil

After a few seconds, pour in the egg mixture. As the eggs set on the bottom, lift the edges to allow the uncooked egg to flow underneath. Continue to cook until mostly set. Invert a plate on top of the pan; turn the plate and pan upside down to turn out the frittata onto the plate. Pour in:

1 teaspoon olive oil

Slide the frittata back into the pan. Cook for 2 or 3 more minutes. Slide onto a plate and serve warm or at room temperature.

VARIATIONS

◆ Add a bunch of sorrel to the chard leaves during the last minute of cooking.

◆ For the chard, substitute broccoli rabe, mustard greens, nettles, or any other greens.

◆ Serve warm on a pool of Simple Tomato Sauce (page 264).

◆ For a delicious sandwich, serve a wedge of frittata with a slice of ham or a few slices of tomato between 2 slices of lightly toasted bread rubbed with garlic.

Soufflés

Dramatic, puffy, and feather-light, with quivering, gilded caps, soufflés are surrounded by an aura of culinary mystery. Surprisingly, beneath the mystery lies a rather simple, but ingenious, dish. In a basic soufflé, a simple white sauce made of flour, butter, and milk is enriched with egg yolks; a flavoring element such as cheese (or fruit or liqueur for a dessert soufflé) is added; and the mixture is lightened with egg whites beaten to many times their original volume. The air trapped in the egg whites expands in the heat of the oven, puffing up the soufflé even more. The only critical point is that a soufflé should be sped to the table the moment it's finished baking. Out of the oven, a steaming soufflé cools quickly and loses its triumphant height.

Here is a basic method to follow to make savory soufflés. Start by making a white sauce, or béchamel: Melt butter in a heavy saucepan. Stir in flour, cook for a minute or two (this mixture is called a *roux)*, and whisk in milk, a little at a time, whisking thoroughly after each addition before adding another. The flour and butter will bind up and then slowly loosen as more milk is added. If you add all the milk at once you are almost guaranteed lumps in the sauce. (If the sauce does get lumpy, push it through a strainer to smooth it.) After the milk is whisked in, bring the sauce to a boil, stirring all the while. This cooks the flour into the milk and fully thickens the sauce. Turn the heat down as low as possible, and simmer for at least 10 minutes, stirring occasionally, to cook out the taste of raw flour. Season the sauce to taste with salt, pepper, nutmeg, and cayenne. Let it cool slightly.

Separate the eggs, stirring the yolks into the béchamel one by one and putting the whites into a large bowl in which they will be beaten later. Take care not to break the yolks: egg whites containing even a tiny bit of yolk refuse to be whipped into a foam as high, stiff, and stable as those without. If there are visible traces of broken yolk in your egg white, you may be able to scoop them out with an eggshell half; if you can't, you may have to separate another egg and save the broken one for some other use. Eggs that are many weeks old have watery whites and fragile yolks, which makes them more difficult to separate than very fresh eggs, with their thick whites and stand-up yolks.

To the béchamel and egg yolks, add grated cheese or other flavoring elements such as a vegetable purée (of leeks, asparagus, or garlic, for example), chopped shellfish, or a few herbs. This mixture is called the

RULE OF THUMB
1¼ cups white sauce
to 1¼ cups cheese or
vegetable purée
to 4 eggs

base of the soufflé. It can be prepared ahead of time and refrigerated, but be sure to take both the base and the egg whites out of the refrigerator at least an hour before baking to come to room temperature.

When ready to cook, preheat the oven to 375°F (or to 400°F if you decide to make individual soufflés rather than one big one). The soufflé needs to bake in the center of the oven. Rearrange the racks, if necessary, to allow plenty of headroom for the soufflé to rise. Butter a baking dish liberally with soft butter. A soufflé can be baked in a traditional soufflé dish, in a shallow gratin dish or other baking dish, or in individual ovenproof cups or porcelain ramekins. Even a flat sheet pan with sides will work; the soufflé won't puff as high, but it will have more surface area to brown. Beat the egg whites vigorously with a wire whisk until they form peaks that are stiff, but still moist and smooth. It's easy to overwhip egg whites with an electric mixer, so pay close attention when the whites start to thicken, and stop and check them frequently. (Overwhipped whites have a chunky granular look to them.)

A copper bowl for beating egg whites does make a difference. A chemical reaction between the eggs and the metal stabilizes the foam.

Stir about one third of the whites into the soufflé base, to lighten it. With a rubber spatula, scrape the rest of the beaten egg whites into the lightened base, and gently fold base and egg whites together without stirring or beating, which would overmix and deflate them. This is important, because the egg whites are responsible for the soufflé's eventual height. To fold, cut straight down through the mixture at the center of the bowl, all the way to the bottom, using the edge of the spatula as a blade. Scrape back to the side on the bottom of the bowl, turning the spatula and bringing it up the side and back over the top with a lifting-and-enclosing motion. Rotate the bowl a little with your other hand and repeat the circular motion of downstroke and enfolding upstroke, rotating the bowl with each stroke, and repeating until there are only a few streaks of white here and there. Gently pour the mixture into the buttered dish, filling it three-quarters full. Bake, undisturbed, until puffed and golden, around 35 to 40 minutes for a large soufflé, and about 10 minutes for individual small ones. A properly cooked soufflé will have a golden crust and a soft tender center.

Sweet soufflés are made in a slightly different manner. Instead of a béchamel, a pastry cream is the base (see page 376) and flavorings such as fruit, chocolate, or a liqueur are added to the cooled pastry cream. When ready to bake, add beaten egg whites and cook as above.

Goat Cheese Soufflé

4 SERVINGS

Melt in a heavy saucepan over medium heat:

5 tablespoons butter

Stir in and cook for 2 minutes:

3 tablespoons flour

Whisk in, little by little, whisking thoroughly between additions:

1 cup milk

Season the béchamel with:

Salt

Fresh-ground black pepper

A pinch of cayenne

1 thyme sprig, leaves only

Cook over low heat, stirring occasionally, for 10 minutes. Remove from the heat and cool slightly. Separate:

4 eggs

Stir the yolks into the white sauce. Add:

4 ounces soft, mild goat cheese

Stir in and taste for salt. It should be ever so slightly too salty to make up for the unsalted whites, which will be added later.

Preheat the oven to 375°F. Butter a 1-quart soufflé dish, or another baking dish such as a gratin dish, with:

1 tablespoon soft butter

Whip the egg whites into moist firm peaks. Stir one third of the whites into the soufflé base. Then gently fold the base into the rest of the egg whites, taking care not to deflate them. Pour the mixture into the buttered dish and bake for 35 to 40 minutes, or until puffed and golden, but still soft in the center and jiggly when shaken gently.

VARIATIONS

◆ Substitute a stronger aged goat cheese for half the mild goat cheese.

◆ Preheat the oven to 400°F. Butter eight 4-ounce ramekins instead of the 1-quart soufflé dish. Fill the ramekins three-quarters full and bake for 10 minutes or until puffed and golden.

◆ Substitute ¾ cup grated Gruyère and ¼ cup grated Parmesan for the goat cheese.

◆ Add ¼ cup Garlic Purée (page 308) along with the cheese.

◆ Evenly sprinkle fine breadcrumbs or finely grated Parmesan cheese onto the buttered inside of the dish.

Tarts, Savory and Sweet

Onion Tart

Apple Tart

Chocolate Tartlets

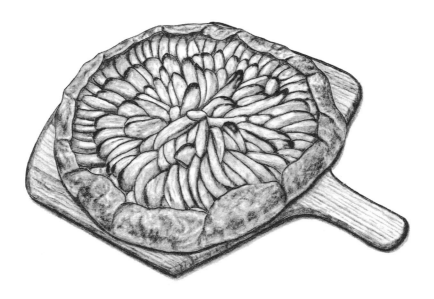

A BUTTERY CRUST with a savory or sweet filling, a tart is a perfect food in the same way a sandwich or a pizza is. My favorite kind of tarts are the flat, crusty, round, and open-faced versions known as galettes. The pastry shell is rolled quite thin, topped with a filling of fruit or vegetables (only about twice as thick as the shell), and baked free-form. The galette is baked until it is crisp and golden and the topping is softened, its flavors concentrated—an ideal marriage of textures and flavors.

Making
Tart Dough

*It turns out that the only
secret to making good
tart dough is practice.*

THE PASTRY determines the outcome of any tart: how it's made, how it's rolled out, and how long it's cooked. The tart dough I make most often is good for both savory and sweet tarts and it makes good pie crust, too. Simply made with flour, butter, and water, the pastry is tender, flaky, and crisp. I avoided making tart dough for years; I found it difficult to make, and I was often disappointed with the results. Then a friend who is an excellent pastry chef explained patiently just how the flour, butter, and water work together, and after a little practice I began to get a feel for the *feel* of the dough, and the look of it, and my tarts got to be consistently good.

As explained in the bread chapter, flour contains a mixture of proteins known as gluten. When mixed with water, these proteins are activated and begin to form a molecular network that makes dough elastic. The more a dough is stirred, or worked, the more the gluten is developed. Gluten is good for bread, which needs a strong supporting network in order to rise, but not so good for tarts: the more the dough is worked, the tougher the pastry will be. That's why it's important not to over-work tart dough or knead it. All-purpose flour is the best flour to use for this recipe; bread flour is too high in gluten and so-called pastry flour and cake flour are too low (which makes the pastry mealy). All-purpose flour has just the right amount of gluten to give the dough a flaky texture. This is where the butter comes in.

Butter adds flavor and richness to the pastry and has important effects on texture as well. When butter is mixed in, it coats some of the flour, isolating the flour from the water—which slows down the activation of gluten, making the pastry more tender. When some of the butter is left in larger, uneven pieces and flattened by rolling, it will *steam* during baking, separating sheets of gluten from one another, and creating a flaky texture. The more butter, the more tender the dough. The more irregular the sizes of the pieces of butter, the flakier the pastry.

When it's mixed into the flour, the butter should be quite cold—refrigerator temperature. If it gets too soft or melts, it makes the dough oily. Have all the ingredients ready before you start: butter chilled and cut into roughly ¼-inch cubes, flour measured, water icy cold. Work the butter into the flour quickly, using your fingertips. If you have one of those tools called a pastry blender, so much the better. The important thing is to work quickly, lightly rubbing the butter and flour together with your fingertips, or chopping and mixing with the pastry blender, for about a minute. (You can use a stand mixer, too, fitted with the paddle attachment, and mix for about a minute at medium-low speed.) Now it's time to add the water.

The water's function is to hydrate the flour, thus activating the gluten. You need enough water to make a cohesive dough that is neither crumbly nor sticky. A dry, crumbly dough is hard to roll out and mealy to eat; wet, sticky dough makes tough pastry. The properties of both flour and butter vary, so the amount of ice-cold water you need to add will also vary. Measure out the amount called for, but don't pour it in all at once. Start by adding about three quarters of the amount. Stir and toss the dough with a fork as you dribble in the water. Avoid working the dough or squeezing it together. (If using a mixer, pour the water down the sides of the bowl while the machine is on low speed, mixing for 30 seconds or less.) Add water until the dough is *just* starting to clump together—if it forms a ball it's too wet. Test it by squeezing together a small handful. If it holds together, there's enough water; if the mass is dry and crumbly, it needs more. Add more water a few drops at a time, stirring lightly between additions.

A few tips to remember: use cold butter, work the butter into the flour lightly and quickly, and add just enough cold water to hold the dough together.

When the dough is the right consistency, gently bring it together into a shaggy ball, working quickly with your fingers (the palms of your hand are much warmer than your fingertips). When making more than one ball of dough, separate the dough into equal parts before forming the balls. Wrap the ball(s) in plastic. (This is a great way to reuse plastic bags from the market.) Once a ball of dough is wrapped in plastic, give it a good squeeze to compact it and flatten it into a disk, pinching the sides together to seal up any cracks that may have formed. Sealing the cracks makes it easier to roll the dough out later. Put the plastic-wrapped disks into the refrigerator to rest for at least an hour before you roll them out. A rest allows the moisture level in the dough to equalize and the gluten to relax, which make it easier to roll out the dough. The dough can be kept in the refrigerator for 2 days, and in the freezer for 2 months. Thaw frozen dough overnight in the refrigerator before using.

Tart and Pie Dough

MAKES TWO 10-OUNCE
BALLS OF DOUGH,
ENOUGH FOR TWO
11-INCH TARTS OR
ONE DOUBLE-CRUST
9-INCH PIE

This recipe is easily halved or doubled.

Have measured:

½ cup ice-cold water

Mix together:

2 cups all-purpose unbleached flour

½ teaspoon salt (omit if using salted butter)

Add:

12 tablespoons (1½ sticks) cold butter, cut into small (¼-inch) cubes

Cut or work the butter into the flour with a pastry blender or your fingertips, leaving some of the butter in fairly large, irregular pieces. This will take 1 or 2 minutes. (Or mix for no more than a minute, at medium-low speed, in a stand mixer fitted with the paddle attachment.) Pour in three quarters of the water, stirring all the while with a fork until the dough begins to form clumps. (In the mixer, turn the speed to low and pour the water down the sides of the bowl, mixing for 30 seconds or less.) Keep adding water if needed. Divide the dough in two, bring each part together into a ball, and wrap each ball in plastic. Compress each ball, and then flatten them into disks. Let rest, refrigerated, for 1 hour or longer.

Rolling Out Tart Dough

TART DOUGH is easiest to roll out when it is malleable, but not soft. If it has been chilling for a number of hours, take it out of the refrigerator for about 20 minutes to soften. This may take more or less time depending on the room's temperature. Choose a surface to roll the dough on that is smooth and cool and where there is enough room to roll out the dough comfortably.

When ready to roll, take the disk of dough, still wrapped in plastic, and flatten it well with your hands, tapping or pinching the edges to seal shut any cracks that may appear. Dust the counter lightly and evenly with flour and place the dough in the middle. Dust the top of the dough generously with flour as well. With the rolling pin, tap firmly across the top of the dough a few times to flatten the disk even more, then begin to roll. Guide the rolling pin from the center of the disk towards the edges, pressing with firm but consistent pressure. After a few rolls, turn the dough over, smooth the flour on the top of the dough, lift it up, and reflour the board. As the dough spreads out, be sure to close up any cracks that appear at the edges by pinching them together. You want the dough to flow out smoothly from under the rolling pin. As the circle gets bigger, keep guiding the rolling pin out from the center, as opposed to rolling back and forth. Think of the dough as a bicycle wheel, and the spokes as the lines to follow while rolling. Give the dough a quarter turn now and then to keep it from sticking, dusting with flour as needed underneath or on top.

If the dough does start to stick, use a pastry scraper to slide gently underneath the edges and loosen the dough from the counter. Carefully fold the dough back and throw some more flour over the countertop. (It's okay to use plenty of flour; just brush it off at the end.) Unfold the dough, and slide it a little to make sure that it is well floured and moving freely. Finish rolling out the dough evenly. Check it for any thick spots and even these areas out.

A circular baking sheet, or pizza pan, is handy to have if you bake a lot of tarts.

Roll the dough a little less than ⅛ inch thick for an open-faced tart. Roll it slightly thicker for a pie or double-crusted tart. Once the dough is rolled, brush off all the extra flour with a soft brush (a kitchen towel will work, if used with a light touch). To move the dough, fold it in half and then in quarters; this keeps it from stretching and tearing when lifted. Transfer the dough onto a baking sheet lined with parchment paper and unfold it. (The parchment paper ensures that the tart will not stick. I highly recommend using it.) Another way to transfer the dough is to roll it onto the rolling pin, then unroll it onto the parchment. Put the dough back in the refrigerator, baking sheet and all, to firm up before filling and finishing. If you are rolling out another piece of pastry, brush the flour evenly back over the counter to reuse. Don't stack the pieces of rolled-out dough on top of each other. Separate them with parchment paper or put them on separate pans.

To prebake a tart or pie shell "blind" (without a filling), line the shell with a piece of foil or parchment paper, then fill the tart with a layer of dried beans reserved for this purpose (or other pie weights). Bake in a 375°F oven for 15 minutes, or until lightly golden around the edge. Take the tart out of the oven and remove the foil and the weights. Return to the oven and cook for another 5 to 7 minutes, until the tart is an even light golden brown.

Savory Tarts

A crisp piece of tart along with a fresh, tangy salad makes an excellent lunch or light dinner.

THERE IS a long list of variations of savory galettes and most of them begin with sautéed onions. Sautéed onions are the perfect foil for the crisp, buttery crust of a tart. When combined with other vegetables, onions add protective moisture and deep flavor as the tart bakes in the oven. The pastry can also be rolled into long thin rectangular tarts, which can be cut into small pieces that make very popular finger food for a party.

Surprisingly, onions vary quite a bit, and not just in appearance. Sometimes they cook quickly and are so juicy they need to be drained before they can be used; other times they take a long time to soften and don't give off any liquid to speak of. Onions with very thin skins are usually much more sweet and juicy, while those with very hard, dark, golden skins tend to take longer to cook. All onions will eventually soften and be delicious, but when given the choice, I recommend selecting large onions that have a delicate, thin, lighter skin. In the summer, when they are in season, sweet Walla Walla, Vidalia, or Bermuda onions make excellent tarts, baking up almost as sweet as honey. In the spring there are fresh onions, or spring onions, that have not been dried and cured, and still have their green stalks attached. Peel them and trim off their stalks, slice them thick, and cook until just soft. The flavor of spring onions is delicate and less sweet than that of mature cured onions.

The right amount of onions cooked to the right consistency is what makes a good tart. Pile the onions into a low-sided, heavy-bottomed pan with a generous amount of fat, and cook them slowly with herbs until soft and tasty; this will take at least 30 minutes. The onions must be cooled before they are spread onto the pastry or they will melt the butter before the tart bakes. The onions should be moist but not dripping wet or the tart will be soggy. If the onions are too juicy, drain them. Save the juice; it can be reduced and served with the tart as a little sauce or added to a vinaigrette.

For a crispier crust, if you have a pizza stone, put it on the bottom rack of the oven to preheat, then bake the tart (on its baking sheet) atop the stone.

If the onions are still juicy, even after draining, sprinkle a little flour over the pastry (avoiding the border), before adding the onions, to soak up some of the juice while the tart cooks. Bake on the lowest rack of the oven for a crust that is crisp and golden brown on the bottom. Check the underside by gently lifting up the tart with a spatula. When the tart is fully baked, slide it off the pan onto a cooling rack to rest. If left on the baking pan to cool, it will steam and the pastry will not stay crisp.

Once you have mastered a basic onion tart, there are many variations you can try: add sliced sweet or hot peppers to the sautéing onions about halfway through cooking; grate some summer squash and stir it into the onions during their last few minutes of sautéing; or, before you fill the tart, while the onions are cooling, stir in either seasoned cherry tomato halves or roasted, peeled, and sliced peppers. You can also top the layer of onions with sliced tomatoes or lightly grilled slices of eggplant. For a sweet and savory tart, mix chopped roasted figs into the onions. Other variations include sprinkling the pastry with grated cheese or brushing it with a slurry of chopped herbs and olive oil before spreading on the onions. Artichoke hearts also can either be sautéed and stirred into the onions, or sliced and baked and arranged on top of them; when the tart comes out of the oven, try painting it with garlic and herb butter. And most of the year you can mix the onions with sautéed greens—collards, chard, spinach, broccoli rabe, or mustard. Or when the tart has only 10 minutes left to bake, top it with anchovies and black olives.

Onion Tart

8 SERVINGS

Heat in a low-sided heavy-bottomed pan:

4 tablespoons olive oil or butter

Add:

6 medium onions (about 2 pounds), peeled and sliced thin

3 thyme sprigs

Cook over medium heat until soft and juicy. This will take from 20 to 30 minutes. Season with:

Salt

Cook for a few minutes more. Put into a bowl to cool. If the onions are very juicy, pour them into a strainer over a bowl to drain. Remove the liquid.

Roll out into a 14-inch circle:

One 10-ounce disk of Tart and Pie Dough (page 174)

Brush off the excess flour, transfer the dough to a baking sheet lined with parchment paper, and let it firm up in the refrigerator for 10 minutes or so. Spread the cooled onions over the dough (removing the thyme branches as you go), leaving a 1½-inch border around the whole circumference of the dough. Fold the border up over the onions. For a shiny, more finished look, mix together and brush the folded dough rim with:

1 egg
1 tablespoon milk or water

Bake on the bottom rack of a preheated 375°F oven for 45 to 50 minutes, or until the crust is golden brown on the bottom. Slide the tart off the pan onto a rack to cool. Serve warm or at room temperature.

Fruit Tarts

WHEN IT IS TIME for dessert, I like to eat fruit. A simple piece of ripe fruit is what I would choose first, but fruit tarts are irresistible, too. Almost any fruit can be made into a tart, either alone or in combination with others. Apples, pears, plums, apricots, peaches, nectarines, cranberries, quince, raspberries, blackberries, huckleberries, all are ideal, and the list goes on and on.

Fruit is best used when ripe—but not so ripe that it is getting soft. Don't hesitate to use bruised or blemished fruit; just discard the damaged parts. With the exception of berries and cherries (which are usually left whole and pitted), the fruit is cut before using. Apricots and small plums (pits removed) and figs can be cut in half and placed cut side up on the pastry. Larger plums and nectarines are better sliced thin. Peaches, apples, and pears should be peeled, pitted or cored, and then sliced. Some fruits, such as quince and dried fruit, need to be poached—gently cooked in sweet syrup—before being sliced and arranged on a tart. Rhubarb can be cut into matchsticks or slices. For best results the fruit should be sliced between ¼ and ⅓ inch thick.

Arrange the fruit on the pastry, leaving a 1½-inch border. The fruit can be scattered evenly over the dough or it can be placed neatly in concentric circles. Apples and other drier fruit should be arranged tightly in overlapping circles. Juicy fruit such as plums and peaches should be one layer deep. Either way, the fruit should be fitted snugly together, one piece placed close to the next, because it will shrink as it cooks. Juicy fruit will give off more liquid as it cooks, making the crust soggy. There are a few things that can be done to mitigate this. The easiest is to scatter a tablespoon or two of flour over the pastry before arranging the fruit on top. Only sprinkle it on the part where the fruit will be arranged, not on the border. The flour can be mixed with sugar, chopped nuts, or ground spices for more flavor. Another way to create a barrier between the pastry and the juice is to spread frangipane (a mixture of almond paste, sugar, and butter) over the pastry; ½ cup is about the right amount for a single tart. Two to three tablespoons of jam can also be spread onto the pastry. This works best for fruit that's only slightly juicy.

For me, tarts are all about the fruit. Try to squeeze as much fruit as possible onto the dough, leaving a small border to fold up for the edge.

Fold the border of dough up over the fruit and brush it generously with melted butter. Sprinkle with sugar, using up to 2 tablespoons. Lightly sprinkle the top of the fruit with more sugar: most fruit will only need 2 or 3 tablespoons. Rhubarb, tart plums, and apricots are exceptions and need a lot more sugar than the others. Taste the fruit as you are assembling the tart. The sweeter it is, the less sugar it will need. Once assembled, the tart can be kept in the refrigerator or freezer until time to bake. It is nice to put a tart into the oven as you are sitting down to dinner: that way it will be ready in time for dessert, still warm from the oven. Bake the tart on the bottom rack of the oven until the bottom of the crust is golden brown. As with savory tarts, it is important that the bottom of the pastry get brown and crisp.

Try any of these variations with the apple tart recipe that follows.

Here are a few suggestions for embellishing any simple fruit tart: After the tart has baked for 30 minutes, sprinkle it with soft berries such as raspberries, huckleberries, or blackberries (first tossed with a little sugar)—this way the berries cook but don't get dried out. Currants, sultanas, or other raisins can be scattered over the crust before arranging the fruit. (If the raisins are very dry, soak them in water and Cognac, then drain them well before putting them on the tart.) And try sprinkling chopped candied citrus peel over the tart when it comes out of the oven.

For added gloss and flavor, glaze the tart after baking. If the fruit is juicy enough, the juice that pools around the fruit during baking can be brushed back over it—a bit like basting a roast with its own juices. A baked fruit tart can also be brushed with a little heated jam, with or without the fruit strained out.

Apple Tart
8 SERVINGS

*Quince poaching liquid
can be reduced to a
delicious russet-colored
glaze for an apple tart.*

Preheat the oven to 400°F.

Peel, core, and slice about ¼ inch thick:

**3 pounds apples (Sierra Beauty, Pippin, Granny Smith
    are good choices)**

Roll out into a 14-inch circle:

One 10-ounce disk of Tart and Pie Dough (page 174)

Brush off any excess flour and transfer the dough to a baking sheet lined with parchment paper. Let it firm up in the refrigerator for 10 minutes or so. Take it out of the refrigerator and lay apple slices end to end in a circle around the circumference, leaving a 1½-inch border. Arrange the remaining apple slices within this circle in tight overlapping concentric circles. The apples should be about 1½ layers thick. Fold the dough border over the apples. Melt:

3 tablespoons butter

Brush the folded dough border generously with butter and then pat the tops of the apples with the rest. Sprinkle the crust with:

2 tablespoons sugar

Sprinkle the apples with:

2 to 3 tablespoons sugar

Bake on the bottom rack of the oven for 45 to 55 minutes, until the crust is golden brown on the bottom. Slide off the pan and cool on a rack.

VARIATIONS

◆ Substitute sliced poached quinces (see page 190) for about half of the apple slices.

◆ Cook 2 of the peeled, cored, and sliced apples in a saucepan with a splash of water until tender. Purée the apples and spread the cooled purée on the pastry (leaving a 1½-inch-wide border). Top with apple slices as above.

◆ Spread the pastry with a few tablespoons of apricot jam before you put on the apples and use warm jam to glaze the tart after baking.

◆ Make a glaze by reducing 1 cup apple juice until thick and syrupy. Flavor with Cognac and lemon juice to taste, and brush over the tart before serving.

Making Sweet Tart Dough

SWEET TART DOUGH, or *pâte sucrée,* is very different from the dough of the previous tarts in this chapter. It is sweet, soft, and almost crumbly instead of crisp and flaky. I use this dough for dessert tarts baked in tart pans with removable bottoms. The pastry is often prebaked so that it will stay crisp when baked with liquid fillings. Some of my favorite tarts of this kind are lemon curd, almond, and chocolate.

Though made from flour and butter, sweet tart dough has the additions of egg and sugar. The ingredients are combined in a process closer to making cookie dough than to that of pastry. In fact, this dough makes delicious thumbprint cookies, little rounds with depressions made by the baker's thumb and filled with lemon curd or jam.

Sweet tart dough is soft and tender for a number of reasons. First, the butter and sugar are creamed (mixed until soft and fluffy) so that they combine thoroughly with the flour, inhibiting the gluten and tenderizing the dough. Finally, the dough is moistened with an egg yolk instead of water, making it even more difficult for the gluten to activate. Nevertheless, the dough can be overworked, so the egg is mixed into the butter to distribute it evenly before the flour is added. Soften the butter for 15 minutes at room temperature before creaming. It needs to be soft enough to stir in the egg yolk, but not so soft that it will melt into the flour and make the pastry oily. Beat the butter until it is soft and fluffy with a wooden spoon (or use a mixer) and then beat in the sugar. Add the egg yolk and vanilla and mix until completely combined. The yolk will be much easier to mix in if it is at room temperature. A cold egg will harden the butter around it. (If your egg is cold, put it in a bowl of warm water for a few minutes before separating it.) Mix in the flour, folding and stirring it into the butter-egg mixture. Don't leave any floury patches in the dough or the pastry will be crackled in these places. The dough will be soft and sticky (sugar makes dough sticky) and needs to be refrigerated for at least 4 hours to firm up before rolling. Gather the dough into a ball and wrap in plastic. Flatten into a disk and chill. The dough can be made and kept in the refrigerator for 2 days or in the freezer for up to 2 months. Let it thaw overnight in the refrigerator before using.

When ready to roll out the dough, take it out of the refrigerator. If it is quite hard, let it sit about 20 minutes to soften. Because the dough is soft and sticky by nature, it is much easier to roll out between 2 sheets of parchment or waxed paper. Cut two 14-inch-square pieces. Flour the bottom piece and center the unwrapped dough on it. Dust the top of the dough with flour and place the other sheet of paper on top. Roll the dough, from the center out, into a 12-inch circle. If the dough sticks to the paper, peel back the paper and dust the dough with a bit more flour. Replace the paper, turn the whole package over, and repeat the dusting on the other side. If the dough gets too soft while rolling, put it on a baking sheet, paper and all, and chill it in the freezer for a few minutes to firm it up.

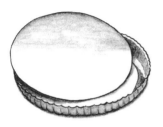

A tart pan with a removable bottom will make unmolding the tart much easier once it is baked.

Continue rolling, flouring when needed, until the dough is about ⅛ inch thick. Let the rolled pastry rest for a few minutes in the refrigerator before using. A 12-inch circle of dough will line a 9-inch tart pan. (A tart pan with a removable bottom will make unmolding the tart much easier once it is baked.) Peel the paper off the circle of dough and, if it is to be baked blind (or empty), lightly prick it all over with a fork. This process is called docking, and it allows the escape of air that otherwise might cause the pastry to bubble up while baking. Invert the dough over the tart pan and remove the other piece of paper. Press the dough gently into the edges. Cut off the excess dough by rubbing your thumb across the top edge of the pan in an outward direction. Press the sides in and up after trimming the dough. (This helps to keep the sides from shrinking down while baking.) Patch any cracks or holes with bits of extra dough. Chill the dough for at least 15 minutes before baking. For smaller tartlets cut the dough ½ inch larger than the diameter of the pans used. Transfer the dough to the tartlet pans with a spatula, pressing the dough evenly over the bottom and sides, and trimming and pressing the sides as above. Excess dough can be rolled out again or made into cookies.

When docked and allowed to rest before baking, this dough will not shrink and does not require any weighting when baked blind. Bake the chilled shells in a preheated 350°F oven for 15 minutes, or until an even light gold in color. Halfway through the baking, remove the tart shells from the oven and lightly pat down any bubbles that may have formed. Let the pastry cool before filling and especially before unmolding.

Sweet Tart Dough (Pâte Sucrée)

MAKES 11 OUNCES OF
DOUGH, ENOUGH FOR
ONE 9-INCH TART,
SIX 4-INCH TARTLETS,
OR 30 COOKIES

Beat together until creamy:

8 tablespoons (1 stick) butter
⅓ cup sugar

Add and mix until completely combined:

¼ teaspoon salt
¼ teaspoon vanilla extract
1 egg yolk

Add:

1¼ cups all-purpose unbleached flour

Mix well, stirring and folding, until there are no dry patches. Chill for at least 4 hours or overnight until firm.

VARIATIONS

◆ Mix 1 teaspoon cinnamon into the flour.
◆ To make thumbprint cookies, roll the dough into 1-inch balls. Roll the balls in sugar and place on a parchment-lined baking sheet about 1 inch apart. Press your thumb into the top of each cookie to make a depression. Bake them in a preheated 350°F oven for 12 minutes, remove from the oven, and fill the depressions with lemon curd or jam. Bake for another 5 minutes, or until light golden. Let cool before serving.

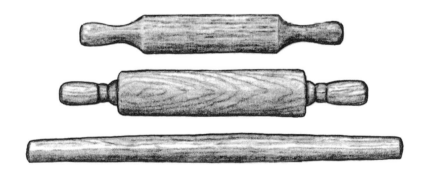

Chocolate Tartlets

MAKES SIX 4-INCH
TARTLETS OR EIGHTEEN
1½-INCH MINI TARTS

*Choose an organic
chocolate with delicious
flavor; the ganache
filling of the tart will
taste just like the
chocolate you select.*

THESE SIMPLE, exquisitely rich, bittersweet chocolate tartlets are beautiful, with shiny surfaces and golden crusts. The prebaked tartlet shells are filled with ganache, a soft chocolate filling made from warm cream and bittersweet chocolate. (Ganache, cooled and thickened, is what chocolate truffles are made from.)

Roll out into a 12-inch circle:

1 disk of Sweet Tart Dough (page 183)

Lightly prick the dough with a fork. Cut six 5-inch circles (for 4-inch tartlets) or eighteen 2-inch circles (for 1½-inch tartlets). Transfer the rounds to 4- or 1½-inch tartlet pans and press the dough into the pans. Cut off the excess dough by rubbing your thumb across the top edge of the pan. Press the sides in and up after trimming the dough. Patch any holes or cracks with a bit of extra dough. Let the tartlet shells rest in the freezer for at least 10 minutes. Prebake the shells in a 350°F oven for 15 minutes, or until they are an even light golden brown. Check the pastry halfway through the cooking and pat down any bubbles that may have formed. Let cool and then unmold.

For the ganache, put into a medium heat-proof bowl:

6 ounces bittersweet chocolate, chopped

Heat just until boiling:

1 cup heavy cream

Pour over the chocolate and let sit for 30 seconds. Stir until the chocolate is melted, but do not overstir or the filling will develop bubbles. Pour into the tartlet shells while it is still quite warm and liquid, very gently tapping and jiggling the pastry shells to even out the filling. Let sit at room temperature for at least an hour to set.

VARIATIONS

◆ This recipe will also make one big tart. Line an 9-inch tart pan with the dough, prebake, and fill with the ganache as above.

◆ Add 2 teaspoons Cognac, brandy, or rum to the chocolate with the hot cream.

◆ Serve with whipped cream; a border of whipped cream piped around the edge is pretty.

Fruit Desserts

Peach Crisp or Cobbler

Poached Pears

Tangerine Ice

THERE IS NO BETTER expression of the season than a piece of ripe fruit. Along with the freshness, sweetness, and beauty it brings to the table, locally grown fruit conveys a powerful sense of place. Once upon a time, when sugary desserts were rare, dessert was virtually synonymous with ripe fruit, served plain; and to me, there is still no better way to end a meal than with the taste of something fresh, clean, aromatic, and naturally sweet. It is exciting to find more and more heirloom and obscure varieties of fruit appearing at farmers' markets, where growers can bring their small harvests to an appreciative public. The farmers' market is also the place where you are more likely to find fruit picked at the peak of ripeness—fruit that is too fragile to withstand the packing and handling required for most commercial venues. Every locale has regional fruit varieties that will make the end of your meal very special indeed, no matter how you serve them—either plain, or transformed into desserts such as warm cobbler or refreshing sherbet.

Fruit for Dessert

Fʀᴜɪᴛ ᴄᴀɴ ʙᴇ given a quick wash and presented whole, prettily arranged in a bowl or on a plate or platter lined with a few fresh grape or fig leaves—prettier still if there are a few fresh leaves attached to the fruit stems or a leafy branch tucked among the fruits. Such a simple still life can be so beautiful when it comes to the table that everyone has to stop and pay attention. In front of each diner, simply set a small plate and, if needed, a knife.

If you prefer, cut up the fruit and serve a bowl of assorted seasonal fruit or a plate of slices of a single kind. Sprinkle a little sugar, orange juice, or wine over the cut fruit. Strawberries in orange juice and sliced peaches chilled in red wine are both exquisite desserts, as is a plate of fresh halved figs scattered with a few raspberries and drizzled with a little honey. Melons are another unforgettable dessert, so luscious and juicy, with so many different kinds to taste, separately or together, their beautiful pastel colors complementing each other. All the soft berries and stone fruits of summer are endlessly combinable: peaches with blackberries, plums with raspberries, and so on. Pears and apples, too, alone or in tandem. In darkest winter, brightness comes from the climates where citrus fruit and dates are ripening. Tangerines and dates are a classic combination. Nuts, toasted or not, are often good with fruit—for example, walnuts with figs and pears, or almonds with apples and dates—and so is cheese. With most cheeses, I particularly like pears and apples, but try other fruits such as figs and dates.

Gathered in season, served at the peak of ripeness, fruit is a perfect reflection of the moment. The best fruit to choose is what looks and tastes best at the market that day. Select fruit that is ripe, unbruised, largely free of blemishes, and aromatic. Smell it. Ask for a taste. With the exception of pears, fruit that is rock hard will never ripen into a prime-tasting example of its variety. Eat fully ripe fruit right away. If you must, keep it in the refrigerator to keep it from overripening, but don't automatically refrigerate it: bear in mind that fruit has a more pronounced aroma and maximum flavor at room temperature. Certain fruits—very ripe strawberries, for example—have an intense perfume when freshly picked and are at their peak only that day. A day or two of refrigeration and the fleeting aroma is gone.

Preserving Fruit

Taste and compare several varieties of a fruit to find those you like best for eating raw and those that are best for cooking.

FRUIT TENDS TO TASTE best and cost the least when it is most abundant, at its seasonal peak. This is the time to put fruit by, preserving it for the winter ahead. Take advantage of the neighbors' trees; of farms where you can pick it yourself; and, best of all, of your own harvest, if you have one. Children love to gather fruit. There is nothing more magical for them than climbing a heavily laden cherry tree, or wandering among raspberry canes bending under the weight of ripe fruit.

Fruit can be preserved, for a matter of days or for many months, in several different ways. One of the easiest is freezing. Berries of all types freeze very well. After checking each one for any mold, spread the berries in a single layer on a tray and freeze them for an hour or two. Transfer the frozen berries to a container or plastic bag that can be tightly sealed; they will last up to 3 months in the freezer. Stone fruit can be quickly cooked with a bit of sugar and puréed to be used later for soufflés, ice cream, and more. The purée can be frozen for several months. A quick fix for fruit that is fast approaching the end of its prime is to cut it up and heat it with a bit of sugar until the juices start to flow. This kind of fruit compote is a favorite dessert in my family, served alone or over ice cream. We like it in the morning, too, on top of pancakes or stirred into a bowl of oatmeal. This compote will last up to a week in the refrigerator.

Fruit syrups, jams, and jellies take more time to cook, but will last a lot longer. These can be made in small amounts—or enlist some friends to help and make a few big batches. Your pantry will be beautiful as well as delicious with all the shining jars and bottles. A fruit paste, sometimes called fruit cheese, is a fruit purée cooked until very, very thick and cooled, usually in a mold. A slice of quince or apple paste with a slice of cheese is a fine finish to a meal. Refrigerated, fruit paste will keep for months. And if you make more than your household can eat, the gift of a jar of homemade jam or a package of fruit paste is always appreciated.

Crisps and Cobblers

CRISPS AND COBBLERS are humble desserts, not too sweet, and full of flavor. A deep layer of fruit is baked under a crunchy topping or cream biscuits, much like a deep-dish pie with a top crust. Every season has fruit to offer: apples and pears in fall and winter, rhubarb and strawberries in the spring, and all the stone fruits and berries of summer.

A crisp topping is a coarse mixture of flour, brown sugar, nuts, and spices, with butter worked into the flour mixture just until it's crumbly. Crisp topping is as easy to make in large batches as it is in small batches, and it freezes very well for up to 2 months. It is a convenient staple to have in the freezer for a quick dessert for an unexpected occasion.

Topped with biscuits, cobblers are less sweet than crisps and best made with juicy fruits. I make simple cream biscuits out of flour and butter worked together, leavened with a little baking powder, and moistened with heavy cream. The dough is rolled out on the thick side and cut into shapes. Once cut, the biscuits can be held in the refrigerator for an hour or two before baking.

Crisps and cobblers work best when the fruit is piled high. For both desserts the fruit is cut into bite-size pieces (⅓-inch-thick slices or 1-inch cubes) and, like fruit pie fillings, tossed with a little flour and a little sugar. Use less sugar for crisp fillings because the crisp topping is so sweet. Tart rhubarb needs quite a bit of sugar, apples need less, and sweet fruits such as peaches need almost none at all. Taste the fruit while you are cutting it and again after it is sugared; you can always add more. The flour thickens the juices that would otherwise be too soupy. It doesn't take much, a tablespoon or two at the most.

A crisp or cobbler is served straight from the dish it has been baked in, so choose an attractive one. Ceramic dishes are best, as metal pans will react with the acid of the fruit. The dish needs to be about 3 inches deep to accommodate a generous layer of fruit. Place the dish on a baking sheet to catch any overflowing juices. Cook until the crisp is dark golden brown and the fruit is bubbling up on the sides; a cobbler's biscuits should be cooked through and golden. If the crisp topping is browning before the fruit is done, place a piece of foil over the top to protect it. Lift off the foil for the last few minutes to recrisp the topping. Serve right away or put back in the oven to warm for a few minutes before serving. Cobblers and crisps are delicious on their own but are even better served with a little cold heavy cream or whipped cream.

Peach Crisp or Cobbler

8 SERVINGS

Peel:

4 pounds ripe peaches

Dip the peaches in boiling water for 10 to 15 seconds, then slip off the skins. Cut the peaches in half, remove the pits, and cut into ⅓-inch-thick slices. There should be about 7 cups fruit. Taste and toss with:

1 tablespoon sugar (if needed)

1½ tablespoons flour

Pile the fruit into a 2-quart baking dish and top with:

3 cups Crisp Topping (recipe follows) or

8 unbaked Cream Biscuits (page 275)

Bake in a 375°F oven for 40 to 55 minutes (rotate once or twice while cooking for even browning) or until the crisp topping or the cream biscuits are golden brown and the fruit is bubbling in the dish.

VARIATIONS

◆ Use 3 pounds peaches and toss the slices with 1 or 2 cups raspberries, blackberries, or blueberries.

◆ Use white peaches and yellow peaches mixed together, or nectarines.

◆ Serve with whipped cream, a pitcher of cold cream, or with ice cream.

Crisp Topping

MAKES 3 CUPS

If you don't want nuts you can leave them out of the crisp topping.

Toast in a 375°F oven for 6 minutes:

⅔ cup nuts (pecans, walnuts, or almonds)

Let cool, then chop coarse.

Put the chopped nuts into a bowl and add:

1¼ cups flour

6 tablespoons brown sugar

1½ tablespoons granulated sugar

¼ teaspoon salt (leave out if using salted butter)

¼ teaspoon ground cinnamon (optional)

Mix well, then add:

12 tablespoons (1½ sticks) butter, cut into small pieces

Work the butter into the flour mixture with your fingers, a pastry blender, or a stand mixer fitted with the paddle attachment. Work just until the mixture comes together and has a crumbly, but not sandy, texture. Chill until ready to use. Crisp topping can be made ahead and refrigerated for a week or so, or frozen for 2 months.

Poaching Fruit

Simply poaching fruit—submerging it in a light syrup and gently simmering until just done—preserves its integrity: it retains its shape and its flavor is enhanced. The poaching liquid can be infused with spices and citrus peel, and wine can be added for flavor. Pears, peaches, plums, apricots, quince, cherries, kumquats, and dried fruit such as apricots, raisins, currants, prunes, and cherries can all be poached. A plain piece of poached fruit is a perfect dessert on its own, but dressed up with vanilla ice cream, a plate of cookies, and raspberry or chocolate sauce, it makes a fancy dish for a special occasion. Simple compotes made of a combination of poached fruits served in their sweet poaching liquid are delightful seasonal desserts. Poached fruit also makes a superb garnish for simple cakes and can be baked into delicious tarts.

Fruit for poaching should not be soft, as you want it to hold its shape after cooking. In fact, fruit that is a bit underripe or otherwise imperfect is improved by poaching. And, conveniently, poaching preserves fruit for a few days, which is a boon when you have an overabundance of fruit that needs to be used. Before poaching, some fruits need preparation. Pears should be peeled: I leave them whole with their stems intact for decoration, but they can be cored and cut in half or into quarters. Bosc, Bartlett, and Anjou are good varieties to poach. Peaches and apricots can be poached whole or cut in half and peeled after cooking. Small flat white peaches are exquisite poached whole. (Crack open a few of the pits, remove the kernels, and add them to the poaching liquid; they add a flavor of almond essence.) Cherries can be pitted or not. Apples should be cored and can be peeled or not, as desired. Some good varieties to poach are: Golden Delicious, Pippin, Sierra Beauty, and Granny Smith. Quinces need to be peeled and cored before going into the syrup and they require much longer cooking. Dried fruit can go directly into the poaching liquid.

Poaching liquid is usually a light sugar syrup. Start with ¼ cup sugar and 1 cup water, adjusting the syrup to your taste and the needs of the fruit. Tart fruit will require a sweeter syrup. You need enough poaching liquid to fully submerge the fruit. Choose a heavy nonreactive pan large enough to hold the poaching liquid and the fruit comfortably. Bring the water and sugar to a boil, stir to dissolve the sugar, and reduce to a simmer. At this point add any flavorings you might be using. I like to add lemon juice and strips of lemon zest, regardless of what fruit I am poaching. A piece of vanilla bean cut in half lengthwise, a cinnamon stick, peppercorns, cloves, or other spices are all possibilities, as are herbs such as rosemary, basil, or thyme. Add more delicate herbs like mint or lemon verbena at the end of cooking to preserve their flavor. Ginger, orange zest, and tea leaves can make tasty infusions. Wine—sweet or dry, red or white—adds fruit and acid. Try a ratio of 2 parts wine to 1 part water. When using a sweet wine such as port or Sauternes, cut back on the sugar in the poaching liquid. If sweetened with honey, brown sugar, or maple sugar, the poaching liquid will be darker and stronger. Another way to flavor the poaching liquid is to add a fruit purée from berries such as raspberries or black currants.

When adding spices and other pungent flavorings to poaching liquid, keep in mind that a little goes a long way, especially with the concentrated flavors of dried fruit.

When the liquid is ready, add the prepared fruit. Some fruits brown quickly once they are exposed to the air (pears and quinces, for example). Add them to the poaching liquid one by one as you peel them. Before poaching, cover the fruit with a circle of parchment paper that has been pierced with a few holes. This will help to keep the fruit submerged while it is cooking. Any fruit sticking up above the liquid may discolor or cook unevenly. Press the paper down on the fruit now and then throughout the cooking. Cook the fruit at a bare simmer until tender but not mushy. Test with a sharp paring knife or toothpick at the thickest part of the fruit. When the knife meets with only slight resistance the fruit is done. The cooking time will vary with each variety of fruit. Ripeness also affects the cooking time: the riper the fruit, the quicker it will cook. (Cooking time can vary wildly, so check the fruit early on to gauge how long it will take.) When poaching more than one kind of fruit, poach each one separately (in the same poaching liquid).

When the fruit is cooked, remove the pan from the heat and let the fruit cool in the syrup. If the fruit is a bit overdone, remove the fruit from the syrup to stop the cooking and allow it to cool separately. Pour the syrup back over the fruit once it is cool. Poached fruit can be served immediately or stored in the refrigerator for up to a week submerged in its poaching liquid in a tightly covered container. As the fruit sits and steeps in the poaching liquid the flavors will intensify. Serve poached fruit cold or reheated in some of its liquid.

The poaching liquid can be transformed into a sauce. Strain the liquid into a heavy nonreactive pan. Boil until reduced to a thick syrup. Add a squeeze of fresh lemon juice or some wine to brighten the flavor.

Poached Pears

4 SERVINGS

Reduced poaching liquid makes a beautiful glaze for a tart or pastry.

Bring to a boil in a heavy-bottomed pan:

4 cups water

1¼ cups sugar

Turn down to a simmer and add:

Zest and juice of 1 lemon

Peel, leaving the stems intact:

4 medium pears (such as Bosc, Bartlett, or Anjou)

Scoop out the small blossom end of each pear and put the pears in the barely simmering sugar syrup. Add more water if needed to cover the pears. Cook the pears for 15 to 40 minutes, depending on variety and ripeness, until tender and translucent but not soft. Test with a sharp paring knife at the thickest part of the pear. Remove from the heat and cool. Serve warm or chilled with some of the poaching liquid, reduced or not.

Store in the refrigerator submerged in the poaching liquid.

VARIATIONS

• Substitute 3 cups dry fruity white or red wine for 3 cups water.

• With the lemon juice and zest, add ½ cinnamon stick broken in pieces and a 2-inch piece of vanilla bean split in half lengthwise.

• Substitute ¾ to 1 cup honey for the sugar.

• Cut the pears into quarters. Peel and core them, removing all the seeds and long strings from the neck. Poach in the syrup for 10 to 20 minutes or until tender.

• Substitute quince for the pears. Quarter, peel, core, and cut into ¼- to ½-inch slices, and poach for about 45 minutes, until tender.

• Serve with whipped cream or crème fraîche, warm chocolate sauce, or raspberry sauce, with or without a garnish of fresh raspberries.

Ice and Sherbet

ICES AND SHERBETS are frozen desserts made from fruit purées or juices. They should be the essence of fruit, with intense, clear flavor. An ice, sometimes called a water ice or *granita*, has a pleasantly grainy texture, while a sherbet or *sorbet* is frozen in an ice-cream maker, giving it a velvety smooth texture.

Fruit and sugar are the basic ingredients in sherbets and ices. They can be enhanced with a touch of vanilla extract or liqueur and a tiny

pinch of salt. The fruit needs to be ripe and full of flavor. Taste it criti-
cally; bland fruit will make bland sorbet or ice. As long as it can be
turned into a juice or purée, any fruit can be frozen into an ice or sherbet. Tender fruit can be puréed while raw in a food mill or food processor and then strained to remove seeds. I usually heat berries with a bit
of sugar just until they start to release their juices before puréeing them.
Harder fruits, such as pears and quinces, need to be cooked until soft
before they can be puréed. You don't have to strain citrus juice: remove
the seeds by hand, and leave the pulp in for more texture and flavor.

Sugar not only adds sweetness, it lowers the freezing temperature of
the mix, which inhibits the formation of ice crystals. This is particularly important for achieving the velvety texture of a sherbet. Chilling
and freezing mutes, or dulls, sweetness. For proper flavor when frozen,
add sugar until the mix tastes overly sweet at room temperature. (For a
very revealing experiment, take 3 separate tablespoons of purée or juice
and add different amounts of sugar to each one. Freeze them, and taste
each one for both sweetness and texture.)

An ice is literally fruit juice or purée that has been frozen. The puréed
fruit or juice is generally sweetened and then poured into a shallow
glass or stainless-steel dish and put to freeze. When adding sugar, go
slowly and test a small spoonful of the mix to see if more sugar is
needed before adding more to the whole batch. You can also freeze a
sample of the mix before freezing the whole lot to verify how it will
taste when frozen. Once the mixture is in the freezer, stir it now and
then to break up the ice crystals and to keep it from separating. The
more often the ice is stirred while it is freezing, the finer the crystals
will be in the end. I like to stir an ice once after the top and sides have
started to freeze, and then again when it is slushy but not solid. When
the ice is solid but still soft when poked, take it from the freezer and
chop it. Scrape across the top down to the bottom with a fork, or use a
pastry scraper and chop up and down and across the pan until the ice is
completely broken up and fluffy. Let the ice re-chill before serving. Give
it a light fluff and scoop it with a fork into a bowl or cup. Serving an ice
with the same fruit that it was made from, either tossed with a bit of
sugar or poached, provides a beautiful contrast of taste and texture.

Sherbet is made much the same way as an ice, but it is frozen in an
ice-cream maker. The important difference is that sherbet needs to be

*You don't need an
ice cream maker to
freeze a granita
or an ice.*

sweeter to acquire the right texture. To find the amount of sweetness required, you should experiment a bit at first and sample small frozen amounts. Once you have done this a few times it will become second nature. Chill the mixture well before putting it into the ice-cream maker. This helps the sherbet freeze quickly, which helps keep the ice crystals small. It is a great treat to make more than one kind of sherbet, either from complementary fruits or from different varieties of the same one, and serve them together.

Tangerine Ice

4 SERVINGS

A Microplane zester is a simple but extraordinarily effective tool for removing the zest from citrus.

Wash and dry:

3 pounds tangerines or mandarins

Grate the zest of 2 tangerines into a saucepan.

Juice the tangerines. There should be about 2¼ cups juice. Pour ½ cup of the juice into a saucepan with the zest and:

⅓ cup sugar

Heat, stirring, just until the sugar is dissolved. Pour into the remaining juice. Taste the mixture and add:

A squeeze of fresh lemon juice (optional)

A tiny pinch of salt

Taste and add more sugar if needed. Pour into a shallow nonreactive pan and freeze. Stir after 1 hour or when the sides and top have developed ice crystals. Stir again after 2 hours or when slushy. Chop when solid but not hard. Transfer to a chilled container.

VARIATIONS

◆ To make sherbet, increase the sugar to ½ cup and chill well. Freeze according to the instructions for your ice-cream maker.

◆ Add a teaspoon or so of Armagnac or Cognac to the mix.

◆ Save the tangerine halves. Scrape out all the membranes and freeze. Scoop frozen sherbet or chopped ice into them and freeze until it's time to serve.

Custard and Ice Cream

Vanilla Pouring Custard

Lemon Curd

Strawberry Ice Cream

THE EASILY MASTERED recipes in this chapter are all about the velvety, smoothing properties of eggs and the simple but delicate process of cooking them to a luscious thickness. You will be able to make innumerable egg-based custards, puddings, sweet sauces, and ice-cream mixes once you've learned the basic techniques. Making ice creams and custards from scratch gives you the versatility to make whatever unusual flavors you might choose (some of my favorites are honey, caramel, and fresh mint), and of course they will be all the better for being made from fresh local organic eggs.

Pouring
Custard

WHEN GENTLY COOKED together in a saucepan, milk, egg yolks, and sugar become a simple pouring custard, or crème anglaise. Served on its own, in a chilled cup, crème anglaise can be a delightfully simple dessert, but more often it is a sauce served to complement sliced fresh fruit, baked and poached fruit, and cakes.

Only the yolks of eggs are used to make pouring custard. When slowly heated, the yolks thicken, adding richness and body to the milk. The standard ratio of egg yolks to milk for custard is 2 yolks to each cup of milk. Separate the eggs, saving the whites for another preparation. Put the egg yolks in a small bowl and mix them lightly, just until they are broken up. Too much stirring or whisking will make them foamy. Heat the milk in a heavy-bottomed pot with sugar and a split vanilla bean. (Vanilla extract can be used instead of vanilla bean, but the flavor will not be quite the same and the visual effect of the tiny black seeds floating in the custard will be lost.)

The milk is heated to dissolve the sugar, steep the vanilla bean, and thicken the yolks. Heat it just to the point where little bubbles are forming around the sides of the pan and the milk is steaming; do not let it boil. When the milk is hot, the egg yolks are added, but first they are thinned and warmed with a bit of the hot milk. Whisk a ladleful of the milk into the yolks and then pour them, stirring all the while, into the hot milk.

Now comes the most important step. If overheated, the eggs yolks will scramble and separate from the milk. To avoid this, stir the hot mixture constantly over medium heat. I like to use a wooden spoon with a bowl that has a flat end, almost like a spatula. Stir in a figure-eight pattern covering the entire bottom of the pan. The bottom of the pan is where the heat is strongest and where overcooking is most likely to happen (this is why it is important to use a heavy-bottomed pan). Don't forget to scrape the corners of the pot, where the sides and bottom come together. Cook the custard just until it thickens and coats the back of the spoon. I find this easier to see with a dark-colored wooden spoon. Run your finger along the length of the back of the spoon. If the mixture stays parted and does not drip back across the line created by your finger, then it is done. The temperature at which this occurs is 170°F. The other visual signal I watch for is when the mixture starts to steam profusely, the way other liquids do right before they are going to boil. Keep checking the custard while you are stirring; it will remain the same for a while and then thicken quickly, almost abruptly, when the proper temperature is reached.

Have a strainer and bowl ready before you start cooking. Once the custard has thickened, immediately remove it from the heat, stir it vigorously for a minute or two, and then pour it through the strainer into the bowl. Stir the custard to cool it further and stop it from cooking. Retrieve the vanilla pod from the strainer and squeeze it into the custard. A lot of seeds and flavor will come out. Serve the custard right away or chill, covering tightly once cold. The custard will thicken even as it cools. Stir well before serving.

For variety pouring custard or crème anglaise can be flavored with fruit purées, espresso, caramel, chocolate, or liquors such as rum, Cognac, or other eaux-de-vie. Flavored pouring custard becomes ice cream when enriched with cream and frozen in an ice-cream maker. The custard can be made slightly thicker with an extra egg yolk, or enriched by substituting half-and-half for part or all of the milk.

Custard can also be baked in the oven rather than on the stovetop. An example is *pots de crème,* rich custards made with cream (or a mixture of cream and half-and-half or milk), in the same ratio of 2 yolks to 1 cup of liquid. Pour the yolk and cream mixture into a heat-proof ceramic baking dish or into little ramekins and bake in a hot-water bath, or *bain-marie,* to protect the custard from the direct heat of the oven. Bake in a 350°F oven until the sides are set but the center of the custard is still loose and jiggly. Remove the baked custards from the water to cool.

Flan and other custards that can be unmolded after being baked are made with egg yolks and whole eggs. The egg whites add body and structure to the custard, allowing it to stand up on its own. Classically flan is made with milk, which makes it a lighter custard. The standard ratio for flan is 1 egg yolk and 1 egg to 1 cup of milk.

Vanilla Pouring Custard (Crème Anglaise)

MAKES 2¼ CUPS

Crème anglaise made with cream is the base for what is known in this country as French vanilla ice cream.

Separate:

4 eggs

Reserve the whites for another purpose. Whisk the yolks just enough to break them up. Pour into a heavy-bottomed pot:

2 cups milk

3 tablespoons sugar

Scrape into the pot the seeds from:

A 2-inch piece of vanilla bean, split lengthwise

Add the vanilla bean. Set a strainer over a heatproof bowl. Heat the milk over medium heat, stirring occasionally to dissolve the sugar. When hot, whisk a little of the milk into the egg yolks and then whisk the yolks into the hot milk. Cook over medium heat, stirring constantly, until the mixture thickens just enough to coat the back of the spoon. Do not let it boil. Remove from the heat and quickly strain. Serve warm or chilled.

VARIATIONS

• Substitute half-and-half for some or all the milk for a richer custard.

• Add one more yolk for a slightly thicker custard.

• Substitute 1 teaspoon vanilla extract for the vanilla bean, adding it after the custard has cooled.

Fruit Curd

FRUIT CURDS, of which lemon curd is a prime example, are a sort of fruit custard, but made without milk or cream. To make lemon curd, a mixture of lemon juice, zest, sugar, eggs, and butter is gently cooked until thick. When cooled, the curd is thick enough to spread. Rich and luscious with the bright tang of lemon, lemon curd is a classic topping for toast or scones, but it is much more versatile than that. Baked in a sweet tart shell it makes an incredible lemon tart, which can be topped with meringue. It can also serve as a filling for cookies, cakes, and pastries (I love Meyer lemon éclairs), or it can be swirled into just-churned French vanilla ice cream.

Lemons are the classic fruit used to make curd, but they are by no means the only one. Any citrus fruit can be used—limes, oranges, grapefruit, tangerines, and so on—as well as purées of berries such as raspberries or blackberries. Mix the zest and juice (in citrus curds, the zest plays as large a part in the flavor as the juice) or berry purée with sugar and eggs and butter, and cook the mixture the same way as an egg custard: in a heavy-bottomed pot, stirring constantly, over medium heat, until it coats the back of a spoon. Take care not to boil the mixture or the eggs will curdle. Pour into a bowl or glass jars to cool. The curd will continue to thicken as it cools. Store, refrigerated, in a tightly sealed container for up to 2 weeks.

Lemon Curd

MAKES 2 CUPS

Wash and dry:

4 lemons

Grate the zest of one of the lemons on the small holes of a grater. Juice the lemons; there should be about ½ cup juice.

Beat until just mixed:

2 eggs

3 egg yolks

2 tablespoons milk

⅓ cup sugar

¼ teaspoon salt (omit if using salted butter)

Stir in the lemon juice and zest and add:

6 tablespoons butter, cut into small pieces

Cook the mixture in a small nonreactive heavy pan, stirring constantly, over medium heat until it is thick enough to coat a spoon. Do not boil or the eggs will curdle. When thick, pour into a bowl or glass jars to cool. Cover and refrigerate.

VARIATIONS

◆ With their sweeter juice and perfumed peel, Meyer lemons make an especially good curd. Make the recipe with the juice of 1 regular lemon and 3 Meyer lemons and the grated zest of 2 Meyer lemons.

◆ To make a frosting, fold lightly sweetened whipped cream into lemon curd. I usually use equal parts of whipped cream and curd.

◆ To make a lemon curd tart, prebake an 9-inch Sweet Tart Dough shell (page 183) and fill with 2 cups lemon curd. Smooth out the curd and bake in a preheated 375°F oven for 15 to 20 minutes or until the lemon curd is set.

Making
Ice Cream

ICE CREAM is universally loved—and homemade ice cream right off the dasher is the most desirable ice cream of all. There are basically two versions. The first is simply sweetened and flavored cream, frozen. The second is a frozen custard made with sweetened cream and egg yolks, which produces a richer, smoother ice cream. They both have their charms, although I lean towards the frozen custard kind.

Ice cream can be made with all cream or a mixture of cream and half-and-half or milk. Flavors tend to be more pronounced in ice cream when it is lightened with half-and-half or milk. Heat the cream to dissolve the sugar (or honey). At this point the cream can be infused with other flavorings, such as vanilla bean, coffee beans, herbs, or finely chopped toasted nuts. Let the flavorings infuse for about 20 minutes, then strain them out, and chill the liquid. Fruit purées and extracts are added after the mixture has cooled. Such solid flavorings as chopped fruit, nuts, or grated chocolate are best stirred in after the ice cream has been frozen; added earlier, they impede the freezing process. To make a custard-based ice cream, strain the warm cream, mix with egg yolks, and cook until thick. Chill well before freezing.

Ice cream can be frozen in a shallow pan or tray but it will have a much smoother texture if frozen in a machine. The constantly moving paddle, or dasher, breaks up the ice crystals and works a small amount of air into the mix as it freezes. There are a variety of ice cream machines on the market. The traditional machines consist of a wooden bucket that holds a metal canister, which can be surrounded by crushed ice and rock salt. The salt lowers the freezing temperature of the ice, making the ice cream freeze more quickly. The canister is fitted with a dasher that is operated by a hand crank or an electric motor. For best results, chill the dasher and canister before adding the ice cream. There are a number of smaller machines that consist of a double-walled canister that is filled with a liquid coolant. The canister is placed in the freezer until the coolant is frozen solid. When ready, it is filled with the mix and fitted with its motor, which turns a scraping arm. The double-insulated canisters are a bit more convenient but take a while to freeze. If you have the space, store the canister in the freezer so it is ready to go whenever you need it. The mix should be very cold before it is added or it may thaw out the canister before the mix has had a chance to freeze. Only fill the canisters about two-thirds full: the mix will expand as it freezes. Ice-cream machines will freeze ice cream in about 30 to 35 minutes.

When just frozen, ice cream is still soft enough that you can stir in such solid flavorings as nuts or candied fruit. The small canister machines have a large hole in the lids for just this purpose. Traditional freezers need to be stopped and opened up. Serve the ice cream right away, or chill it for a few hours to harden further. In a traditional machine you can leave the ice cream in its ice-packed canister right in its bucket (add more ice to cover the top), but don't leave it in the insulated canister-type machine, which won't be cold enough to harden the ice cream. Instead, transfer the soft ice cream to a chilled container and put it in the freezer. Pack the ice cream tightly to discourage the formation of any ice crystals. Ice cream will maintain its full flavor for up to a week, but it will lose its sublime texture. When it has frozen quite hard, take the ice cream out of the freezer for a few minutes before serving, for easier scooping.

Strawberry Ice Cream

MAKES 1 QUART

In a small bowl whisk briefly, just enough to break up:

3 egg yolks

Measure into a heavy-bottomed pot:

¾ cup half-and-half

½ cup sugar

Set a strainer over a heat-proof bowl. Heat the half-and-half over medium heat, stirring occasionally to dissolve the sugar. When hot, whisk a little of the hot half-and-half into the egg yolks and then whisk the warmed yolks into the hot mixture. Cook over medium heat, stirring constantly, until the mixture thickens and coats the back of the spoon. Do not let it boil. Remove from the heat and quickly strain. Add:

¾ cup heavy cream

Cover the mixture and chill.

Wash, dry, and hull:

1½ pints strawberries

Mash with a potato masher or purée in a food mill. Stir in:

¼ cup sugar

Let the strawberries macerate in their own juices, stirring occasionally, until the sugar has melted. Add the berries to the cold cream mixture and flavor with:

A couple drops of vanilla extract

A pinch of salt

Chill thoroughly, and freeze in an ice-cream machine according to the manufacturer's instructions.

VARIATIONS

• For heightened flavor, add 1 or 2 teaspoons kirsch (cherry eau-de-vie) at the same time as the vanilla.

• Purée 1½ pints raspberries, blackberries, mulberries (my favorite!), or other soft berries, and strain the purée to remove the seeds. Use in place of the strawberries. With the exception of raspberries, the berries should be warmed until they just begin to release their juices before puréeing. Add a squeeze of fresh lemon juice, if needed.

• Substitute 1½ cups mashed peeled peaches or nectarines for the strawberries.

• Substitute 1½ cups plum or pear purée for the strawberries. Before puréeing sliced plums or pears, heat them with the sugar and a bit of water just until soft.

• This recipe will work without the egg yolks: the ice cream will be lighter and the texture will be grainier and less creamy.

Cookies and Cake

Ginger Snaps

Anise-Almond Biscotti

1-2-3-4 Cake

EVERYBODY HAS A BIRTHDAY, and everybody deserves a homemade birthday cake—or at least a few homemade birthday cookies. And birthdays are only one of the holiday occasions that call out in our imaginations for something baked by loving hands at home. For children, simple home baking provides a wonderful introduction to the kitchen: it teaches basic lessons in organization, measurement, mixing, oven use, and cleanup. For many cooks, baking cookies was the spark that ignited a lifelong passion for cooking. Even people who generally shy away from baking (people like me, in other words) need a short lesson in cookies and cake.

Making Cookies

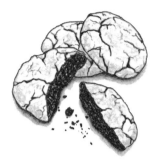

A VAST ARRAY of cookie recipes spring from one basic formula: butter and sugar are beaten together, eggs are stirred in for moisture, and flour is mixed in at the end. The consistency of the resulting cookie dough can range from one firm enough to roll out and cut, to a dough soft enough to drop from a spoon right onto a baking sheet, to a very wet dough moistened only with egg whites that has to be piped and thinly spread with a knife onto a baking sheet. (A charming cookie called a *langue de chat,* or cat's tongue, is made from this last kind of dough.)

Beating butter and sugar together until fluffy and light-colored is called creaming. Sugar is added, and the beating continues until the mixture is light and fluffy again. The creaming process aerates the butter: air bubbles are literally forced into the butter mixture. These air bubbles expand during the baking, making the cookies light and tender. Butter can be creamed by hand or with a mixer. If using a mixer, the butter and sugar can be added at the same time. Mix at medium-high speed for 2 or 3 minutes (if using a stand mixer, use the paddle attachment). Stop the machine once or twice to scrape down the sides to ensure that all the sugar gets incorporated into the butter evenly. In a pinch, cold butter can be used: just put it in the mixing bowl by itself and beat until soft before adding the sugar. The butter has to be soft to cream properly.

Once the butter and sugar are creamed together, add the eggs and mix well. If using a mixer, scrape down the sides of the bowl as needed. It is important that the eggs be at room temperature, too. If they are added cold, the butter will seize up, deflating the air bubbles, and the dough will resist thorough mixing. Add liquid flavorings and sweeteners such as vanilla extract, liquors, molasses, and honey along with the eggs.

Flour is the last ingredient to be added. Be sure to measure the flour the same way every time. This will make your baking more consistent. I recommend this method: Stir the flour up to fluff it. Use a dry measuring cup, the flat-topped kind that fills to the brim, and either scoop up the flour with it or spoon the flour into it; then draw a spatula or knife across the top of the cup to level the flour. Don't tap the cup or the flour will compact. Add the flour to the butter and eggs and stir it in until just mixed. You want all the flour to be completely mixed in, but too much stirring will activate the gluten in the flour and make the cookies tough. Mix salt, ground spices, and baking powder or baking

I became a better baker when I learned to fluff the flour and measure it consistently.

soda into the flour before it is added to the cookie dough. Chunky fla-vorings such as chopped nuts, chocolate, or dried fruit should be stirred in gently after the flour has been mixed in.

Dough for drop cookies can be baked right away or chilled and baked later. Cookies that are to be shaped or rolled out often require chilling first to firm up the dough. Many cookie doughs can be rolled into logs, chilled, and then sliced into neat cookies to bake. Shape the logs into ovals, squares, or rectangles for different shapes. The logs can be frozen for up to 2 months and the sliced cookies require no defrost-ing before baking. Slice off as many cookies as needed and return the rest to the freezer for later.

Professional half-sheet pans make an enormous difference for baking cookies evenly without browning the bottoms.

To bake cookies properly it is worth investing in one or two heavy baking sheets. They help the cookies to bake evenly, particularly by keeping them from browning too much on the bottom. An oven ther-mometer is helpful for determining your oven's actual temperature. I like to line baking sheets with parchment paper or a silicone mat, both of which keep cookies from sticking and make cleanup much easier. The parchment paper can be reused from batch to batch.

Bake the cookies in the center of a preheated oven. Adjust your oven racks if necessary. Every oven has a hot spot where the cookies will bake more quickly. To compensate for this, rotate the baking sheets halfway through the baking. Turn the baking sheets around, both front to back and top to bottom, switching oven racks. If the cookies are browning too quickly on the bottom, slide another baking sheet under-neath the hot one to slow it down. Cookies at the edges of a baking sheet may bake more quickly; if so, remove them when they are done and return the rest to the oven to finish. Let the cookies cool completely before storing.

Ginger Snaps

MAKES THIRTY
2-INCH COOKIES

*Ginger snaps make great
ice cream sandwiches.*

Preheat the oven to 350°F.

Measure into a bowl and stir together:

2 cups flour

1½ teaspoons baking soda

½ teaspoon salt

2 teaspoons cinnamon

1½ teaspoons ground ginger

In another bowl, beat until soft and fluffy:

11 tablespoons (1 stick plus 3 tablespoons) butter, softened

Add:

⅔ cup sugar

Cream the mixture until light and fluffy. Stir in, mixing well:

½ teaspoon vanilla extract

¼ cup molasses

1 egg, at room temperature

Stir in the dry ingredients. Don't overmix, but make sure they are completely incorporated. Wrap the dough in plastic and chill for 2 hours. On a lightly floured board, roll out the dough ⅛ to ¼ inch thick. Cut out the cookies with a floured cutter and place them 1½ inches apart on a baking sheet lined with parchment paper or a silicone mat. Bake until puffed and set, about 10 minutes. Let the cookies cool for 1 to 2 minutes before removing from the pan.

VARIATIONS

• Roll the dough into 2 logs 1½ inches in diameter, wrap in plastic wrap, and chill for at least 2 hours in the refrigerator or 30 minutes in the freezer. When cold, cut into ¼-inch-thick coins, place them 1½ inches apart on a lined baking sheet, and bake as above. The cookies can be dipped in sugar before baking, if desired.

• Roll the dough into 1-inch balls, place them 3 inches apart on a lined baking sheet, and flatten them with a flat-bottomed glass dipped in sugar.

• Add ½ teaspoon fresh-ground black pepper to the flour mixture for a spicier cookie.

Biscotti

Biscotti, plain or dipped in bittersweet chocolate, served with a bowl of cherries or tangerines are a perfect ending to a meal.

IN ITALIAN, *biscotti* means "twice-cooked." Biscotti are baked first in long loaves, then sliced into thick cookies, and baked again until lightly toasted. The cookies are crisp and dry, and store well; and I like the fact that they are not extremely sweet. Various ingredients such as nuts, chocolate, spices, liquor, and dried fruits are added for flavor. I make biscotti flavored with lightly toasted almonds and aniseed. They go equally well with a cup of coffee or tea or a glass of wine.

The biscotti recipe I use most often has no butter. Eggs and sugar are beaten together until they increase in volume, turn light in color, and form a ribbon when you lift up the whisk or beaters. This means the mixture will fall back onto itself slowly and thickly in a ribbon-like pattern. When the eggs are warm it will take about 3 or 4 minutes to beat the eggs to this point; when they are cold, it can take up to 10 minutes. If you have forgotten to take the eggs out of the refrigerator in advance, warm them for a few minutes in their shells in a bowl of almost-hot water.

Air trapped in the beaten egg mixture lightens the texture of biscotti. Be careful to stir in the flour only until it is just incorporated, and then gently fold in the other ingredients so as not to deflate the eggs. Form the dough into long loaves on a baking sheet lined with parchment paper. The dough will be very wet and sticky. Wet your hands before touching it to keep them from sticking. Use a spoon and your hands to smooth the logs. Bake them until golden and set. When removed from the oven, the loaves are quite delicate until cooled. Carefully pull the whole sheet of paper with the loaves right onto a cooling rack. When cool, slice the loaves with a long serrated bread knife (on a diagonal, for longer cookies). Spread the cookies out on the baking sheet and bake again until golden and toasted. They will keep for up to a month in an airtight container.

Anise–Almond Biscotti

MAKES ABOUT
40 COOKIES

Preheat the oven to 350°F.

Spread out on a baking sheet and toast in the oven for 5 minutes:

1½ cups whole almonds

Let cool and coarsely chop.

Measure and stir together:

2¼ cups unbleached all-purpose flour

1 teaspoon baking powder

¾ teaspoon aniseed

In another bowl, combine:

3 eggs, at room temperature

1 cup sugar

¼ teaspoon lemon zest

Beat together until the mixture forms a ribbon. Stir in the flour mixture until just incorporated and then gently fold in the almonds.

On a parchment-paper-lined baking sheet, form the dough into two 3-inch-wide loaves, about 3 inches apart. Smooth the loaves with damp hands. Bake for 25 minutes, or until lightly golden. Remove the loaves from the oven and let cool for about 10 minutes. Lower the oven temperature to 300°F. Cut the cooled loaves into ½-inch-thick cookies and place cut side down on 2 baking sheets. Cook for 10 minutes, turn the cookies over, and cook for another 10 minutes, or until golden brown.

VARIATIONS

◆ Omit the almonds and use 1 cup raisins and 1 cup walnuts instead. Other nuts and dried fruits may be used in the same quantities.

◆ Add ½ cup chopped candied citrus peel.

◆ Use a spice other than anise, such as fennel or coriander, or omit the spices entirely and increase the amount of grated zest to 1 teaspoon.

Making a Cake

1-2-3-4
1 cup butter
2 cups sugar
3 cups flour
4 eggs

It's a satisfying thing, knowing how to make a classic buttery, delicate cake from scratch. A 1-2-3-4 cake is a version of a traditional recipe the name of which refers to the quantities of butter, sugar, flour, and eggs—the cake's principal ingredients. The cake has wonderful flavor, and the texture is moist and tender, the two qualities that make a cake great. Unadorned, it makes a simple tea cake perfectly suited for a garnish of fresh fruit; decorated, it can be anything from a birthday cake to a wedding cake to individual cupcakes.

Baking requires more precision than most other types of cooking and it is enormously helpful to gather and measure your ingredients carefully at the outset. The first steps to baking a cake are preparing the pan, preheating the oven, and assembling the ingredients. To prepare the cake pan, first butter the inside, spreading softened butter thinly and evenly with a butter wrapper, a brush, or your fingers. To ensure that the cake does not stick to the bottom, line it with parchment paper: trace the bottom of the pan on a piece of parchment paper, cut it out, and put it into the pan. Butter the piece of parchment paper as well. The recipe may also say to flour the pan. To do so, put a couple of tablespoons of flour (or cocoa, for chocolate cakes) into the pan and carefully rotate it to distribute the flour evenly over the butter. Once all the butter has been coated with flour, invert the pan and tap out all the excess.

Bake cakes in a preheated oven. The first few minutes of baking determine how a cake will rise. When the oven is not up to temperature, the rising is inhibited. Preheat the oven for at least 15 minutes and check the temperature with an oven thermometer before putting the cake in to bake.

Having all your ingredients measured and at room temperature before you start makes the whole process smoother and easier, and you'll be less likely to make mistakes. Room-temperature ingredients are essential. Adding cold ingredients will cause the batter to "seize," or shrink and deflate, which will compromise the cake's texture, making it dense instead of light. Butter needs to be soft; take it out of the refrigerator to soften for at least 30 minutes. It will soften faster if you cut it up into small pieces. Measuring out the milk and separating the eggs ahead of time will give them time to warm up.

The flour is mixed with salt and a chemical leavener, either baking powder or baking soda. For a lighter, more delicate cake, use cake flour;

it is made from soft wheat, which has a lower protein content, and is milled very fine. Pastry flour is the next-best thing. All-purpose flour can be used, too, but the texture of the cake will be heavy and coarse; cake flour makes a big difference. The most accurate measure of flour is by weight, but most recipes in the United States use measurements in volume. The amount of flour added to a cake makes a big difference in its final texture so, for consistency, try to measure the flour exactly the same way every time. For delicate cakes I suggest sifting more flour than the recipe calls for before you measure it. Sifting aerates the flour and makes it easier to mix, which helps to keep the cake light. Scoop or spoon the flour into the measuring cup (use a dry measuring cup, with a flat rim and no pour spout) and scrape a spatula or knife across the top of the cup to level it. Don't compact the flour by tapping the cup or smashing the flour down. After sifting and measuring, stir the other dry ingredients into the flour. Many recipes instruct you to sift the dry ingredients together, but stirring does a better job of mixing the ingredients.

The first step of assembling the batter is to cream the softened butter with sugar. Beat the butter and sugar until the mixture is soft and fluffy and very light in color. If you do this with an electric mixer the butter and sugar can be beaten together from the start, but when beating by hand beat the butter well first before adding the sugar. Creaming the butter and sugar will take 5 to 10 minutes. Don't skimp on this: it is the key to a soft, voluminous, tender cake. The sugar cuts into the butter, creating air pockets, and as the butter gets lighter, the air pockets expand and multiply. This aerated mixture is the foundation of the cake. Room-temperature egg yolks are beaten in one at a time and each is thoroughly incorporated before the next is added. The mixture may start to look a little curdled after all the yolks are added, but don't worry; adding the flour will rectify this in the end.

Next, the flour mixture and room-temperature milk are mixed in alternately, starting and ending with the flour. For best results, use a sifter or a fine-meshed sieve and add the flour mixture to the batter by thirds. The flour doesn't have to be completely mixed in before the next addition of milk. Mix only until the milk and flour are just incorporated. The milk activates the gluten in the flour and overmixing will develop it, toughening the cake. Whip the egg whites into stiff but moist

Baking powder is a leavening agent that reacts to liquid and heat and creates carbon dioxide gas, which expands the bubbles created by the creaming process, causing the cake to rise. Baking powder loses its effectiveness after six months to a year, so be sure to check the date on the can when you buy it or mark it yourself.

peaks. Stir one third of the whites into the batter to loosen it, then gently fold in the rest. Pour the batter into the prepared pan; it should be no more than two-thirds full to allow room for the cake to rise.

For best results, bake the cake in the center of the oven; adjust the racks if necessary. If possible, don't disturb the cake during the first 15 minutes of baking. Opening the oven lowers the heat significantly and the change in temperature could cause the cake to fall. After this initial cooking, the structure of the cake is pretty well set and much more stable. Start testing for doneness when the cake is well risen and golden and is pulling away from the sides of the pan. Poke a wooden toothpick or skewer into the center of the cake. The cake is done when the toothpick comes out clean with no batter sticking to it. Let the cake cool before taking it out of the pan.

This 1-2-3-4 cake is very moist and can be made a day ahead. For best results, store it in its pan, tightly covered. Unmold it and decorate it the day you serve it. To unmold the cake slide a knife around the edges of the cake pan. Invert the cake onto a plate. Peel off the parchment paper and invert the cake onto another plate.

1-2-3-4 Cake

MAKES TWO
9-INCH ROUND CAKES

This recipe is easily cut in half or doubled. For a one-layer cake, I usually make half this recipe.

Preheat the oven to 350°F.

Butter the cake pans and line the bottom of each with parchment paper. Butter the paper and dust the pans with flour, tapping out the excess. Separate:

4 eggs

Measure:

1 cup milk

Sift and then measure:

3 cups cake flour

Stir in:

4 teaspoons baking powder

½ teaspoon salt (use ¼ teaspoon if using salted butter)

In another bowl, beat until light and fluffy:

1 cup (2 sticks) butter, softened

Add:

2 cups sugar

Cream until light and fluffy. Beat in the 4 egg yolks, one at a time, and:

1 teaspoon vanilla extract

When well mixed, add the flour mixture and milk alternately, starting and ending with one third of the flour. Stir just until the flour is incorporated. In another bowl, whisk the egg whites to soft peaks. Stir one third of the egg whites into the batter, then gently fold in the rest. Pour the batter into the prepared pans and bake until a toothpick inserted into the center comes out clean, 30 to 40 minutes.

VARIATIONS

• This quantity of batter can be divided among 3 cake pans to make 3 layers; it also makes 24 cupcakes using buttered and floured muffin tins, or 30 cupcakes using paper liners; or it can be baked in a 12- by 18-inch half-sheet pan to make a sheet cake. Bake the cupcakes and the sheet cake for about 20 minutes.

• For lemon cake, add 1 tablespoon finely grated lemon zest and 2 teaspoons lemon juice to the batter. Frost with equal parts lemon curd and whipped cream folded together.

• For orange cake, add 1 tablespoon finely grated orange zest and 2 teaspoons orange juice to the batter. Fill with whipped cream and sliced strawberries.

Part II:

At the Table

Recipes for Cooking Every Day

A Little Something . . .

Roasted Almonds with Herbs

MAKES 1½ CUPS

Preheat the oven to 375°F. Measure into a bowl:

1½ teaspoons hot water
½ teaspoon salt

Stir to dissolve the salt. Add and toss together:

1½ cups almonds
3 thyme sprigs, leaves only
1 winter savory sprig, leaves only

Pour into a cast-iron skillet or baking dish large enough to hold the almonds in mostly a single layer. Roast for 15 to 20 minutes, stirring every 5 minutes or so, until the insides are golden brown. (Cut one open to see.) Once nuts start to brown they can burn very quickly. Watch out! Remove from the oven and pour into a mixing bowl. While still warm, toss with:

2 teaspoons olive oil

Taste and add more salt if needed.

VARIATIONS

♦ Try different herbs: marjoram leaves, and chopped sage leaves, for example.
♦ Try different nuts: walnuts, hazelnuts, and pecans are good this way.
♦ Roast the nuts dry without the salted water. Oil and salt them after roasting.

Warm Olives

MAKES 1 CUP

Simply rinsing olives and warming them a little refreshes their flavor; adding some herbs and garlic and a little zest makes them even more delightful.

Rinse in a strainer under running water:

1 cup olives with pits (use an assortment of flavors and colors)

Set aside to drain.
Heat, in a small heavy pan:

2 teaspoons olive oil

Add the drained olives with:

1 garlic clove, peeled and quartered
1 chile, fresh or dried
3 thyme or savory sprigs
2 strips of orange or lemon zest

Cook over low heat, stirring occasionally, for 5 minutes, or until the olives are warm all the way through. Turn off the heat and leave them in the warm pan for a few minutes before serving. Serve warm, if possible. They can easily be reheated.

VARIATIONS

♦ Substitute other herbs for the thyme or savory.
♦ Add whole seeds such as fennel, cumin, caraway, or black mustard seed.
♦ Add a few pinches of cayenne or paprika.

Marinated Chard

3 TO 4 SERVINGS

You can prepare any greens this way—rapini, mustard greens, beet tops, spinach, rocket, kale—but cook them separately, because they all have different cooking times. The sturdiest greens, such as kale, take longest. Once cooked, they can be mixed together in any combination, dressed with this simple olive oil marinade, piled warm on croutons, or cooled and wrapped in slices of prosciutto.

Wash:

1 bunch (about 12 ounces) of chard

One at a time, grasp the stems in one hand and strip the leaves off with the other. (Reserve the stems for another use, such as a gratin.) Cut the leaves into 2-inch pieces. Heat a heavy sauté pan or skillet over medium-high heat. Pour in:

1 tablespoon olive oil

Add the chopped greens and sprinkle with:

Salt

Cook, stirring often, until the greens are tender, about 5 minutes. The residual water clinging to the leaves from washing is usually enough to keep them moist; if not, add a splash of water during the cooking. Remove the greens from the pan and let cool. Squeeze out any excess moisture and transfer to a bowl. Dress with:

1 tablespoon olive oil
1 garlic clove, chopped fine
A squeeze of lemon juice
A pinch of dried chile flakes

Taste, adjust the seasoning, and serve.

Tapenade

MAKES ABOUT ⅔ CUP

Mix together:

½ cup black olives
  (niçoise, Nyon, or dry-cured),
  pitted and coarsely chopped
1 tablespoon capers, rinsed, drained,
  and coarsely chopped
2 salt-packed anchovies,
  soaked, boned, and chopped
1 garlic clove, peeled and split with
  germ removed, chopped fine or
  pounded to a purée
1 savory sprig, leaves only, chopped
½ teaspoon brandy (optional)
¼ cup olive oil

Taste and add, if necessary:

Salt

Let sit at room temperature for 30 minutes before serving to allow the flavors to marry.

VARIATIONS
• Stir in 2 tablespoons roasted chopped almonds.
• Add ¼ teaspoon grated orange zest.
• Substitute green olives or use a mixture of green and black.

Roasted Sweet Peppers

4 SERVINGS

Preheat the oven to 450°F. Wash and dry:

3 whole medium fleshy bell peppers or
  pimientos

Arrange on a rimmed baking sheet with at least ½ inch of space between each pepper for even browning. Roast in the oven, checking every 5 minutes. Turn them as they begin to brown. Keep turning until the skin is blistered and black and the peppers are soft but not completely falling apart, about 35 minutes. If the skin is done but the pepper is still firm, place the pepper in a covered container to steam. Allow to cool.

Cut the peppers in half and scrape out the ribs and seeds. Peel off the skin. Tear or cut the flesh into ½-inch strips.

Marinate with:

1 small garlic clove,
  pounded to a purée
1 tablespoon olive oil
1 teaspoon vinegar
1 teaspoon chopped fresh marjoram
Fresh-ground black pepper
Salt to taste

Serve at room temperature as part of an antipasto platter or warm with grilled meat or fowl.

VARIATION
• For a smoky flavor, grill over medium-hot coals instead of cooking in the oven.

Marinated Cheese with Herbs and Olive Oil

MAKES 6 OUNCES

Any soft mild white cheese will work here. Fresh goat cheese shaped into logs or rounds, feta, even a stiff yogurt cheese like labneh would work. This cheese makes a nice spread for croutons or a tasty garnish for a salad.

Cut into ½-inch rounds, slices, or wedges:
   6 ounces goat or feta cheese
Place in a nonreactive container and add:
   ¾ cup extra-virgin olive oil
   3 to 4 thyme sprigs
   2 to 3 bay leaves
Cover tightly and refrigerate for at least 1 day or up to 1 week.

VARIATIONS

◆ Use different herbs such as rosemary, marjoram, oregano, savory, or hyssop.
◆ Add a couple of dried hot peppers for a bit of heat.
◆ Add some whole spices such as black peppercorns, fennel, anise, cumin, or coriander.
◆ Add ¼ cup rinsed and drained niçoise olives with the herbs.
◆ Gently cook 2 or 3 peeled, halved garlic cloves in half of the olive oil until tender but not brown. Let the oil cool and pour over the cheese with the cooked garlic and the remaining oil.
◆ Remove the cheese from the oil, pat dry breadcrumbs all over the surface, and toast in a hot oven until brown and crisp, about 5 to 10 minutes. Serve with a garlicky salad.

Eggplant Caviar

MAKES 2 CUPS

Preheat the oven to 400°F.
Cut in half lengthwise:
   2 medium eggplants
Sprinkle the cut surfaces with:
   Salt
   Fresh-ground black pepper
   Olive oil
Place cut side down on a baking sheet and roast until soft. Test for doneness at the stem end; the eggplant should be very soft. Remove from the oven and let cool. Scrape the flesh out of the skins into a bowl and stir vigorously to loosen into a purée.
Add:
   2 tablespoons fresh lemon juice
   ¼ cup olive oil
   Salt
   Fresh-ground black pepper
   1 garlic clove,
      peeled and pounded to a purée
   2 to 4 tablespoons chopped parsley or
      cilantro
Mix well and taste, adding more salt and lemon as needed.

VARIATIONS

◆ Use 2 tablespoons chopped mint in place of parsley or cilantro.
◆ Add ½ teaspoon crushed toasted coriander seeds. To toast, heat whole coriander seeds in a heavy pan over medium heat until slightly brown. Crush in a mortar and pestle or under a heavy pan.
◆ Add a pinch or two of dried chile flakes.
◆ For a smoky flavor, keep one eggplant whole and char it over hot coals or the open flame of a burner until tender. Cut in half, scrape out the flesh, and combine with the other ingredients.

Stuffed Eggs

MAKES 12 HALF EGGS

This is a very simple approach to a classic deviled egg, but I like them without a lot of spices and things that cover up the good egg flavor. I sprinkle them with chopped fresh herbs just before serving.

Fill a medium-size pot with water and bring to a boil. Add:

6 eggs, at room temperature

Simmer for 9 minutes, then drain the eggs and chill in ice water until cooled.

Peel, cut in half lengthwise, and carefully scoop the yolks into a mixing bowl. Set the whites on a platter, cut side up, and sprinkle with:

Salt

Fresh-ground black pepper

With a fork, mash the yolks with:

3 tablespoons homemade mayonnaise (see page 46)

1 teaspoon Dijon mustard

Salt

Fresh-ground black pepper

If the yolk mixture is very thick, add cold water by the teaspoonful until the consistency is right. Taste for seasoning; fill the whites with the yolk mixture. If not serving within an hour, refrigerate until ready to eat. Before serving, garnish with chopped tender herbs such as chives and parsley.

VARIATIONS

◆ Substitute a mixture of soft butter and olive oil for the mayonnaise.

◆ Add paprika to the yolk mixture or sprinkle it over the stuffed eggs, or both.

◆ Add chopped herbs such as parsley, chervil, chives, mint, tarragon, or cilantro to the yolk mixture.

◆ Add pounded garlic to the yolk mixture and garnish each stuffed egg with an anchovy fillet.

◆ Add chopped capers or olives to the yolk mixture.

Guacamole

4 SERVINGS

There are many varieties of avocados, and all may be used, but the Hass avocado is the ideal choice. The flesh has a rich, nutty, and herby taste. It is a good keeper, it peels easily, and the pit is easily removed. An avocado is ripe when it yields to the gentle pressure of your thumb.

Cut in half and remove pits from:

2 ripe avocados

Scoop the flesh out of the skins with a spoon into a mortar and mash it roughly with a pestle. Stir in:

1 tablespoon fresh lime juice

2 tablespoons finely chopped onion

2 tablespoons chopped cilantro

Salt

Taste and add more salt and lime juice as needed.

VARIATION

◆ For a spicy guacamole, add a jalapeño or serrano pepper, seeded and finely diced.

Fresh-Pickled Vegetables

A good tasty use for a variety of vegetables is vinegar pickles. Unlike fermented pickles, which take weeks or months, these are ready to eat in a few minutes and will keep for a week. These pickles can be used in a variety of ways and are good to have on hand to brighten up a charcuterie plate—or as an hors d'oeuvre on their own. Prepare the pickling solution by combining all the ingredients listed below and bringing them to a boil. Cook each type of vegetable separately in this boiling brine, scooping them out when they are cooked but still a little bit crisp. Set them aside to cool. Once all the vegetables are cooked and cooled, and the pickling solution has cooled to room temperature, combine the vegetables, transfer to jars or another covered container, cover with the pickle brine, and refrigerate.

Use this method to pickle little florets of cauliflower, sliced carrots, quartered pearl or cipolline onions, halved okra pods, small turnips cut into wedges with some of their stems still attached, whole green beans, small cubes of celery root, and more. Sometimes I just slice red onions very thin and pour the boiling brine over them. By the time they cool they will have cooked just enough, and they are delicious served with smoked fish and new potatoes.

Feel free to alter the ingredients of the brine: try using red instead of white vinegar, or adding a bit of saffron, or other kinds of dried chiles, or fresh slices of jalapeño.

For about 3½ cups pickling brine, combine and bring to a boil:

1½ cups white wine vinegar
1¾ cups water
2½ tablespoons sugar
½ bay leaf

4 thyme sprigs
**Half a dried cayenne pepper or a
    pinch of dried chile flakes**
½ teaspoon coriander seeds
2 whole cloves
1 garlic clove, peeled and cut in half
A big pinch of salt

Cheese Puffs (Gougères)

MAKES ABOUT 40 SMALL OR 20 LARGE CHEESE PUFFS

My friend Lulu from Bandol often serves these—usually the variation with anchovies. Hot from the oven, they are perfection with chilled rosé wine.

Heat, without boiling, in a heavy-bottomed saucepan:

½ cup water
**3 tablespoons butter, cut into small
    pieces**
½ teaspoon salt

When the butter has melted, stir in, all at once:

½ cup flour

Keep stirring vigorously until the mixture coheres and pulls away from the sides of the pan. Keep stirring for another minute over the heat, then transfer to a mixing bowl and allow to cool slightly. (Stirring will speed up the cooling process.)

Beat in, one at a time:

2 eggs

Beat in the first egg thoroughly before adding the next. Stir in:

3 ounces Gruyère cheese, grated (about ¾ cup)

Preheat the oven to 400°F. Line 2 baking sheets with parchment paper (not necessary, but it makes cleanup easier). Spoon the dough onto the baking sheets in spoonfuls either 1 or 2 inches in diameter and 1½ inches apart. You can also pipe out the puffs with a pastry bag with a ½-inch plain tip.

Bake undisturbed for 10 minutes, at 400°F. Lower the temperature to 375°F and bake for 15 minutes more. The puffs should be golden brown and crisp on the outside. With a sharp pointed knife, pierce each warm puff with a small slit to let out the steam, which helps them stay crisp. Serve right away. The puffs can be recrisped and reheated in a 375°F oven for 3 minutes.

VARIATION

◆ In place of the cheese, use 2 or 3 salt-packed anchovies, soaked, filleted, and chopped.

Buckwheat Pancakes (Blinis)

4 SERVINGS

The batter is made in two stages. First a sponge is made (a mixture of milk, flour, egg yolks, and sugar that starts the yeast going and develops extra flavor) and then more milk and flour are added after the first rise.

Heat until lukewarm:
6 tablespoons milk
Stir in:
¾ teaspoon dry yeast
Stir together in a large bowl:
¼ cup buckwheat flour
¼ cup all-purpose flour
1 teaspoon sugar
¼ teaspoon salt

Mix the warm milk and yeast into:
2 egg yolks
Stir this into the dry ingredients until well mixed. Cover and let rise in a warm place until doubled in bulk, about 1 hour.
When the sponge has risen, mix together:
¼ cup buckwheat flour
¼ cup all-purpose flour
Add to the sponge, a little at a time, alternating with:
6 tablespoons milk, at room temperature
Mix well to make a smooth batter. Let rise again until doubled in bulk, about 1 hour. The batter can sit for 4 or 5 hours at a cool room temperature.

When it's time to fry the blinis, beat to soft peaks:
2 egg whites
Fold into the batter just until incorporated.

Drop the batter by the spoonful onto a hot, lightly buttered griddle. Blinis cook much more quickly than other pancakes, and they should be flipped as soon as they start to dry out around the edge but before all the bubbles on the surface have popped, less than a couple of minutes. Cook on the other side just long enough to color slightly.

Blinis are traditionally served with melted butter and crème fraîche spooned onto them while they are warm, with such savory toppings as smoked salmon, bottarga, caviar, and chives, or with applesauce or jam.

VARIATION

◆ Blinis are wonderful for breakfast. Make the batter the day before and refrigerate after the second rise. The next morning, let the batter come to room temperature, fold in the egg whites, and cook. Serve them with warm apricot jam.

Oysters, Raw and Cooked

The best-tasting oysters are perfectly fresh, alive, and just out of the water. They taste of the pure vitality of the ocean, and they are best when oceans are at their coldest. As the water warms during the summer months, oysters spawn and their flesh can be creamy and unpleasant. Oysters should be tightly closed when purchased. Store them in the refrigerator in a bag or container that is not airtight, so they can breathe.

When serving oysters on the half shell, shuck them right before they are to be eaten. Take care when shucking oysters. Protect your hand with a towel or heavy glove, and only use a proper oyster shucker or knife, not a sharp knife. Put a dish towel on a firm surface and place the oyster on the towel with the deep-cupped half of the shell on the bottom. Fold the towel over the front edge of the shell and insert the oyster knife into the back of the shell at the hinge. Twist the oyster knife back and forth while pushing in to pop open the hinge. Once the shell is open, slide the knife along the inside of the top shell, cutting the muscle that holds the two half shells together. Take care to keep the knife in contact with the shell so only the muscle is cut and the flesh of the oyster is left intact and beautiful. Discard the top shell and slide the oyster knife along the inside of the bottom shell to separate it from

that shell as well. Pick out any bits of shell and place the shucked oysters on a bed of crushed ice, taking care to preserve as much of the delicious liquor as possible (ice can be easily crushed, in a bag with a hammer or in a food processor).

I like to serve oysters on the half shell with lemon wedges and a ramekin of mignonette sauce. To make mignonette sauce, mince 1 small shallot and mix with 3 tablespoons white wine vinegar, 3 tablespoons dry white wine or Champagne, and fresh-ground black pepper.

To cook oysters, first take off their top shells, as you would for raw oysters. To keep them steady, set them on a bed of rock salt in an ovenproof dish. They can be flavored in many ways: with a spoonful of spicy salsa; with herb butter; with garlic butter and breadcrumbs; or with bits of cooked bacon and chives. A simple favorite is to mix chopped shallot, butter, fresh-ground black pepper, parsley, and lemon zest and juice. Put a spoonful on each oyster and bake at 400°F until just firm and hot, 6 to 8 minutes. Serve them right away with fresh bread or croutons.

Oysters can also be opened on the grill (page 155) and eaten out of their shells, and they can be taken out of their shells raw and fried in fresh breadcrumbs (page 62).

Sauces

(CONTINUED)

SEE ALSO

Vinaigrette 44

Aïoli (Garlic Mayonnaise) 47

Salsa Verde 45

Herb Butter 48

Fried Herbs and Toasted Breadcrumbs 63

Simple Tomato Sauce 264

Tartar Sauce

MAKES ABOUT 1 CUP

Serve this sauce with breaded fried sole or oysters.

Combine in a mixing bowl:

1 egg yolk
1 teaspoon white wine vinegar
½ teaspoon water
A pinch of salt

Mix well with a whisk. Into a cup with a pour spout, measure about:

¾ cup olive oil

Slowly dribble the oil into the egg yolk mixture, whisking constantly. As the egg yolk absorbs the oil, the sauce will thicken, lighten in color, and become opaque; this will happen rather quickly. You can then add the oil a little faster, whisking all the while. If the mayonnaise becomes too thick, thin it with a bit of water or vinegar. When all the oil has been added, stir in:

1 tablespoon chopped capers
1 tablespoon chopped cornichon or
  gherkin (not sweet pickle)
1 tablespoon chopped parsley
1 teaspoon chopped tarragon
1 teaspoon chopped chives
1 tablespoon chopped chervil

Season to taste with:

Salt
Fresh-ground black pepper

Add more vinegar if desired. Let the tartar sauce sit for 30 minutes to let the flavors emerge and marry.

VARIATION

◆ Substitute 2 teaspoons fresh lemon juice and ¼ teaspoon grated lemon zest for the white wine vinegar.

White Sauce (Béchamel Sauce)

MAKES 2 CUPS

This is the basic white sauce used in lasagna, vegetable gratins, and savory soufflés.

Melt in a heavy-bottomed pot:

3 tablespoons butter

Stir in:

3 tablespoons flour

Cook over medium heat for 3 minutes. Add, bit by bit, whisking constantly:

2 cups milk

To avoid lumps, completely whisk in each addition of milk before adding the next. If, despite this, the sauce is lumpy, strain it through a sieve after all the milk has been added, and return to the burner to cook. Bring slowly to a boil, stirring all the time. Turn down to a bare simmer (use a flame tamer if necessary) and cook for 20 to 30 minutes, stirring occasionally to keep the sauce from sticking. Season with:

Salt
A pinch of nutmeg (optional)
A pinch of cayenne (optional)

Use right away or keep warm. (The sauce will solidify when cool.)

VARIATIONS

◆ To make a thicker sauce for a soufflé, use more flour and less milk: 4 tablespoons butter, 4 tablespoons flour, and 1½ cups milk.
◆ When making a vegetable gratin, replace up to 1 cup of the milk with vegetable cooking water (either the water the vegetables were cooked in or the water squeezed from cooked greens).

Pan Gravy

MAKES ABOUT 1½ CUPS

Pan gravy is classically made with the drippings of a roast. This method applies to any number of roasted meats: beef, lamb, pork, chicken, turkey. It's easiest to make the gravy right in the pan that the meat was roasted in.

Remove the roast from the pan and transfer to a warm place. Pour or skim off all but:

1 tablespoon fat

Put the pan over a low flame and stir in:

1 tablespoon unbleached flour

Cook for a few minutes, stirring constantly, and then add slowly, whisking all the while to avoid lumps:

1½ cups broth or water

Keep cooking the gravy, stirring all the while, until it reaches a boil. Be sure to scrape up all the brown bits stuck to the bottom of the pan; they contribute lots of flavor to the sauce. Season with:

Salt

Fresh-ground black pepper

Pour through a strainer if there are lumps.

Beef Reduction Sauce

MAKES ABOUT 1 CUP

This is best made from a variety of bones: knuckles add body from cartilage and tendons, shanks, and neck bones add meaty flavor (the meat from shanks can be cut off and used as the meat to brown). Don't skimp on either meat or bones. They both add specific flavors and qualities that the sauce needs.

Arrange on a heavy-duty baking sheet or in a roasting pan:

3 pounds beef bones, preferably a mixture of meaty bones and knuckles

Roast in a 400°F oven until quite brown, about 40 to 50 minutes. While the bones are roasting, put a heavy stockpot over medium heat. When hot, add:

2 tablespoons olive oil

½ pound beef, such as shank, shin, or chuck, cut into 1-inch pieces

Brown the meat well, stirring now and then. When well browned, pour off most of the fat and add:

1 carrot,
    peeled and cut into large pieces
1 onion,
    peeled and cut into large pieces
1 celery stalk, cut into large pieces
A pinch of salt

Cook, stirring now and then, until the vegetables are wilted. Be sure to not let the bottom of the pan burn. Add:

¼ teaspoon black peppercorns
1 whole clove
2 allspice berries
3 thyme sprigs
A few parsley stems
1 cup dry red wine

Stir well, scraping up any brown bits clinging to the bottom of the pan. Cook the wine until it has reduced significantly. Add the browned bones and:

5 cups chicken or beef broth

Bring the liquid to a boil, reduce to a simmer, and skim any foam that has collected on the surface. Pour off the fat from the pan the bones were browned in. If there are any brown bits sticking to it, add a bit of broth from the pot, scrape them up, and tip the liquid back into the pot. Cook, at a simmer, for 3 to 4 hours. Strain, pressing well on the meat and vegetables to extract all the juices. Skim off any fat and pour into a shallow pan to reduce. Cook at a rapid boil until reduced to 1 cup. Season with salt to taste.

◆ Use white wine instead of red.

◆ Use 3 pounds lamb bones (1 pound of which is meaty neck bone) and ¼ pound lamb meat instead of beef bones and meat.

◆ Use 3 pounds pork bones and ½ pound pork meat instead of beef.

◆ Use 1 chicken carcass and 2 or 3 whole legs instead of beef bones and meat. Chop up the carcass before browning for maximum flavor extraction.

◆ Instead of beef, use 1 duck carcass and about ½ pound meaty duck scraps such as tenderloins or legs. Chop up the carcass before browning.

Bolognese Sauce

MAKES ABOUT 3 CUPS

This sauce is time-consuming to make, so consider doubling the recipe. It's especially good with hand-cut fresh egg noodles (see page 89) or in lasagna (see page 270).

Heat in a large heavy-bottomed pot:

1 tablespoon olive oil

Add:

2 ounces pancetta, diced fine

Cook over medium heat until lightly browned, about 5 minutes. Add:

1 small onion, diced fine
1 celery stalk, diced fine
1 carrot, diced fine
2 garlic cloves, finely chopped
5 sage leaves
2 thyme sprigs
1 bay leaf

Cook over medium heat, stirring occasionally, until tender, about 12 minutes.

While the vegetables are cooking, heat in a large heavy-bottomed pan, preferably cast iron:

1 tablespoon olive oil

Add and brown over medium-high heat, in two batches:

1 pound skirt steak, cut into ⅛-inch cubes
4 ounces pork shoulder, coarsely ground

Cook until the meat is a nice chestnut color. Once all the meat is browned, pour in:

1 cup dry white wine

Reduce the wine by half, scraping the brown bits off the bottom of the pan. Add the browned meat and the deglazing juices to the tender vegetables with:

2 tablespoons tomato paste
Salt

Measure and stir together:

2 cups beef or chicken broth
1½ cups milk

Pour enough of this liquid into the pot to bring it to the level of the meat and vegetables. Simmer gently until the meat is very tender, about 1½ hours. As the liquid reduces, keep topping it up with the rest of the broth and milk, and skimming the fat that rises to the surface.

When the meat is tender, remove the sauce from the heat and season to taste with more salt, if needed, and:

Fresh-ground black pepper

VARIATIONS

◆ Include ¼ cup dried porcini, soaked, drained, and chopped fine, with the diced vegetables.

◆ Other cuts of beef can be used instead of skirt steak. Chuck or hanging tenderloin will make a delicious sauce, although hanging tenderloin will require at least an hour more of cooking time to become tender. During the additional cooking time it may be necessary to add more broth or milk to keep the sauce from becoming too dry.

Mushroom Ragù

MAKES ABOUT 2 CUPS

This is a rich, deep-flavored pasta sauce, like Bolognese—but meatless.

Heat in a large, heavy skillet:

2 tablespoons olive oil

Add and cook over medium heat, until very tender:

1 large yellow onion, peeled and diced fine

1 large carrot, peeled and diced fine

2 celery stalks, diced fine

Salt

When cooked through, with no crunch but with little or no browning, add:

6 thyme sprigs, leaves picked from the stems

6 parsley sprigs, leaves only, chopped

1 bay leaf

Cook for 1 minute. Add and cook for 5 minutes:

½ cup diced tomatoes

Set aside. Carefully clean and slice:

2 pounds mushrooms (choose a mixture of two or three types: chanterelles, black trumpets, hedgehogs, brown or white button mushrooms)

If the mushrooms are very dirty, it will be necessary to wash them (crunching down on dirt and sand is very unpleasant). The mushrooms may take on some water, but it will be thrown off shortly after they hit the hot pan. As they cook, the mushrooms will give off liquid; let the juices boil away or tip off the juices and set them aside. Continue cooking the mushrooms until lightly browned (you may need to add a little more oil or butter). The reserved juices can be added back to the sauce later in place of some of the water or broth. Sauté each type of mushroom separately, until tender and lightly browned in:

Olive oil and a little butter

Turn the cooked mushrooms onto a cutting board and chop to the size of the cooked vegetables. Combine with the vegetables and herbs in the large skillet and add:

½ cup cream or crème fraîche

1 cup water or chicken broth

Bring to a simmer and cook for 15 minutes. Taste for salt and add as needed. Moisten with more liquid if too thick.

VARIATION

◆ Add ½ cup peas or cooked greens such as spinach, rocket, or chard to the sauce with the broth and cream.

Beurre Blanc (Warm Butter Sauce)

MAKES 1 CUP

Bring to a boil in a small heavy-bottomed pot:

2 shallots, diced fine

¼ cup white wine vinegar

½ cup dry white wine

A few black peppercorns

A pinch of salt

Cook until the liquid is almost completely gone (as the liquid gets low, reduce the heat). Remove from the heat when the shallots are still moist but not floating in liquid. (This step can be done far in advance.) Put the pan over a very low heat. Bit by bit, whisk in:

14 tablespoons (1¾ sticks) butter, cut into small pieces

Wait until each addition is mostly melted and incorporated before adding more. Monitor the heat; the sauce should be warm while the butter is being added but not hot or the sauce will separate. Oddly enough it will also separate if the sauce gets too cool while the butter is being added. Once all the butter has been incorporated, taste for salt and add more as needed. Thin with a splash of fresh wine, some broth, or even water; the added liquid helps keep the sauce from breaking or separating and makes it lighter. Strain if desired. Serve immediately or keep warm in a double boiler over warm, but not hot, water, or in a warmed thermos.

VARIATIONS

• Flavor the sauce with chopped herbs, capers, or nasturtiums.

• Add whole spices, such as coriander or fennel seeds, along with the peppercorns.

• A simpler sauce can be made by putting 3 tablespoons wine, lemon juice, or even water in a pan, bringing to a boil, and swirling or whisking in 4 tablespoons (½ stick) butter, cut into small pieces, and a pinch of salt.

Béarnaise Sauce

MAKES ABOUT ½ CUP

Béarnaise is a luxurious sauce flavored with shallots and tarragon, which give it a tart edge. It elevates a grilled steak or roast beef from delicious to divine.

Combine in a small heavy pot:

1 shallot, peeled and minced
2 tablespoons chopped chervil
2 tablespoons chopped tarragon
A pinch of salt
A few black peppercorns
3 tablespoons white wine vinegar
6 tablespoons dry white wine

Bring to a boil and cook until reduced to 2 tablespoons. Strain into a bowl, pressing as much liquid from the solids as possible. Discard the solids.

Separate into a medium-size nonreactive heat-proof bowl:

2 egg yolks

Add the strained reduction to the eggs and mix well. Place the bowl over a pot of hot but not boiling water. Be sure that the bottom of the bowl is not touching the water. Whisk the eggs for a minute and then slowly add, whisking all the while, in a small stream:

6 tablespoons (¾ stick) unsalted
**   butter, melted**

If the sauce gets too thick, add a teaspoon of warm water. The sauce should be warm but never hot. If overheated, the sauce will separate or the yolks will scramble. When all the butter has been added, stir in:

1 to 1½ tablespoons chopped tarragon
A pinch of cayenne

Taste for salt and correct as needed. Serve immediately or hold the finished sauce over warm, but not hot, water, or in a warmed thermos.

VARIATIONS

• Substitute other herbs (such as mint, basil, or chives) for the tarragon.

• To make a hollandaise sauce, omit the tarragon-shallot reduction and whisk the egg yolks together with 1 tablespoon warm water and 2 teaspoons fresh lemon juice. Add the butter as above and finish with salt and more lemon juice as desired.

Bagna Cauda

MAKES ABOUT 1 CUP

Bagna cauda means "warm bath" in an Italian dialect. Don't let the anchovies steer you away. The strong flavors of garlic and anchovy are suspended in perfect balance in warm butter and olive oil. It is a delightful dipping sauce for raw vegetables, and it makes a tasty sauce for grilled vegetables and grilled or baked fish.

Soak in water for 5 minutes:
> **5 salt-packed anchovies**

Debone them and chop the fillets. There should be about 2 tablespoons.

Heat some water to a simmer in the bottom of a double boiler or small pot.

Put the anchovies in the top of the double boiler or in a medium-size nonreactive heat-proof bowl set over the simmering water and add:
> **6 tablespoons (¾ stick) butter**
> **⅓ cup extra-virgin olive oil**
> **3 garlic cloves,**
> **peeled and sliced very thin**
> **Zest of 1 lemon**
> **¼ teaspoon fresh-ground black pepper**

Heat and stir until the butter is melted. Taste and add as needed:
> **Salt**

Pesto

MAKES ABOUT 1½ CUPS

Pesto is my favorite sauce to make. I love the sensory experience of pounding it and smelling it and tasting it as I go. Pesto is more than a pasta sauce: it's delicious on sliced tomatoes, as a dipping sauce for vegetables, on a pizza, or as a sauce for grilled chicken and vegetables.

Pick the leaves from:
> **1 bunch of basil, to yield about**
> **1 lightly packed cup**

In a mortar and pestle, pound to a paste:
> **1 garlic clove, peeled**
> **Salt**

Add and continue to pound:
> **¼ cup pine nuts, lightly toasted**

Add:
> **¼ cup grated Parmesan cheese**

Transfer this mixture to a bowl. Coarsely chop the basil leaves and put them in the mortar. Pound the leaves to a paste. Return the pounded pine nut mixture to the mortar. Pound the leaves and pine nut mixture together. Continue pounding as you gradually pour in:
> **½ cup extra-virgin olive oil**

Taste for salt and adjust if necessary.

VARIATIONS

◆ Substitute parsley or rocket for some or all of the basil.

◆ Substitute grated pecorino cheese for half of the Parmesan.

◆ Use walnuts instead of pine nuts.

Gremolata and Persillade

Gremolata is a mixture of chopped parsley, garlic, and lemon zest. Persillade (pronounced "per-see-odd") is simply chopped parsley and garlic. Although these are not technically sauces, I use them as a fresh bright finish to sprinkle over roasted or braised meats, pastas, and anything grilled.

To make gremolata, mix together:

3 tablespoons chopped parsley
**1 teaspoon grated or finely chopped
   lemon zest**
2 garlic cloves, finely chopped

For persillade, combine the parsley and garlic, and omit the lemon zest.

Fresh Tomato Salsa

MAKES ABOUT 1 CUP

This salsa is so easy to make and tastes so much better than anything you can buy in a jar! Use fresh ripe tomatoes in the summer and canned whole tomatoes the rest of the year.

Core and cut into medium dice:

**2 medium ripe tomatoes or 4 canned
   whole tomatoes**

Put in a bowl with:

1 garlic clove, peeled and chopped fine
½ white or red onion, diced fine
**6 cilantro sprigs (stems and leaves),
   chopped**

Juice of ½ lime
Salt

Stir gently and add more salt and lime juice as needed. Let sit for 5 minutes to allow the flavors to develop.

VARIATIONS

• Add 1 jalapeño or serrano chile, chopped fine.
• Add ¼ teaspoon crushed toasted cumin seeds.
• Fold in ½ avocado cut into medium dice.

Peach Salsa

MAKES ABOUT 1½ CUPS

This salsa is a fresh complement to grilled or baked fish or fish tacos.

Peel:

2 ripe peaches

Dip the peaches in boiling water for 10 to 15 seconds. Slip off the skins, cut the flesh away from the pits, and cut into medium dice. Add:

½ small red onion, diced fine
**1 serrano or jalapeño chile, seeds and
   veins removed, diced fine**
Juice of 1 lime
Salt
1 to 2 tablespoons chopped cilantro

Stir together and taste for salt, heat, and acid. Adjust with more salt, chile, and lime juice as needed.

VARIATIONS

• Substitute other fruits for the peaches: papaya, mango, or melon.
• Substitute 2 green onions instead of the red onion.
• Add 1 small avocado, peeled, pit removed, and cut into medium dice.

Tomatillo Salsa

MAKES 2 CUPS

This bright-tasting sauce is a great accompaniment to grilled foods of all descriptions—steak, chicken, shrimp, or vegetables—and it is also wonderful as a dip for tortilla chips or as a sauce for tamales.

Remove the husks from:

1 pound tomatillos (about 12 medium)

Rinse them and put them in a saucepan with water barely covering. Add a pinch of salt, bring to a boil, lower the heat, and simmer until just soft, about 4 to 5 minutes. Drain, reserving the cooking liquid. Measure ½ cup of the cooking liquid into a blender with:

2 jalapeño or serrano chiles,
  seeded and sliced
1 cup chopped cilantro leaves and
  stems
1 garlic clove, sliced
Salt

Add the cooked tomatillos and blend briefly. The sauce should have a coarse texture. Taste for salt and add more as needed. Let the sauce sit to develop the flavors. It will thicken as it cools and may be thinned with more of the cooking liquid.

VARIATIONS

◆ For a more spicy salsa, add another jalapeño or serrano chile.

◆ This salsa is also delicious with a mashed medium avocado mixed in.

◆ Make the sauce with chopped raw tomatillos and with water instead of the cooking liquid.

◆ If you have the opportunity, substitute the rarer purple tomatillos, which are a little sweeter and especially wonderful used raw.

Cucumber–Yogurt Sauce

MAKES ABOUT 1½ CUPS

This sauce is a version of a raita, the cooling South Asian yogurt sauce, which is often seasoned with cumin seed, cinnamon, and cayenne. Try different varieties of cucumber such as lemon, Armenian, or Japanese. If the cucumbers have large seeds, use a spoon to scrape them out after you cut the cucumbers in half. A cool growing season sometimes yields bitter cucumbers, so taste each cucumber; a bitter cucumber will spoil the sauce.

Peel, halve, and slice into half-moons:

1 medium cucumber

Toss in a medium-size bowl with:

A pinch of salt

Allow to sit for 10 minutes. Drain off any liquid that has collected. Stir in:

¾ cup whole-milk yogurt
1 small garlic clove,
  pounded to a purée
1 tablespoon olive oil
2 mint sprigs,
  leaves only, cut in chiffonade

VARIATIONS

◆ Grate the cucumber instead of slicing it, for a smoother sauce.

◆ For a little spice, add a pinch of pulverized dried red pepper such as marash or cayenne.

Harissa

MAKES ABOUT ¾ CUP

This North African condiment is made from puréed sweet peppers and chiles. Use it to spice up a soup, roast meat, or grilled vegetables; as a sandwich spread; or as a sauce with rice or couscous dishes.

Toast in a hot oven or on a hot griddle until puffed and fragrant:

5 dried ancho chiles (about 2 ounces)

Take care to not burn them. Remove and discard the stems and seeds. Put the chiles in a small bowl, cover them with boiling water, and let them soak for about 20 minutes, then drain.

Roast over an open flame until the skin is thoroughly blackened and blistered:

1 large red bell pepper

Set the blackened pepper aside covered with a towel or sealed in a paper bag for 5 minutes or so to steam and loosen the skin. Peel the pepper, discarding the stem, seeds, and skin.

In a blender or food processor, purée the soaked, drained chiles and peeled pepper to a smooth thick paste with:

4 garlic cloves, peeled
Salt
¾ cup olive oil
1 teaspoon red wine vinegar

If desired, thin the sauce with a bit of water. Store in the refrigerator for up to 3 weeks under a film of oil.

VARIATIONS

• Add cayenne pepper to taste for a spicier harissa.
• Add ½ teaspoon each toasted and ground cumin and coriander seeds, and ¼ teaspoon caraway seeds.

Chermoula

MAKES ABOUT ¾ CUP

This is a variation of a North African condiment. It is redolent of coriander and complements saffron rice with vegetables or fish.

Put in a blender:

One 1-inch piece of fresh ginger, peeled
1 serrano chile, seeds and veins removed
½ cup extra-virgin olive oil
Salt

Blend until smooth and add:

⅓ cup flat-leaf parsley leaves
½ cup cilantro leaves and stems

Blend until the leaves are chopped, but there is still some texture. Pour into a bowl and season with:

Juice of ½ lemon
1 garlic clove, pounded to a purée

Taste for salt and acid and adjust as desired. Let sit for 10 minutes for the flavors to marry.

VARIATIONS

• Add ½ onion, peeled and diced, with the ginger and chile.
• To use as a marinade for fish or chicken, make the chermoula with only ¼ cup oil.
• Add ½ teaspoon ground toasted cumin or coriander seeds.

Crème Fraîche

MAKES 1 CUP

Crème fraîche is heavy cream that has been cultured and thickened with a live enzyme like the one found in buttermilk. It is thick and smooth with a rich tangy flavor. The advantage of cooking with crème fraîche (as opposed to sour cream) is that it will not separate when boiled. Crème fraîche is easy to make and is amazingly versatile. Stir it into a vinaigrette for a creamy, tangy dressing. Flavor it with herbs and a touch of salt for a perfect garnish for a soup. Use it to thicken and enrich a pasta sauce or braise. A potato gratin is sublime when made with crème fraîche. For dessert it can be sweetened with sugar, honey, or maple syrup to make a simple sauce. It can be whipped to make a soft whipped cream (be sure not to overwhip it; it will become grainy, just like heavy cream).

Mix with melted chocolate for a great frosting (page 386). And it makes delicious ice cream.

Into a clean glass jar pour:
**1 cup heavy cream
(do not use ultra-pasteurized)**
Add and stir well:
1 tablespoon cultured buttermilk
Cover the jar loosely and let the cream sit at room temperature for 24 hours or so, or until the cream thickens. The time this takes will depend on the ambient room temperature. When thickened, cover the jar tightly and store in the refrigerator. Crème fraîche will continue to thicken and become tangier as it ages. Stir thick crème fraîche to thin it. If very thick it can be thinned with milk or water. Crème fraîche may be stored for up to 10 days in the refrigerator.

Salads

(CONTINUED)

Cauliflower Salad with Olives and Capers 247

Cucumbers with Cream and Mint 247

Lentil Salad 248

Tabbouleh Salad 248

SEE ALSO

Garden Lettuce Salad 51

Greek Salad 53

Orange and Olive Salad 55

Poached Egg with Curly Endive Salad 143

Rocket Salad with Parmesan

4 SERVINGS

Rocket and arugula are both common names for the spicy salad plant *Eruca vesicaria*, which has dark green, lobed leaves that taste nutty and peppery.

Trim off any tough stems from:

4 large handfuls of rocket

Wash and spin dry, then keep cool.

To make the vinaigrette, mix:

1 tablespoon red wine vinegar (or a mixture of sherry vinegar and red wine vinegar)

Salt

Fresh-ground black pepper

Whisk in:

3 to 4 tablespoons extra-virgin olive oil

Start with the smaller amount of oil and taste the dressing with a leaf of the rocket. Add more oil and salt to taste. When ready to serve, toss the rocket with the vinaigrette.

With a sharp, sturdy vegetable peeler cut thin curls of:

Parmesan cheese or another hard grating cheese such as pecorino

Scatter the cheese curls over the top of the salad and serve.

VARIATIONS

• Toast ¼ cup hazelnuts in a 350°F oven until brown. Rub the hot nuts in a kitchen towel to remove the skins. Chop and toss with the rocket. Pine nuts, walnuts, or pecans are delicious, too.

• Peel and thinly slice 1 or 2 persimmons (see note, page 240) and tuck the slices in the rocket salad.

Hearts of Romaine with Creamy Dressing

4 SERVINGS

This salad is best made with whole uncut leaves of romaine. You may need to remove quite a few of the large outer leaves to expose the smaller pale green sweet leaves at the heart. There are tender small varieties called Little Gem and Winter Density that make incredible salads. Look for them at your farmers' market.

Remove the outer darker green leaves from:

2 heads of romaine lettuce

Cut off the stem end and separate the leaves. Wash them thoroughly and spin-dry in batches.

To make the dressing, stir together in a large bowl:

1 tablespoon white wine vinegar

Grated zest of 1 lemon

1 tablespoon fresh lemon juice

Salt

Fresh-ground black pepper

Taste, and adjust as needed. Whisk in:

3 tablespoons extra-virgin olive oil

3 tablespoons heavy cream

Taste for salt and acid and adjust if needed. Gently toss the lettuce with the dressing, making sure each leaf is evenly coated.

VARIATIONS

• A couple of salt-packed anchovies, rinsed, filleted, and chopped, are a great addition to the dressing.

• Some or all of the following herbs are delicious chopped and scattered over the salad: basil, chervil, chives, and tarragon.

• This dressing is equally suitable for butter or Bibb lettuces and for frisée and radicchio.

Caesar Salad

4 SERVINGS

Remove the outer darker green leaves, leaving only the smaller light green leaves, from:

2 heads of romaine lettuce

Cut off the stem ends and separate into leaves. Keep the small leaves at the heart intact, and tear the larger leaves in pieces. Wash well and spin dry in batches. Keep cool until ready to dress.

Cut into small cubes, about ½-inch square:

3 ounces day-old country-style bread

You should have about 20 cubes. Toss in a bowl with:

1½ tablespoons extra-virgin olive oil
Salt

Spread on a baking sheet and toast in a 350°F oven for 10 to 12 minutes, or until golden brown, stirring the croutons occasionally for even browning.

To make the dressing, mix in a small bowl:

1 tablespoon red wine vinegar
1 tablespoon fresh lemon juice
2 garlic cloves, pounded to a purée
2 teaspoons chopped salt-packed anchovies (about 2 to 3 fillets)
Salt
Fresh-ground black pepper

Whisk in:

¼ cup extra-virgin olive oil

Right before serving the salad, grate:

½ cup Parmesan cheese (about 1 ounce)

Whisk into the dressing:

1 egg yolk

Add a small handful of the grated cheese and whisk until thick. Taste for salt and acid with a piece of romaine. Adjust the seasoning as needed. Put the romaine in a large bowl, pour three quarters of the dressing over the salad, and toss. Taste and add more if needed. Add most of the rest of the grated cheese and toss lightly. Arrange the salad on a large plate. Toss the croutons in the bowl, scraping up the last of the dressing, and then scatter them over the salad. Garnish with the last of the cheese and a final grind of pepper.

Chicken Salad

MAKES ABOUT 2½ CUPS

First, make a mayonnaise. Whisk together in a large bowl:

1 egg yolk
¼ teaspoon white wine vinegar
A pinch of salt

Pour in, in a slow steady stream, whisking all the while:

¾ cup olive oil

Stir into the mayonnaise:

2 cups roasted or poached chicken meat cut into ¼-inch pieces
2 tablespoons chives or scallions sliced very thin
2 celery stalks, diced fine
1 tablespoon capers, rinsed, drained, and coarsely chopped
Salt
Fresh-ground black pepper

Taste and adjust the salt as needed. Serve in a sandwich or on a bed of lettuce that has been dressed with a simple vinaigrette.

VARIATIONS

◆ Add a pinch of cayenne for a bit of spice.
◆ Substitute diced cucumber for the celery.
◆ Add chopped hard-cooked egg.
◆ Add pounded garlic to the mayonnaise.
◆ Add a few chopped pitted green olives.
◆ Stir in chopped tender herbs such as chervil, parsley, tarragon, or basil.

Chopped Salad

A chopped salad is a mixture of thinly sliced or chopped greens and sliced or chopped vegetables, egg, cheese, meat, or fish, all tossed with a vinaigrette. The best-known chopped salad is the Cobb salad, which generally includes avocado, bacon, chicken, blue cheese, tomato, and egg. However, the only absolutely required ingredient for a chopped salad is crunchy, crisp salad greens. Romaine, Little Gems, escarole, radicchio, or iceberg will work. Darker greens like spinach, rocket, or cress are nice as well.

Wash the greens, but don't chop them until you are ready to dress the salad. A red wine vinaigrette, with a little mustard to help it stick to the ingredients, is a good starting point. The addition of a little cream or crème fraîche enriches the dressing and pairs well with slightly bitter greens. In addition, pounded garlic, anchovy, and even a few capers are all delicious mixed into the vinaigrette.

Of course, the choice of dressing is influenced by the chopped ingredients. In spring, thinly sliced fennel, snap peas, and a few walnuts or almonds with a light, creamy dressing make a fresh, bright-tasting salad. In summertime, tomatoes, cucumbers, gypsy or bell peppers, and avocado are all candidates for a chopped salad. For ripe flavors like these, a simple red wine vinaigrette with a little pounded garlic and a handful of torn basil and mint leaves is just right. Diced pink or golden beets are beautiful in chopped salad, but red beets will bleed color into all the other ingredients. Chopped boiled eggs are good in just about any chopped salad, either mixed in or sprinkled over.

For any chopped salad, assemble all your chopped ingredients except the lettuces and dress them with vinaigrette, salt, and pepper. Next chop the washed and dried lettuce leaves, add them to the bowl, and toss them all together with more dressing. Taste, adjust the seasoning, and serve.

Jicama Salad with Orange and Cilantro

4 SERVINGS

Peel and cut in half lengthwise:
>   **1 small jicama (about ½ pound)**

Cut into ¼-inch-thick slices. Cut the slices into ¼-inch-wide sticks.

Peel with a sharp knife down to the flesh, removing all the rind and membrane:
>   **2 oranges**

Slice into ¼-inch-thick rounds and remove the seeds. Arrange the jicama and orange slices on a plate. Sprinkle with:
>   **A pinch of paprika or spicy chile powder (ancho or guajillo)**

Make a dressing by whisking together:
>   **Juice of 1 lime**
>   **Salt**
>   **2 tablespoons extra-virgin olive oil**

Pour over the jicama and oranges. Sprinkle with:
>   **1 to 2 tablespoons chopped cilantro**

VARIATION

◆ Add ¼ cup sliced radishes. Taste and add more lime juice if needed.

Persimmon and Pomegranate Salad

4 SERVINGS

There are two varieties of persimmons available on the market, fuyu and hachiya. Fuyu are round and flat and are eaten while still crisp; they make colorful and tasty salads. Hachiya are elongated with a pointy tip, and are tannic until ripe and very, very soft.

Cut the tops from and peel:

3 ripe medium fuyu persimmons

Slice them thin or cut into small wedges, removing any seeds you find. Arrange the wedges on a plate.

Hold, cut side down, over a bowl:

½ pomegranate

Pound on the back of the fruit with a large spoon to dislodge the seeds. Pick out and discard any white pith that may have fallen out with the seeds. Sprinkle the seeds over the persimmon wedges.

For a simple vinaigrette, mix together:

1 tablespoon sherry or red wine
   vinegar
Salt
Fresh-ground black pepper

Stir to dissolve the salt and then whisk in:

3 tablespoons extra-virgin olive oil

Taste and correct the salt and acid as needed. Spoon the vinaigrette over the fruit and serve.

VARIATION

◆ Toss 4 small handfuls of lettuce with half the vinaigrette. (I prefer lettuces such as arugula, frisée, escarole, radicchio, or Belgian endive.) Arrange the lettuce on the plate and then arrange the fruit and nuts, if using, over the lettuce. Pour the rest of the vinaigrette over, and garnish with toasted walnuts.

Grapefruit and Avocado Salad

4 SERVINGS

Peel with a sharp knife down to the flesh, removing all the rind and membrane:

2 medium ruby grapefruit

Cut the sections free, slicing carefully along the partitioning membranes. Squeeze the juice from the membranes. Measure 2 tablespoons of the juice into a small bowl. Stir in:

1 teaspoon white wine vinegar
Salt
Fresh-ground black pepper

Whisk in:

2 tablespoons extra-virgin olive oil

Taste and adjust the acid and salt.

Cut in half and remove the pit from:

2 medium Hass avocados

Peel the halves and cut into ¼-inch slices. Sprinkle lightly with salt. Arrange the grapefruit sections and avocado slices alternately on a plate and spoon the vinaigrette over.

VARIATIONS

◆ Garnish with watercress or chervil.

◆ Double the amount of vinaigrette and dress 4 small handfuls of arugula separately with half of the vinaigrette. Arrange the avocado and grapefruit on top, and spoon the remaining vinaigrette over the fruit.

◆ For the avocados, substitute 2 large or 4 small artichokes. Trim off all the leaves, remove the chokes, and cook the hearts until tender in salted boiling water. Slice and marinate in a couple spoonfuls of the vinaigrette.

◆ Slice thin 1 small sweet spring onion. Marinate in a spoonful of vinaigrette. Scatter over the arranged salad before spooning on the dressing.

Sliced Tomatoes with Basil

4 SERVINGS

Look for all the different colors, sizes, and flavors of tomatoes at the farmers' market all through tomato season—July, August, and September. Mix them together, sliced or wedged, for a strikingly beautiful salad.

Wash and core:

4 medium tomatoes (about 1¼ pounds)

Cut into ¼-inch slices and arrange on a plate. Season with:

Salt

Neatly stack and roll into a long thin cylinder:

5 basil leaves

Cut across the cylinder of leaves with a pair of scissors or a knife, making long thin slices (a chiffonade). Scatter the chiffonade over the tomatoes and then drizzle the salad with:

2 to 3 tablespoons extra-virgin olive oil

VARIATIONS

◆ Cut ½ pound fresh mozzarella, feta, or queso fresco into thin slices. Tuck the slices of cheese between the slices of seasoned tomato and finish with the basil and oil.

◆ Make a vinaigrette to use in place of the olive oil. Mix together 1 shallot, minced; 1 tablespoon red wine vinegar; salt and fresh-ground pepper; and a sprig of fresh basil. Let macerate for 15 minutes or so. Remove the basil and whisk in 3 or 4 tablespoons extra-virgin olive oil.

◆ Use different herbs in place of the basil such as summer savory, mint, marjoram, and parsley.

◆ Cut a few cherry tomatoes in half and dress with a bit of salt and oil or vinaigrette. Scatter over the sliced tomatoes with the basil.

Green Bean and Cherry Tomato Salad

4 SERVINGS

Cherry tomatoes and beans come in many sizes and colors. Mix them all together. You can include shell beans, too. The beans can be cooked and cooled in advance.

Snap off the stem ends (and pull off the tails, if dry or tough) of:

½ pound green beans (haricot vert, young Blue Lake, Kentucky Wonder, or a similar variety)

Cook until tender in salted boiling water. Drain and immediately spread them out on a sheet pan or plate to cool.

Stem and cut in half:

½ pound cherry tomatoes

Stir together in a large bowl:

1 small shallot, diced fine
1 tablespoon red wine vinegar
Salt and fresh-ground black pepper

Taste and adjust if necessary. Let sit for 15 minutes or more. Then whisk in:

¼ cup extra-virgin olive oil

Adjust the acid and salt as needed. Toss the cherry tomatoes with the vinaigrette. Taste. Add the green beans, and:

6 basil leaves, cut into chiffonade (optional)

Toss gently. Taste for seasoning and add salt and vinegar as needed.

VARIATIONS

◆ Add chopped black olives to the dressing.

◆ The green beans alone make a lovely salad. They are particularly good tossed with the basil and lots of chopped parsley.

◆ Roasted red peppers, peeled and sliced, may be substituted for the cherry tomatoes.

Niçoise Salad

4 SERVINGS

This composed salad is based on a recipe from Provence. It makes a delightful lunch or light dinner. The summer vegetables are set off by the piquant anchovies and rich hard-cooked egg.

Soak and fillet:

3 salt-packed anchovies

Cut the fillets lengthwise into strips and coat them with a bit of olive oil.

Wash and core:

¾ pound ripe tomatoes

Cut into small wedges and season with:

Salt

Blanch in salted boiling water until tender:

¼ pound green beans, trimmed

Drain and lay out to cool.

Cut into thin strips:

**1 sweet red pepper, cut in half,
        stem, seeds, and veins removed**

Peel and cut into bite-size wedges, large pieces, or slices:

2 medium or 1 large cucumber

Place in a saucepan of water and bring to a boil:

2 eggs

Cook at a gentle boil for 5 minutes, then cool in cold water.

Mix together in a small bowl:

**1½ tablespoons red wine vinegar
Salt
Fresh-ground black pepper
1 garlic clove, peeled and crushed**

Stir to dissolve the salt and then let sit a few minutes to macerate. Whisk in:

**4 tablespoons extra-virgin olive oil
5 basil leaves, chopped**

Taste for salt and acid and adjust as necessary.

Peel the eggs and cut them into quarters.

Season the cucumbers, peppers, and green beans with salt and then toss with three quarters of the vinaigrette. Arrange on a plate. Dress the tomatoes, tossing gently, and arrange around the vegetables. Garnish the salad with the eggs and the strips of anchovy fillet.

VARIATIONS

⬧ For a more substantial salad, grill or pan sear ¾ pound fresh tuna, leaving it quite rare. Break the tuna into pieces, dress with a bit of the vinaigrette, and arrange on the plate with the vegetables.

⬧ Serve the salad on a bed of lettuce or arugula.

⬧ Roast the peppers, then peel and seed them, and cut into strips.

Leeks Vinaigrette

4 SERVINGS

Leeks are at their best in the cold months, when lettuce is scarce. Dressed with this mustardy vinaigrette, they make a bright winter salad.

Trim and clean (see page 258):

**12 small leeks (less than 1 inch in
        diameter) or 6 medium leeks**

Cook for 7 to 12 minutes, or until tender, in abundant salted boiling water. To test for doneness, use a sharp knife to pierce the thickest part of the root end. If the leek is tender it will offer no resistance. When the leeks are done, carefully lift them out, drain them, and set them aside to cool.

To make the vinaigrette, mix together in a small bowl:

**1 tablespoon red wine vinegar
2 teaspoons Dijon mustard**

Salt

Fresh-ground black pepper

Whisk in:

¼ cup extra-virgin olive oil

Taste and adjust the seasoning as needed.

Squeeze the cooled leeks gently to remove any excess water. Cut larger leeks lengthwise into halves or quarters. Gently toss the leeks with a pinch of salt. When ready to serve, arrange on a plate, spoon the vinaigrette over, and turn gently to coat. Sprinkle with:

1 tablespoon chopped parsley or chervil

VARIATIONS

◆ Coarsely chop 1½ hard-cooked eggs and scatter over the top with the parsley.

◆ Coarsely chop or slice 4 salt-packed anchovy fillets and scatter over the top with the parsley.

◆ Oil, season, and grill the cooked leeks over medium coals before dressing.

Celery Root Rémoulade

4 SERVINGS

Serve this winter salad alongside other little salads, such as marinated beets, carrot salad, or arugula salad.

Cut away all the brown skin and small roots from:

1 medium celery root (about 1 pound)

Rinse. With a sharp knife or mandoline, cut the celery root into ⅛-inch-thick slices. Cut the slices into thin matchstick-size pieces. (This is called a julienne of celery root.) Toss with:

Salt

1 teaspoon white wine vinegar

Mix together in a small bowl:

2 tablespoons crème fraîche

2 teaspoons Dijon mustard

Juice of ½ lemon

2 teaspoons extra-virgin olive oil

Salt

Fresh-ground black pepper

Stir well. Pour over the celery root and toss to coat. Taste for salt and acid. The salad can be served right away or refrigerated for up to a day.

VARIATIONS

◆ Add other raw julienned root vegetables, such as rutabaga, carrot, or radish, to the salad.

◆ Sprinkle with chopped parsley, chervil, or mint.

◆ Toss together with a rocket salad.

◆ For the crème fraîche, substitute 1 egg yolk and whisk in 3 tablespoons olive oil.

Marinated Beet Salad

4 SERVINGS

Beets of different colors make a very beautiful salad. Dress the red ones separately so their color doesn't bleed all over the others.

Trim the greens to ½ inch from:

**1 pound beets
(red, Chioggia, golden, or white)**

Wash thoroughly. Put them in a baking dish with a little water (enough to cover the bottom of the dish to a depth of ⅛ inch) and sprinkle with:

Salt

Cover tightly and bake the beets in a 350°F oven until they can be easily pierced with a sharp knife, 30 minutes to 1 hour, depending on their size. Uncover and cool. Cut off the tops and roots and slip off the skins. Cut the peeled beets into small wedges or ¼-inch dice and sprinkle with:

**1 teaspoon vinegar (red wine, sherry, or white wine vinegar)
Salt**

Let stand for a few minutes to allow the beets to absorb the flavor. Taste and add more salt or vinegar as needed. Toss with:

1 to 2 teaspoons extra-virgin olive oil

Serve alone, or with other salads.

VARIATIONS

• Substitute fresh orange juice for some of the vinegar and toss with grated orange zest.

• Toss with 1 tablespoon chopped fresh herbs such as mint, tarragon, or cilantro.

• Add ½ teaspoon grated fresh ginger with the olive oil.

• Bake the beets with 1 teaspoon fennel or cumin seeds sprinkled over them.

• Toss with a small amount of nut oil instead of olive oil. Walnut oil is particularly tasty with beets.

Coleslaw

4 SERVINGS

Use green cabbage, red cabbage, savoy cabbage, or napa cabbage. Each one is tasty, and each will make a slightly different salad.

Tear off and discard the tough outer leaves of:

1 small cabbage

Cut into quarters and remove the core. Turn cut side down and slice crosswise into thin shreds.

Mix together in a large bowl with:

**½ small red onion,
sliced as thin as possible
Salt**

Prepare a vinaigrette by mixing together:

**1 tablespoon cider or wine vinegar
Salt
Fresh-ground black pepper**

Stir to dissolve the salt and then whisk in:

4 tablespoons olive oil

Taste for acid and salt and adjust as desired. Pour the dressing over the cabbage and onions and mix well. Taste again for salt and acid. Eat right away or let it sit for a while to let the flavors permeate and the cabbage soften.

VARIATIONS

• Quarter and core 1 apple; slice thin or dice and mix in with the cabbage and onions.

• Stir in 2 to 3 tablespoons chopped parsley or other tender herbs at the end.

• Add ¼ cup celery root, peeled and cut into a matchstick julienne.

• Mix in a couple of thinly sliced jalapeño or serrano peppers (seeds and stems removed), substitute lime juice for the vinegar, and stir in 1 tablespoon chopped cilantro at the end.

• Stir in ¼ cup homemade mayonnaise (see page 46) in place of the olive oil.

Potato Salad

4 SERVINGS

Yellow potatoes such as Yellow Finn and Yukon Gold have very good flavor and texture for potato salad. Don't use baking potatoes such as russets; they will fall apart.

Cook in salted boiling water until tender (there should be very little or no resistance when poked with a small sharp knife):

> **1½ pounds waxy potatoes (Yellow Finn, Yukon Gold, or red creamers)**

Drain, cool, peel, and cut into bite-size pieces. Place in a mixing bowl.

Cook in simmering water for 9 minutes:

> **2 eggs, at room temperature**

Cool in cold water and peel.

Mix together:

> **1 tablespoon wine, cider, or rice wine vinegar**
> **Salt**
> **Fresh-ground black pepper**

Pour over the potatoes, stir gently, and let sit for 7 minutes or so to allow the potatoes to absorb the vinegar. Add:

> **½ red onion, cut into small dice or very thinly sliced**
> **¼ cup extra-virgin olive oil**

Mix carefully. Taste for salt and vinegar, and add more as needed.

Chop the eggs and gently stir into the potatoes with:

> **1 tablespoon chopped chives**
> **1 tablespoon chopped parsley**

VARIATIONS

◆ Use ⅓ cup homemade mayonnaise (see page 46) instead of the olive oil.
◆ Substitute ¼ cup crème fraîche for the olive oil.
◆ Stir in 2 tablespoons soaked, drained, and chopped capers.

◆ Peel, cut, and dress the potatoes with salt and vinegar while still hot. Sauté 2 or 3 pieces of bacon cut into small pieces. Substitute 1 tablespoon bacon fat for 1 tablespoon of the olive oil. Pour the fat over the potatoes with the herbs and bacon and serve warm. Omit the eggs or serve as a garnish on top.

Carrot Salad

4 SERVINGS

My daughter always loved this salad and I would often make a tiny version for her lunch and change the shapes for variety: grated, thin curls (cut with a peeler), matchsticks, or slices.

Peel and grate:

> **1 pound carrots**

Make the vinaigrette by stirring together in a small bowl:

> **1 teaspoon red wine vinegar**
> **2 teaspoons fresh lemon juice**
> **Salt**
> **Fresh-ground black pepper**

Whisk in:

> **¼ cup olive oil**

Taste and adjust as necessary. Toss the carrots with the dressing and:

> **2 tablespoons chopped parsley**

Let the salad stand for 10 minutes. Taste again and, if needed, add more salt, lemon juice, or oil.

VARIATIONS

◆ Instead of grating the carrots, cut them into a fine julienne or slice them very thin.
◆ Add 2 tablespoons fresh orange juice.

Moroccan Carrot Salad with Ginger

4 SERVINGS

This salad tastes best when the carrots have time to marinate and absorb the flavors of the spices.

Peel and cut into little batons about 2 inches long and ¼ inch square:

4 large carrots

Cook in salted boiling water until almost tender; they should be pliable, but still crisp in the center. Drain and season with:

Salt

In a small bowl, mix together:

½ teaspoon each cumin and coriander, toasted and ground

One 1-inch piece of fresh ginger, peeled and finely grated

A pinch of cayenne

Pour over the warm carrots and toss gently. Marinate for a few hours or in the refrigerator overnight. Just before serving whisk together:

Juice of ½ lime

2 tablespoons extra-virgin olive oil

2 tablespoons chopped cilantro or parsley

Pour over the carrots and toss gently. Taste for seasoning and add salt and lime juice as needed.

VARIATIONS

◆ Garnish with green or black olives.

◆ Use mint instead of cilantro or parsley.

Shaved Fennel Salad

4 SERVINGS

Fennel makes a very delicate salad when sliced paper-thin. It can be difficult to cut the fennel very thin with a knife, so instead I reach for my plastic Japanese mandoline. But watch your fingertips and use the guard!

Trim off the tops and root ends from:

2 fennel bulbs

Save a few feathery leaves for garnish. Pull off and discard any discolored or dehydrated outer layers.

To make the dressing, stir together:

2 tablespoons fresh lemon juice

Grated zest of ¼ lemon

1 teaspoon white wine vinegar

Salt

Fresh-ground black pepper

Whisk in:

3 tablespoons extra-virgin olive oil

Taste and adjust with salt and lemon juice as needed. When ready to serve, thinly slice the fennel crosswise. A small Japanese mandoline makes this job easy and gives pretty results. Toss the fennel with the dressing. Taste and adjust the seasoning if needed. If you like, garnish with:

1 teaspoon chopped fennel tops

VARIATIONS

◆ Parmesan cheese curls, sliced with a vegetable peeler, make a wonderful garnish.

◆ Use Meyer lemons when available and double the amount of zest.

◆ Add 1½ tablespoons chopped green olives to the dressing.

◆ Mix 2 tablespoons parsley leaves in with the fennel.

◆ Sweet peppers, celery, and radishes can be sliced and tossed with the fennel (singly or all together).

Cauliflower Salad with Olives and Capers

4 SERVINGS

This makes an exciting salad for the middle of winter.

Trim the leaves and core from:

1 medium cauliflower

Break apart or cut into small florets. Cook until just done in salted boiling water. Drain and let cool.

Stir together in a large bowl:

Juice of 1 lemon

Salt

Fresh-ground black pepper

Whisk in:

3 tablespoons extra-virgin olive oil

Add the cauliflower and toss with the dressing. Taste and add salt and lemon as needed. Add:

¼ cup olives,

pitted and coarsely chopped

2 tablespoons chopped parsley

1 tablespoon capers,

rinsed and chopped

Toss gently.

VARIATIONS

◆ Leave out the capers and add ¼ cup sliced radishes.

◆ Instead of—or in addition to—parsley, try marjoram, basil, or mint.

Cucumbers with Cream and Mint

4 SERVINGS

There are many varieties of cucumbers, each with its own flavor and texture. I especially like Armenian, Japanese, and lemon cucumbers.

Peel and slice:

2 cucumbers

If the seeds are large and tough, cut the cucumbers in half lengthwise and scoop out the seeds with a spoon before slicing. Place in a medium-size bowl and sprinkle with:

Salt

In another bowl, combine:

¼ cup heavy cream

3 tablespoons olive oil

Juice of ½ lemon

Fresh-ground black pepper

Stir well. If water has accumulated with the cucumbers, drain it off. Pour the dressing over the sliced cucumbers and combine. Coarsely chop:

3 mint sprigs, leaves only

and toss with the cucumbers. Taste and adjust the salt as needed. Serve cool.

VARIATIONS

◆ Add pounded garlic to the dressing.

◆ Serve alongside sliced beets dressed with oil and vinegar.

◆ Grate or dice the cucumbers and serve as a sauce over baked salmon.

◆ Parsley, chervil, basil, or cilantro can be substituted for the mint.

◆ Substitute plain yogurt for the cream.

◆ Add spices such as cumin, coriander, or mustard seeds to the dressing.

Lentil Salad

4 SERVINGS

French green lentils or black Beluga lentils are the best varieties to use for lentil salads because they have lots of flavor and they hold their shape when cooked.

Sort and rinse:
1 cup lentils
Cover with water by 3 inches and bring to a boil. Turn down to a simmer and cook until tender all the way through (adding more water if necessary), about 30 minutes. Drain and reserve ½ cup of the cooking liquid. Toss the lentils with:
1 tablespoon red wine vinegar
Salt
Fresh-ground black pepper
Let sit for 5 minutes. Taste and add more salt and vinegar if needed. Add:
3 tablespoons extra-virgin olive oil
¼ cup thinly sliced scallions or
    3 tablespoons finely diced shallot
3 tablespoons chopped parsley
Stir to combine. If the lentils seem dry and are hard to stir, loosen them with a bit of the reserved cooking liquid.

VARIATIONS
• Add ½ cup diced cucumber.
• Dice very fine ¼ cup each of carrot, celery, and onion. Cook until tender in a couple spoonfuls of olive oil. Cool and stir into the salad in place of the scallions or shallots.
• Garnish with ½ cup crumbled goat or feta cheese.
• Toast and crush ½ teaspoon cumin seeds and add to the salad. Substitute cilantro for the parsley.
• Dice ¼ cup flavorful sweet peppers, season with salt, and let stand to soften. Stir in with the scallions or shallots.

Tabbouleh Salad

4 SERVINGS

Tabbouleh is a Lebanese salad made with bulgur wheat, chopped herbs, and tomatoes. It is a spectacular salad, green and fresh, with more herbs than grain. Bulgur wheat is made from wheat grains that have been parboiled or steamed and then dried. It requires only quick cooking or soaking.

Cover by 1 inch with cold water:
½ cup bulgur wheat
Soak for 20 minutes to plump the grains, then drain in a sieve. While the bulgur is soaking, prepare the other ingredients. Chop:
1½ large bunches of parsley
    (about 1½ cups, chopped)
1 bunch of mint
    (about ⅓ cup, chopped)
1 bunch of scallions, white and green
    parts (about 1 cup, chopped)
Mix the herbs in a large bowl with:
2 ripe medium tomatoes,
    cored and diced small
With your hands, squeeze the soaked bulgur to remove as much water as possible and mix it into the chopped herbs and tomatoes, along with:
Juice of 1 lemon
Salt
¼ cup extra-virgin olive oil
Mix well. Taste and add more salt, lemon juice, or oil if needed. Let rest for about 1 hour before serving to allow the bulgur to absorb the flavors. If you like, serve garnished with romaine leaves to use as scoops for eating the salad.

Soup

Beef Broth 251

New Garlic and Semolina Soup 251

Garlic Broth with Sage and Parsley 252

Tortilla Soup 252

Chicken Noodle Soup 253

Turkey Soup with Kale 254

Curly Kale and Potato Soup 254

Turnip and Turnip Greens Soup 255

Bean and Pasta Soup 256

White Bean and Butternut Squash Soup 257

Spicy Cauliflower Soup 257

Leek and Potato Soup 258

Spring Pea Soup 258

Red Pepper Soup 259

Sweet Corn Soup 259

Spicy Summer Squash Soup with Yogurt and Mint 260

Gazpacho 260

Tomato Soup 261

Onion Panade 262

(CONTINUED)

SEE ALSO

Beef Broth

MAKES ABOUT 3 QUARTS

This is a simple beef broth that's good for moistening beef braises and stews and soups.

Place on a heavy-duty baking sheet or in a roasting pan:

4 pounds beef bones, preferably a mixture of meaty bones and knuckles

Roast in a 400°F oven until brown, about 25 minutes. Turn the bones over, then add to the roasting pan:

1 carrot, peeled and cut into large pieces

1 onion, peeled and cut into large pieces

1 celery stalk, cut into large pieces

Roast for another 25 minutes. Put the bones and vegetables into a large pot with:

A few black peppercorns

3 thyme sprigs

2 tomatoes, quartered (optional)

A few parsley stems

Cover with 1 gallon water. Bring to a boil and turn down to a simmer. Skim off all the foam. Simmer for 6 hours. Check the level of the liquid and add more water if it drops below the level of the bones. Strain and skim the fat. Allow to cool before covering. Store in the refrigerator for up to 1 week or freeze for up to 2 months.

New Garlic and Semolina Soup

MAKES ABOUT 2 QUARTS; 4 TO 6 SERVINGS

Semolina, coarsely ground durum wheat, turns simple, homemade chicken broth into a more substantial, silky textured soup.

In a heavy soup pot, bring to a boil:

2 quarts chicken broth

1 herb bouquet, tied with cotton string (a few sprigs of thyme and parsley, and a bay leaf)

Salt

Stirring constantly with a whisk, sprinkle in:

½ cup semolina

Lower the heat and continue stirring until the semolina is suspended in the broth and no longer settles to the bottom, about 5 minutes. Add:

3 green garlic plants (bulbs and stalks), trimmed of green parts and chopped fine

Cook at a simmer, stirring occasionally with a wooden spoon, for 20 minutes. Discard the herb bouquet, taste for salt, adjust as needed, and serve hot.

VARIATIONS

◆ Add cooked, chopped spinach to the bowl when serving.

◆ Float shavings of Parmesan or pecorino cheese on top of each serving.

◆ Float a little herb butter on top of each serving.

◆ Add 1 cup shelled peas or thinly sliced snap peas after 13 minutes of cooking.

Garlic Broth with Sage and Parsley

This is a time-honored restorative soup made with broth, or even water, infused with the vitality of garlic and herbs. As the saying goes, "Garlic is as good as ten mothers."

Make this soup in the early spring with immature green garlic or later in the spring and early summer when garlic has just been pulled from the ground and the cloves are just set.

Peel and slice fresh garlic:

> **2 to 3 teaspoons sliced green garlic, or 1 or 2 sliced cloves per cup of broth**

Bring some light chicken broth to a boil with a few leaves of fresh sage. Once it comes to a boil use a skimmer to remove the sage leaves (if the sage cooks too long, the broth will become bitter and dark). Add the garlic to the broth along with salt to taste. Cook for about 5 minutes. Drizzle olive oil over a toasted slice of day-old bread, put it in a bowl, ladle soup over the bread, add a pinch of coarsely chopped parsley, and serve. For a heartier soup, poach an egg in the broth and serve it on top of the bread.

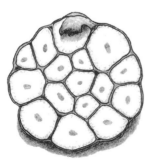

Tortilla Soup

MAKES 2 QUARTS; 4 TO 6 SERVINGS

This is a classic Mexican soup that is brought to the table with a variety of serve-yourself garnishes.

Heat to a simmer:

> **1½ quarts chicken broth**

Add:

> **1 chicken breast half (with skin and bones for best flavor)**

Cook at a bare simmer until the chicken is done, about 20 minutes. Turn off the heat, transfer the breast to a plate, and let cool. Remove and discard the skin and bones and shred the meat.

Into an 8-inch heavy-bottomed skillet over medium-high heat, pour:

> **½ cup peanut or vegetable oil**

Then add:

> **4 corn tortillas, cut into ½-inch strips**

Fry in small batches until golden brown and crispy. Drain on paper towels and season with salt.

In a large heavy pot, heat:

> **2 tablespoons olive oil**

Add:

> **1 Anaheim green pepper, seeded and thinly sliced**
> **½ medium yellow onion, thinly sliced**
> **2 garlic cloves, thinly sliced**
> **Salt**

Cook until soft, about 5 minutes. Pour in the hot broth, then add:

> **2 tomatoes, peeled, seeded, and diced; or 3 small canned whole tomatoes, diced (juice included)**
> **1 dried chipotle chile, seeds removed**
> **Salt**

Bring to a boil and then turn down to a simmer and cook for 30 minutes.

Add the shredded chicken meat and heat through, but do not boil. Taste for salt and adjust as needed.

Serve the soup with the crispy tortilla strips and little bowls of the following garnishes:

½ cup chopped cilantro

6 lime wedges

About 4 ounces crumbled queso fresco or grated Monterey Jack cheese

½ cup peeled and shredded jicama

½ cup julienned radish

1 cubed avocado

VARIATIONS

◆ Add 1½ teaspoons chopped fresh Mexican oregano to the broth.

◆ Pickled jalapeño and red onion are also great garnishes.

◆ Cooked and drained black beans and sautéed chard can be added to make a more substantial soup.

Chicken Noodle Soup

MAKES 1½ QUARTS; 4 SERVINGS

This soup is what I want to eat when I'm feeling under the weather. It is light, clean, and full of flavor.

Combine in a large pot:

1 chicken breast half (with skin and bones for best flavor)

1 quart chicken broth

Bring to a boil and then turn down to a simmer. Skim any foam from the top of the liquid. Add:

½ medium onion, peeled and sliced

½ carrot, peeled and sliced

½ celery stalk, trimmed and sliced

¼ parsnip, peeled and sliced

1 parsley sprig

Cook at a gentle simmer for 40 minutes. Turn the broth off and carefully lift the chicken out of the broth and let cool. Strain the broth through a fine strainer and discard the vegetables. Skim off the fat and add salt to taste.

When the breast is cool, remove the skin and any bones and shred the meat into bite-size pieces. Put the meat into a bowl and cover with a spoonful or two of broth to keep the meat from drying.

Meanwhile bring a pot of salted water to a rapid boil. Add:

1 ounce fettuccine noodles, broken or cut into bite-size pieces

Cook until tender, then drain in a colander and rinse in cold water.

Put in a heavy stockpot:

3 tablespoons diced onions

3 tablespoons diced carrots

3 tablespoons diced celery

2 tablespoons diced parsnip

Salt

Cover with 2 cups of the chicken broth and cook at a gentle simmer until tender, about 15 minutes. Once the vegetables have finished cooking add the remaining broth, the cooked noodles, and the shredded chicken meat. Taste and adjust with salt as needed.

Just before serving, stir in:

1 teaspoon chopped fresh dill

Turkey Soup with Kale

MAKES 3 QUARTS; 6 TO 8 SERVINGS

This is a good soup to make the day after Thanksgiving.

Pick all the meat from:

1 roasted turkey carcass

Coarsely chop the meat and set aside. Break up the carcass and put it in a large stockpot with:

½ onion, peeled
½ carrot, peeled
½ celery stalk
6 thyme sprigs
3 parsley sprigs
1 bay leaf
3 quarts water

Bring to a boil, reduce to a simmer, skim, and cook for 2 hours. Meanwhile, heat, in a large soup pot:

2 tablespoons olive oil

Add and cook, over medium heat, until very tender:

1½ onions, peeled and diced
1½ carrots, peeled and diced
1½ celery stalks, diced
Salt

Bring a pot of salted water to a boil and add:

1 bunch of kale, leaves torn from the stems and coarsely chopped

Cook until tender, about 5 to 10 minutes. Drain and set aside. Put a colander over the pot of diced vegetables and strain the turkey broth through it directly into the soup pot. Simmer for 10 minutes or so, add the turkey meat and kale, taste for seasoning and adjust if necessary, and serve hot.

VARIATIONS

◆ Sautéed mushrooms (especially porcini) added just before serving give a luxurious flavor and texture to this humble soup.

◆ Some of the kale can be sautéed with garlic and dried chile flakes and floated atop the soup on a slice of toasted bread.

◆ Add cooked rice or pasta just before serving.

◆ Fry a little diced pancetta in the soup pot before adding the diced vegetables.

Curly Kale and Potato Soup

MAKES 2 QUARTS; 4 TO 6 SERVINGS

Remove the tough stems from the leaves of:

1 large bunch of kale, curly or Russian

Wash, drain well, and coarsely chop.
Heat in a heavy soup pot:

¼ cup extra-virgin olive oil

Add:

2 onions, sliced thin

Cook over medium heat, stirring occasionally, until soft, tender, and slightly browned, about 12 minutes.

While the onions are cooking, peel, cut in half, and cut into ¼-inch-thick slices:

1 pound potatoes
(Yellow Finn or Yukon Gold)

When the onions are cooked, stir in:

4 garlic cloves, chopped

Cook the garlic for a couple of minutes, then add the potatoes and chopped kale. Stir, then add:

A large pinch of salt

Cook for 5 minutes, stirring occasionally. Pour in:

6 cups chicken broth

Raise the heat, bring to a boil, then immediately reduce the heat to a simmer and cook for 30 minutes, or until the kale and potatoes are tender. Taste the soup and add more salt if necessary. Serve hot and garnish each serving with:

Extra-virgin olive oil
**Parmesan or other hard cheese,
  freshly grated**

VARIATIONS

◆ Slice ½ pound linguiça, chorizo, or a spicy garlic sausage. Brown in the oil before adding the onions; remove when brown. Add to the soup with the kale.

◆ Garnish with croutons. Cut bread into ½-inch cubes, toss with olive oil and salt, and bake until golden in a 350°F oven, about 12 minutes.

◆ Add 1½ cups cooked white beans 10 minutes before the soup is finished.

Turnip and Turnip Greens Soup

MAKES 2 QUARTS; 4 TO 6 SERVINGS

Young turnips with their greens are in the markets in spring and fall. The two together make a delicious soup or side dish.

Remove the greens from:
  **2 bunches of young turnips with
    greens**
Trim and discard the stems from the greens. Wash and drain the greens and cut them into ½-inch strips.

  Trim the roots from the turnips. If needed peel the turnips (taste one to judge if the skins are tough), and slice thin.
Warm in a heavy pot over medium heat:
  3 tablespoons butter or olive oil
Add:
  1 onion, sliced thin
Cook until soft, about 12 minutes. Add the sliced turnips with:
  1 bay leaf
  2 thyme sprigs
  Salt
Cook for 5 minutes or so, stirring occasionally. Cover with:
  6 cups chicken broth
Bring to a boil, then turn the soup down to a simmer and cook for 10 minutes. Add the turnip greens and cook for another 10 minutes or until the greens are tender. Taste for salt and add more as needed.

VARIATIONS

◆ Add a small piece of prosciutto or smoked bacon with the sliced turnips and herbs.

◆ Garnish the soup with grated Parmesan.

◆ Cook the soup in water instead of broth and stir in a couple tablespoons of butter or olive oil at the end for richness.

Bean and Pasta Soup

MAKES 2 QUARTS; 4 TO 6 SERVINGS

Italy's national dish, *pasta e fagioli,* is easy to make and is a wonderful way to serve fresh shell beans (see page 76). Most any kind of fresh shell bean will do, but cranberry and cannellini beans are traditional choices.

Shell:

2 pounds fresh shell beans

Put the shelled beans in a pot and cover with water to a depth of 1½ inches. Bring to a boil, turn down to a simmer, and cook the beans until soft but not falling apart. Start checking after 20 minutes. When soft, season to taste with:

Salt

While the beans are cooking, heat in a heavy-bottomed soup pot:

⅓ cup olive oil

Add:

⅓ cup finely diced onion
¼ cup finely diced carrot
¼ cup finely diced celery
A pinch of dried chile flakes
**2 teaspoons coarsely chopped fresh
    sage leaves**

Cook until soft over medium heat, stirring occasionally, about 12 minutes. Add:

4 garlic cloves, coarsely chopped
Salt

Cook for a few minutes, then add:

**1 pound ripe tomatoes, peeled,
    seeded, and diced or one 12-ounce
    can whole tomatoes, drained and
    chopped**

Cook for another 5 minutes, then add the beans with just enough bean liquid to cover. Cook over low heat, stirring now and then, until the beans are very tender, about 15 minutes.

Meanwhile, cook until tender in abundant boiling salted water:

**¼ pound pasta (broken noodles or
    small shapes)**

Remove one third of the beans and mash them or purée them in a food mill. Stir the cooked and drained pasta and the puréed beans into the soup and cook for 5 minutes. Thin the soup with bean liquid as needed. Check for salt and add more as needed. Serve garnished with:

Extra-virgin olive oil
Parmesan cheese, grated

VARIATION

◆ Use 1 cup dried beans, cooked (see page 78), instead of fresh shell beans.

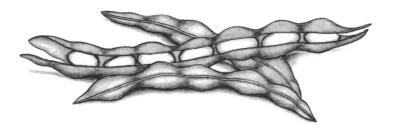

White Bean and Butternut Squash Soup

MAKES 2 QUARTS; 4 TO 6 SERVINGS

Soak in 4 cups water overnight:

**1 cup dried white beans
(such as cannellini, haricot blanc,
or navy beans)**

Drain and put in a large pot with:

**3 cups chicken broth
4 cups water**

Bring to a boil, then lower the heat, and simmer until the beans are tender. Start checking after 45 minutes. Season to taste when cooked.

Heat in a heavy-bottomed pot:

2 tablespoons olive oil or duck fat

Add:

**2 onions, sliced thin
3 or 4 sage leaves
1 bay leaf**

Cook over medium heat until tender, about 15 minutes. Stir in:

**1 medium butternut squash,
peeled and cut into ½-inch cubes
Salt**

Cook for 5 minutes. Drain the beans and add 6 cups of their cooking liquid to the squash and onions. Cook at a simmer until the squash starts to become tender. Add the beans and keep cooking until the squash is very soft. Taste and adjust the seasoning if necessary.

VARIATIONS

• Serve hot soup over thickly sliced country-style or levain bread that has been brushed with duck fat or olive oil and toasted until crisp and golden brown.
• Use other varieties of winter squash: Delicata, acorn, kabocha, French pumpkin.

Spicy Cauliflower Soup

MAKES 2 QUARTS; 4 TO 6 SERVINGS

This is an unusually spicy and full-flavored soup; if necessary, adjust the pungent spices to your comfort level.

Heat, in a heavy-bottomed soup pot:

¼ cup olive oil

Add and cook, stirring often, over medium heat:

**1 onion, peeled and diced
1 carrot, peeled and diced
1 teaspoon coriander seeds, crushed
1 teaspoon cumin seeds, crushed
1 teaspoon chile powder
¼ teaspoon turmeric
¼ teaspoon dried chile flakes
Salt
Fresh-ground black pepper**

When very soft but not browned, add:

**6 cilantro sprigs, coarsely chopped
1 large head of cauliflower, trimmed of
green leaves and coarsely chopped
(about 6 cups)
3 cups chicken broth
3 cups water**

Raise the heat and bring to a boil, stirring occasionally. Reduce the heat to a simmer and cook until the cauliflower is very tender, about 30 minutes. Stir vigorously with a spoon or whisk to coarsely purée the soup. You may need to add more broth or water to thin the soup if it is too thick. Taste, adjust the seasoning if necessary, and serve hot. Garnish each serving with:

**Yogurt
Chopped cilantro or mint
A squeeze of lime juice**

VARIATIONS

• For a richer soup, use all chicken broth. For a lighter, vegetarian soup, use all water.

Leek and Potato Soup

MAKES 2 QUARTS; 4 TO 6 SERVINGS

Trim off the root end and the tough upper greens from:

2 pounds leeks

Cut the trimmed leeks in half lengthwise and slice thin. Rinse in a bowl of cold water. Lift the leeks out of the water to drain.

Melt over medium heat in a heavy-bottomed pot:

3 tablespoons butter

Add the leeks along with:

2 thyme sprigs
1 bay leaf
Salt

Cook until soft, about 10 minutes. Add:

1 pound yellow potatoes, peeled,
halved or quartered, and sliced

Cook the potatoes for 4 minutes, then add:

6 cups water

Bring to a boil and turn down to a simmer. Cook until the vegetables are tender, but not falling apart, about 30 minutes. When done, stir in:

⅓ cup crème fraîche or heavy cream

Do not boil once the cream is added. Check the seasoning and adjust to taste. Remove the bay leaf and thyme before serving.

VARIATIONS

• Garnish with fresh-ground black pepper and some chopped chives.

• For a heartier soup, use broth instead of water.

• Remove the bay leaf and the herb sprigs and purée the soup before stirring in the cream.

• Omit the cream, purée the soup before serving, and garnish with a pat of parsley butter (see page 48).

Spring Pea Soup

MAKES ABOUT 2 QUARTS; 4 TO 6 SERVINGS

This is one of the soups that I think are best made with water rather than broth, so nothing interferes with the sweet, delicate flavor of the peas.

Heat, in a heavy-bottomed soup pot:

3 tablespoons butter

Add and cook over medium heat, stirring often:

1 large onion, sliced thin
Salt

When very soft but not browned, pour in and bring to a boil:

5 cups water

When the water boils, add:

3 cups shelled very fresh sweet peas
(about 2 pounds)

Cook at a simmer, stirring occasionally, until the peas are tender, about 5 minutes. Purée the soup in batches in a blender. Fill the blender only one third of the way up and pulse to get started to avoid hot soup splashing out of the top. Taste, adjust seasoning, and serve. If you are not going to serve the soup right away, pour the puréed soup into a bowl set over an ice bath to chill it quickly and preserve the bright green color. Stir frequently and carefully when reheating to avoid scorching.

VARIATIONS

• Pass the purée through a sieve or food mill for a smooth texture.

• Spring Pea Soup can be served hot or cold, and with a variety of garnishes: crème fraîche or yogurt and mint; buttery croutons; and herbs such as chervil, tarragon, or chives.

Red Pepper Soup

MAKES 2 QUARTS; 4 TO 6 SERVINGS

Yellow bell peppers also work very well in this soup, but green peppers are not sweet enough. You can even make two batches of soup, one red, one yellow, and ladle them into bowls for a yin-and-yang effect.

Heat, in a heavy-bottomed soup pot:
  1 tablespoon olive oil
Add and cook, stirring often, over medium heat:
  1 large onion, sliced fine
  2 red bell peppers, cut in half, seeds
    and veins removed, and sliced fine
  Salt
When very soft but not browned, add:
  2 garlic cloves, peeled and chopped
  6 thyme sprigs, leaves only
Cook for 4 minutes more, then add:
  ¼ cup short-grain rice
  4 cups chicken broth
  2 cups water
  1 teaspoon red wine vinegar
Raise the heat and bring to a boil, stirring occasionally. Reduce the heat to a simmer and cook until the rice is tender, about 20 minutes. Allow to cool slightly, and then purée in a blender until very smooth and velvety. Thin the soup with broth or water if it is too thick. Taste for seasoning, adjust as needed, and serve hot.

VARIATIONS
◆ Add some fresh or dried hot chiles to the soup.
◆ Garnish bowls of the pepper soup with crème fraîche and chopped herbs such as chives, basil, or parsley.
◆ Cut the peppers into medium dice, omit the rice, and use all chicken broth. Serve without puréeing.

Sweet Corn Soup

MAKES 1½ QUARTS; 4 SERVINGS

This is a no-fail soup as long as you have fresh sweet corn. I make it all summer and vary it with different garnishes through the season.

Melt in a heavy-bottomed pot over medium heat:
  4 tablespoons (½ stick) butter
Add:
  1 onion, diced
Cook until soft, without browning, about 15 minutes. Season with:
  Salt
Meanwhile, shuck:
  5 ears corn
Cut the kernels from the cobs. Add the kernels to the cooked onions and cook for 2 to 3 minutes. Cover with:
  1 quart water
Bring to a boil. Immediately lower the heat to a simmer and cook until the corn is just done, about 5 minutes. Remove from the heat and purée in small batches in a blender. (Be careful when blending hot soup in a jug blender and always make sure there is an air vent to allow the steam to escape.) Strain the soup through a medium-mesh strainer to remove any tough skins. Taste and adjust for salt as needed.

VARIATIONS
◆ Garnish with crème fraîche seasoned with chopped savory, salt, and pepper.
◆ Garnish with chopped nasturtium petals or nasturtium butter (chopped nasturtium petals worked into soft butter seasoned with salt and pepper).
◆ Garnish with a purée of roasted sweet or chile pepper enriched with butter or cream.

Spicy Summer Squash Soup with Yogurt and Mint

MAKES ABOUT 2 QUARTS; 4 TO 6 SERVINGS

Heat, in a heavy-bottomed soup pot:

¼ cup olive oil

Add and cook, stirring often, over medium heat:

1 large onion, sliced fine
A pinch of saffron threads
1 teaspoon cumin seeds
1 teaspoon coriander seeds
¼ teaspoon turmeric
1 teaspoon sweet paprika
½ teaspoon cayenne pepper
2 garlic cloves, peeled and sliced

Cook until very soft but not browned. If the onions or garlic start to stick, turn down the heat, and add a splash of water to the pot.

While the onions are cooking, wash in cold water:

5 medium green or yellow summer squash

Cut into thick (¾-inch) slices. When the onions are done, add the squash to the pot with:

Salt

Cook for 2 minutes, then pour in:

3 cups chicken broth
3 cups water

Bring to a boil, reduce to a simmer, and cook until the squash is tender, about 15 minutes. Meanwhile, make the yogurt and mint garnish. Cut into julienne:

4 mint sprigs, leaves only

In a medium-size mortar, pound half of the julienned mint to a paste. Stir in the remaining mint and:

2 tablespoons olive oil
⅔ cup yogurt
Salt

Let the soup cool a bit, then purée in a blender until very smooth. (Take care when blending hot soup to leave a vent for the steam to escape.) Reheat, thin with a little water if necessary, taste, adjust the seasoning, and serve hot with a spoonful of yogurt and mint. Pass around:

Lime wedges

at the table, if you want.

Gazpacho

MAKES ABOUT 3 QUARTS; 6 TO 8 SERVINGS

This is not a particularly traditional version of this recipe, but if you have ripe delicious tomatoes, it makes a beautiful piquant summer soup—a sort of liquid salad—that's worth all the grating, pounding, and dicing. For a light summer meal, add a few shrimp—or other fish or shellfish—to the soup.

Soak in a bowl of hot water for 15 minutes:

1 dried ancho chile

Drain and crush to a paste with a medium-size mortar and pestle. Remove and set aside.

In another bowl, soak in cold water for 2 minutes:

2 cups crustless cubes of day-old country-style white bread

Drain and squeeze out the excess water.

In the mortar and pestle, pound together into a paste:

2 garlic cloves
A pinch of salt

Add the soaked bread, pound until smooth, and set aside.

Cut in half horizontally:

5 pounds ripe tomatoes

Over a bowl, grate the cut sides of the tomatoes on the medium holes of a box grater until only the skin is left. Discard the skins. Pass the pulp through a strainer to remove seeds, if you like. Stir the chile purée and the bread paste into the tomato pulp in a large bowl. Add:

¼ cup extra-virgin olive oil
Salt

Refrigerate until well chilled. To speed this up you can set the bowl in another, larger bowl filled with ice. Taste for seasoning before serving and add more salt if needed.

Make a relish to garnish the soup. Mix together:

½ pound cherry tomatoes, halved
1 cucumber, peeled and diced
1 yellow bell pepper, seeded and diced
½ red onion, diced
A handful each of chopped chervil and basil
2 tablespoons red wine vinegar
¼ cup extra-virgin olive oil
Salt
Fresh-ground black pepper

Divide the chilled soup among 6 to 8 bowls and add a generous spoonful of relish to each bowl.

Tomato Soup

MAKES ABOUT 1½ QUARTS; 4 SERVINGS

This is a soup for the height of summer, when tomatoes are abundant and perfectly ripe.

Warm a heavy-bottomed pan. Add:

2 tablespoons olive oil
1 tablespoon butter
1 medium onion, sliced
1 small leek, white and light green parts, sliced
A pinch of salt

Cover and cook until soft but not brown. Add water to keep from browning if necessary. Add:

2 garlic cloves, peeled and sliced

Cook for about 2 minutes, then add:

2 pounds ripe tomatoes (about 10 medium tomatoes), washed, cored, and sliced
1 scant tablespoon white rice
A large pinch of salt
½ bay leaf
1 small sprig of savory, thyme, or basil

Cook over medium heat, stirring occasionally, until the tomatoes fall apart. Add:

1 cup water
1 tablespoon butter

Continue cooking for another 10 minutes, until the rice is tender. Remove the herb sprig. Carefully ladle the soup into a blender not more than one-third full. Blend until smooth, about 1 minute. Pass the puréed soup through a medium strainer to remove skins and seeds. Taste for salt. Add more water if the soup is too thick.

VARIATIONS

◆ Omit the rice for a thinner soup.
◆ Garnish the soup with crème fraîche and mint, or with buttered croutons, or with torn basil or finely cut chives and olive oil.

Onion Panade

4 SERVINGS

A panade is a thick soup made of layers of bread, vegetables, and cheese moistened with broth or water and baked until soft and golden. This onion panade is a hearty, homey soup bursting with sweet onion flavor.

Peel and slice thin:
> **1½ pounds onions
> (about 4 cups, sliced)**

Heat in a heavy-bottomed pan:
> **¼ cup butter or olive oil**

Add the onions with:
> **2 or 3 thyme sprigs**

Cook over medium-low heat until quite soft, about 30 minutes. Turn the heat up slightly and cook the onions, stirring occasionally, until a medium golden brown, about 15 minutes.

Add to taste:
> **Salt**

While the onions are cooking, cut into thin slices:
> **⅓ loaf day-old country-style bread**

Place the slices on a baking sheet in a 350°F oven until dry but not brown, about 5 minutes.

Grate and mix together:
> **⅓ cup Parmesan cheese
> ¼ cup Gruyère cheese**

Assemble the soup: Make a layer of bread slices in the bottom of a 1½-quart baking dish. Spread half the onions onto the bread slices and sprinkle with about one third of the cheese. Make another layer of bread slices and cover with the rest of the onions and another third of the cheese. Make a final layer of bread slices and sprinkle with the remaining cheese.

Heat:
> **3 to 4 cups beef broth or chicken broth**

Pour the broth into the dish, pouring carefully down the side of the dish so as not to disturb the layers, until the top layer of bread starts to float. Dot the top with:
> **2 tablespoons butter**

Cover and bake in a 350°F oven for 45 minutes, then uncover the dish and bake for another 20 to 30 minutes, or until the top is golden brown and crisp.

VARIATIONS

⁕ Peel and seed 1 small butternut or 2 Delicata squash and slice thin. Layer the slices between the bread.

⁕ Add a few chopped dried mushrooms to the hot broth.

⁕ For a simple onion soup, add the broth to the browned onions and simmer for 15 minutes. Taste and adjust the seasoning. If you like, garnish with buttery croutons and grated Gruyère cheese.

Pasta

Pasta with Tomato Sauce

Pasta with tomato sauce is another standby. Tomato sauces range from those made simply, with raw tomatoes, to those flavored variously with bacon, capers, anchovies, or chiles and herbs. What is most important is to use flavorful (organic) tomatoes. Fresh tomatoes should be ripe and juicy with real flavor. If not, canned whole tomatoes are a better choice.

Most of the recipes for tomato sauce that follow call for tomatoes that have been peeled and seeded. To do this, plunge cored tomatoes into boiling water until their skins are loose, anywhere from 15 seconds to a minute. Lift the tomatoes out of the hot water and plunge them into a bowl of ice-cold water to stop the cooking. Drain and peel. Cut the tomatoes in half horizontally and coax the seeds out into a bowl. Strain the seeds and save the juice.

To cook 1 pound of pasta, which will make 6 servings or 4 generous servings, bring at least 4 quarts well-salted water to a boil. Cook the pasta at a rapid boil until tender. When done, drain it, reserving a small amount (about ½ cup) of the cooking water. Toss the pasta with 2 cups warm tomato sauce. Add a touch of the cooking water if the noodles seem to be sticking together or the sauce is too thick. Taste and add salt if needed. Plate the pasta and garnish with grated cheese and chopped herbs, if desired. Another way to serve the pasta is to toss the noodles with olive oil and grated cheese, plate them, and then spoon the sauce over the noodles.

Simple Tomato Sauce

MAKES ABOUT 2 CUPS

This can be used only as a fresh sauce for pasta, but also as an element in many different dishes. When tomatoes are abundant, this is a good sauce to make in quantity and freeze or can. If you are going to pass the sauce through a food mill, there's no need to peel and seed the tomatoes beforehand. The food mill will strain out all the skins and seeds.

Peel, seed, and dice (see left):
  2 pounds ripe tomatoes
Save the juice, strain out the seeds, and add the juice to the diced tomatoes.
Peel:
  5 large garlic cloves
Smash them and chop coarse.

Put a heavy-bottomed pot over medium heat and when hot, pour in:
  ¼ cup extra-virgin olive oil
Add the garlic and when it starts to sizzle, immediately add the tomatoes and their juice with a large pinch of:
  Salt
Cook at a simmer for 15 minutes. For a smooth sauce, pass through a food mill.

VARIATIONS

◆ Add a handful of chopped parsley, marjoram, or oregano or a chiffonade of basil leaves to the sauce a couple of minutes before it is done.

◆ Sauté 1 small diced onion in the oil before adding the garlic.

◆ When tomatoes are out of season, use canned tomatoes: Drain, saving the juice, one 28-ounce can whole peeled tomatoes. Chop the tomatoes coarse and cook them with their juice.

◆ Add a whole dried chile or a pinch of dried chile flakes for spice.

Raw Tomato Sauce

MAKES ABOUT 2 CUPS

This recipe is only for tomatoes that are at their absolute peak: dead ripe and full of flavor.

Core and cut into medium dice:

2 pounds ripe tomatoes

Put them in a bowl and toss them with:

Salt
¼ cup torn basil leaves
⅓ cup extra-virgin olive oil

Cover the bowl tightly and set aside for at least 1 hour before tossing with hot fresh-cooked, drained pasta.

VARIATIONS

• Add a pinch of dried chile flakes for spice.
◆ For a more refined sauce, peel and seed the tomatoes before dicing them. Strain the seeds out of the juice and pour it into the bowl with the diced tomato.

Tomato Sauce with Bacon and Onion

MAKES ABOUT 2 CUPS

Bucatini is the classic pasta for this sauce.

Into a heavy pan over medium heat, pour:

2 tablespoons olive oil

Add:

3 slices bacon (or pancetta),
cut into ¼-inch pieces

Cook until the fat is rendered and the meat is lightly browned. Remove the meat and set aside. Add to the fat left in the pan:

1 large onion, peeled and sliced thin

Cook, stirring now and then, until soft, about 10 minutes. Add:

6 ripe medium tomatoes,
peeled, seeded, and chopped, or
8 canned whole tomatoes, drained
and chopped
Salt

Cook for 10 minutes over low heat. Add the reserved bacon and cook for another 2 or 3 minutes. Taste for salt and adjust as needed.

VARIATIONS

◆ Instead of tomatoes, use 1½ cups Simple Tomato Sauce (opposite) and cook for only 4 minutes.
◆ After the onions have cooked, pour in ⅓ cup white wine, and reduce over medium heat until the liquid has almost completely evaporated. Add the tomatoes and proceed with the rest of the recipe.
◆ When the sauce is nearly done, stir in a small handful of chopped parsley or a chiffonade of basil leaves.

Spicy Tomato Sauce with Capers, Anchovies, and Olives

MAKES ABOUT 2 CUPS

This is the sauce you need to make pasta alla puttanesca, a specialty of Naples.

Into a heavy saucepan over medium heat, pour:

⅓ cup olive oil

Add:

6 garlic cloves, chopped

When they start to sizzle add:

1 cup Simple Tomato Sauce (page 264)

3 tablespoons capers, rinsed, drained, and chopped

¼ cup pitted black olives, chopped

¼ teaspoon (or more) dried chile flakes

¼ cup chopped parsley

Cook for 5 minutes and add:

3 salt-packed anchovies, soaked, filleted, and chopped

Cook for a minute or two. Taste for salt and adjust as needed.

Fusilli with Tomato Sauce, Eggplant, and Ricotta Salata

4 SERVINGS

Trim and cut into thin slices:

1 pound Japanese or other small eggplant

Salt and let drain for 15 minutes. Heat in a heavy pan:

½ cup olive oil

Pat the eggplant dry and fry until golden brown in the hot oil. Drain and season with:

Salt

In a large saucepan, heat together:

2 cups Simple Tomato Sauce (page 264)

¼ cup basil chiffonade

Cook in abundant salted boiling water:

¾ pound fusilli

Drain, reserving ½ cup water, and toss with the tomato sauce and the fried eggplant. Taste for salt and thin with pasta water as needed. Serve, garnished with:

¼ pound grated ricotta salata or pecorino cheese

Pappardelle with Bolognese Sauce

4 SERVINGS

The wide, hand-cut fresh egg noodles called pappardelle are classically sauced with ragùs and hearty sauces like this one.

Roll out, not too thin:

1 recipe Fresh Pasta (page 89)

Cut into ¾-inch-wide noodles. Toss the noodles with extra flour and lay them out on a plate or baking sheet, cover them with a towel, and refrigerate until ready to use.

Bring a large pot of salted water to a boil.

Grate:

2 to 3 ounces Parmesan (about ½ cup)

In a small saucepan over low heat, warm:

2 cups Bolognese Sauce (page 227)

Cook the noodles in the boiling water for 3 or 4 minutes, until al dente. While the noodles are cooking, melt in a large sauté pan:

2 to 3 tablespoons butter

Turn off the heat. Drain the noodles, reserving a small amount of the hot pasta water. Put the noodles into the warm pan with the butter and toss with two thirds of the grated cheese and:

Salt

Moisten with a bit of the pasta water if needed. Divide the noodles among 4 pasta bowls or place on a warm platter. Spoon the sauce over the noodles. Sprinkle with the rest of the cheese and:

1 tablespoon chopped parsley

Serve immediately.

VARIATIONS

• Add about half the Bolognese sauce when you toss the noodles with the butter and two thirds of the cheese, and spoon over the rest when you plate the noodles, as above.

• For the Bolognese sauce, substitute Mushroom Ragù (page 228).

Fusilli with Greens and Sausage

4 SERVINGS

I love the flavors of spicy garlicky sausage together with nutty greens such as broccoli rabe. Besides fusilli noodles, penne rigate, orecchiette, or any other large toothy pasta shape is good for this sauce.

Trim and wash:

1 large bunch of broccoli rabe, chard, or kale

Chop coarse and cook until tender in salted boiling water. Drain well, saving the cooking water to cook the pasta in, if you like. Form into small balls:

½ pound Fennel Sausage (page 358), or ½ pound Italian sausage, casings removed

Heat in a heavy-bottomed pan:

2 tablespoons olive oil

Add the sausage and cook over medium heat until browned and cooked through, about 6 to 8 minutes. Remove the sausage and add to the pan:

1 large onion, sliced thin

Sauté, tossing now and then, over medium-high heat until the onions soften and caramelize a bit. Season with:

Salt

Fresh-ground black pepper

A pinch of dried chile flakes

Add the cooked greens and sausage and cook for a few minutes, tossing and stirring. Taste for salt and adjust as needed.

Bring a large pot of salted water to a boil. Add:

¾ pound fusilli, orecchiette, or penne rigate

Cook al dente, then drain and return to the pan. Toss the pasta with a bit of salt and:

Extra-virgin olive oil

Plate and top with the sauce, drizzle with olive oil, and sprinkle with:

½ cup grated pecorino or Parmesan cheese

Serve immediately.

VARIATIONS

• Omit the sausage and increase the amount of olive oil the onions are cooked in.

• Instead of cooking the greens in boiling water, add them to the onions with a bit of water and cook until tender.

Pasta al Pesto

4 SERVINGS

The trick to saucing pasta with pesto is to loosen the noodles with hot pasta water. It makes all the difference.

Cook in abundant salted boiling water:

¾ pound dry pasta (linguine, spaghettini, fedelini, trofie), or Fresh Pasta (page 89)

Cook al dente. Drain, reserving 1 cup of the cooking water.

Return the pasta to the pot or place in a large warm bowl and toss with:

1½ cups Pesto (page 230)
Salt

Mix about ½ cup of the reserved hot pasta water into the noodles. Taste and add more salt or water if needed. Plate and garnish with:

Freshly grated Parmesan cheese

Serve immediately.

VARIATIONS

◆ Place a layer of sliced, salted, ripe tomatoes on the plate before plating the pasta.
◆ Trim ½ pound green beans. Cook separately in salted boiling water and add to the boiling pasta for the last minute, to reheat; toss the noodles and beans with the pesto sauce.
◆ Peel and cut ½ pound potatoes into small cubes. Cook separately. Heat the cooked potatoes in the pasta water in the last minute the pasta is cooking. Toss with the noodles and pesto.

Linguine with Clams

4 SERVINGS

This pasta works well with little clams in their shells or with large clams steamed open, removed from their shells, and chopped.

Wash well under cold water:

2 pounds small clams

If they are sandy, soak them in abundant cold water for 30 minutes. Drain well.

Heat a large pot of salted water to a boil. Heat in a heavy-bottomed pan:

1 tablespoon extra-virgin olive oil

When hot, add the clams and:

5 garlic cloves, chopped fine
A large pinch of dried chile flakes
½ cup white wine

Cover and cook over medium-high until the clams open, about 6 or 7 minutes. Meanwhile cook al dente, in the salted boiling water:

¾ pound linguine

When the clams have opened, stir in:

1 tablespoon chopped parsley
3 tablespoons extra-virgin olive oil

Drain the noodles well, toss with the clam sauce and more salt, if needed, and serve.

VARIATIONS

◆ Use mussels instead of clams.
◆ Before you add the clams to the pot, add 1 medium fennel bulb, trimmed and chopped fine. Cook over medium heat until almost soft, about 5 minutes, and add the clams and herbs as above, but omit the wine and add ½ cup Simple Tomato Sauce (page 264).
◆ If using larger clams, steam them open and remove them from their shells. Chop the clams and return them with their liquor to the sauce with the parsley.

Spicy Squid Spaghettini

4 SERVINGS

Trim and clean (see page 344):

1½ pounds squid

Reserve the tentacles and cut the bodies into ¼-inch rings. Season both with:

Salt

Fresh-ground black pepper

Bring a large pot of salted water to a boil. Add:

¾ pound spaghettini

Cook al dente. A few minutes before the pasta is done, put a large heavy pan over medium-high heat. When the pan is hot, pour in:

2 tablespoons olive oil

Add the tentacles, toss, and cook for 30 seconds. Turn up the heat and add the rings. Continue to cook, tossing now and then, for another 2 minutes. Then add:

3 garlic cloves, minced

¼ teaspoon dried chile flakes

2 tablespoons chopped parsley or basil

2 tablespoons extra-virgin olive oil

Remove the pan from the heat and add:

A squeeze of lemon juice

Taste for salt and lemon and adjust as needed.

When the pasta is done, drain, reserving some of the water. Toss the pasta with salt, olive oil, and the squid, and add pasta water as needed to loosen the pasta.

VARIATIONS

• Garnish with ½ cup toasted breadcrumbs.

• Add 1 tablespoon chopped capers with the dried chile flakes and garlic.

• Sauté a sliced onion in olive oil until soft. Season with salt and add to the squid with the dried chile flakes and garlic.

• Garnish with a drizzle of Aïoli (page 47) thinned with a bit of water.

• Serve the sautéed squid without the pasta as an hors d'oeuvre.

Fedelini with Summer Squash, Walnuts, and Herbs

4 SERVINGS

Any variety or combination of summer squash will do for this recipe. Use more than one color for a more vibrant dish.

Preheat the oven to 350°F and lightly toast:

¼ cup walnuts

for 8 to 10 minutes. Let cool and coarsely chop.

Trim the ends from:

1 pound summer squash

Cut into julienne with a knife or mandoline. Heat in a heavy pan:

2 tablespoons olive oil

Add the julienned squash and sauté over medium-high, tossing the squash in the pan, until tender and lightly browned. Season with:

Salt

Fresh-ground black pepper

**3 tablespoons chopped marjoram,
    basil, or parsley**

Cook in abundant salted boiling water:

¾ pound fedelini

Drain, reserving some of the cooking water. Toss the noodles with the seasoned squash, a splash of the cooking water, and:

Toasted walnuts or pine nuts

Taste and correct the seasoning, and add more pasta water if needed. Plate and garnish, if desired, with:

Freshly grated Parmesan cheese

VARIATION

• Instead of the herbs, stir in a couple tablespoons of pesto.

Spinach Lasagna

8 SERVINGS

The difference between good lasagna and divine lasagna is making it with silky, fresh pasta.

Prepare:

1 recipe Fresh Pasta (page 89)
2 cups Simple Tomato Sauce (page 264)
1½ cups White Sauce (Béchamel Sauce; page 225)

Remove the large stems from:

1 bunch of spinach (about ½ pound)

Wash well and drain.

Pour into a skillet over medium heat:

1 teaspoon olive oil

Add the spinach and season with:

Salt

Cook until almost wilted. Add:

1 garlic clove, peeled and chopped fine

Cook for a minute or two more. Set aside to cool. Gather the spinach into a ball, squeeze to remove excess moisture, and chop fine. Mix with:

½ pound ricotta cheese
1 tablespoon olive oil
Salt

In a bowl combine the white sauce with:

¼ cup freshly grated Parmesan cheese
A pinch of grated nutmeg
Salt

Roll out the pasta into 5- to 6-inch-long sheets. Cook al dente in abundant salted boiling water. Drain, rinse under cold water, drain again, and put in a bowl. To prevent the lasagne from sticking to one another, lightly coat them with:

1 tablespoon olive oil

Oil a 10- by 12-inch baking dish, and begin to assemble the lasagna. Spread a few spoonfuls of the white sauce on the bottom of the dish. Lay out a single layer of pasta, trimming as needed to fit the dish, and spread with a third of the ricotta mixture. Add another layer of pasta and spoon in half of the tomato sauce. Add another layer of pasta and pour over half the white sauce and top with another layer of pasta. Repeat until you have 7 pasta layers—3 with ricotta, 2 with tomato sauce, and 2 with white sauce—and end with a final top layer of pasta. Drizzle olive oil over the top, cover with foil, and bake in a 400°F oven for 20 minutes. Remove the foil and sprinkle with:

2 tablespoons freshly grated Parmesan cheese

Bake for 10 to 15 minutes more, until bubbling and golden brown. Remove from the oven and allow to rest for 5 minutes before serving. Lasagna can be assembled ahead of time and baked later. Take it out of the refrigerator an hour before baking.

VARIATIONS

◆ Substitute Bolognese Sauce (page 227) or Mushroom Ragù (page 228) for the tomato sauce.

◆ For the spinach, substitute other greens, such as chard, escarole, or rocket.

◆ Add sliced mozzarella to the ricotta layers.

◆ In summer, substitute slices of ripe tomatoes for the tomato sauce. Stir pesto instead of spinach into the ricotta.

◆ A simpler lasagna-like baked pasta can be made by cutting the pasta into big squares and cooking as above. Spoon some tomato sauce on the bottom of a baking dish, place a square of pasta on the sauce, add some ricotta and Parmesan cheese, and fold the pasta over to form a triangle shape. Repeat with more squares of pasta, overlapping the triangles; top with more sauce; sprinkle generously with Parmesan; and bake for 15 to 20 minutes in a 450°F oven until bubbly and crisp at the edges.

Ricotta and Herb Ravioli

4 SERVINGS

This recipe is for a simple filling that works equally well as a stuffing for cannelloni or squash blossoms. The stuffed blossoms can be poached or baked.

In a bowl mix together:
> **1 cup ricotta cheese**
> **2 garlic cloves, chopped fine**
> **1 tablespoon extra-virgin olive oil or softened butter**
> **1 egg**
> **⅓ cup freshly grated Parmesan cheese**
> **2 tablespoons mixed chopped herbs such as marjoram, basil, thyme, savory, parsley, or sage**
> **Salt**
> **Fresh-ground black pepper**

Taste the mixture for salt and correct as needed.
Roll out:
> **1 recipe Fresh Pasta (page 89)**

To make ravioli, roll out the pasta fairly thin and cut into sheets about 14 inches long. Keep the stack of well-floured pasta sheets under a towel to keep them from drying as you work with one sheet at a time. Pipe or spoon 1 tablespoon of the ricotta and herb filling along the lower third of a sheet of pasta. Keep about 1½ inches between each blob of filling. Spray very lightly with a fine mist of water. Fold the upper half of the pasta over the lower half; then, starting at the fold, gently coax all the air out of the ravioli, pressing the two layers of pasta together with your fingertips. When the sheet of ravioli has been formed and pressed, use a zigzag rolling cutter to cut off the bottom edge and to cut between each portion of filling. Separate the ravioli and lay them out on a sheet pan sprinkled with flour; make sure they aren't touching each other or they will stick together. Cover with a towel or parchment paper and refrigerate until ready to cook. Keep refrigerated right up to the time of cooking to prevent the filling from seeping through the pasta, which can cause the ravioli to stick to the pan.

Cook the ravioli in salted simmering water for 5 to 6 minutes, until the pasta is done. Drain and serve on a platter or in individual bowls. In a small saucepan melt:
> **1 to 2 tablespoons butter**

Pour over the pasta and sprinkle with:
> **Freshly grated Parmesan cheese**

Serve hot.

VARIATIONS

◆ Wash and stem 1 bunch of chard or spinach. Cook in butter until soft. Cool, squeeze out all the excess water, chop well, and stir into the ricotta mixture. Reduce the amount of chopped herbs to 2 teaspoons.

◆ For a different sauce, cook a few whole sage leaves in butter over medium heat until the butter is slightly brown and the leaves are crisp.

(continued)

◆ Sauce the ravioli with Simple Tomato Sauce (page 264) instead of melted butter.

◆ Serve in bowls with a ladle of hot broth poured over.

◆ For cannelloni use ½ recipe pasta; roll and cut the sheets into rectangles about 4 by 3 inches. Cook in salted boiling water until done, cool in cold water, and lay the rectangles out on a cloth. Pipe or spoon a couple of tablespoons of filling lengthwise along one third of a rectangle of pasta. Gently roll the pasta to form a large straw. Place the cannelloni, seam side down, in a buttered baking dish. Cover with 1½ cups Simple Tomato Sauce (page 264) and bake for 20 minutes at 400°F.

Cheese and Pasta Gratin

4 SERVINGS

This gratin (macaroni and cheese by another name) is good to make when you find yourself with the ends of several types of cheeses. Almost any cheese works, except mozzarella, which gets a little stringy, and blue cheeses, which can take over the dish. I love Gruyère for macaroni and cheese, and cheddar, Jack, and Cantal are all good, too.

Melt, in a heavy skillet:

3 tablespoons butter

Add:

3 tablespoons flour

Cook over very low heat, stirring with a whisk for 3 minutes. The roux should bubble gently.

Whisking constantly, add, little by little:

2½ cups milk

Continue whisking until the sauce has the consistency of thick cream. Add:

Salt to taste

Raise the heat to medium, switch to a wooden spoon, and stir continuously until the sauce begins to simmer. Lower the heat and cook, stirring occasionally, for 10 minutes.

Melt in a heavy ovenproof skillet:

1 tablespoon butter

Add:

1½ cups fresh breadcrumbs (see page 62)

Toss the crumbs to coat with butter and toast in a 350°F oven for 10 to 15 minutes, stirring them every 5 minutes, until lightly browned.

Turn off the heat under the white sauce and stir in:

8 ounces grated cheese

Cook al dente in abundant salted boiling water:

¾ pound short-cut pasta (macaroni, fusilli, penne)

Drain and pour into a buttered gratin dish. Pour the cheese sauce over the pasta and mix until it is well coated. Taste for salt, and adjust as needed. Scatter the toasted breadcrumbs over the top and bake in a 400°F oven for 15 minutes, or until the crumbs are golden brown and the sauce is bubbling.

VARIATIONS

◆ Stir together the pasta and the sauce and serve right away instead of finishing in the oven.

◆ Stir in diced ham or prosciutto.

Breads and Grains

Cornbread

MAKES ONE 8- OR 9-INCH ROUND OR
SQUARE LOAF

Preheat the oven to 425°F.

Butter an 8- or 9-inch baking dish or cast-iron skillet.

Mix together:

¾ cup cornmeal
1 cup unbleached all-purpose flour
1 tablespoon sugar (optional)
1 tablespoon baking powder
¾ teaspoon salt

Pour into a 2-cup measuring cup:

1 cup milk

Whisk in:

1 egg

Make a well in the dry ingredients, pour in the egg and milk mixture, and whisk or stir until well mixed and smooth. Stir in:

4 tablespoons (½ stick) butter, melted

Pour the batter into the prepared pan and bake for 20 minutes, or until the cornbread is brown on top and a toothpick inserted in the middle comes out clean.

VARIATIONS

• Pour the batter into 12 buttered muffin tins and bake for 12 to 15 minutes.

• For denser cornbread, reverse the amounts of cornmeal and flour, using 1 cup cornmeal and ¾ cup flour. Or use only cornmeal.

• For a crispier crust, put the cast-iron pan in the oven while it is preheating, with 1 tablespoon butter (or, for more flavor, 1 tablespoon bacon drippings). When the pan is hot, take it out of the oven, tilt it to distribute the fat evenly, and then pour in the batter.

• To make buttermilk cornbread, use 1¼ cups buttermilk instead of the milk and instead of 1 tablespoon baking powder, use 2 teaspoons baking powder and ½ teaspoon baking soda.

Soda Bread

MAKES 1 LOAF

Soda bread is the national bread of Ireland and is made with baking soda for leavening instead of yeast. It is traditionally baked on a hearthstone or in a Dutch oven in the embers of a fire. From beginning to end, this recipe takes no more than an hour.

Preheat the oven to 450°F.

Measure and mix together in a large bowl:

3¾ cups unbleached all-purpose flour
1 teaspoon salt
1 teaspoon baking soda

Measure:

2 cups buttermilk

Make a well in the dry ingredients and pour in 1½ cups of the buttermilk. Stir, adding more buttermilk if needed; the dough should be soft, but not wet or sticky. Turn the dough out onto a floured surface and knead just enough to bring the dough together. Turn it over and pat it into a round loaf about 1½ inches high. Place on a baking sheet and cut a cross into the top of the loaf with a knife. Cut fairly deeply into the bread, being sure to cut all the way to the edges; this helps the bread to rise properly. Bake for 15 minutes, lower the temperature to 400°F, and bake for another 30 minutes, or until done. To test, tap the bread on the bottom: it will sound hollow when done.

VARIATION

• For brown soda bread, use 3 cups whole-wheat flour and ¾ cup unbleached all-purpose flour.

Cream Biscuits

MAKES EIGHT 1½-INCH BISCUITS

Cream biscuits are melt-in-your-mouth delicious on their own for breakfast, served with Fried Chicken (page 347) and savory stews, for desserts baked in a cobbler with juicy fruit (see page 178), or in the classic Strawberry Shortcake (page 365).

Preheat the oven to 400°F.
Stir together in a large bowl:

> **1½ cups all-purpose flour**
> **¼ teaspoon salt**
> **4 teaspoons sugar (optional)**
> **2 teaspoons baking powder**

Add:

> **6 tablespoons (¾ stick) cold butter,
> cut into small pieces**

Cut the butter into the flour with your fingers or a pastry blender until they are the size of small peas. Measure:

> **¾ cup heavy cream**

Remove 1 tablespoon and set aside. Lightly stir in the remainder of the cream with a fork until the mixture just comes together. Without overworking it, lightly knead the dough a couple of times in the bowl, turn it out onto a lightly floured board, and roll out about ¾ inch thick. Cut into eight 1½-inch circles or squares. Reroll the scraps if necessary.

Place the biscuits on a baking sheet lined with parchment paper and lightly brush the tops with the reserved tablespoon of cream. Bake for 17 minutes or until cooked through and golden.

Scones

MAKES 8 SCONES

You can put this dough together in just a few minutes. These scones are surprisingly light and are delicious as an after-school snack or with afternoon tea.

Preheat the oven to 400°F.
Measure and mix together in a large bowl:

> **2 cups unbleached whole-wheat pastry
> flour**
> **2½ teaspoons baking powder**
> **½ teaspoon salt**
> **¼ cup sugar**

Stir in:

> **1⅓ cups cream**

Mix until the dough just starts to come together; it will be sticky. Turn it out onto a floured surface and knead briefly, just enough to bring the dough completely together. Pat it into an 8-inch circle. Brush with:

> **2 tablespoons butter, melted**

And sprinkle with:

> **1½ tablespoons sugar**

Cut the circle into 8 wedges and place the wedges 1 inch apart on a baking sheet lined with parchment paper or a silicone liner. Bake for 17 minutes or until golden brown.

VARIATIONS

• To the dry ingredients, add ½ cup chopped dried fruit (apricots, nectarines, or pears) or whole dried cherries, cranberries, raisins, or currants.

• Add the grated zest of a lemon or an orange.

• Cut out individual scones with a round cutter, or cut the scones into smaller shapes.

• Substitute unbleached all-purpose flour for whole-wheat flour.

Buttermilk Pancakes

4 TO 6 SERVINGS

For different flavors, use different flours; they can be mixed and matched at will, as long as half of the flour is whole-wheat pastry flour, to keep them light.

In a large bowl, measure and mix together:

¾ cup whole-wheat pastry flour
¾ cup mixed whole-grain flours (such as whole wheat, spelt, cornmeal, rye, or buckwheat)
1 teaspoon baking powder
1 teaspoon baking soda
1 tablespoon sugar (optional)
1 teaspoon salt

Separate:

2 eggs

In a large measuring cup, measure:

1¾ cups buttermilk

Whisk the egg yolks into the buttermilk. Make a well in the dry ingredients, pour in the buttermilk mixture, and stir until just mixed. Add:

6 tablespoons (¾ stick) butter, melted

Stir well. In another bowl, beat the egg whites until they form soft peaks, then fold them into the batter. If the batter is too thick, add more buttermilk.

Spoon the batter onto a preheated griddle, cooking a single pancake first to see if the griddle is the right temperature. Cook until the undersides of the pancakes are golden brown. Turn them over and cook until done.

VARIATIONS

◆ For the buttermilk, substitute a mixture of yogurt and milk. Or make the pancakes with regular milk: use 1½ cups milk, omit the baking soda, and use 2 teaspoons baking powder instead.

◆ For very tender pancakes, use 4 tablespoons (½ stick) butter and ¼ cup sour cream or crème fraîche.

◆ Unbleached all-purpose flour can be substituted for the whole-grain flour.

◆ Peel and coarsely chop 1 banana and fold into the finished batter or stir in 1 cup blueberries.

Whole-Grain Waffles

MAKES ABOUT 8 WAFFLES

In a large bowl, measure and mix together:

1 cup whole-wheat pastry flour
1 cup mixed whole-grain flours (such as whole wheat, spelt, cornmeal, rye, or buckwheat)
1½ teaspoons baking powder
1 teaspoon baking soda
½ teaspoon salt
1 tablespoon sugar (optional)

In a large measuring cup, measure:

2 cups buttermilk

Whisk in thoroughly:

3 eggs

Pour the buttermilk and egg mixture into the dry ingredients and stir until just mixed. Pour in:

8 tablespoons (1 stick) butter, melted

and stir until well mixed. If necessary, thin with more buttermilk: the batter should pour off the spoon. Cook in a preheated waffle iron until crisp and golden.

VARIATION

◆ To make waffles with regular milk, increase the baking powder to 2½ teaspoons and omit the baking soda.

Couscous

Couscous can be cooked instantly with a bit of boiling water, but for more flavor and a great texture it is worthwhile to steam it the way they do in Morocco.

Allow about ¼ cup uncooked couscous per person. Wash the couscous thoroughly in abundant water. Drain and spread out in a large shallow pan. Let the couscous rest for 15 minutes, then rub your hands through the couscous to break up any lumps.

Set up a steamer. Add some aromatics such as ginger, garlic, herbs, and spices to the water. For 4 servings, put 1 cup couscous in the steamer basket (if the holes are large, line the basket with cheesecloth), cover, and steam for 20 minutes. Transfer the couscous back to the pan and break up any lumps with the back of a spoon. Sprinkle with ½ cup water and about ½ teaspoon salt. Mix in, using your fingers like a rake. Add 1 teaspoon butter and mix in with your fingers. Let the couscous rest for 15 minutes and steam again for 15 to 20 minutes. (The couscous can sit for some time before this final steaming.) Cover the couscous with a damp towel to keep it moist, and work out any lumps with your fingers.

Sushi Rice

MAKES 4 CUPS

I love a dinner of make-it-yourself sushi. I put a large bowl of sushi rice on the table with squares of toasted nori, thinly sliced fish and vegetables, and some pickled ginger and wasabi. Everyone rolls his own and eats them out of hand.

Wash well in a few changes of cold water:
2 cups short-grained Japanese-style rice
Drain well, place in a heavy-bottomed pots and cover with:
2¼ cups water
Cover the pot with a tight-fitting lid, bring to a boil, and reduce immediately to low heat. Cook the rice for 15 minutes. Turn off the heat, and let the rice sit for another 10 minutes.

While the rice is cooking, make the seasoning mixture. Mix together:
1 tablespoon rice wine vinegar
¼ teaspoon salt
1 teaspoon sugar
Stir until the sugar is dissolved.

When the rice is cooked, turn it out into a bowl, and pour the seasoning mixture over the rice. Gently stir with a wooden paddle, using a cutting action, until the rice is evenly coated. Let the rice cool before using.

Farro Salad with Shallots and Parsley

4 SERVINGS

Farro is a delicious, nutty-tasting whole grain with a flavor like a cross between wheat berries and barley. It cooks quickly (almost as fast as rice) and can be served boiled, plain, or marinated in a salad; or it can be prepared in the same way as a risotto. I usually cook 1½ cups of farro at a time. I serve half of it warm as a side dish and the other half the next day as a salad.

Bring to a boil:
   6 cups salted water
Add:
   ¾ cup farro
Simmer for 20 to 25 minutes or until tender. Drain and transfer to a bowl. Sprinkle with:
   1 tablespoon red wine vinegar
   Salt
Stir and taste. Add more salt or vinegar if needed. Stir in:
   1 small shallot or 2 scallions, diced
      fine
   2 tablespoons chopped parsley
   3 tablespoons extra-virgin olive oil
   Fresh-ground black pepper
Serve at room temperature, or chilled.

VARIATIONS
◆ Wheat berries and spelt can be cooked and served in the same manner. Wheat berries take longer to cook, sometimes up to 50 minutes. Start checking after 20 minutes.
◆ Cilantro or basil can be substituted for the parsley.
◆ Diced cucumbers or halved cherry tomatoes can be added in season.
◆ Sherry vinegar or lemon juice can substitute for part or all of the red wine vinegar.

Eggs and Cheese

Hard-Cooked and Soft-Cooked Eggs

"Hard-boiled" eggs shouldn't be hard, nor should they be boiled, exactly, so I prefer to call them "hard-cooked." Here is my preferred method for cooking eggs so that their yolks will be just set, and golden and moist at the center. Let the eggs sit at room temperature while bringing a pot of water to a boil. Turn the water down to a simmer and gently lower the eggs into the water with a slotted spoon. Adjust the temperature so the water stays just below a simmer, and cook for 9 minutes. Lift the eggs out of the water and plunge them immediately into ice water. Crack them all over when they're cool enough to handle and peel away the shells. The 9-minute rule is a reliable guideline, but remember, timing is bound to be approximate because your eggs may be slightly larger or smaller and colder or warmer.

A soft-cooked egg can be cooked the same way, but for only about 5 minutes or so. Eat it warm, straight from the shell.

Fried Eggs

The key to frying eggs is finding the right pan—mine is a well-seasoned, 10-inch cast-iron pan—and taking care of it. Wipe it clean after you use it, or wash it with water if there's any food stuck on it, but keep it out of soapy water and the dishwasher, and keep it dry.

Warm a cast-iron pan over medium heat. After a minute or so turn the heat to low and add a piece of butter or a splash of olive oil. Tilt and swirl the pan to cover the bottom of the pan with the melting butter or oil. Gently crack open the egg into the pan. Lightly salt and pepper the egg and cook until the white is almost completely set. Gently coax a spatula under the egg. With a smooth motion turn it over in the pan without breaking the yolk; this is difficult with a slow-cooked egg because the yolk is still quite tender. Season the egg again with salt and pepper. For a very runny yolk, cook for just a few seconds more. For a firmer yolk, cook for another minute or so. For those who do not like their yolks the least bit runny, break the yolk just before flipping the egg over, turn off the heat, and allow the egg to be cooked until done by the residual heat of the pan.

Scrambled Eggs

Crack 1 or 2 eggs per person into a bowl. Choose a heavy-bottomed pan of a size such that the eggs will be about ½ inch deep in the pan. (A 10-inch skillet is perfect for scrambling a dozen eggs.) Heat the pan over medium heat for a few minutes. This is key: a properly heated pan will keep the eggs from sticking. Meanwhile, lightly beat or stir the eggs together. If they are stirred or beaten too much the eggs will be runny and won't have as much body when cooked. Season them with salt and pepper (and chopped herbs, if you like), using a generous pinch of salt for every 2 eggs. When the pan is hot, add a hazelnut-size piece of butter for every 2 eggs. When the butter is almost finished foaming, pour in the eggs. Let the eggs cook undisturbed for a few moments; when you see them start to set, begin to push the eggs around in the pan, allowing liquid egg to flow out over the hot pan. Cook the scrambled eggs until they're just a little looser than you like them (I like mine very moist); they will continue cooking when you take them off the heat. Serve immediately.

Egg Salad

4 SERVINGS

Hard-cooked eggs that are chopped and stirred into salads hold up better when cooked a little longer than hard-cooked eggs served intact.

Cook in simmering water for 10 minutes:

6 eggs, at room temperature

Cool in ice-cold water and peel. Chop the eggs coarse.

Mix together:

**2 teaspoons capers,
rinsed, drained, and chopped
1 tablespoon chopped parsley
2 tablespoons chopped scallions,
spring onions, shallots, or chives
Salt
Fresh-ground black pepper
A pinch of cayenne
⅓ cup homemade mayonnaise
(see page 46)**

Add the chopped eggs to the flavored mayonnaise. Mix well, taste and adjust the seasoning, if necessary, and add, if you like, a few drops of:

Vinegar or lemon juice

VARIATIONS

◆ Add 2 teaspoons Dijon mustard

◆ Use Aïoli (page 47) instead of plain mayonnaise.

◆ Add ½ cup diced celery, or cucumbers, or both.

Quesadillas

4 SERVINGS

Quesadillas, cheese-filled tortillas cooked until crisp and melted, are a simple quick pick-me-up. They are a standby for hungry kids after school. Served with rice, beans, and salsa, they make a complete lunch or dinner.

Gather together:

**8 corn or flour tortillas
1 cup grated mild melting cheese such
as Monterey Jack**

Sprinkle the cheese over 4 of the tortillas and then top with the remaining 4 tortillas.

In a heavy-bottomed skillet over medium heat, melt:

½ teaspoon butter

When hot, put in a quesadilla and cook until golden. Turn over and cook until the second side is golden and the cheese is melted. Hold in a warm oven and repeat with the other quesadillas.

VARIATIONS

◆ Sprinkle chopped cilantro over the grated cheese before topping with the second tortilla, or put a few slices of roasted peppers or chiles in with the cheese.

◆ After cooking, put a spoonful of salsa, mild or spicy, or sour cream, or Guacamole (page 219) on the quesadilla.

◆ The tortillas can be cooked dry in a hot skillet without the butter, if you prefer.

Grilled Cheese Sandwich

Made with good bread and Gruyère cheese, and fried in fresh butter, a grilled cheese sandwich is as good as a sandwich gets.

Slice country-style bread and cover half the bread slices with three layers of very thin slices of Gruyère cheese. Top with the remaining slices of bread. Put a heavy skillet (cast iron works best) over medium-low heat to warm through. Spread the tops of the sandwiches with softened butter or olive oil. (If the butter is cold, cut thin slivers of butter to scatter over the top.) When the pan is hot, put in the sandwiches, buttered side down, and cook until golden brown. If the bread is browning too quickly and threatening to burn, turn the heat down. Spread the top slices of the sandwiches with more butter or oil. Turn the sandwiches over and cook until the second side is golden brown and the cheese is melted. I like to lay 3 or 4 sage leaves over the butter on each side before frying. The leaves brown and crisp in the butter and are laminated onto the bread. When the sandwiches are cooked and crisp, rub the bread with a peeled garlic clove.

Onion Custard Pie

MAKES ONE 9-INCH PIE

This pie makes a good picnic breakfast.

Roll out into a 12-inch round:
10 ounces Pie Dough (page 174)
Line a 9-inch tart or pie pan with the dough, folding the edges in to make double-thick sides. Press the sides in well and prick the bottom all over with a fork. Refrigerate for at least 1 hour.

Preheat the oven to 375°F. To keep the dough from shrinking while it bakes, line the shell with a piece of foil or parchment paper, then fill the tart with a layer of dried beans (or other pie weights). This is known as baking blind. Bake for 15 minutes or until lightly golden around the edge. Take the tart out of the oven; remove the foil and the weights. Return to the oven and cook for another 5 to 7 minutes, until the pastry is an even light golden brown.

Heat in a heavy-bottomed skillet:
4 tablespoons (½ stick) butter
When melted add:
4 onions, peeled and sliced thin
Cook over medium heat until soft and golden, about 20 to 30 minutes. Season with:
Salt
Fresh-ground black pepper
Remove from the pan and spread on a plate to cool. Mix together:
1½ cups half-and-half
2 eggs
2 egg yolks
½ cup grated Gruyère cheese
Salt
Fresh-ground black pepper
A pinch of cayenne
When the onions have cooled, spread them in the baked tart shell, pour in the custard mixture, and bake at 375°F for 35 to 40 minutes or until the top is puffed and golden brown.

VARIATIONS
• Sauté the onions with a few sprigs of fresh herbs such as thyme, savory, or marjoram.
• Cut 4 slices bacon into small pieces and cook until just crisp. Drain and sprinkle over the bottom of the tart shell before adding the onions.
• Try another cheese instead of Gruyère.
• Add to the custard 2 cups sautéed, chopped greens in place of half of the onions.

Vegetables

(CONTINUED)

(CONTINUED)

◆ Artichokes

Artichokes are the flower buds of a domesticated thistle plant. There are large green globe artichokes, small violet ones, and purple ones. Some are smooth, without a single thorn, and some have leaves tipped with sharp, treacherous spikes. Each variety has its own unique flavor. Artichokes are best when young and freshly harvested. A more mature artichoke will have a larger choke (the hairy interior) and tougher flesh. Look for brightly colored, tightly closed artichokes with stems that look freshly cut, not shriveled.

Artichokes can be cooked whole or pared down to their pale-colored hearts. To pare large artichokes, pull off all of the small leaves (petals, really) along the stem. Then with a heavy sharp knife, cut away the top of the artichoke to about 1 inch above the base. With a small sharp knife, pare away all the dark green from the stem, base, and outer leaves. Scoop out the choke with a small spoon. If you're not cooking the artichoke heart right away, rub it with a cut lemon or submerge it in water acidulated with lemon juice or vinegar to prevent the cut surfaces from oxidizing and turning dark brown.

Small young artichokes are prepared similarly; break off the outer leaves until you reach the light green interior leaves with darker green tips. Cut the tops of the leaves off at the point where the two colors meet. Pare away the dark green parts of the stem and base. Don't be timid about trimming away all of the dark green leaves and parts of the artichoke, as they are fibrous and will not soften, no matter how long they are cooked. Once again, if the artichokes are to be cooked fairly soon they don't need to be treated, but otherwise rub them with a cut lemon or put them in a bowl of acidulated water.

Artichokes Boiled or Steamed

Trim off the cut end of the stem of each artichoke and cut off any thorns from the leaves. You can do this easily with a pair of scissors. Plunge the artichokes into abundant rapidly boiling salted water and cook until tender, about 30 minutes for large artichokes. Test for doneness by probing the bottom of the artichoke around the stem with a small sharp knife or skewer. To steam, prepare the artichoke the same way and steam, tightly covered, over rapidly boiling water. Serve with a ramekin of melted butter or homemade mayonnaise—plain or flavored with lemon, garlic, and herbs (see page 47).

Braised Artichokes

4 SERVINGS

The combination of artichokes, green garlic, colorful spring onions, and flowering thyme makes a delectable braise.

Trim:

12 small artichokes, or 4 medium
artichokes (1½ to 2 pounds)

One at a time, cut off the top third of the artichokes. Pull off the tough outer leaves to expose the light green tender leaves. With a paring knife, trim away the dark green base of the leaves and the outer layer of the stems and cut off the end of the stem. Cut the artichokes into quarters lengthwise (cut larger artichokes into eighths) and cut out the chokes. To prevent discoloring, rub the cut artichokes all over with:

1 lemon, cut in half

Trim off the roots and upper stalks from:

1 green garlic stalk
1 spring onion

Cut the garlic and onion in half lengthwise and slice thin. In a medium saucepan, warm over low heat:

3 tablespoons olive oil

Add the garlic and onion and:

3 or 4 thyme sprigs

Cook gently for about 5 minutes, then add the prepared artichokes. Stir and continue cooking for 2 or 3 minutes. Season with:

Salt
Fresh-ground black pepper

Add:

¼ cup white wine
¼ cup water

Cover and cook gently for 20 minutes or so, stirring occasionally, until tender and saucy. Taste for salt and finish with:

2 tablespoons extra-virgin olive oil

Sautéed Artichokes with Onions, Garlic, and Herbs

4 SERVINGS

Pour into a heavy pan over medium heat:

1½ tablespoons olive oil

When hot, add:

1 small onion, diced

Cook until soft, about 7 minutes. Remove from the pan.

While the onions are cooking, trim:

12 to 15 very small artichokes
(about 1½ pounds)

Slice thin. In the same pan the onions were cooked in, heat:

1½ tablespoons olive oil

Add the sliced artichokes and cook over medium heat, stirring occasionally, until tender and browned, about 10 minutes. Add the onions and:

3 garlic cloves, chopped
3 tablespoons chopped herbs
(such as thyme, marjoram,
oregano, savory, or parsley)
Salt
Fresh-ground black pepper

Cook for about 2 minutes. Taste for salt and adjust as needed.

VARIATIONS

✦ With the garlic add 2 tablespoons capers, rinsed, drained, and chopped, and, for a little heat, a pinch or two of dried chile flakes.

✦ Use 3 large artichokes. Trim them down to the edible hearts, remove the chokes, and slice thin. Cook the sliced artichokes as above. If they brown before they're tender, add a little water with the onions and herbs to finish cooking them.

◆ Asparagus

SEASON: SPRING

Asparagus comes in three colors: green, purple, and white. The green and purple varieties taste very much the same and the purple, when cooked, turns dark green. White asparagus, which doesn't turn green because it is grown protected from the sun, is much more rare and expensive, and it has a milder flavor. Asparagus is best when the tips (the blossom ends) are tightly closed, and its flavor is sweetest when freshly harvested. Look for smooth-skinned, brightly colored spears with fresh (not dried-out looking) cut ends and compact tips.

To prepare asparagus, grasp each spear and bend it until it snaps. The spear will break at the natural point where it becomes tender. I prefer fat asparagus stalks to thin ones because once they are peeled they are sweeter and less grassy-tasting than the skinny ones. The trick is to use a peeler that removes paper-thin layers of skin, exposing pale green flesh, not white. This is unnecessary if the spears are quite thin, or if they are going to be cut into small pieces. Start about 1 inch below the blossom tip and peel down along the spear towards the cut end.

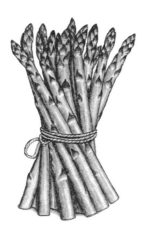

Cooking Asparagus

To boil asparagus, snap the ends off and peel. Cook the asparagus uncovered in a large pot of salted boiling water until just tender, about 3½ minutes (less for skinnier ones). Drain and serve hot or at room temperature (to cool, spread them out on a towel).

To steam asparagus, put peeled asparagus in a steamer over boiling water for about 3 minutes or until just tender.

For grilled asparagus, brush cooked boiled asparagus lightly with olive oil and season with salt and pepper. Grill over a bed of medium-hot coals, turning often, until warmed through and a little browned from the grill.

To roast asparagus, place uncooked peeled spears in one layer on a baking pan with sides. Drizzle with olive oil and sprinkle with salt. Roll the spears back and forth to coat them with oil and salt. Roast in a 400°F oven until tender, about 9 to 11 minutes. Turn the spears once, halfway through the cooking.

Serve asparagus warm or at room temperature with herb mayonnaise (see page 47), Vinaigrette (page 44), Salsa Verde (page 45), or Beurre Blanc (page 228); or drizzle with extra-virgin olive oil and sprinkle with chopped hard-cooked egg and crisped pancetta or shavings of Parmesan cheese. Asparagus is delicious in risotto (see page 290), and combined with other vegetables (see page 316).

Asparagus and Lemon Risotto

4 SERVINGS

For an overview and more detailed instructions for making risotto, see page 103.

Snap off the ends of:

1 pound asparagus

Cut the spears on the diagonal into ¼-inch pieces.
Remove the zest from:

1 lemon

Cut the lemon in half and squeeze the juice. Melt in a heavy-bottomed 2½- to 3-quart saucepan over medium heat:

2 tablespoons butter

Add:

1 small onion, diced fine

Cook until the onion is soft and translucent, about 10 minutes.
Add:

1½ cups risotto rice (Arborio, Carnaroli, Baldo, or Vialone Nano)

Cook the rice, stirring now and then, until translucent, about 4 minutes. Do not let it brown.

Meanwhile, bring to a boil and then turn off:

5 cups chicken broth

Stir the lemon zest into the sautéed rice, then pour in:

½ cup dry white wine

Cook, stirring fairly often, until all the wine is absorbed. Add 1 cup of the warm chicken broth and cook at a vigorous simmer, stirring occasionally. When the rice starts to get thick, pour in another ½ cup of the broth and add some salt (how much depends on the saltiness of the broth). Keep adding broth, ½ cup at a time, every time the rice thickens. Do not let the rice dry out. After 12 minutes stir in the cut asparagus. Cook un-

til the rice is tender but still has a firm core, 20 to 30 minutes in all. When the rice is just about done, stir in half the lemon juice and:

1 tablespoon butter

⅓ cup grated Parmesan cheese

Stir vigorously to develop the creamy starch. Taste for salt and lemon juice, adding more as needed. Turn off the heat, let the risotto sit uncovered for 2 minutes, and serve. Add a splash of broth if the rice becomes too thick.

VARIATIONS

❖ Stir 2 or 3 tablespoons chopped chervil or parsley into the risotto before serving.

❖ Clean 1 pound scallops, removing the small muscle (the "foot") attached to their sides. If they are very large scallops, cut them in half horizontally—so that you end up with 2 thinner disks of scallop. Stir the scallops into the risotto 5 minutes before it has finished cooking.

❖ Add 1 pound peas, shelled, 10 minutes before the risotto has finished cooking. Garnish with chopped chervil or a few fresh spearmint leaves cut into thin ribbons.

❖ For a winter squash risotto, omit the lemon and asparagus. Peel ½ small butternut squash and remove the seeds and strings from the inner cavity. Cut into small dice. Heat 2 tablespoons butter in a heavy-bottomed pan, add the squash with a few leaves of fresh sage, and season with salt. Cook over medium-low heat until the squash is just done, cooked through but not soft. Add the cooked squash 5 minutes before the risotto has finished cooking. (Alternatively, add sage to the sautéing onions and stir the raw diced squash into the risotto with the second addition of broth.) This works well with parsnips, carrots, and celery root also.

◆ For a potato and pancetta risotto, omit the lemon and asparagus. Peel and dice small 2 large yellow potatoes. Dice 2 slices pancetta. Add the pancetta to the onions while they are sautéing. Stir the potatoes into the rice with the first addition of broth.

◆ For a grilled radicchio risotto, omit the lemon and asparagus, and just before serving, stir in about 2 cups chopped grilled radicchio (see page 312).

◆ Beans

For information about dried and fresh shell beans and how to select and prepare them, see Beans, Dried and Fresh, page 75.

◆ Green Beans

SEASON: EARLY SUMMER THROUGH FALL

Green beans are beans harvested while the pods are still tender and edible and the seeds within are immature. There are many, many delicious varieties: Blue Lake and Kentucky Wonder beans, wide romano beans (both yellow and green), yellow wax beans, purple and cream-colored Dragon's Tongue beans, and the tender little French beans called haricots verts, to name only a few. Choose fresh, bright, crisp beans. They should snap quickly when bent and should have only the tiniest of seeds inside. Use the beans quickly to enjoy their best flavor. To prepare them, give them a rinse, and then snap or cut off

the stem end. It is not necessary to remove the tail end unless the beans are very stringy or the ends are desiccated.

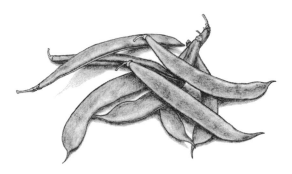

Romano Beans with Marjoram
4 SERVINGS

Large flat romano beans are one of the summer vegetables I most look forward to for their irresistible beany flavor. Don't hold back on the marjoram; the fresh pungent flavor of the herb is a wonderful complement to the beans.

Trim and discard the stem ends of:
> **1 pound romano beans**

Cut the beans into 1-inch lengths; they are pretty when you cut them on a slight diagonal. Cook the beans until tender in abundant salted boiling water. Drain the beans and toss them with:
> **Salt**
> **Extra-virgin olive oil**
> **¼ cup chopped fresh marjoram**

Taste for salt and serve.

VARIATIONS
◆ Finish with a squeeze of lemon juice.
◆ Use butter instead of olive oil.
◆ Use other kinds of tender beans.

Fresh Shell Bean and Green Bean Ragout

4 SERVINGS

A mixture of fresh green beans (haricots verts, yellow wax beans, romano beans, or Blue Lake beans) makes this dish both beautiful and tasty. Each variety cooks in a different amount of time, so cook them separately. The same water can be used. Cook yellow wax beans first, to preserve their color. A variety of shell beans can be used as well, but once again, be sure to cook different beans separately.

Shell:

1 pound fresh shell beans (such as cranberry, cannellini, or flageolet)

Cook the beans in lightly salted boiling water until creamy and tender. Start checking after 15 minutes. When they are done, let the beans cool in their cooking liquid.

Meanwhile, snap off the stem ends, and pull off the tails if dry or tough, from:

¾ pound green beans

Cut into 1-inch bite-size pieces. Cook until tender in salted boiling water, drain, and spread out on a baking sheet or plate to cool.

Heat in a heavy-bottomed pan over medium heat:

2 tablespoons olive oil

Add:

1 onion, diced

Cook until translucent, about 10 minutes, then add:

2 garlic cloves, peeled and chopped
2 teaspoons chopped savory, marjoram, or parsley
Salt
Fresh-ground black pepper

Cook for 4 minutes. Drain the shell beans, reserving their cooking liquid. Stir the shell beans and ¾ cup of their liquid into the onions. Raise the heat and bring to a boil. Stir in the green beans and return to a boil. Turn down the heat and cook for another minute or so to warm the beans through. Taste for salt and add more as needed. Serve with a drizzle of:

Extra-virgin olive oil

Green Beans with Toasted Almonds and Lemon

4 SERVINGS

This is a wonderful side dish for pan-fried fish.

Trim the stem end from:

1 pound green beans

Melt, in a heavy pan, over medium heat:

3 tablespoons butter

When the foam has begun to subside, add:

¼ cup sliced almonds

Cook, stirring fairly often, until the almonds begin to brown. Turn off the heat and add:

Juice of ½ lemon
Salt

Cook the beans until tender in salted boiling water. Drain well and toss with the almonds and butter. Taste for salt and adjust as needed.

VARIATIONS

◆ Substitute chopped pecans or hazelnuts for the almonds.
◆ Use romano beans or Dragon's Tongue beans instead of tender green beans.
◆ Add a clove of finely chopped garlic to the butter just before adding the beans.

Hummus

MAKES ABOUT 2 CUPS

Homemade hummus is very easy to make. If you don't have any tahini (a paste made from sesame seeds), a chickpea purée without it is still quite delicious. Just add more olive oil.

Soak for 8 hours or overnight:

¾ cup dried chickpeas

Drain and cook in plenty of water until quite tender, 1 to 2 hours. Drain the cooked beans, reserving ¼ cup of the cooking liquid. Purée with a food mill or in a food processor or blender.

Stir in:

¼ cup tahini (sesame seed paste)
¼ cup fresh lemon juice
2 garlic cloves,
peeled and pounded to a purée
1 tablespoon extra-virgin olive oil
Salt

Mix until smooth, adding some of the cooking liquid if needed.

VARIATIONS

◆ Stir in ¼ teaspoon ground cumin and cayenne to taste.

◆ Garnish with a drizzle of olive oil that has been mixed with ground cumin and cayenne.

◆ For very smooth hummus, peel the chickpeas after they're cooked.

Refried Beans

4 SERVINGS (ABOUT 2 CUPS)

Freshly rendered lard is the traditional fat for refried beans. Look for it at Latin American markets.

In a heavy pan over medium heat, melt:

3 or 4 tablespoons nonhydrogenated lard

When hot, add:

½ medium onion, diced

Cook the onion until soft, about 7 minutes. Add:

2 cups cooked pinto or black beans
¼ cup bean cooking liquid
Salt

Cook for a few minutes. Mash the beans with a bean or potato masher. Add more bean cooking liquid if needed: the consistency should be a little on the thin side, because the mashed beans will thicken as they sit. Taste for salt and serve.

VARIATIONS

◆ Lard or bacon fat is very tasty in these beans, but olive oil can be used instead.

◆ Two or three chopped garlic cloves may be added to the cooked onions a minute before adding the beans.

◆ Broccoli

SEASON: EARLY SPRING, FALL, AND LATE WINTER

The part of the broccoli plant that we eat is the unopened budding sprout, meaning that broccoli is, more or less, a big unopened flower. The most typical variety of broccoli is green and fairly large. Other types include sprouting broccoli, which produces small, dark green sprouts that are harvested individually. Romanesco broccoli looks a little otherworldly; it is chartreuse-green with a conical head made of pointy spiraling florets. There is also purple broccoli, some of which has such compact heads that it looks more like cauliflower than broccoli. Select broccoli that is brightly colored and firm, with compact heads that are not wilted, yellow, or blooming. Remove the florets from the main stem and cut or break them up as desired. Trim the end of the stems, and when they are large, peel them with a paring knife or peeler. Cut the peeled stems into sticks or slices.

Steamed Broccoli with Garlic, Butter, and Lemon

4 SERVINGS

Cut the thick stems from a large bunch of broccoli. Peel and trim the stems and cut them in pieces. Cut the tops into florets. Steam the prepared broccoli until tender. While the broccoli is steaming, melt a few tablespoons of butter in a small heavy pan; add 2 or 3 garlic cloves, chopped or pounded, and some salt. Cook just until the butter starts to bubble. Turn off the heat and add a big squeeze of lemon juice. Remove the broccoli from the steamer to a serving bowl, pour the flavored butter over the plated broccoli, and serve. For variety, add chopped marjoram or oregano to the hot butter. Use half butter and half extra-virgin olive oil instead of all butter.

Long-Cooked Broccoli

MAKES 2½ CUPS

Long-cooked broccoli is cooked until it resembles a coarse purée. It's delicious on croutons, tossed with pasta, or as a side dish.

Cut the stems from the florets of:
    1½ pounds broccoli
Trim off and discard the dry ends of the stems, and peel the rest and slice thin. Divide or chop the florets into small pieces. Warm in a heavy-bottomed pot over medium heat:
    6 tablespoons olive oil
Add the broccoli with:
    6 garlic cloves, peeled and sliced
    A pinch of dried chile flakes (optional)
    Salt
Cook for a few minutes, stirring occasionally. Add:
    1 cup water
and bring to a boil. Lower the heat to a bare simmer, cover the pot tightly, and cook until very tender, about 1 hour. Stir occasionally and add water if the broccoli starts to dry out and stick. When the broccoli is completely tender, stir briskly (the broccoli will be falling apart) and season with:
    Juice of 1 lemon
Taste for seasoning and add salt, lemon juice, or oil as needed.

• Brussels Sprouts

SEASON: FALL AND WINTER

Brussels sprouts look like tiny cabbages, and indeed they are part of the cabbage family. Though they come in both red and green, the green variety is by far the more common. Brussels sprouts grow on tall, heavy stalks and make quite a dramatic sight when sold still on the stalk at the farmers' market. Choose smaller sprouts that are tightly closed, bright in color, and have no yellowing leaves. They should feel firm and heavy for their size.

To prepare the sprouts, remove and discard any damaged outer leaves and trim the stem, cutting it close up to the bottom of the sprout. Brussels sprouts can be cooked whole or cut up, or all the leaves can be separated from the core. Give the prepared sprouts a quick wash and drain them before using.

Brussels Sprouts Gratin

4 SERVINGS

Trim the outer leaves and stems from:

1 pound Brussels sprouts

Cook them until tender in abundant salted boiling water, about 10 to 12 minutes. Drain the sprouts well and chop coarse.
Into a heavy pan over medium heat, put:

**2 slices bacon or 3 slices pancetta,
cut into ½-inch pieces**

Cook until just rendered and limp. Add the chopped sprouts. Season with:

Salt

Fresh-ground black pepper

Stir and cook for a few minutes. Butter a gratin or baking dish. Add the sprouts and bacon and spread evenly. Pour over:

**½ cup half-and-half, or a mixture of
half-and-half and heavy cream**

Sprinkle evenly over the sprouts:

⅓ cup fresh breadcrumbs (see page 62)

Top with:

Thin shavings of butter

Bake in a 400°F oven for 20 to 25 minutes or until the crumbs are golden and the liquid is bubbling.

VARIATION

• Add chopped thyme and garlic to the sprouts with the bacon.

Sautéed Brussels Sprouts with Bacon and Onions

4 SERVINGS

Trim away any damaged outer leaves and cut off the stems from:

1 pound Brussels sprouts

If the sprouts are very small, cut them in half; otherwise cut them into quarters. Cook the sprouts until tender, in abundant salted boiling water. Drain well.
Heat a heavy pan over medium heat. Add:

1 tablespoon olive oil

2 slices bacon, cut into 1-inch pieces

Cook the bacon until rendered and brown, but not crisp. Remove the bacon with a slotted spoon. To the fat in the pan, add:

1 small onion, diced

2 thyme or savory sprigs

Cook the onion until soft but not browned. Season with:

Salt

A squeeze of lemon juice (optional)

Turn the heat to medium-high, add the drained sprouts, and cook, tossing or stirring occasionally, until the sprouts are warmed through and starting to brown a bit. Add the bacon and toss. Check for seasoning and adjust as needed.

(continued)

VARIATIONS
* Omit the bacon.
* A minute before adding the sprouts, add 2 finely chopped garlic cloves to the onions.
* Toss the finished sprouts with a spoonful of chopped fresh thyme leaves.
* This same dish can be made with Brussels sprouts leaves. Cut out the stems from the sprouts and separate them into their leaves. Thinly slice the compact centers. Don't boil the leaves. Add them after the onions are cooked and salted. Cook for 2 minutes. Pour in chicken broth to a depth of about ¼ inch, cover the pan, and cook at a simmer until the leaves are tender, about 10 to 15 minutes.

* Cabbage

SEASON: YEAR-ROUND, BEST IN FALL AND WINTER

The most common type of cabbage is round, smooth-leafed green cabbage, but there are many other varieties to choose from. Smooth-leafed cabbage can be green or red, round, conical, or even flat. Each has a different flavor and texture. I find red cabbage to be a bit more pungent in flavor and to have thicker, tougher leaves. Savoy cabbage is round with thin, light yellow-green, crinkled leaves; it is my favorite for braising. Napa cabbage is an elongated light green cabbage with very tender leaves that have broad, light-colored ribs. This cabbage cooks quickly and makes a great coleslaw. Other cabbages include Asian varieties, bok choy, tat-soi, and mizuna to name a few. These are loose-leaved and dark green in color and are best suited for cooking (except young mizuna, which is an excellent salad green).

When choosing cabbages, select brightly colored, compact heads. They should be firm and feel heavy. Loose-leafed cabbages should not be yellowing or wilted. Remove and discard any damaged or wilting outer leaves. Remove the core from headed cabbage. This is unnecessary for the loose-leafed varieties.

Braised Savoy Cabbage

4 SERVINGS

Braised savoy cabbage is a versatile and stellar winter dish, served either by itself or as an accompaniment to braised duck or chicken or fried sausage.

Remove the tough outer leaves of:
   1 large or 2 small savoy cabbages
Cut the heads in half, and then into quarters. Cut out the cores and cut the quarters into thick slices. Season with:
   Salt
   Fresh-ground black pepper
Heat in a heavy pan:
   2 tablespoons olive oil
Add:
   1 carrot, peeled and diced small
   1 onion, peeled and diced small
   1 celery stalk, diced small
Cook over medium heat for about 7 minutes or until soft, then add:
   1 bay leaf
   2 thyme sprigs
   2 garlic cloves, chopped
   Salt
Cook for another minute and then stir in the seasoned sliced cabbage along with:
   ½ cup white wine, dry or sweet
Cover and cook until the wine is mostly gone, about 8 minutes. Add:
   ½ cup chicken broth or water
Bring the liquid to a boil, turn down to a simmer, cover the pan, and cook for about

15 minutes more, until the cabbage is tender. Stir the cabbage two or three times during the cooking. Taste before serving and add salt or white wine vinegar as needed.

VARIATIONS

• Brown 2 slices bacon cut into small pieces in the oil before adding the vegetables.
• Cook 4 pork sausages and add to the cabbage for the last 5 minutes of cooking.
• Peel 4 potatoes and cook until tender in salted boiling water. Add to the cabbage during the final 5 minutes of cooking.
• Another way to braise cabbage: Cut the quarters into wedges. Heat the oil in the pan and add the wedges and brown on one side. Omit the diced carrot, onion, and celery and add the herbs, garlic, salt, wine, and broth, and cook until tender. For richness add a couple of tablespoons of butter as well.

Homemade Sauerkraut

MAKES ABOUT 1 QUART

If you've never had homemade sauerkraut before, it will be a revelation. And it is easy to make at home: the longer it ferments, the softer the texture and the more intense the flavor. The rule-of-thumb ratio is 1½ teaspoons salt per pound of cabbage.

Remove any damaged outer leaves from:
  1 large, firm, green or red cabbage
Cut the cabbage in half and remove the core. Cut the halves into quarters and slice the quarters as thin as possible. You should have about 5 cups of shredded cabbage. Put the shredded cabbage into a bowl with:
  3½ teaspoons sea salt
  1 teaspoon caraway seeds (optional)
Thoroughly work the salt into the cabbage with your fingers until the cabbage begins to release juices. Pack the cabbage into a non-reactive container, such as a 2-quart glass jar. Press the cabbage down as you are packing it in. There should be enough liquid to cover the cabbage. If not, top it up with a brine made from:
  1 cup filtered water
  1 tablespoon salt
Place a weight over the cabbage to keep it submerged under the brine (see Note). Cover the jar loosely with a dish towel. Let the cabbage ferment at room temperature for 1 week or so. Remove any scum that may appear on the surface of the brine. At this point taste the sauerkraut. If you like the flavor, remove the weight, cover the jar, and refrigerate. Otherwise, let it continue to ferment until it reaches the desired flavor. The sauerkraut will keep in the refrigerator for up to 6 weeks.

Note: The weight can be anything clean and heavy: a rock resting on a plate slightly smaller in diameter than the container, a small jar filled with water, or a water-filled plastic bag (well secured so it won't leak). The important thing is to hold the cabbage down below the level of the brine.

Buttered Cabbage

Any cabbage will work for this recipe—green, savoy, red, or napa. Trim the cabbage of any damaged outer leaves. Cut the head in half and remove the core. Cut the halves into quarters and slice thin. Put the sliced cabbage in a pan with a large knob of butter, salt to taste, and ½ inch of water. Bring to a boil, cover the pan, turn down the heat, and cook at a simmer until the cabbage is tender. Taste for salt and butter and adjust as needed.

◆ Carrots

SEASON: YEAR-ROUND, BEST IN SPRING AND FALL

Carrots are a fundamental staple of the kitchen. They are part of the culinary triumvirate of carrot, celery, and onion that is the basis of so many broths, braises, and stews. Carrots are available year-round, though they do have specific seasons regionally. Here in California they are at their sweetest and juiciest in late spring and fall. Look for fresh carrots that have been grown locally and harvested recently with their greens still attached. The difference in taste between such a carrot and one already peeled, cut, and sealed in a plastic bag is enormous. A fresh carrot will cook better and add more flavor to your food. There are many varieties of carrots; some of them are not even orange. Check out your local farmers' market to see what is growing in your area. When you buy carrots with their tops intact, remove them before putting them in the refrigerator. The carrots will keep better without them.

Glazed Carrots

This is more of a general method rather than a recipe. Peel the carrots and cut them into slices or sticks. Put them in a heavy pot or pan and add water to come about halfway up the carrots (don't pile them higher than an inch or so in the pan; use a larger pan if you have to). Add a good pinch of salt and a couple of teaspoons of butter per serving. Bring the water to a boil, turn down the heat so the water is simmering, and cover the pan. Cook until the carrots are tender. Take off the lid and let the liquid boil down until it has made a buttery sauce that coats the carrots. Remove the carrots from the pan immediately as the sauce will continue to reduce in the hot pan. If it reduces too much, it will separate; add a bit of water to bring it back together. Oil can be used instead of butter, but it won't make as thick a glaze. Right at the end of the cooking, stir in a spoonful of chopped cilantro, parsley, or basil.

Carrot Purée with Caraway and Cumin

4 SERVINGS

Algerian in origin, this recipe makes a colorful, tasty hors d'oeuvre. Serve it at room temperature with toasted croutons or pita bread and marinated olives. Warm, it makes a great side dish with baked fish and Chermoula (page 233).

Bring a large pot of salted water to a boil. Add:
> **1½ pounds carrots, peeled and cut into ½-inch-thick slices**
> **2 garlic cloves, peeled**

Cook until the carrots are tender. Drain. Heat in a small heavy pan:
> **2 teaspoons olive oil**

Add:
> **½ onion, diced fine**

Cook until soft, about 7 minutes. Crush in a mortar and pestle or under a heavy skillet:
> **½ teaspoon ground cumin**
> **¼ teaspoon ground caraway**

Add to the sautéed onions with:
> **Salt**

Add the drained cooked carrots and garlic and cook for a couple minutes more. Off the heat, mash into a coarse purée with a potato masher or fork. Add:
> **1 to 2 teaspoons fresh lemon juice**

and taste for salt. Adjust as needed. If you like, garnish with:
> **Chopped cilantro**

◆ Cauliflower

SEASON: SPRING AND FALL

Cauliflower is a bunched mass of flower stems. The mass of flowers is referred to as the curd. Cauliflower is typically white, but there are green and purple varieties as well. The leaves are the best indicator of a cauliflower's freshness. Look for bright fresh leaves, and heads with tight, brightly colored curd. There should be no brown spots; these are signs of age, as is a coarse-textured curd. Wash the cauliflower well. Trim away any damaged leaves, but leave the nice ones, as they are actually quite tasty.

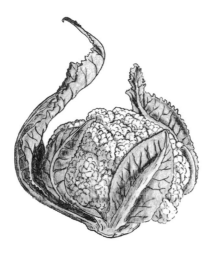

Roasted Sliced Cauliflower

Trim and wash cauliflower and cut across the whole head into ¼-inch-thick slices. Lay out the slices in a single layer on a baking sheet, brush with oil, and season with salt and pepper. Roast in a 400°F oven until tender and starting to brown, about 20 minutes. Sprinkle the slices with chopped fresh herbs or crushed whole spices, for variety.

Steamed Cauliflower

Cauliflower can be steamed whole or cut up into florets. When steaming whole, it's best to cut out the core unless the cauliflower is very small. Turn the cauliflower upside down and carefully cut out a deep cone shape with a sharp, sturdy paring knife, making a complete circle around the central stem. Pull out and discard the core. Steam the cauliflower until it's tender. Steamed cauliflower can be flavored in many ways: Heat extra-virgin olive oil in a small heavy pan. Add 2 pounded garlic cloves; a spoonful of rinsed and drained capers; a spoonful of chopped fresh marjoram, oregano, or parsley (or a mixture); salt; and fresh-ground black pepper and cook until the garlic is just warmed through. Pour over the warm cauliflower. Or serve the cooked cauliflower, warm or at room temperature, with Bagna Cauda (page 230). Or arrange the steamed cauliflower in a gratin or baking dish, spoon melted butter over it, and cover it with sliced cheese (Gruyère, cheddar, or fresh pecorino, for example). Bake in a 350°F oven until the cheese melts into the cauliflower.

◆ Celery and Celery Root

SEASON: CELERY, YEAR-ROUND;
CELERY ROOT, FALL AND WINTER

Celery and celery root were developed from the same plant but now they are two distinct varieties. Celery is one of the staples of the kitchen, used to flavor soups, broths, and braises. It is also quite tasty as a vegetable dish and offers lots of crunch in salads. Celery has a powerful flavor, especially the leaves. Use it judiciously when cooking; too much celery flavor can be unpleasant in a broth, for example. Look for fresh, bright stalks when selecting celery. The outer stalks are best used for flavoring and the inner lighter ones for eating.

Celery root, also called celeriac, has only a few short stalks and leaves; it is the large round knobby root that is eaten both cooked and raw. Its flavor is mild and sweet. Select smaller, firm, heavy roots that have fresh vibrant leaves. Avoid roots that have brownish, rusty stains or blemishes; these tend to be bitter. Trim the top and bottom of the roots and cut away the tough brown skin. If you are not using it right away, wrap it in a damp cloth to keep it from turning brown.

Braised Celery

4 SERVINGS

Remove the tough outer stalks of:

1 head of celery

Trim the root end close to the bottom of the stalks and cut off the leafy tops. Pull off the outer stalks to expose the pale green heart. Cut the group of stalks at the heart in half lengthwise, and then in half again as wedges. Line up all the stalks and cut in half crosswise.

Into a heavy pan over medium heat, pour:

2 tablespoons olive oil

Add:

1 small onion, sliced thin

2 or 3 thyme sprigs

Cook for 5 minutes. Add the celery. Cook for 5 to 7 minutes, until the onions and celery have browned a little. Season with:

Salt

Add:

1 cup chicken or beef broth

Bring to a boil. Lower the heat to a simmer. Cover the pan and cook until the celery is tender. The sauce should be thick and coat the celery; if not, uncover the pan, raise the heat, and reduce the liquid as much as needed. Taste for salt and serve.

VARIATION

◆ For a milder dish, blanch the celery for 7 minutes in salted boiling water before browning it with the onions.

Celery Root and Potato Purée

4 SERVINGS

The flavors of celery root and potato combine so perfectly that they form a new flavor all its own. Not only are they delicious together in purées, but they also make an excellent gratin (see Potato Gratin, page 318).

Peel and cut into large pieces:

1 pound potatoes,
  preferably a yellow-fleshed variety
  such as Yellow Finn or Yukon Gold

Cook until soft in salted boiling water.

Drain. Pass the potatoes through a ricer or food mill and return to the pot. For a chunkier consistency smash with a potato masher right in the pot. Stir in:

2 tablespoons butter

Peel, cut in half, and slice fairly thin:

1 medium celery root (about ¾ pound)

Melt in a heavy-bottomed pan over medium-low heat:

3 tablespoons butter

Add the celery root with:

Salt

Cover tightly and cook until quite soft, 12 to 15 minutes, stirring now and then. Lower the heat if the celery root starts to brown. Pass through a food mill, or, for a smoother version, purée in a blender. Stir into the potatoes. If the purée is too thick, thin with:

Milk

Taste and add salt or more butter if needed.

◆ Corn

SEASON: SUMMER

Sweet corn comes in an array of yellows and whites. There are ears that are full of white kernels, yellow kernels, or both yellow and white. The open-pollinated varieties begin to lose sweetness, converting sugar to starch from the moment they are picked. Modern hybrids have been bred to keep their sweetness for a few days, but some argue that these varieties are too sweet and lack "corn flavor." What better way to decide than by experimenting with a few varieties to discover your own favorites?

No matter the variety, corn is still best eaten fresh, the day it's picked. Look at the cut end to gauge the freshness. Select ears that are plump, juicy, and bright in color, with a fresh cut. The brown silk may look a little sticky on a very fresh ear of corn. Don't be put off if there is a worm at the tip—not that one wishes for a worm, but its presence is a healthy sign that the farmer is not using pesticides. If you can't eat it immediately, store corn in the refrigerator, unhusked.

Shuck corn right before you cook it, removing the husk and all the silk. If there has been a worm visitor, slice off the evidence; no harm has been done to the rest of the ear. To remove the kernels from the cob, hold onto the stem end, pointing the tip of the ear down, and run your knife down the cob, cutting off the kernels. The trick is to gauge the right depth at which to cut—not so deep as to take some of the cob with the kernel, but not so shallow that too much of the kernel is left behind. It is less messy if you tip your ear into a roasting pan to catch all the kernels as they are shaved off. If you wish, rub the cob with the back of the knife to remove all the corn milk from the kernel bits left behind.

Corn on the Cob

Corn on the cob is one of the simplest ways to enjoy summer eating. Shuck the ears of corn: tear off the husks and wipe the corn silk away with a kitchen towel. Cook the ears in a large quantity of boiling salted water for 4 minutes or so. (Or grill them, as on page 159.) Remove, drain, and serve with butter, salt, and pepper.

You can also serve corn on the cob with butter, salt, lime wedges, and ground dried ancho chiles; or with a compound butter made of softened butter, chopped parsley, chopped savory, and finely sliced scallions. (To grind dried ancho chiles, first remove their seeds and veins and then pulverize the chiles in a mortar and pestle or in a spice grinder.)

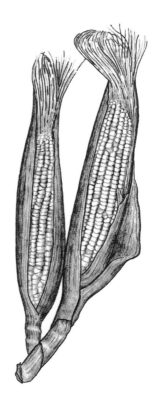

Corn Hash

4 SERVINGS

This corn hash has an exciting and lively combination of flavors: sweet corn, tart lime, and spicy peppers. It goes with all kinds of summertime dishes.

Shuck and remove the kernels from:
> **4 ears sweet corn**
> **(about 2 cups kernels)**

Melt in a heavy skillet, over medium heat:
> **2 tablespoons butter**

Add:
> **1 small red onion, diced**
> **1 small hot chile (serrano or jalapeño),**
> **cut in two, seeds and veins**
> **removed, and diced very fine**

Cook for 3 or 4 minutes, to soften.
Add:
> **Salt**

Cook for another minute, then turn up the heat to medium-high and pour in the corn kernels. Cook for a few minutes, tossing or stirring, until the corn is cooked. If needed, moisten with a splash of water. Season with:
> **A squeeze of lime juice**
> **1 tablespoon chopped cilantro**

Taste and adjust the seasoning with more salt and lime juice, if needed.

VARIATIONS
• Use sweet pepper in place of the spicy chile.
• Use basil or parsley instead of cilantro.
• Green onions or scallions can be used in place of the onions. Cook for only a minute or so with the chile.
• Finish the hash with a knob of flavorful Herb Butter (page 48).

Succotash

4 SERVINGS

The traditional combination for succotash is lima beans and corn, but any other kind of shell bean will be delicious, too.

Shell:
> **1 pound fresh lima beans or other**
> **fresh shell beans**

Place the beans in a pot with water to cover by 1½ inches. Cook until tender; start checking after 10 minutes. Season with:
> **Salt**

Meanwhile shuck:
> **4 ears sweet corn**

Slice off the kernels with a sharp knife. You should have about 2 cups.
Melt in a heavy pot over medium heat:
> **3 tablespoons butter**

Add:
> **1 small onion, peeled and diced**
> **2 to 3 thyme sprigs**

Cook for 5 minutes and add:
> **2 small summer squash, diced**
> **Salt**

Cook for another 5 minutes, add the corn, and after 1 minute add the drained cooked beans. Cook for 3 or 4 minutes, until the corn has cooked through. Check the seasoning and adjust as needed. Stir in:
> **2 teaspoons chopped parsley**

VARIATIONS
• Add 2 garlic cloves, chopped fine, at the same time as the corn.
• Add 2 teaspoons chopped basil or summer savory with the chopped parsley.
• Add 1 diced sweet pepper to the onions and cook for 3 minutes before adding the diced squash.
• A few minutes before adding the corn, add 2 tomatoes, peeled, seeded, and diced.

◆ Eggplant

SEASON: MIDSUMMER TO EARLY FALL

The most common eggplant is the large, purple, oval-shaped globe eggplant, but there are plenty of other varieties to choose from. Globe eggplants range from small to large and from dark purple to the more uncommon white-and-purple striped Rosa Bianca. Smaller, thinner eggplants, usually called Asian eggplants, range in color from dark to light purple, and from short to quite long. There are many more obscure varieties, including eggplants as small as marbles and eggplants that are bright orange and red. Unless otherwise indicated, most recipes can be made with any variety.

Eggplant is best when the skin is bright and shiny, the fruit is firm, and the cap and stem are fresh looking. A dull, matte skin is an indication that the eggplant is too mature or that it has been in storage too long, or both.

Wash the eggplant and trim off and discard the cap and blossom end. It is not necessary to peel most eggplant because the skin is usually quite thin and tender. Many recipes ask you to salt eggplant to rid it of its bitterness, but I find that small eggplant don't require this; nor do most large ones for that matter, as long as their seeds are small and tender. However, eggplant has a sponge-like ability to soak up a great deal of oil as it cooks. Salting eggplant before cooking will rid it of some of its internal moisture, which will help reduce the amount of oil it is able to absorb. To further lighten a dish, eggplant can be tossed with oil and baked instead of fried.

Roasted Eggplant

Eggplant can be roasted whole, cut in half, or cut in wedges. Large eggplant are most commonly roasted whole or in halves to make a purée. Cut the eggplant in half and with a sharp knife score the flesh in a cross-hatch pattern. Season with salt and pepper. Place the eggplant cut side down on an oiled sheet pan. Put whole eggplant directly on the oiled sheet pan. Roast at 400°F until the eggplant is soft, always testing at the stem end. Scoop out the tender flesh.

Eggplant can also be roasted in slices or wedges to serve warm as a side dish or marinated as part of an antipasto or salad. First trim off the stem and blossom ends and then cut the eggplant lengthwise into thick wedges or crosswise into fairly thick slices (½ inch thick is good). When cut too thin, the wedges and slices will dry out before they have cooked through. Salt the pieces generously and let them stand for a few minutes. Meanwhile heat the oven to 400°F and oil a baking sheet or shallow pan. Lay the pieces flat on the pan and then oil the upper side. Bake for 20 to 35 minutes, depending on the size of the wedges or slices. The eggplant is done when it is soft all over and brown on the underside. If the pieces are sticking, let them cool for a few moments and they will be easier to lift. Serve right away, or dress with wine vinegar, slices of garlic, chopped herbs, extra-virgin olive oil, salt, and fresh-ground black pepper and serve at room temperature.

Caponata

MAKES ABOUT 4 CUPS

Caponata is a Sicilian recipe for a sweet-and-sour vegetable stew made with eggplant and tomatoes. It is good served cold as an appetizer or as part of an antipasto plate, or hot, as a side dish with roasted meats or fish.

Trim and cut into 1-inch cubes:

2 medium eggplants

Season with salt and put into a colander to drain for 15 minutes or so.

In a heavy pot over medium heat, warm:

1 tablespoon olive oil

Add enough eggplant cubes to cover the bottom of the pan and sauté until golden. Remove and continue sautéing batches of the eggplant, adding more oil as needed. After removing the last batch of eggplant, add a bit more oil and sauté until golden:

⅔ cup thinly sliced celery

Remove from the pan and set aside. Add to the pan:

1 tablespoon olive oil

1 small onion, diced

Cook, stirring occasionally, until soft and translucent, about 7 minutes. Add:

1½ cups Simple Tomato Sauce
(page 264)

Cook for another 7 minutes. Stir in the cooked eggplant and celery, then add:

⅓ cup green olives, pitted

2 to 3 tablespoons capers,
rinsed and drained

2 salt-packed anchovies,
rinsed, filleted, and chopped

¼ cup red wine vinegar

1½ teaspoons sugar

Cook for a final 10 minutes. Taste and add more salt, vinegar, or sugar as desired. Caponata tastes even better the next day.

VARIATIONS

◆ Garnish with ¼ cup chopped basil.

◆ Garnish with 3 tablespoons toasted pine nuts.

◆ For a lighter version of this dish, toss the salted and drained eggplant with 2 tablespoons olive oil, spread on a baking sheet, and bake in a 375°F oven until golden brown, about 30 minutes.

Grilled Eggplant

4 SERVINGS

Prepare a medium-hot fire under a clean grill. Trim the stem ends off and cut into ⅓-inch slices:

4 Japanese eggplants or
1 large globe eggplant

Using a pastry brush, brush the slices lightly on both sides with:

Olive oil

Sprinkle with:

Salt

When the fire is ready, wipe the grill with oil and arrange the eggplant slices on it. Grill about 3 minutes on each side, until the eggplant is soft to the touch. Serve warm, with grilled fish and Salsa Verde (page 45), for example; or at room temperature, with Farro Salad with Shallots and Parsley (page 278) and Cucumber-Yogurt Sauce (page 232).

◆ Fava Beans

SEASON: EARLY SPRING TO EARLY SUMMER

For tips on shelling, skinning, and preparing fresh fava beans, see page 82.

Fava Bean Ragout

4 SERVINGS

Shell:

2 pounds fava beans

Cook in boiling water for 1 minute or so and then cool in ice water. Drain and pop the beans out of their skins.

Heat in a heavy-bottomed saucepan:

1 tablespoon olive oil or butter

Add:

**2 small spring onions,
trimmed and sliced crosswise**

Cook over medium heat until soft, about 4 minutes. Add the peeled fava beans and:

**1 small green garlic,
trimmed and sliced crosswise**

Salt

Pour in enough water to come up ¼ inch in the pan. Bring to a boil and then turn down to a simmer. Cook for 4 minutes or until the fava beans are tender. Add:

2 tablespoons extra-virgin olive oil or butter

2 teaspoons chopped parsley or chervil

Swirl to combine. Taste for salt and adjust as needed.

VARIATIONS

◆ Substitute peas for half of the fava beans.

◆ A small onion can be used instead of the spring onions.

◆ Fennel

SEASON: SPRING, EARLY SUMMER, AND FALL

Fennel is among the most versatile of vegetables: it's good whether it's eaten raw in salads, or cooked in any number of ways, and I use it as an aromatic vegetable, often instead of celery, in mirepoix (diced carrot, onion, and celery) and other preparations. Cultivated fennel forms a compact, pale white bulb that is topped with fibrous green stalks and feathery leaves. The flavor is reminiscent of anise or licorice. Look for firm, undamaged bulbs that have no signs of drying or shrinking. The fronds should be fresh and vibrant.

To prepare fennel, trim away the darker fibrous stalks and bottom end, and remove any outer layers that are tough or blemished. Fennel should be cut close to the time it is needed, as it will oxidize and brown over time. Cover cut fennel with a damp cloth to protect it. Many recipes ask you to remove the core, but I don't find it necessary; on the contrary, I like the taste of the core and find it quite tender. The feathery dark green fennel leaves can be stripped from the stalks and chopped to use as a flavorful garnish.

Wild fennel is an uncultivated variety of fennel that does not produce a bulb. Its leaves, flowers, pollen, and seeds are all very flavorful and useful in stuffings, marinades, garnishes, and sauces. If it grows in your region, forage for it in the wild.

Braised Fennel

4 SERVINGS

Trim:

2 or 3 fennel bulbs

Trim away the root end, cut off the leafy tops and fibrous stalks, and peel away any bruised outer layers. Cut each bulb in half and then into three or four wedges. In a heavy-bottomed pan, heat 2 cups water with:

¼ cup white wine (optional)
Fennel tops
4 thyme sprigs
4 savory sprigs
1 bay leaf
½ teaspoon fennel seeds, crushed
Salt

Bring to a boil and turn down to a simmer. Pour in:

3 tablespoons extra-virgin olive oil

Add the fennel and cook, turning now and then, until tender, about 10 to 12 minutes. If the water boils away before the fennel is done, add more water. Taste for salt and add as needed along with:

A squeeze of lemon juice

VARIATIONS

♦ Brown the fennel wedges in a little olive oil before adding the water, wine, and spices.

♦ Artichokes can be cooked the same way. Trim them into wedges with the stem attached, if possible. While the artichokes are simmering, cover with a piece of parchment paper to keep them from discoloring.

Sautéed Fennel

Cut off the leafy tops and fibrous stalks and trim off the root ends from fennel bulbs. If you want, save some of the feathery leaves to chop and use later to garnish the dish before serving. Peel away any bruised outer layers. Cut the bulbs in half and then slice fairly thin. Heat a heavy skillet over medium-high heat. Pour in enough oil to coat the bottom generously and add the cut fennel. Let the fennel brown for a few minutes undisturbed. Start tossing or stirring occasionally and continue to cook until the fennel is tender. Season with salt, fresh-ground black pepper, and the chopped fennel leaves. Finish with a squeeze of lemon juice or a pinch of dried chile flakes.

Fennel Gratin

4 SERVINGS

This is a gratin made with a thin white sauce (béchamel), rather than one layered with milk, or with cream and broth. I use this method to cook other vegetables, such as cauliflower, wilted greens, or asparagus.

Trim:

2 large or 3 medium fennel bulbs

Cut them in half and then into wedges. Cook the wedges in salted boiling water until tender, about 5 minutes. Reserve some of the cooking liquid. Make a thin white sauce. Heat in a small heavy pot:

2 tablespoons butter

Stir in:

1½ tablespoons flour

Cook over medium heat for 3 minutes. Add bit by bit, whisking constantly:

⅓ cup milk

⅓ cup fennel blanching liquid

To avoid lumps, whisk in each addition of liquid completely before adding the next. If lumps do occur, strain the sauce, after all the liquid has been added, and return to the burner to cook. Bring slowly to a boil, stirring constantly. Turn down to a bare simmer (use a flame tamer if necessary) and cook for 15 to 20 minutes, stirring occasionally. Season with:

Salt

A pinch of ground nutmeg

A pinch of cayenne (optional)

½ cup grated Parmesan cheese

Preheat the oven to 375°F.

Liberally butter a baking or gratin dish big enough to hold the fennel wedges in one compact layer. Arrange the fennel in the dish and pour the sauce over it. Bake for 20 minutes or until bubbling and browned on top.

✦ Garlic

SEASON: SPRING, SUMMER, FALL

I couldn't cook without garlic. I use it raw and cooked in all manner of dishes. Many varieties of garlic are available, each with its own individual flavor, some with white skins and some with red skins. In the spring, you can also find immature or green garlic. It looks a lot like a leek and its flavor is a little milder and subtler than that of mature garlic. Green garlic tastes great and can be used in all its phases of development. As green garlic starts to mature, the bulb of cloves begins to form, but the skin will still be moist and tender. To prepare green garlic, trim off the root end and remove any damaged or dried outer layers. Use all the white parts of the plant and the tender, light green parts of the stalk.

Mature garlic starts coming to market in summer. Look for firm, tight heads of garlic that are hard and heavy. Garlic has a definite season and eventually starts to sprout; the germ inside each clove starts to turn green and grow. When it has been in storage too long, it may become oxidized, turning yellow with an unpleasant odor. If the clove has started to sprout, cut it in half and remove the green germ from the center. Do not use cloves that have begun to turn yellow.

I find the easiest way to peel garlic is to press down on the head with the heel of my palm to separate it into individual cloves. Use a sharp paring knife to cut off the tip and butt end of a clove and peel off the skin. I prefer not to smash garlic unless I am going to use it right away. Garlic begins to oxidize immediately and should not remain exposed to the air once it has been smashed or cut. Chopped or pounded garlic can be kept a short time under a bit of oil.

Roasted Garlic

This is best when made with firm, fresh heads of garlic that have not begun to sprout. Peel away only the outer dry papery skin of each head of garlic, but don't separate the cloves from the head. Arrange the heads of garlic in a single layer, root side down, in an earthenware baking dish or heavy oven-proof pan that holds them snugly. Pour in chicken broth or water to a depth of ¼ inch. Drizzle the heads with olive oil, and sprinkle with salt. For more flavor add a couple sprigs of thyme or savory and a few peppercorns. Cover tightly and bake in a 375°F oven. Check after 20 minutes. When done, the garlic should be soft and tender; if not, continue baking a little longer. When tender, drizzle with a bit more olive oil and roast, uncovered, for another 7 minutes. Roasted garlic is best served right away with toasted bread and, if you want, a little goat cheese and some olives. Pull apart the cloves, squeeze out the garlic purée onto the bread, and dip the bread into the roasting juices.

Garlic Purée

MAKES ABOUT ½ CUP

Garlic purée is delicious stirred into mashed potatoes or a soufflé base. It makes a tasty compound butter with a bit of salt and will make a gravy taste sublime.

Separate into cloves and peel:
    2 heads of garlic
If the cloves have started to sprout, cut them in half and remove the sprouting green germ. Put the garlic cloves in a small heavy saucepan. Add:
    ¾ cup chicken broth or water
    1½ tablespoons butter or olive oil
    2 to 3 thyme or savory sprigs
    A pinch of salt
Bring the liquid to a boil, reduce to a simmer, cover the pan, and cook until the garlic is very tender, 10 to 15 minutes. Check on the simmering garlic now and then and add more chicken broth or water if needed. When the garlic is tender, drain, reserving the liquid. Mash the garlic or pass it through a food mill. Thin the purée with the reserved liquid. Don't toss out any leftover liquid; it is very tasty.

VARIATIONS

◆ This can be made without peeling the garlic. The garlic cloves take a bit longer to cook and must be puréed in a food mill to separate the flesh from the skins.

◆ Use 1 cup sliced green garlic instead of garlic cloves. Use ½ cup broth or water and cook until tender, about 5 minutes.

• Leafy Greens and Chicories

SEASON: LATE SPRING THROUGH WINTER

Leafy greens include chard, kale, broccoli rabe, collards, spinach, as well as the tops of beets and turnips. There are many varieties of each of these, rainbow chard, Swiss chard, red Russian kale, laciniato kale, and Bloomsdale spinach just to name a few. Select greens that are vibrant, perky, and fresh looking. Avoid buying them in bags already washed and prepared. Whatever time is saved with these convenience items is completely offset by the greater flavor and freshness of locally harvested greens.

Except for chard, the stems of leafy greens should be stripped off and discarded. To do this, hold on to the stem and then grasp the bottom of the leaf and pull it towards the leaf tip while pulling away on the stem with the other hand. The leaves may also be cut from the stem with a small sharp paring knife. The wide ribs of chard leaves can be saved and cooked; they do have a longer cooking time than the leaves, and they need to be separated and cooked apart or ahead. Wash all greens well in abundant water and drain.

Chicories are the family that includes radicchio, escarole, Belgian endive, and frisée. These greens are pleasantly bitter—and not always green: radicchio is usually red, and Belgian endive is a pale, pale yellow green. The hearts of leafy varieties such as escarole and curly endive are almost white. All chicories make delightful salads, and some are sturdy enough to braise and grill. They all should have brightly colored, fresh outer leaves. The headed varieties such as Belgian endive and some varieties of radicchio should be firm and tightly closed.

To prepare chicories for salads, tear off and discard the outer dark leaves, which can be tough and bitter. Separate the leaves and wash and dry them well. Belgian endive will brown very quickly and should be trimmed and cut just before being used. To prepare chicories for braising and grilling, the tightly headed varieties can be cut in half or in wedges.

Wilted Chard with Onion

4 SERVINGS

Wash thoroughly and drain:
   1 large bunch of chard
Pull the leaves from the ribs. Trim the ends from the ribs and then cut them into thin slices. Cut the leaves into wide ribbons.
Heat in a heavy pan:
   2 tablespoons olive oil
Add:
   1 onion, diced
Cook over medium heat, stirring occasionally until soft, about 5 minutes. Add the chard ribs and continue cooking for 3 minutes. Add the chard leaves and:
   Salt
Cook, stirring now and then, until the leaves are tender. Add a little bit of water if the pan gets dry and the onions begin to stick and brown.

VARIATIONS

• Use only 1 tablespoon olive oil, and before adding the onions, add 2 slices bacon cut into 1-inch pieces. Cook until the bacon is beginning to brown, take it out of the pan, and add the onions. Return the cooked bacon to the pan with the chard.

• Add a pinch of dried chile flakes for a bit of spice.

Chard Gratin

4 SERVINGS

Wash and stem:

1½ bunches of chard

Save half the stems and slice them thin. Bring 2 quarts of salted water to a boil and cook the sliced stems for 2 minutes. Add the chard leaves and cook until tender, about 3 minutes. Drain and cool. Gently squeeze out the excess liquid from the stems and leaves and coarsely chop them.

Toss together:

1 cup fresh breadcrumbs (see page 62)
2 teaspoons melted butter

Toast on a baking sheet in a 350°F oven, stirring now and then, until lightly brown, about 10 minutes.

Melt over medium heat in a heavy-bottomed pan:

1½ tablespoons butter

Add:

1 onion, diced

Cook over medium heat until translucent, about 5 minutes. Stir in the chard and:

Salt

Cook for 3 minutes. Sprinkle with:

2 teaspoons flour

Stir well and add:

½ cup milk
A little freshly grated nutmeg

Cook for 5 minutes, stirring occasionally. Add more milk if the mixture gets too thick. The chard should be moist but not floating in liquid. Taste and add salt if needed.

Butter a small baking dish. Spread the chard mixture evenly in the dish and dot with:

2 teaspoons butter

Sprinkle the breadcrumbs evenly over the top. Bake in a 350°F oven until the gratin is golden and bubbling, 20 to 30 minutes.

VARIATION

◆ Substitute 1½ pounds spinach for the chard. Wilt the spinach in a pan with a little butter and water. Cool and squeeze out the excess liquid, as above.

Chard with Parmesan

I was amazed to discover how a little Parmesan and butter transforms plain wilted chard. Try it and see.

Pull the leaves from the ribs of one or more bunches of chard. Discard the ribs (or save them for another dish), wash the leaves, and cook until tender in abundant salted boiling water, 4 minutes or so. Drain the leaves, cool, squeeze out most of their excess water, and chop coarse. For every bunch of chard, melt 3 tablespoons butter in a heavy pan over medium heat. Add the chopped chard and salt to taste. Heat through and for each bunch of chard stir in a generous handful of freshly grated Parmesan cheese. Remove from the heat and serve.

Broccoli Rabe with Garlic and Hot Pepper

4 TO 6 SERVINGS

This is one of my favorite greens. It has an assertive flavor that is bitter, nutty, sweet, and *green*. The stems have a great texture that's both juicy and chewy. It calls out for garlic and strong flavorings such as hot pepper, anchovies, and vinegar.

Stem:

**2 bunches of broccoli rabe
(about 1¼ pounds)**

Cut off and discard any woody parts of the stems. Cut the rest of the stems into ½-inch-long pieces. Slice the leafy parts into 1-inch ribbons. Wash the greens in cold water and drain.

Into a wide sauté pan over medium heat, pour:

3 tablespoons olive oil

When hot, add:

**1 dried cayenne pepper, sliced coarse,
or a pinch of dried chile flakes
3 garlic cloves, coarsely chopped**

Stir once, then quickly toss in the broccoli rabe and season with:

Salt

If all the broccoli rabe won't fit in the pan, wait until some of it is wilted before adding the rest. The residual water from washing the greens should be enough to cook them, but if the pan gets too dry and starts to sizzle, add more water. The toughness of broccoli rabe varies wildly. Cooking it until tender can take anywhere from 4 to 12 minutes. Keep checking for tenderness and seasoning. Just before serving stir in:

1 tablespoon extra-virgin olive oil

Braised Belgian Endive

4 SERVINGS

I love endive cooked this way. It is so succulent and really does melt in your mouth. Serve it with all kinds of roasted meats and poached or baked fish.

Trim off the root ends and remove any discolored outer leaves of:

4 Belgian endive

Cut in half lengthwise and season well with:

Salt

Melt in a heavy-bottomed skillet:

2 tablespoons butter

Add the endive, cut side down, and cook over medium heat until nicely browned. This can be done in batches, adding more butter with each batch. The pan will brown, which is fine; just don't allow it to blacken. If it does, wash it out before adding the next batch. Place the endive, browned sides up, in a baking dish just large enough to hold them in a single layer. Pour in:

About 1 cup chicken broth

The broth should be about ½ inch deep in the dish. Cover tightly and bake in a 400°F oven until tender, about 20 minutes. Check for doneness by probing the core with a sharp knife.

VARIATIONS

◆ Wrap each endive half in a thin slice of pancetta or bacon before browning. Brown the wrapped endives on both sides, using more butter if necessary, and braise as above.

◆ Place the cut endives in a baking dish and pour in about ¾ cup cream, season with salt and pepper, and cook until tender, brown, and bubbling.

Grilled Radicchio with Garlic Vinaigrette

This is one of the most delicious ways to eat radicchio, especially with grilled meats, or mixed into a risotto or pasta dish.

Wash and trim the radicchio. Cut leafy varieties shaped like heads of romaine, such as Rossa di Treviso, lengthwise into halves or quarters; round heads shaped like cabbages, such as Rossa di Verona, are best cut into 6 or 8 wedges. Put the cut radicchio in a bowl, drizzle with olive oil, season with salt and fresh-ground black pepper, and gently toss to coat evenly.

Grill the radicchio over a medium-hot fire, turning frequently until wilted and tender throughout, about 10 minutes. The time will vary according to the type and size of the radicchio and the heat of the fire. The outer leaves may get crispy, which is very tasty. When done, sauce the radicchio with a garlicky vinaigrette made with red wine and balsamic vinegars. Serve warm or at room temperature.

VARIATION

◆ Instead of grilled, the radicchio can be broiled, oven roasted, or pan fried until tender and witted.

Creamed Spinach

4 SERVINGS

Stem, wash, and drain:

1 pound spinach

Melt in a heavy pan over medium heat:

2 tablespoons butter

Add:

1 medium onion, diced small

Cook until tender, about 7 minutes, then add the spinach and cook until just wilted. If there is a lot of liquid in the pan, bunch the spinach to one side, press it to squeeze out as much liquid as possible, and pour it off. Return the pan to the stove and add:

Salt

⅓ cup heavy cream or crème fraîche

Cook at a boil until the cream has reduced and thickened around the spinach. Taste for salt and adjust as needed and finish with:

Fresh-ground black or white pepper

VARIATIONS

◆ Add 2 garlic cloves, chopped fine, with the salt and cream.

◆ Finish the dish with a squeeze of lemon juice or a sprinkle of wine vinegar.

◆ Add ⅛ teaspoon or so of freshly grated nutmeg with the salt and cream.

◆ Use ½ cup White Sauce (Béchamel Sauce; page 225) in place of the cream, and simmer gently for 5 minutes.

✦ Mushrooms

SEASON: YEAR-ROUND

Edible wild mushrooms grow almost everywhere. Their flavors are woodsy, earthy, and complex; their textures, pleasantly meaty and chewy. They are a tasty and rewarding food for foragers; chanterelles, morels, boletus, and oyster mushrooms are among the common varieties that are easy to identify. However, never eat mushrooms you have gathered in the wild unless you know exactly what you are doing and can positively identify your mushrooms. Take no chances. Investigate your local resources—an amateur mycological society or a mushroom expert at your local college or university—to learn about the growing habits of wild mushrooms and how to identify them.

Where wild mushrooms are abundant they are gathered by commercial pickers and sold in markets. Buy wild mushrooms that look fresh and alive, without any signs or smells of mold or rot. Store them in a paper bag in the refrigerator and eat them as soon as possible. Clean them carefully. If they are not too muddy or sandy, you can use a paring knife to carve away irregularities and discolorations and use a damp cloth to wipe away any dirt that can't be scraped off. Trim away the stem ends and any blemished places. Especially dirty mushrooms may need to be quickly dunked in cold water to get rid of the dirt and grit of the wild, but don't let them soak or they will absorb a lot of water. Drain them well.

Common cultivated mushrooms—both the white ones and the brown cremini—can now be found organically grown. Look for smaller mushrooms that have tightly closed caps. Trim the stem ends and wipe the caps clean; no further washing is needed.

Sautéed Mushrooms

Put a skillet over high heat. When it's very hot, add enough olive oil to coat the pan. Quickly add the mushrooms and a sprinkle of salt. If the mushrooms give off so much water that they start simmering in liquid instead of sautéing, tip off the excess liquid and save it for another use. Domestic mushrooms will have less moisture and should be cooked over lower heat. You may have to add a bit more oil at this point. Continue sautéing the mushrooms until they begin to brown and are tender to the bite. If you have more than one kind of mushroom, sauté each kind separately before combining them. When they are ready, you can add a splash of cream or a spoonful of crème fraîche and cook until just hot. Or add chopped thyme and garlic or a sprinkling of Gremolata (page 231) and sauté gently for a moment before serving on croutons, alongside grilled meat, or inside an omelet—or as a pasta sauce.

✦ Onions

SEASON: YEAR-ROUND,

BEST IN SPRING THROUGH FALL

Onions are a fundamental ingredient that gives background sweetness and depth to an endless number of soups, sauces, stews, and vegetable dishes. Different kinds of onion come to market at different times. The most common onion—the yellow onion with brown, dry, papery skin—is held in storage and available year-round. Spring onions—fresh onions with bulbs and intact green tops—are harvested and sold in spring. They are tender and mild and wonderful to cook with. The sweet onion varieties (which include Walla Walla, Maui, and Vidalia onions) start to mature in the early summer; these are big onions with pale yellow papery skins, but they do not store well. The height of summer is also the height of onion season, and the market is crowded with scallions and recently harvested onions. (Scallions have green tops, like spring onions, but they lack bulbs.) Look for spring onions and scallions that are bright and shiny with fresh-looking greens. Roots should be fresh and white, not withered. Dry, cured onions should be hard, with crackly, papery skins.

To prepare spring onions, trim away the green tops, root end, and any dry or damaged outer layers. To prepare cured onions, make shallow cone-shaped cuts to remove the stem and root ends. Unless you want to slice horizontal onion rings, cut the onion in half lengthwise and peel away the papery skin (it is much easier to peel an onion after it has been cut in two). Tiny onions are easier to peel if you soak them for a minute or two in warm water to hydrate their skins; just do this right before you peel them. Slice or chop onions right before you need them: onions oxidize and start losing their best flavors soon after they are cut. Use a sharp knife, to avoid mashing and bruising them. If they are to be used for a salad, submerge sliced onions in ice water to preserve them. (This will also help tame the raw flavor of a hot, pungent onion.)

The sweet and salty combination of onion and anchovy is particularly delicious, especially in an Onion Tart (page 177).

Baked Sliced Onions

Peel firm, juicy onions and slice them crosswise ¼ inch thick. Figure 2 to 3 slices per person. Brush a baking sheet with olive oil and place the onion slices on it in a single layer. Season the slices with salt and turn them over. Brush the exposed sides of the onions with more oil, season with salt, and bake them in a 375°F oven for 30 minutes or until tender and browned on their undersides. Serve the onions as is, or marinate them in a spoonful or two of vinaigrette. These are good warm as a side vegetable and at room temperature as part of a salad or antipasto plate.

Grilled Onions

Prepare a medium-hot fire in an outdoor grill and place the grate over it to preheat. Peel some onions and slice them crosswise ¼ to ½ inch thick. Thread them on a skewer for easier grilling by placing an onion slice flat on the table, holding a skewer parallel to the table, and carefully pushing it into and through the center of the slice. The skewered onion slice will look like a large lollipop. Two or three slices will fit onto one skewer. Brush the onions with olive oil and season with salt. Clean the grill grate well and wipe it with a cloth (or layers of paper towels) moistened with oil. Arrange the onions on the grill and cook for about 4 minutes on each side. If the onions are not yet tender, continue grilling them until they are, turning as often as needed to keep them from burning. Serve warm or at room temperature, either plain or with a simple vinaigrette or sauce.

After grilling a piece of meat or fish, the fire is usually still hot and just right for grilling onions and a few slices of bread. They are a wonderful accompaniment to grilled meat, especially hamburgers.

✦ Parsnips

SEASON: LATE FALL AND WINTER

Parsnips look like large ivory-colored carrots. They are indeed related to carrots, but biting into a raw parsnip is not a good idea: they are almost inedible. When cooked, however, the flavor of parsnips is nutty and sweet. They are wonderful roasted or mashed, by themselves or with other vegetables, and they add a deep, complex note to broths and soups. At the market look for medium-size, firm, smooth-skinned parsnips; when you peel small ones, there's not much parsnip left to eat, and very large ones have a woody core that needs to be removed. Prepare parsnips just like carrots, peeling away the skin and trimming off both ends.

Parsnip or Root Vegetable Purée

Any number of root vegetables can be used to make this purée. Parsnips alone make a sweet purée with a lovely creamy yellow color. Turnips cook quickly and make a loose nutty purée. Carrots, celery root, rutabagas, and kohlrabi can all be turned into a purée as well. Peel and cut the vegetables into large pieces. Cook in salted boiling water until tender. Purée in a food mill and enrich with butter, cream, or olive oil. Celery root and turnips, cut into smaller pieces, can be cooked in butter or olive oil, covered, over low heat without any water. Stir often and lower the heat if the pan starts to scorch.

A purée may be made from a combination of root vegetables; celery root, carrots, and rutabagas make a delicious combination, and turnips and kohlrabi are also nice together. Puréed potatoes are especially tasty mixed with celery root or parsnip purée. When making combination purées it is best to cook the vegetables separately since they all require different cooking times. They can then be puréed together.

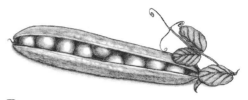

✦ Peas

SEASON: SPRING AND EARLY SUMMER

Shelling peas (or English peas), snap peas, and snow peas are the three most common varieties. Shelling peas are shelled, and only the peas within are eaten. Snap peas and snow peas are eaten pod and all. The tender shoots or tips of the pea vines are good to eat as well. All peas taste best when harvested while young and tender. They are the sweetest at this stage, as the sugars have not yet transformed to starch. Shelling peas have a very short season; they are only around while the cool weather of spring is here. Snap peas and snow peas can tolerate a bit of heat and will last into the early summer.

Select peas that are vibrant and firm, with shiny pods. When very fresh the pods will actually squeak as they are rubbed together. Smaller peas of any variety will be tastier than larger ones. The edible-pod varieties, especially snow peas, are best when the peas are tiny, almost undeveloped. As they mature and become too stringy to eat whole, sugar snap peas can be shucked like shelling peas.

To prepare snap and snow peas, snap back each end and pull it down the side of the pod to remove any strings. Pea shoots need only to be picked over for any yellow leaves and then rinsed and drained before being sautéed or steamed.

Green Pea and Asparagus Ragout

4 SERVINGS

Shell:

¾ pound green peas

Snap the ends from:

¾ pound asparagus

Slice, on a slight diagonal, into slices between ⅛ and ¼ inch thick. Leave the tips 1½ inches long; split them in half lengthwise if they are thick. Melt, in a heavy pan over medium heat:

2 tablespoons butter

Add:

3 spring onions, trimmed and sliced (about ¾ cup)

Cook for 4 or 5 minutes, until soft. Add the sliced asparagus and shelled peas with:

½ cup water

Salt

Cook for 4 or 5 minutes, or until the vegetables are tender. Swirl in:

1 tablespoon butter

1 tablespoon chopped parsley or chervil

Taste for salt and adjust as needed.

VARIATIONS

◆ Tender young fava beans can be substituted for some or all of the peas.

◆ Use sugar snap peas trimmed and sliced on the diagonal instead of the shelling peas.

◆ Slice 1 or 2 stalks of green garlic and add with the asparagus and peas.

Buttered Peas

The easiest, and maybe the best, way to serve tender shelling peas is to shell them and then cook them in ½ inch or so of salted boiling water. Peas take longer to cook than you might expect; I find they take around 4 minutes. Keep tasting them, and drain them when they are done to your liking. Put a large pat of butter on them and a sprinkle of salt, stir together, and serve immediately. If you have it available, chervil is wonderful chopped and stirred in. A slice or two of prosciutto or other ham can be julienned and stirred in with the butter, which makes a lovely pasta sauce for fresh or dried egg noodles. Another way to cook peas, one dear to the French, is to heat the water, then add salt and a few butter lettuce leaves along with the peas. When the peas are tender, swirl in butter to make a sauce around the peas and lettuce. The peas can also be cooked in olive oil instead of butter.

All of these ways of cooking shelled peas apply to sugar snap peas. Cook them whole, or cut in half lengthwise or diagonally so that they mix well with sauce.

◆ Peppers

SEASON: MIDSUMMER THROUGH FALL

There is a spectacular array of varieties and colors of sweet peppers and chiles, all from the same genus. For the most part, sweet peppers are larger and fleshier than spicy chiles. All peppers start out green and then change colors as they ripen; the palette extends from green to purple to red with all the shades of yellow and orange in between. The most common sweet pepper is the bell pepper, but there are many others: Hungarian wax peppers, which are small and pale yellow; lipstick peppers, also small, in brilliant shades of red-orange; larger, less fleshy gypsy peppers; tiny red cherry peppers; long pointy Corno di Toro peppers; and fat fleshy pimientos, to name just a few. All these peppers are sweet, but they have many nuances in flavor as well and are especially suited to the Mediterranean cooking of the South of France, Italy, and Spain. Select peppers that have ripened beyond the immature green stage. A green pepper has not had the chance to develop its full flavor and is much harder to digest. Peppers are tasty whether raw or cooked, roasted or peeled. There are even more varieties of chile peppers. They vary in flavor and spiciness as well as size and color. Chiles are eaten immature and green, fully mature, and dried.

Choose shiny, bright, fresh peppers and chiles. Avoid any that have spots or blisters on their skin. Peppers and chiles are prepared the same way, regardless of size: either roast them whole to remove the skins and remove the cap, internal veins, and seeds (the veins and seeds are the spiciest part of a chile); or cut them up without cooking them first, removing the cap and stem, carving off the tough internal veins, and shaking out all the seeds. When using dried chiles, split them open and discard the seeds and stems. They can be toasted briefly in a hot oven or pan and then rehydrated in water for a sauce or can be added directly to a stew.

Sautéed Peppers with Capers

4 SERVINGS

Sautéed peppers are good on pizzas and pastas, in omelets, or on croutons. If you like, mix hot and sweet peppers.

Cut in half:

3 sweet peppers, preferably of different colors and types

Trim the stem end and remove the seeds and the ribs inside the peppers. Slice thin. Peel and slice thin:

1 onion

Heat in a heavy pan:

3 tablespoons olive oil

Add the onion and cook over medium heat, stirring occasionally, for 4 minutes. Add the peppers and season with:

Salt

Cook for another 4 to 6 minutes, or until the peppers begin to soften. Stir in:

2 to 3 garlic cloves, chopped

1 tablespoon capers, rinsed, drained, and chopped coarse

Cook for another few minutes, turning down the heat if the pan begins to brown. Taste for salt and adjust as needed. When the peppers are done toss with:

1 tablespoon chopped basil or parsley (or both)

Serve lightly drizzled with:

Extra-virgin olive oil

◆ Potatoes

SEASON: SPRING AND FALL

Baking potatoes, boiling potatoes, new potatoes, and fingerling potatoes—there are many kinds of each to choose from, some yellow, some blue or red. The red-skinned potatoes often called boiling potatoes have dense, white, waxy flesh that holds its shape when boiled. They won't do very well for baking and make terrible mashed potatoes, turning gluey when mashed. Baking potatoes usually have light brown skins with white flesh that is dry and fluffy when cooked. These are best for baking and for French fries. Kennebecs and russets are common varieties.

The tastiest, most versatile potatoes are the yellow-fleshed varieties such as Yellow Finn, German Butterball, and Yukon Gold.

The flesh of these potatoes has a texture between that of a baker and a boiler. They have enough waxy starch to hold together when boiled, but not so much that they can't be mashed—and best of all they are full of flavor, much more so than any white-fleshed variety.

New potatoes are those that are dug while the plants are still green in the fields and have thin shaggy skins. They are a real treat. Fingerlings are smaller potatoes shaped, as you might guess, like long thin fingers. Some delicious varieties to try are Russian Banana, German, and Ruby Crescent.

Select potatoes that are firm and free of discolored spots. Don't buy potatoes that have green on the skin. This is caused by exposure to light and may indicate the presence of solanine, which is toxic. The green may be peeled away, but it is better to avoid having to do so. Store potatoes in a bag or cupboard away from any light. New potatoes and fingerlings never need to be peeled; just wash them well before cooking. Other potatoes should be peeled, depending on the recipe and your wishes. Once peeled, potatoes should be kept submerged in water to keep them from turning brown.

Potato Gratin

4 SERVINGS

I like this best when the potatoes are sliced quite thin (a mandoline makes this easy): that way the potato slices are less likely to curl up and burn on the edges. Yukon Gold and other waxy, yellow-fleshed potatoes keep their texture in a gratin; floury potatoes like russets fall apart.

Rub a 9- by 12-inch gratin dish with:
   Butter
Peel and slice about ¹⁄₁₆ inch thick:
   **4 large yellow potatoes
   (about 1½ pounds)**
Make a layer of potato slices in the gratin dish, overlapping them slightly, like shingles. Sprinkle with:
   Salt and fresh-ground black pepper
Continue to layer the potato slices, seasoning each layer, until the potatoes are used up. You should have two or, at the most, three layers. Carefully pour over the potatoes:
   1 cup milk
The liquid should come up to the bottom of the top layer of potatoes. Add more if necessary. Generously dot the top of the potatoes with:
   3 tablespoons butter, cut into pieces
Bake in a 350°F oven until browned and bubbling, about 1 hour. Halfway through the baking, take the gratin dish out of the oven and press the potatoes flat with a metal spatula to keep the top moist. Return to the oven and keep checking. The gratin is done when the potatoes are soft and the top is golden brown.

VARIATIONS
◆ Peel and smash a garlic clove and rub it all over the inside of the gratin dish before buttering it.

• Use duck fat instead of butter.

• Use heavy cream or a mixture of half-and-half and cream. Omit the butter.

• Substitute celery root, parsnip, or turnip slices for up to half the potatoes.

• Add chopped herbs such as thyme, parsley, chives, or chervil between the layers.

• Sauté mushrooms, sorrel, spinach, or leeks, and layer them between the potato slices.

• Sprinkle grated Gruyère or Parmesan cheese on each layer and sprinkle more on top for the last 15 minutes of baking.

Pan-Fried Potatoes

4 SERVINGS

Peel and cut into ¾-inch cubes:

1½ pounds yellow potatoes,
such as Yellow Finn or Yukon Gold,
or russet potatoes

Cut the potatoes as uniformly as possible so they will cook evenly. Bring a pot of salted water to a boil and cook the potatoes until they are just cooked through and tender but not falling apart. Drain the potatoes and let them sit for a few minutes to dry and cool.

Heat in a heavy-bottomed pan, preferably cast iron:

½ cup olive oil

When the oil is hot, add the potatoes and cook over medium heat, stirring and tossing regularly, until golden, about 15 minutes. Season with:

Salt

Serve immediately.

VARIATIONS

• Fry the potatoes in half olive oil and half clarified butter or duck fat.

• Cut the potatoes into small dice, about ⅜ inch. Do not boil them first and fry them until crispy, tossing regularly.

Mashed Potatoes

4 SERVINGS

Boil, in well-salted water, for 15 to 20 minutes, until fully cooked through:

1½ pounds yellow or russet potatoes
(or a mixture), cut in medium-size
pieces

Test the potatoes by cutting a piece in half and checking the center. It should be tender, flaky, and dry. Drain the potatoes well and leave them in the colander to steam for a few minutes. Meanwhile, in the now-empty pot, heat:

½ cup whole milk or potato-cooking
water

Return the drained potatoes to the pot. Add:

4 tablespoons butter, cut into pieces

With a potato masher or wooden spoon, mash the potatoes over low heat, to keep them hot. Season with:

Salt, to taste

Add more milk, if the mashed potatoes are too stiff.

VARIATIONS

• Substitute extra-virgin olive oil for the butter.

• Squeeze Roasted Garlic (page 308) out of the skins and into the mashed potatoes.

• Stir quickly sautéed sliced scallions into the mashed potatoes.

• Cook other root vegetables separately (carrots, celery root, turnips, or parsnips), and mash them with the potatoes.

• For a smooth purée, pass the cooked potatoes through a food mill instead of mashing them.

• Form cold leftover mashed potatoes into patties and pan-fry them the next morning to eat with eggs.

◆ Sweet Potatoes and Yams

SEASON: LATE FALL THROUGH WINTER

Sweet potatoes and yams are virtually interchangeable in the kitchen. Sweet potatoes have pale-yellow, dry, nutty-flavored flesh. Jewel and garnet are the two most common kinds of yam; both have reddish to purple-colored skin and brilliant orange, sweet, moist flesh. Look for firm, unblemished sweet potatoes or yams. They continue to sweeten after harvest, but they don't store well and they tend to spoil fairly quickly. Wash them and roast them whole in the skin or peel them to roast, steam, or fry.

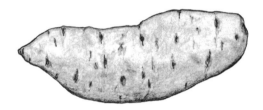

Sweet Potatoes with Lime

The small, purple-fleshed Hawaiian sweet potatoes that are sometimes found in the market are especially good this way. Choose firm, fresh sweet potatoes. Wash and scrub them well. Bake in a 375°F oven until tender, about 1 hour. When they are done, split the potatoes open, dot with butter, sprinkle with salt, and squeeze lime juice over them. Scatter a handful of coarsely chopped cilantro over them, if you like.

Moroccan Sweet Potato Salad

4 SERVINGS

Peel:

2 sweet potatoes (about 1 pound)

Cut into large cubes and toss with:

Olive oil
Salt

Spread out in a baking dish and roast until tender in a 375°F oven. When done, remove from the oven and let cool. Meanwhile prepare a marinade. Whisk together:

A pinch of saffron threads
½ teaspoon grated fresh ginger
A pinch of ground cumin
1 teaspoon paprika
Salt
2 tablespoons fresh lemon juice
3 tablespoons extra-virgin olive oil

Stir in:

2 tablespoons chopped cilantro
  (stems and leaves)
1 tablespoon chopped parsley (leaves)

Spoon the marinade over the lukewarm sweet potatoes and let sit for 30 minutes, stirring now and then. Taste for salt and adjust as needed. Serve at room temperature.

VARIATIONS

◆ Add 1 tablespoon coarsely chopped green olives.

◆ Add the zest of ½ lemon to the marinade.

◆ For a slightly different marinade, cook ½ onion, diced fine, in a little olive oil with the ginger and saffron, until soft but not brown, about 7 minutes. Transfer the onion to a bowl, add the rest of the marinade ingredients, and proceed as above.

◆ Tomatoes

SEASON: SUMMER

Nothing compares with a vine-ripened, fragrant, colorful tomato. Farmers' markets (and your own backyard!) are the best places to go for tomatoes. Most of the supermarket varieties sold year-round have been bred for structure and not flavor. They can be shipped around the world, but they won't make a tasty meal. There are many, many tomatoes to choose from. Little cherry tomatoes ripen quickly and are the first to market. They come in many colors; the golden and red ones are the most flavorful. Plum tomatoes are good for sauce. And then come all the other types, many of them called "heirloom tomatoes" to remind us that they are tomatoes our forebears planted in the days before produce was shipped globally. There are yellow, golden, orange, green, purple, striped, and, yes, red tomatoes to choose from. They come in as many sizes as there are colors.

Choose deeply colored tomatoes that are neither soft nor too firm. Tomatoes will continue to ripen off the vine, and do so best out of direct sunlight. Don't put your tomatoes in the refrigerator; the cold really steals their flavor. Wash the tomatoes and cut out a cone at the stem end to remove the core. If the skin is thick, tomatoes may be better peeled. To peel, plunge them into rapidly boiling water and remove them once the skin is loosened, which will take between 15 seconds and a minute or so (check the tomatoes often to know when to pull them out). Cool the tomatoes quickly in ice-cold water and slip off the skins. To seed a tomato, cut it in half horizontally and gently squeeze each half, coaxing the seeds out of each little cavity with your fingers. The juice can be strained to use in cooking, or to drink.

Tomato Confit

4 SERVINGS

Cooking tomatoes this way concentrates and intensifies their flavor. Each one is like a spoonful of sweet sauce.

Preheat the oven to 350°F. Peel and core:
4 medium tomatoes
In the bottom of a baking dish just large enough to hold the tomatoes snugly, scatter:
A few basil sprigs
Arrange the tomatoes core side down on top of the basil. Sprinkle with:
Salt
Add:
About ½ cup olive oil
Bake for about 50 minutes. The tomatoes are done when lightly browned on top and completely tender. Remove them carefully when serving. The oil left behind can be saved to add to a vinaigrette or other sauce.

Baked Stuffed Tomatoes

Small sweet late-season tomatoes, especially the Early Girl variety, are wonderful for stuffing and baking. You can peel the tomatoes for a more delicate texture, but it is optional. Make a stuffing of fresh breadcrumbs (using country-style bread), chopped garlic, and lots of fresh basil. Piccolo fino basil, a spicy and very small-leafed variety, is especially good. Core the tomatoes, cut them in half horizontally, and remove the seeds. Season the insides with salt and pepper, and fill the cavities with the breadcrumb mixture, pressing it in well and mounding it on top. Fit the tomatoes snugly in a shallow earthenware dish and drizzle each one with olive oil. Bake at 375°F for 30 minutes or so, until nicely browned.

Ratatouille

6 TO 8 SERVINGS

For a very colorful ratatouille use different colored peppers, squash, and tomatoes. Don't hesitate to double this recipe, as any ratatouille left over will taste even better the next day.

Cut into ½-inch cubes:

1 medium eggplant

Toss the cubes with:

Salt

Set the cubes in a colander to drain for about 20 minutes.

Heat in a heavy-bottomed pot:

2 tablespoons olive oil

Pat the eggplant dry, add to the pan, and cook over medium heat, stirring frequently, until golden. Add a bit more oil if the eggplant absorbs all the oil and sticks to the bottom of the pan. Remove the eggplant when done and set aside. Pour in:

2 tablespoons olive oil

Add:

2 medium onions, cut into ½-inch dice

Cook for about 7 minutes, or until soft and translucent. Add:

4 to 6 garlic cloves, chopped
½ bunch of basil, tied in a bouquet
   with kitchen twine
Salt
A pinch of dried chile flakes

Cook for 2 or 3 minutes, then stir in:

2 sweet peppers, cut into ½-inch dice

Cook for a few minutes, then add:

3 medium summer squash,
   cut into ½-inch dice

Cook for a few more minutes, then stir in:

3 ripe medium tomatoes,
   cut into ½-inch dice

Cook for 10 minutes longer, then stir in the eggplant and cook for 10 to 15 minutes more, until all the vegetables are soft. Remove the bouquet of basil, pressing on it to extract all its flavors, and adjust the seasoning with salt.

Stir in:

6 basil leaves, chopped
Extra-virgin olive oil

Serve warm or cold.

VARIATIONS

• Cook all of the vegetables, except the tomatoes, separately until tender and then stir them together with the tomatoes, herbs, garlic, and salt. Heat through and serve.
• For Ratatouille of Grilled Vegetables, see page 160.

Winter Roasted Tomatoes

This is a very simple preparation to satisfy that wintertime craving for deep tomato flavor. Exact proportions are unimportant.

Choose a wide, shallow earthenware dish and pour in olive oil to cover the bottom. Over the oil spread a diced onion, 2 or 3 garlic cloves sliced thin, and a scattering of fresh herb leaves, such as marjoram, parsley, rosemary, or basil. Season with salt. Drain a large can of organic whole tomatoes (drink the juice or save for another use), and arrange the tomatoes in a single layer over the onions, garlic, and herbs. Season with salt and pepper, sprinkle with a little sugar, and drizzle with olive oil. Bake, uncovered, at 275°F for 4 to 5 hours. Coarsely cut up the tomatoes and serve as a sauce with warm pasta, roasted meats and beans, or whatever you like. The tomatoes are also delicious served on crusty bread as an hors d'oeuvre.

◆ Turnips and Rutabagas

SEASON: FALL THROUGH SPRING

Turnips are related to arugula and radishes. They share a little of their nutty heat, but they are sweeter. They come in many colors: the most common are the purple-topped white variety and the all-white Tokyo turnip. Sautéed or steamed, turnip tops make tasty greens, too, and in fact some varieties are grown only for their greens.

Turnips can be found year-round but are sweetest and most tender when they are freshly harvested. Early spring and fall is the time to look for small, tender turnips with their greens still attached. These can be cooked whole, and they often don't need to be peeled. As the turnips mature, their skin becomes thicker and tougher and the flavor more pungent. Hot weather makes turnips tough and bitter. Look for smooth-skinned, bright, shiny, firm turnips with fresh greens. The tiniest turnips can be cooked with their greens still attached and need no more preparation than a thorough washing. The greens should be cut off of larger turnips, but you can leave an inch or so of stem for color. Taste to decide if the skin is tender enough to leave in place. Large turnips should be peeled and trimmed completely; peel deeply, removing some flesh along with the skin.

Rutabagas belong to another species, a cross between the turnip and cabbage. Also known as swedes, they resemble large yellow turnips with purplish tops. They are a little starchier than turnips, but they develop a good sweet flavor after the cold has set in. They are prepared and cooked like large turnips.

Buttered Turnips

Turnips have quite a bit of internal moisture and can be cooked without any water at all. This recipe works well with large or small turnips. Peel the turnips if they need it and cut them into medium pieces. Smaller turnips can be left whole or just cut in half. Put them in a heavy pan with a big pinch of salt and a large pat of butter. Cover and cook the turnips until tender over medium heat, stirring every now and then. If the pan starts to brown, turn down the heat. Serve them as is, or mash them with a touch of fresh butter. Turnips can also be sliced and cooked uncovered over higher heat to brown them on purpose; they are delicious caramelized like this. Keep an eye on them to make sure that they don't brown so much that the flavor becomes bitter.

Steamed Turnips and Turnip Greens

When you find small turnips with fresh greens still attached it is nice to cook them together. Wash the turnips thoroughly and remove any yellowed or damaged leaves. Leave the greens on the turnips and cut off the root. If they are on the large side, cut the turnips in halves or quarters. Put the turnips and their greens in a heavy pan with a pinch of salt and add water to a depth of about ¼ inch. Cook the turnips, covered, over medium-high heat until both the turnips and their greens are tender, anywhere from 3 to 6 minutes. Lift the turnips out of the water and serve with a sprinkle of salt and a little butter or extra-virgin olive oil.

Large turnips are good cooked with their greens, too. Cut off the greens, leaving an inch or so of stems on the turnips. Peel the turnips and cut into wedges. Strip the leaves off the stems. Put the turnips in a pan with the leaves on top, and cook in a little water as above.

◆ Winter Squash

SEASON: LATE FALL THROUGH LATE WINTER

Pumpkin, Delicata, acorn, butternut, spaghetti, and kabocha are a few of the many sweet-fleshed winter squashes available in the markets. These are all squashes that are eaten after they have matured and their skins or rinds have hardened. Squash continues to sweeten off the vine. Choose unblemished squash that are firm and heavy. They don't need to be refrigerated unless they have been cut open. Cut squash in half carefully with a heavy knife on a stable surface. Scoop out the seeds and fiber from the inside cavity. The halves can be roasted until tender, cut side down, or they can be peeled (a swivel-bladed vegetable peeler will work on most squash) and cut up to roast, steam, or sauté. They're delicious made into soup, by themselves or with other vegetables in a flavorful broth, or puréed.

Winter Squash Purée

Sweet squash purée makes a fine filling for ravioli or as a substitute for pumpkin in a pie. Choose your favorite variety of squash. Cut the squash in half and scoop out the seeds. Place the halves cut side down on an oiled or parchment-paper-lined baking sheet. Bake in a 350°F oven until the squash is tender throughout. The time will vary depending on the type of squash you have chosen. Remove from the oven, let cool, and then scoop the flesh from the peel. Purée in a food mill or mash with a spoon or potato masher. Season the purée with oil or butter and salt and a little cream, if desired. For variety, stir in some diced ripe pear to the purée or garnish with fried sage leaves.

Roasted Butternut Squash

Peel 1 small butternut squash, cut it in half, and remove the seeds. Cut into ¼-inch dice. Put the squash in a shallow earthenware baking dish, sprinkle with salt, drizzle with extra-virgin olive oil, add a few torn sage leaves, toss well, and bake in a 350°F oven until soft and lightly browned on top, about 1½ hours. For variety, instead of sage leaves, toss the squash with 4 garlic cloves, chopped fine, and ¼ cup chopped parsley.

⬥ Zucchini and Other Summer Squash

SEASON: SUMMER

The most common summer squashes are green zucchini, the light green flying-saucer-shaped pattypan, and the gooseneck-shaped yellow crookneck. More obscure varieties with different flavors and textures can be found at farmers' markets. One of my favorites is Costata Romanesco, a ribbed, mottled-green, zucchini-shaped squash. It has a sweet flavor and a texture that doesn't break down while cooking. Choose small, firm squash with bright skin. Larger ones tend to be watery and seedy. Wash the squashes or rub them clean with a damp cloth. Trim off and discard both the blossom and stem ends. Once cut, squash can be stored in the refrigerator under a damp towel for several hours. The blossoms of summer squash are good to eat as well. Trim off their stems and shake them well to rid them of any bugs they may be harboring. Chop the blossoms, sauté them, and add to an omelet, a pasta sauce, or a risotto. Or cook them whole, stuffed with cheese perhaps, and poached, baked, or dipped in a simple batter and fried.

Summer Squash Gratin

4 SERVINGS

Preheat the oven to 375°F. Wash, dry, and trim the ends from:

6 medium summer squash,
   all one kind or a variety, for color

Slice the squash very thin. A Japanese mandoline makes this job easier. Cut into a chiffonade:

Leaves from a few basil sprigs

Arrange a layer of squash in a medium-size baking or gratin dish. It is best if you can make three layers. Sprinkle with the basil chiffonade and:

Salt
Fresh-ground black pepper

Repeat with the remaining squash to make two more layers, sprinkling each with basil, salt, and pepper. Pour in:

½ cup cream
½ cup half-and-half

The liquid should just come up to the top of the squash. Bake until bubbling and browned on top, about 1 hour. For even browning, press down on the squash with a spatula once or twice while the gratin is cooking.

VARIATIONS

⬥ Layer 2 thinly sliced garlic cloves with the basil.

⬥ Sprinkle ¼ cup Parmesan or other grating cheese on the layers while assembling the gratin.

⬥ Use other herbs such as summer savory, marjoram, or parsley in place of the basil.

⬥ For a nondairy version, sauté 1 onion, sliced, in olive oil until soft, about 10 minutes. Season with sliced garlic, salt, and the basil or other herbs. Place the onions in the bottom of the gratin and layer on the squash, seasoning with salt as you go. Drizzle with olive oil. Cover with a piece of parchment paper and cook until the squash is translucent. Take off the parchment, press the squash down with a spatula, and bake until tender and lightly browned on top.

Zucchini Ragout with Bacon and Tomato

4 SERVINGS

Clean and cut the ends from:

**4 to 6 small zucchini, preferably firm
Costata Romanesco**

Cut into ¼-inch slices and toss with:

Salt

Place in a colander to drain.
Heat in a heavy-bottomed pan:

2 tablespoons olive oil.

Add:

**2 slices bacon or pancetta,
cut into small pieces
1 onion, peeled and diced**

Cook for 10 minutes, until tender, then add:

**¾ pound tomatoes,
peeled, seeded, and diced**

Cook for 7 minutes or until the tomatoes begin to break down. Add the sliced zucchini and cook, stirring occasionally, until the zucchini is tender and the sauce is thick. Turn the heat down if the sauce is boiling rapidly or if it starts to stick. At the last few minutes season with:

**Fresh-ground black pepper
2 teaspoons chopped parsley
2 teaspoons chopped basil**

Taste for salt, add some if needed, and serve warm or at room temperature as an antipasto dish or on top of grilled or toasted bread rubbed with a garlic clove.

Sautéed Grated Zucchini with Marjoram

4 SERVINGS

Rinse, dry, and trim the ends of:

1 pound zucchini

Grate them on the large holes of a box grater (or use the julienne blade of a mandoline). Layer the zucchini into a mixing bowl, salting each layer lightly, and let stand for 20 minutes or so. (Gauge the salt by taste; the zucchini should taste highly seasoned but not salty.) Drain the zucchini in a sieve or colander, squeezing tightly to remove as much liquid as possible. Into a heavy-bottomed sauté pan, over medium-high heat, pour:

2 tablespoons olive oil or butter

Add the drained zucchini and sauté, tossing frequently until lightly browned, about 7 minutes. Spread it out in the pan with a wooden spoon to help it brown. When the squash is cooked, take the pan off the heat and stir in:

**3 tablespoons coarsely chopped fresh
marjoram leaves (or leaves and
flowers)
1 garlic clove pounded to a purée**

Serve hot or at room temperature.

Fish and Shellfish

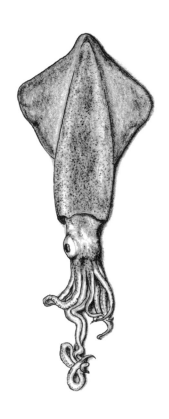

Buying Fish

Fish is one of the last wild foods we see regularly on the dinner table, but our oceans are endangered. It is important to be informed and consider the ramifications of our buying decisions carefully. The sustainability of fisheries is a complicated issue; you have to stay up to date to know which fish are safe to eat. As fishing worldwide has become increasingly industrialized, many small-scale fishing operations have been forced out of business and whole fisheries have been pushed to the edge of collapse. The ocean's stocks are plummeting, in part, because vast numbers of young fish are being turned into meal to feed farmed fish and shrimp. Salmon and shrimp farms also pollute coastal waters—not to mention the adverse effects of the drugs and dyes that are fed to these animals. The choices we make as consumers and cooks will have an effect on the recovery or further decline of our ocean resources.

To stay informed I turn to my fishmonger, Paul Johnson of Monterey Fish, who has dedicated himself to these topics and their intricacies. He has a wonderful Web site (www.webseafood.com) filled with related articles, essays, and links. Another good resource is the Monterey Bay Aquarium's Seafood Watch (www.mybayaq.org/cr/sea foodwatch.asp), a consumer's guide to sustainable seafood choices.

Baked Fish

Just about any type of fish can be baked, whether whole, cut into steaks, or filleted. Season the fish with salt and place it in an oiled baking dish or on an oiled rimmed baking sheet; the fish may give off some liquid as it bakes so it is best to use something with sides. Bake fillets and steaks in a hot oven, about 425°F. Whole fish, which will take longer to cook, should bake in a 375°F oven. Most fillets are done when they are just cooked through at the center, the flesh opaque but still moist. Some exceptions are tuna, albacore, and salmon, which are much tastier when cooked medium rare with the flesh still translucent in the center. When cooked on the bone, whole or in steaks, all types of fish need to be cooked until the flesh can be lifted from the bones, but just to this point and no longer. It is important to not overcook fish or it will become dry and tough. Fillets cook fairly quickly: depending on the thickness, they take from 7 to 10 minutes. A good gauge for cooking whole fish is 10 minutes per inch of thickness measured at the thickest part of the fish. Whole fish can be slashed diagonally to the bone to speed up the cooking. These are only rough guides and you should check the fish often while it is cooking to judge its doneness. Gauge the doneness by pushing in the flesh with your finger. It will feel soft when underdone; as it cooks and sets it will begin to feel a bit springy. Don't hesitate to cut into it to know for sure.

Besides a basic seasoning of salt, you can add a splash of wine and a drizzle of extra-virgin olive oil or a pat of butter for more flavor and moisture. The fish also can be infused with a marinade before baking; marinades can be made from herbs, spices, citrus zest and juice, and olive oil. Fillets and steaks can be painted or smeared with Pesto (page 230), Chermoula (page 233), or other flavorful sauces before they are slipped into the oven. Wrap whole fish or fillets in aromatic fig or grape leaves or in branches of lime, lemon, or fennel so the leaves can perfume the fish and help trap moisture. Fish can also be baked in a juicy sauce such as a tomato sauce, seasoned sautéed onions, or a vegetable ragout. Add 5 minutes or so to the cooking time when baking fish in sauce.

Baked Wild Salmon with Herb Butter

4 SERVINGS

Salmon fillets have easy-to-spot pin bones—a row of thin white rib-like bones that extends from behind the gills to the fish's midsection. Rub your fingers over the flesh to locate these bones; use a pair of needle-nosed pliers to pull them out of the flesh.

Prepare:
> **½ cup Herb Butter (page 48)**

Pull any pin bones from:
> **1 to 1½ pounds wild salmon fillet,**
> **cut into 4- to 6-ounce pieces**

Refrigerate until ready to cook.

Preheat the oven to 425°F and remove the herb butter from the refrigerator to soften. Season the salmon with:
> **Salt**
> **Fresh-ground black pepper**

Oil a baking dish or a rimmed baking sheet and place the pieces of salmon in it, skin side down. Brush or drizzle with oil. Bake until the flesh is just set and still pink in the center, 7 to 10 minutes, depending on the thickness of the fillets. Spoon some of the soft herb butter over each piece of fish and pass the rest in a small bowl.

VARIATIONS

◆ Add 4 chopped salt-packed anchovy fillets to the herb butter.

◆ Another way to bake salmon is to slow roast it. Keep the salmon in one piece with its skin on. Oil a baking dish or a rimmed baking sheet and cover the bottom with a layer of fresh herb sprigs. Place the seasoned salmon skin side down on the herbs. Oil the top of the salmon and bake at 225°F for about 30 minutes. The salmon will be just set and incredibly succulent and tender. This is delicious served at room temperature with a vinaigrette made with lemon juice and zest.

◆ If you have access to fresh fig leaves, this is a must. Although the leaf is not eaten, it suffuses the fish with a delightful coconut aroma. Season and oil the salmon fillets, wrap each piece in a clean fig leaf, and bake as above.

Steamed Fish

Steaming is a wonderful way to cook fish. It preserves the natural pristine flavor of the fish and the delicate texture of the flesh, especially of flaky white-fleshed fish such as haddock, halibut, sole, and salmon. Season the fish and cook in a steamer over simmering water in a closed pot. Aromatics—herbs, spices, and vegetables—can be added to the water for more flavor. Cook the fish until the flesh is set and no longer translucent in the center—except salmon, which is best if its center is still translucent. Steaming has the added benefit of retaining all the internal moisture of the fish, but don't overcook the fish or it will dry out. Like baked fish, fish to be steamed can be wrapped in aromatic leaves or branches. Steamed fish goes particularly well with sauces such as Salsa Verde (page 45) and Pesto (page 230) and any butter sauce.

Steamed Sole with Beurre Blanc

4 SERVINGS

Steamed sole is ethereally light and beurre blanc (butter sauce) adds acid and richness. Other tasty sauces to consider are Salsa Verde (page 45) or an herb butter (see page 48) or, for a very pure meal, a simple drizzle of extra-virgin olive oil and a squeeze of lemon.

Trim any bones or skin from:

    **1½ pounds sole fillets
       (petrale, rex, lemon, or Dover)**

Season the fillets with:

    Salt

Prepare:

    **1 cup Beurre Blanc (Warm Butter
      Sauce; page 228)**

Set aside over a pot of warm (but not hot) water or in a thermos to keep warm.

Fill a pot with water to a depth of about 2 inches and bring to a boil. Arrange the fillets in a steamer and place over the boiling water. Cook until set but still moist. This will take from 4 to 7 minutes, depending on the thickness of the fish. Remove the steamer from the pot and transfer the fish to a warm serving plate or individual plates. Spoon the beurre blanc over the fish.

Garnish with:

    **2 tablespoons chopped fresh tender
      herbs, such as chervil, parsley,
      chives, or tarragon**

VARIATION

✦ If nasturtiums are available, remove the green stems from a handful, chop the flowers, and stir them into the finished butter sauce. They add a wonderful color and flavor that complements the sole.

Pan-Fried Fish

Pan-frying is best for thinner fillets and steaks, or for whole fish that are no more than 1 inch thick. Season the fish with salt and pepper and other seasonings such as chopped fresh herbs or crushed spices as desired. For skinless fillets, heat a heavy sauté or frying pan until quite hot; add just enough oil, clarified butter, or a mix of oil and whole butter to cover the bottom of the pan. Carefully add the fish and cook over medium-high heat for 3 minutes (4 to 5 minutes for whole fish) and then turn. Cook for another 3 minutes and test for doneness. Remove the fish from the pan when it is just slightly underdone, as it will continue cooking in the residual heat. When cooking fish with skin, add more fat to the pan, about ⅛ inch deep. Put the fish into the pan skin side down. The skin will shrink while it cooks, pulling the fish up from the bottom of the pan. To keep the skin next to the hot pan (which is necessary to crisp it), weigh the fillets down with a foil-wrapped skillet that is slightly smaller than the one used for the cooking. This will hold the fillets flat and ensure even crisping of the skin. Cook the fillets on their skin for the majority of the time, about 5 to 7 minutes, depending on their thickness, then turn them and cook on the flesh side for just another minute or two, or until done. Remember that the pan must be quite hot before the fish is added; this will keep it from sticking. Also, don't crowd the fish or it will sweat and give off liquid, ruining any chances of browning and crisping. Lastly, don't overcook the fish.

A quick pan sauce can be made after you have removed the fish and poured off the cooking fat. Add tomato sauce to the hot pan and stir in all the brown bits left on the pan for added flavor, or deglaze the hot pan with wine or lemon juice and finish with a swirl of butter or extra-virgin olive oil and a handful of herbs. Add a handful of toasted nuts for flavor and texture.

Pan-Fried Striped Bass with Lemon Sauce

4 SERVINGS

The striped bass fishery, once endangered, has fully recovered and is now flourishing. This fish is especially delicious with its skin left on and sautéed until brown and crispy.

For the sauce, whisk together:

¼ cup extra-virgin olive oil
¼ teaspoon lemon zest
2 tablespoons fresh lemon juice
Salt
Fresh-ground black pepper

Taste for salt and lemon juice and adjust as desired. The sauce will separate as it sits; this is not a problem.

Season:

4 pieces striped bass,
skin on (4 to 6 ounces each)

with:

Salt
Fresh-ground black pepper

Choose a heavy-bottomed pan for frying the fish. Take another, slightly smaller pan that will fit into the pan for the fish, and wrap its bottom with foil. This pan will be used as a weight to hold the fish flat against the frying pan to ensure that all of the skin will cook and crisp. (You will see the fish contract when it goes into the hot pan, as the skin shrinks on contact with the heat.) Warm the larger pan over medium-high heat. When hot, pour in:

Olive oil, enough to generously coat the bottom

Add the pieces of bass, skin side down, and place the foil-wrapped pan on top of the fish. Cook until the skin is brown and crispy, about 7 minutes. Check now and then to see that the fish is indeed browning, but not overbrowning. Adjust the heat up or down to speed up or slow down the cooking as needed. When the skin is browned, remove the top pan and turn the fish. Cook for another minute or so, until the fish is just cooked through, but is still moist and tender inside. Meanwhile whisk the lemon sauce together again and pour it onto a warm plate. Serve the fish skin side up, on top of the sauce.

VARIATIONS

• Garnish the fish with a couple spoonfuls of chopped tender herbs such as parsley, chives, chervil, cilantro, or basil.

• Soak, rinse, and squeeze dry a tablespoon or so of capers. When the fish is cooked add the capers to the hot pan and sauté for a minute or two. Remove with a slotted spoon and scatter over the fish.

• Make a Beurre Blanc (Warm Butter Sauce; page 228) instead of the olive oil sauce.

Grilled Tuna with Grilled Bread and Aïoli

4 SERVINGS

Prepare:

1 cup Aïoli
(Garlic Mayonnaise; page 47)

Thin slightly with water. The sauce should flow from the spoon but still be quite thick. Cut about ½ inch thick:

6 slices country-style bread

Brush with:

Olive oil

Meanwhile prepare a bed of hot coals. When the grill is clean and hot, brush:

4 pieces tuna (4 to 6 ounces each)

with:

Olive oil

Season with:

Salt
Fresh-ground black pepper

Place on the grill and cook for about 3 minutes on each side. Tuna cooks quickly and tastes best rare, when it is still quite red in the center. When cooked all the way through it is dry. The timing will vary depending on how thick your pieces of fish are. Don't hesitate to cut into a piece to see how done it is. When the fish is cooked, remove it from the grill to a warm plate. Put the bread slices on the grill and cook until toasted on each side. Spoon some aïoli over each piece of fish and serve with the grilled bread and some:

Lemon wedges

VARIATIONS

• Serve with Tapenade (page 217) instead of aïoli. Thin the tapenade slightly with extra-virgin olive oil.

• Serve with Salsa Verde (page 45) instead of aïoli. Salsa verde made with a good amount of marjoram in place of some of the parsley is particularly tasty with tuna.

• Crush 2 teaspoons fennel or cumin seeds and add to the salt and pepper when seasoning the fish.

Fresh-Cured Sardines

4 SERVINGS

If beautifully fresh sardines are not available, substitute mackerel, fresh anchovies, or thinly sliced tuna.

Ask your fishmonger to scale and fillet:
  12 fresh sardines
Season the fillets well with:
  Salt
  Fresh-ground black pepper
Arrange the fillets snugly in a dish and strew with:
  1 garlic clove, sliced thin
  ½ lemon, sliced thin
  2 teaspoons red wine vinegar
  A few branches of fresh herbs (savory, parsley, thyme, or marjoram)
  2 bay leaves
Squeeze the juice from the other half of the lemon over the fillets and then pour over:
  3 tablespoons extra-virgin olive oil
Let sit for 1 hour before serving. Well-chilled, the sardines will keep for 2 days. Serve on croutons or buttered fresh bread with a spoonful of the marinade.

VARIATIONS

◆ Cut ½-inch slices of baguette or other bread and spoon some of the marinade over each slice. Then place a fillet on top, skin side up, cutting the fillets to fit if needed. Toast for 4 minutes in a 450°F oven.
◆ Grill the cured fillets over a hot fire for a minute or two on each side.

Fish Tartare

4 SERVINGS

Many fish can be served raw as tartare: tuna, albacore, halibut, and salmon, for example. It is exceptionally important to use impeccably fresh fish; be sure to tell your fishmonger that you intend to eat the fish raw. At home, keep the fish chilled over ice at all times. Cut the fish on a clean board with a sharp knife, and put the cut-up fish in a bowl nestled in a larger bowl filled with ice. For an ample appetizer, figure on ½ pound of fish for 4 people; you will need more if serving the tartare as a main dish.

To cut the fish, first slice it very thin across the grain, removing any fibrous connective tissue. Cut the slices into a thin julienne, and then cut the julienne crosswise into fine dice. The fish can be cut ahead and covered tightly with plastic wrap to keep it from drying out. Stir in the other ingredients just before serving. Serve fish tartare on little croutons or endive leaves, or on a bed of simply dressed greens.

Cut into fine dice:
  ½ pound perfectly fresh fish
Keep refrigerated over ice. Just before serving, mix together in a small bowl:
  Zest of ½ lime
  Juice of 1½ limes
  ¼ teaspoon coriander seeds, crushed
  2 tablespoons extra-virgin olive oil
Toss the diced fish with a little salt, then add the lime juice mixture, and toss again. Stir in:
  1½ tablespoons chopped cilantro
Taste and adjust with salt and lime juice as needed.

VARIATIONS

◆ For the lime juice and coriander mixture, substitute 1 tablespoon fresh lemon juice,

2 tablespoons extra-virgin olive oil, 2 teaspoons rinsed and chopped capers, salt, and 2 teaspoons chopped basil, mint, or marjoram for the cilantro.

• For the lime juice and coriander mixture, substitute 1 tablespoon fresh lemon juice, 2 tablespoons extra-virgin olive oil, ½ teaspoon freshly grated ginger, fresh-ground black pepper, a pinch of cayenne, salt, and 2 teaspoons chopped shiso leaf or parsley for the cilantro.

Court Bouillon

MAKES ABOUT 1 QUART

A court bouillon is a quickly made aromatic vegetable broth for poaching fish. (In French, *bouillon* means "broth," and *court* means "short.")

In a large heavy pot, combine and bring to a boil:

> **1½ cups dry white wine**
> **4 cups water**
> **2 carrots, peeled and sliced**
> **1 celery stalk, sliced**
> **2 onions, peeled and sliced**
> **1 bay leaf**
> **7 black peppercorns**
> **6 coriander seeds**
> **3 thyme sprigs**
> **A handful of parsley stems**
> **2 teaspoons salt**

Skim off any rising scum. Turn down the heat and simmer for 45 minutes. Strain, discarding the solids.

VARIATION

• If there's no white wine, substitute about 2 tablespoons good white wine vinegar.

Fish Stock

MAKES 1 QUART

Fish stock is a delicate broth, cooked briefly and gently for best flavor. Bones and heads are used for flavor and body. They should be washed and cleaned of gills and organs to make a clear, clean-tasting stock. White-fleshed fish are best; salmon, mackerel, or other oily fish have too strong a flavor. If not buying whole fish, ask your fishmonger for clean heads and bones for making stock.

Rinse and clean:

> **1½ to 2 pounds fish bones and heads (gills removed), from white-fleshed fish only**

Put the bones and heads in a large heavy pot (if necessary, chop them so they fit) with:

> **1½ cups dry white wine**
> **8 cups water**
> **Salt**

Bring to a boil and turn down immediately to a simmer. Skim any foam that rises to the surface and add:

> **1 carrot, peeled and sliced**
> **1 medium onion, peeled and sliced**
> **1 small celery stalk, sliced, leaves removed**
> **¼ teaspoon black peppercorns**
> **Parsley stems**

Cook, barely simmering, for 45 minutes. Strain, discarding the solids. If not using right away, allow to cool, cover tightly, and refrigerate. Fish stock will keep for a day or two in the refrigerator, but it tastes best the day it is made.

VARIATIONS

• Use red wine instead of white, if appropriate (for a red wine fish stew, for example).

• Include a tomato or two with the vegetables.

Provençal-Style Fish Soup with Rouille

8 TO 10 SERVINGS

This is more than a soup; it is a generous meal fit for a gathering, and it has everything I love about food and flavor. I learned to make it from my French "mother," Lulu. It's one of the longest recipes in the book, but taken in parts it is not hard to make. I think of it as several steps: first make a fish stock, then prepare the fish and shellfish; make the rouille (garlic mayonnaise flavored with pepper purée); make the soup base with vegetables and the fish stock; toast garlic croutons; and finally put it all together, cooking the fish and shellfish in the deeply flavored soup base, and serve it with rouille and croutons to pass at the table.

To make the fish stock, rinse and clean:

3 pounds fish bones and heads (gills removed), white-fleshed fish only

If necessary, chop the bones so they will fit in a large heavy pot. Prepare:

1 onion, peeled and sliced
1 small carrot, peeled and sliced
**1 small fennel bulb,
    trimmed and sliced**
**3 medium tomatoes,
    cored and coarsely chopped**
**1 head of garlic,
    cut in half horizontally**

Put a large heavy pot over medium-high heat and pour in:

**Olive oil, enough to cover the bottom
    of the pan**

Add the fish bones and sauté for 2 minutes and then add the prepared vegetables with:

¼ teaspoon black peppercorns
¼ teaspoon fennel seeds
¼ teaspoon coriander seeds

**A few sprigs of fresh herbs
    (such as fennel tops, wild fennel,
    savory, thyme, or parsley)**
1 bay leaf
A pinch of saffron threads

Continue to cook for a few more minutes, until the vegetables start to soften. Pour over:

2 cups dry white wine

Bring to a boil and cook for a couple of minutes, then add:

1½ quarts water
Salt

Bring to a boil and immediately turn down to a simmer. Skim off the foam that rises to the surface. Cook at a simmer for 45 minutes and then strain.

Meanwhile trim away any bones from:

**2 pounds assorted fish fillets
    (rockfish, ling cod, halibut, or
    sea robin, or any combination)**

Add the bones to the simmering fish stock. Cut the fillets into 2- or 3-inch pieces and marinate in:

**Extra-virgin olive oil, just enough to
    coat the fish**
**2 tablespoons chopped fennel tops,
    wild fennel, or parsley**
**4 garlic cloves,
    crushed and coarsely chopped**
Salt

Scrub and remove the beards from:

1 pound mussels

Prepare:

Rouille (opposite)

For the soup base, heat a heavy soup pot over medium heat and pour in:

3 tablespoons olive oil

When hot, add:

1 medium onion, diced fine

Cook for 5 minutes and add:

**1 leek, white part only,
    cleaned, rinsed, and diced**

**1 medium fennel bulb,
trimmed and diced**

A pinch of saffron threads

Cook, stirring now and then, until soft, about 7 minutes; do not brown. Add:

Salt

**4 or 5 medium tomatoes
(about ¾ pound), peeled, seeded,
and diced**

Cook for another 3 or 4 minutes. Pour in the strained fish stock and bring to a boil. Turn down to a simmer and cook for 5 minutes. Taste for salt and adjust. This can be done ahead of time, and in fact, it tastes better if this soup base of stock and vegetables has a chance to sit for a while before you add the fish.

Prepare the croutons. Brush:

8 to 10 slices country-style bread

with:

Olive oil

Lay the oiled bread on a baking sheet and toast in a 375°F oven for 10 minutes, or until golden brown. Rub the croutons with:

1 garlic clove, peeled

When ready to finish and serve the soup, bring the soup base to a simmer and add the fish. Cook for 3 minutes, then add the mussels. Cook at a simmer until the shellfish open their shells. Taste the soup for salt and adjust as necessary. Serve with the croutons and rouille to pass at the table.

VARIATIONS

◆ Add ¾ pound shrimp, unpeeled or peeled, with the mussels. (If you peel the shrimp first, add the peels to the simmering stock.)

◆ Use small clams in combination with the mussels.

Rouille

MAKES ABOUT 1½ CUPS

Roast or grill:

1 large or 2 small sweet peppers

Peel and seed the peppers, and with a mortar and pestle pound (or process) into a purée.

Transfer the peppers to a bowl, then add to the mortar:

3 garlic cloves

Salt

Pound into a purée, then stir in:

A pinch of cayenne pepper

1 egg yolk

½ teaspoon water

When combined, add in a slow steady stream, whisking all the while:

1 cup olive oil

Stir in the pepper purée. Taste for salt and adjust if necessary. Refrigerate the rouille if you're not using it within the hour.

VARIATION

◆ For more piquancy, use dried ancho chiles (or another dried chile) in place of or in combination with the sweet peppers. Toast dried chiles in a 400°F oven for 4 minutes, then soak in boiling water for 10 minutes or so. Drain and purée. Pass through a strainer to remove the tough skins.

Bourride

4 SERVINGS

Bourride is another Provençal fish soup, this one thickened with garlic mayonnaise. The broth is smooth, luxurious, and redolent of garlic.

First make a fish stock. Heat together in a heavy pot:

1 pound bones from white-fleshed fish, washed and cut into pieces
½ leek, white part only, cleaned, sliced, and rinsed
½ small onion, sliced
½ fennel bulb, trimmed and sliced
4 garlic cloves, peeled and smashed
¾ cup dry white wine
A few black peppercorns
1 bay leaf
2 or 3 thyme sprigs
A big pinch of salt
4 cups water

Bring to a boil and then turn immediately down to a simmer. Skim well and cook for 45 minutes. Strain through a fine sieve; discard the bones and vegetables.

While the stock is cooking make a very rich garlic mayonnaise. Mix together:

2 egg yolks
1 teaspoon water

Whisk in, in a slow steady stream:

⅓ cup extra-virgin olive oil

Stir in:

4 garlic cloves, pounded to a paste with a pinch of salt

Prepare the croutons. Brush:

4 slices country-style bread

with:

Olive oil

Lay the oiled bread on a baking sheet and toast in a 375°F oven for 10 minutes, or until golden brown. Rub the croutons with:

1 garlic clove, peeled

Trim, removing any bones, and cut into 3-inch pieces:

1 pound firm white-fleshed fish (rockfish, ling cod, angler, or halibut)

Season with:

Salt

Pour the strained stock into a heavy pot and bring to a boil. Immediately reduce to a simmer and add the seasoned fish. Poach the fish gently for 6 minutes or until just cooked through. Remove the fish to a bowl with a slotted spoon and keep warm. Pour a few ladles of hot broth into the garlic mayonnaise and then whisk the thinned mayonnaise into the broth. Cook, stirring constantly, over medium heat until the broth is thickened and coats the spoon. Do not let the soup boil or it will curdle. Put the fish into warm bowls and pour the thickened broth over it. Garnish with the croutons.

VARIATIONS

‣ Sauté together until soft 1 small onion, 1 small leek, and 1 small fennel bulb, all sliced very thin. Season with salt and add to the broth with the fish.
‣ At the same time as the fish, add 1 pound mussels, washed and beards removed.

Clam Chowder with Buttered Croutons

4 SERVINGS

Wash well and drain:

2 pounds clams

Place in a heavy pot with ⅓ cup water. Cover and cook over medium-high heat until the clams open. Remove the clams from the pot. When cool, remove the clams from their shells. If they are big clams, chop them;

otherwise, leave them whole. Strain the liquor left in the pot through a couple layers of cheesecloth.

Peel and cut into small cubes:

¼ pound potatoes
(about ¾ cup, cubed)

Cook the potatoes in salted boiling water until almost done. Drain and set aside.

Heat in a heavy soup pot:

2 teaspoons butter

When melted, add:

1½ slices bacon, cut crosswise into
¼-inch pieces

Cook over medium heat until almost crisp. Remove the bacon pieces and add:

1 onion, diced fine
2 thyme sprigs, leaves only

Cook for a few minutes and add:

1 small celery stalk, diced fine

Continue cooking, stirring now and then, until the onions are soft and golden. Season with:

Salt
Fresh-ground black pepper

Add the potatoes and bacon and cook for a couple of minutes. Add the clams with their liquor. Heat to a boil, immediately turn down to a simmer, and cook until the potatoes are soft, about 3 or 4 minutes. Pour in:

¾ cup milk
⅓ cup cream

Heat gently, but do not allow the chowder to come to a boil. Taste for seasoning and adjust as needed. Serve garnished with:

Buttered croutons (see page 58)
Fresh-ground black pepper

VARIATIONS

◆ Use mussels instead of clams.

◆ Make a fish chowder. Cut fish fillets into bite-size pieces and use water or fish stock instead of the clam liquor.

◆ Crab and Lobster

When selecting live crabs from tanks at the market, choose lively ones that feel heavy. Keep them refrigerated and cook them as soon as possible; it's important to cook them while they are still alive. Once out of water, they start to decline.

The easiest way to cook crab is to boil it. Bring an abundant quantity of water to a boil, enough so that the crabs will be easily submerged. (You may only have a pot roomy enough for one or two large crabs, such as Dungeness; if you have more crabs, boil them one or two at a time.) Throw in a lot of salt; the water should taste salty. When it has reached a rolling boil, pick up the live crab between its back legs (to stay clear of its pinching front claws) and drop it in. Start timing the cooking from the moment the crab enters the boiling water. Keep the heat turned up all the way, but don't worry if it never comes back to a boil. The amount of time the crab will take to cook will be anywhere from 12 to 15 minutes for a Dungeness crab, to just a few minutes for a small blue crab. Ask your fishmongers for their advice, or look online; there are many Web sites with information about cooking and cleaning the many different varieties.

The cooked crabs can be cleaned and eaten right away, or cooled briefly in cold water and stored in the refrigerator for up to 2 days. Serve cracked crab with melted butter or homemade mayonnaise (see page 47), with a squeeze of lemon for a little zing. I like to serve a garlic mayonnaise (see page 47) flavored with the orange crab butter (or tomalley) that is found under the shell. Be sure to taste the crab butter first and use it only if it is not bitter.

To clean a crab, turn it onto its back and

pry up the triangular apron. Pull and twist it off the body. Turn the crab over and grasp it by the corner of the top shell or carapace. Pull it off with a twisting motion. Remove the lungs, the feathery fingers that run along the sides, and the mouth. Scoop out and save the tomalley or crab butter if you like, discarding the white intestine. Rinse the crab clean under cold running water. Split the crab in two (or not) and crack the claws with a mallet or crab cracker. Large crab can be reheated after they have been cooked, cleaned, and cracked; the meat can be picked out or the crab can be reheated later. (The delicate pointed tip at the end of a crab leg is the perfect tool for picking the crabmeat from the shells.) To reheat the crab, brush with melted butter or oil (flavored with herbs and spices if you want) and heat for 5 to 7 minutes in a 400°F or hotter oven, just long enough to heat the crab through.

Much of the foregoing advice for cooking crab applies to lobster. Choose lively, heavy lobsters and cook them as soon as you can. Cook lobsters in abundant salted boiling water for 7 minutes. Put the lobster in head first and start timing from the moment it enters the water. Turn the heat down to a simmer if a boil is reached before the time is up (a rolling boil toughens the meat). Cooking lobsters too long also makes the meat tough, so keep an eye on the clock. If you are going to reheat the lobster or add it to a sauté or other dish, cook the lobster for only 5 minutes. Drain the cooked lobster and either serve it right away or cool it down under cold running water or in an ice bath for a few minutes.

Lobster can be left whole or split down the middle, or it can be broken down into claws, knuckles, and tails. To do this, twist the tail away from the head and twist off the claws. Crack the claws with a mallet or crab cracker and remove the meat. With a pair of kitchen shears, make a cut down the soft, nearly transparent shell on the underside of the tail. Using a towel to protect your hands, grasp both sides of the tail and bend them back, splitting open the shell along the cut. Pull out the lobster meat. You can also cut the tail in two lengthwise to remove the meat.

Some recipes call for cooking a raw lobster cut in pieces. To kill a live lobster, place it on its back and, holding its head with a towel, make a cut with a heavy sharp knife at the base of its head. The tail can be split or left whole.

Female lobsters occasionally have roe in their abdomen; this is called the coral. It turns bright red when cooked and is very tasty. The green liver or tomalley is found in all lobsters; it is edible and can be used to flavor a sauce.

Crab Cakes
4 SERVINGS

These are a seasonal treat here in California when local Dungeness crab is available (roughly late November through June). Two Dungeness crabs will yield a pound of picked crabmeat, more or less; use as many blue crabs or other crabs as needed to yield the same, or purchase freshly picked crabmeat.

Bring a large pot of generously salted water to a boil. Carefully drop in:

2 live Dungeness crabs

Boil for 15 minutes. Remove the crabs and let them drain and cool. When cool enough to handle, pull off the large top shell and remove the fibrous lungs. Rinse lightly, pull off the legs, and split the main body in half down the center. Crack the legs, and pick the crabmeat clean from all the bodies and legs. Put the meat in a bowl. Gently go through the picked meat with your fingers to remove any last stray bits of shell. Refrigerate until ready to use.

Make some clarified butter. Melt in a small heavy pot over medium heat:

5 tablespoons unsalted butter

Cook the butter until it has separated and the milk solids are just turning a light golden brown. Pour through a fine strainer to remove the milk solids.

Prepare:

1 cup mayonnaise (see page 46)

Stir in:

2 tablespoons chopped chives

2 tablespoons chopped parsley

2 tablespoons chopped chervil

1 tablespoon fresh lemon juice

Salt

A pinch of cayenne

Stir the mayonnaise into the crabmeat, mixing gently but thoroughly. Taste and adjust the lemon juice and salt as needed. Form the mixture into 8 patties. Roll the patties to coat in:

1½ cups fresh breadcrumbs made from *pain de mie* or another firm white bread (see page 62)

Warm a heavy-bottomed pan (cast iron works well) over medium heat. Pour in the clarified butter. When the butter is hot, add the crab cakes and fry until golden brown, about 4 minutes on each side. Turn down the heat if the crumbs start to burn.

VARIATIONS

◆ Serve with Tartar Sauce (page 225), Aïoli (Garlic Mayonnaise; page 47), or lemon mayonnaise (see page 47).

◆ Serve with Shaved Fennel Salad (page 246) or garden salad.

◆ For fish cakes, use 2 cups chopped firm white fish fillet such as halibut, haddock, or ling cod in place of the crab.

Grilled Lobster

4 SERVINGS

Prepare:

½ cup Herb Butter (page 48)

Bring a large pot of generously salted water to a boil. (It should taste as salty as seawater.) Drop in:

4 lobsters (about 1 to 1½ pounds each)

Cook for 1 minute. Plunge into a bowl of cold water to stop the cooking. Drain after 1 minute.

Crack the claws with the blunt back of a heavy knife. Lay each lobster on its back and make a lengthwise cut splitting the tail meat open but leaving the top shell intact. Remove the sand sac and vein from the tail. Stuff 2 spoonfuls of herb butter into the tail.

Meanwhile prepare a medium-hot bed of coals. When the fire is ready, put the lobsters on the grill, split side up, and grill for 4 minutes on each side. Serve hot and pass lemon wedges and the rest of the herb butter (melted, if you desire).

◆ Scallops

The scallops we usually see in markets are the meaty round white adductor muscles that open and close scallop shells, propelling them through the water. Their roe, known as the coral, is also delicious, although it is rarely sold in this country; ask your fishmonger. Fresh scallops should smell sweet and should not be floating in liquid; if they are, they are definitely not fresh. Scallops can be cooked in many ways—fried, sautéed, poached, steamed, grilled, or baked—or eaten raw, in a ceviche or as scallop tartare. They are mild in flavor and best in simple preparations. (All scallops are sweet, but tiny bay scallops are especially so.)

Before cooking scallops, remove the small vertical band of muscle attached to the side of the scallop. (This is sometimes called the foot.) Because scallops can absorb a great deal of liquid, don't rinse them unless absolutely necessary. They cook very quickly: bay scallops take only a minute or two and larger scallops take only four to six. Large scallops to be sautéed or gratinéed can be cut horizontally into two or three disks before cooking. For a salad, cut them after they have been cooked.

Sautéed Scallops with Salsa Verde

4 SERVINGS

Prepare:
   ½ cup Salsa Verde (page 45)
Remove the small muscle (the "foot") attached to the side of:
   1 pound sea scallops
Season the scallops with:
   Salt
   Fresh-ground black pepper

Warm a heavy-bottomed pan over medium-high heat; when hot, pour in:
   Olive oil to coat the bottom of the pan
Turn the heat up to high and add the scallops in a single layer. Don't crowd the pan or they will sweat and not brown. Cook the scallops for 2 to 3 minutes on each side. Do this in as many batches as necessary, keeping the cooked scallops warm while you finish. When all the scallops are cooked, spoon the salsa verde over them and serve immediately.

VARIATIONS
◆ Use bay scallops instead of sea scallops. Cook for 3 or 4 minutes, tossing them in the pan as they cook.
◆ Thread the seasoned scallops onto skewers, brush with oil, and grill over a medium-hot fire for 2 to 3 minutes on each side.

◆ Shrimp

Industrial shrimp farming takes a heavy toll on coastal areas. Whenever possible, buy fresh, sustainably harvested wild shrimp. These taste the best and are the best for the environment. Shrimp is a delicate food that should be cooked soon after it is purchased. Keep it stored over ice until ready to use. Shrimp is sold by size (large, jumbo, bay, etc.), and some are labeled with numbers that express the number of shrimp to a pound (16-20 means a pound will yield 16 to 20 shrimp, for example).

Either peeled or left in the shell, shrimp can be grilled, baked, steamed, boiled, or sautéed. As they cook they turn bright pink or red, depending on the variety. This change of color is the sign that they are done. In their shells, most shrimp will cook in three or four minutes; when peeled, shrimp cook in just a minute or two. Keep a close eye on shrimp while they are cooking.

When cooking shrimp in the shell, season it generously; the seasoning needs to penetrate the shell to flavor the meat inside. (The shell itself also flavors the shrimp.) Leave unpeeled shrimp whole when boiling or sautéing. When grilling, baking, or broiling unpeeled shrimp, you can first butterfly (or split) them. Turn the shrimp on its back and cut lengthwise, through the underside to the back shell, leaving the two halves connected. Flatten the shrimp. For easy grilling, skewer the butterflied shrimp, season them, and brush with oil or butter.

To peel shrimp, split the shell by gently prying it apart and away with your thumbs, from the underside out. The last joint of the shell and the tail can be left on for color if you want. All shrimp have a sand vein that runs the length of the tail on the dorsal side. The sand veins of large shrimp are sometimes gritty when full. When full, the vein will look dark and should be removed (it is not necessary to remove it when empty). Without cutting too deeply, run your knife down the center of the back of the shrimp, scrape the vein out of the cut, and discard it.

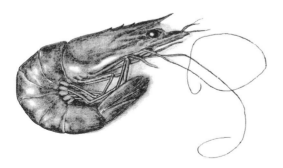

Sautéed Shrimp with Garlic and Parsley

4 SERVINGS

I prefer shrimp sautéed in their shells. Peeling with your fingers at the table is a bit messy (some would say fun), but the flavor the shells impart makes it all worthwhile.

Season:
   1 pound shrimp
with:
   Salt
   Fresh-ground black pepper
Season the shrimp liberally because the seasoning needs to penetrate the shell.
Peel and chop:
   4 garlic cloves
Cover with a bit of olive oil to keep from oxidizing. Pick the leaves from:
   6 parsley sprigs
Chop the leaves; you should have at least 3 tablespoons.

Heat a heavy-bottomed skillet. When hot, pour in:
   2 tablespoons extra-virgin olive oil
Turn the heat up to high and add the seasoned shrimp. Cook, tossing the shrimp frequently, until the shells start to turn pink, about 3 minutes. Turn off the heat and toss in the chopped garlic and parsley. Toss the shrimp in the pan until well coated with the garlic and parsley. Serve immediately.

VARIATIONS
• Add 4 sliced scallions to the shrimp with the garlic and parsley.
• Add a large pinch of dried chile flakes.
• For the parsley, substitute chopped cilantro or a chiffonade of basil leaves.
• Peel and devein the shrimp before cooking.

◆ Squid

Squid, or calamari as it is sometimes called, is not only inexpensive and delicious, but also abundant in our oceans, which makes it an excellent choice for the table. Choose squid that is pristine and fresh. The skin should be shimmering and translucent, the eyes crystal clear, and the scent fresh and sweet.

Squid needs to be cleaned before cooking. First trim off the tentacles, cutting as close to the eyes as possible for maximum yield. The tentacles encircle the tough, inedible mouth or beak. To remove it, gently squeeze the tentacles where they were separated from the body and the beak will pop out. Lay the squid flat and, while holding on to the tail end, run the dull side of a paring knife firmly over the body, from tail to head, pressing out the insides and the transparent quill, a feather-shaped bonelike structure that runs the length of the squid. If the quill breaks in the body, cut off the tip of the tail and push it out that way. I don't remove the skin; I like the way it looks. Don't rinse squid; it absorbs a great deal of water in the process. The body may be left whole for stuffing, grilling, or roasting, or cut into rings for sautéing, frying, or making into a stew.

Squid has a very high protein content, and its flesh becomes elastic and tough as it cooks. To keep squid tender, cook it quickly over high heat, for no longer than 3 or 4 minutes. The squid will be cooked, but the meat will not have had time to toughen. An alternative is to stew it in liquid over low heat for at least 30 minutes. The long cooking eventually softens the protein, and the squid will be tender again.

Grilled Squid

4 SERVINGS

I like to serve grilled squid as an hors d'oeuvre or along with other grilled fish or as part of an array of fish and vegetables and Aïoli (page 47). The aroma of the squid cooking on the grill is irresistible.

Clean (see left):

1 pound small squid

Season and marinate the bodies and tentacles in:

2 to 3 tablespoons olive oil
Salt
Fresh-ground black pepper
Dried chile flakes
**2 tablespoons chopped fresh
    marjoram or parsley**

The squid is easier to grill on skewers, with the bodies and tentacles cooked separately. Thread the bodies onto bamboo skewers across the opening so that they lie flat, and skewer the tentacles across the thickest part of the ring. Grill the skewers of squid over a hot fire. If small they will only take a few minutes on each side. Turn more frequently if the fire is quite hot; it is ideal if they get a little crisp on the outside and remain tender on the inside. Serve hot or at room temperature.

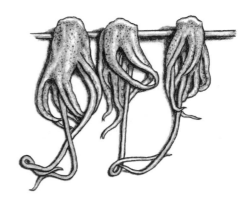

Poultry

Chicken Cooked Under a Brick 346

Fried Chicken 347

Sautéed Chicken Livers 347

Grilled Whole Chicken 348

Grilled Duck Breast 348

Braised Duck Legs with Leeks and Green Olives 349

Roast Duck 350

Roast Turkey 350

SEE ALSO

Roast Chicken 110

Braised Chicken Legs 131

Chicken Cooked Under a Brick

This is the classic Italian dish known as *pollo al mattone.* Cooking chicken under a heavy weight results in an exceptionally crispy skin.

This version is for legs that have been boned, leaving the thigh and drumstick attached. You may be able to persuade your butcher to do this for you. If not, use a very sharp boning or paring knife to cut through the skin and tendons all the way around the "ankle" of the drumstick. With the fleshy side of the leg facing up, starting at the ankle, cut down along one side of the bone, keeping your knife against it and cutting along its entire length to the joint. Continue along the thigh bone out to the ball at its end. Pull the flesh back to expose the bone as you cut along the other side, pulling the flesh away as you go and working your knife under the bones so that the meat is attached only at the joint. Bend the ends of the bones together and carefully cut away the remaining flesh around the joint: be careful not to nick the skin, which is very close to the bone at this point. The bones can be saved for making broth.

Season the boned legs well with salt and pepper, and, if you want, dried chile flakes and coarsely chopped herbs such as thyme, rosemary, savory, or sage. Put a cast-iron skillet over medium heat. When hot, add a tablespoon of olive oil, then quickly and carefully place the chicken legs in the pan with the skin side down. Arrange the chicken so that all the skin is in contact with the skillet. Wrap another skillet of the same size with aluminum foil to use as a weight. Place the foil-wrapped skillet on top of the chicken. This will press all of the skin into contact with the hot skillet surface below

and give it extra crispness. Adjust the heat so that the chicken is sizzling at medium. The aim is to thoroughly brown and crisp the skin and render some of the fat without burning the skin or overcooking the meat. Lift the weight and check the skin on one of the legs after a few minutes to see how it's doing. If it's darkening very quickly, lower the heat a bit. If the skin is still pale, raise it a little. By the time the skin is well browned and crispy, about 10 to 12 minutes, the meat will be nearly cooked through. Remove the weight and carefully turn the legs over; there will be a lot of rendered fat by this point, some of which you can pour or spoon off. Do not replace the weight on the skin side or it will lose its crispness. Cook for a few minutes more to finish the legs, and serve hot.

VARIATIONS

• The boned chicken legs can be cooked on the grill, over a medium fire, under a weight as well.

• Boneless chicken breasts can be cooked in the same way. The cooking time will be shorter.

Fried Chicken

SERVES 4

Season, at least 1 hour ahead of time, or overnight if possible:

> **2 chicken breast halves, bone in and skin on**
> **2 chicken legs, skin on**

with:

> **Salt**
> **Fresh-ground black pepper**

Cut each breast into 2 pieces and cut the leg in two through the joint, separating the drumstick from the thigh. Place the 8 pieces of chicken in a bowl and cover with:

> **2 cups buttermilk**

Let sit for 20 minutes. Put a large cast-iron pan over medium heat.
Pour in 1 inch of:

> **Peanut or vegetable oil**

For dredging the chicken pieces, mix together in a pie pan:

> **About 2 cups flour**
> **A pinch of cayenne (optional)**
> **Salt**
> **Fresh-ground black pepper**

Test to see if the oil is hot enough by dipping a finger in the buttermilk and then the flour. Drop a bit of the wet flour into the oil. If it sizzles and floats around the pan, the oil is ready. Dip the pieces of chicken into the flour and turn them over a few times to coat them evenly and completely. Carefully slip the floured chicken pieces into the hot oil. The chicken should fit in a single layer without being too crowded. Fry in batches if necessary, keeping the pieces from the first batch warm in a very low oven. Cook, turning occasionally, until browned and cooked through, about 15 minutes. Cut into a piece and check for doneness. Drain the cooked chicken well on a rack or paper towels.

VARIATIONS

✦ Up to half the flour can be replaced with cornmeal for a crunchier texture.
✦ Use boneless breast and leg meat; they will cook more quickly.
✦ For a thinner coating, omit the buttermilk. Mix the seasoned flour in a large paper bag, add the chicken pieces, and shake. Remove the floured chicken and let it dry for 30 minutes before cooking.

Sautéed Chicken Livers

4 SERVINGS

Trim ½ pound chicken livers of fat and connective tissue. Trim off and discard any green markings on the livers, which may be residue from the gall bladder and is very bitter. Cut the livers in two where the two lobes separate naturally. Season with salt and fresh-ground black pepper. Heat olive oil or butter in a heavy pan over medium-high heat. When hot, add the livers (don't crowd them in the pan) and cook on one side for 3 minutes. Turn the livers and cook for another 2 minutes or so. Livers have a milder taste when they are still pink inside. For added flavor, add a minced shallot to the pan after turning the livers. If you like, once the livers are cooked, remove them from the pan and pour in 2 tablespoons brandy or wine, to deglaze the pan. Finish by swirling in a pat of butter. This is good warm, or it can be cooled and mashed with softened butter to make a simple liver pâté.

For a quick hors d'oeuvre, cook one or two livers as above. Slice and serve on buttered croutons topped with a few drops of balsamic vinegar and chopped parsley.

Grilled Whole Chicken

4 SERVINGS

The day before cooking, if possible, remove the backbone from (or ask your butcher to do this):

1 chicken (about 3½ to 4 pounds)

Use a pair of poultry shears or a knife to cut through the thigh joint and rib bones along either side of the backbone. Turn the chicken breast side up and flatten the bird by pressing down on the breastbone with the palm of your hand, pushing until you hear the bone snap. Brush the bird lightly with:

Olive oil

Season all over with:

Salt

Fresh-ground black pepper

Cover and refrigerate. Remove the chicken from the refrigerator an hour before you are ready to grill. Prepare a bed of coals and let them burn down until medium-hot (the coals should be covered with white ash). Clean the grate and set it 5 or 6 inches above the coals to heat. Place the bird on the hot grill, bone side down, and cook until browned, about 10 to 15 minutes. Turn and cook until the skin is brown and crispy, about 10 to 15 minutes. Turn again and continue cooking, turning every 5 minutes until done. Depending on the fire this will take from 30 to 40 minutes total. Check at the thigh bone to gauge the doneness. Keep an eye out for flare-ups and overbrowning. Move the chicken to a cooler place on the grill if it is cooking too quickly, or turn it more frequently from the start. Remove from the grill when done and let rest for 10 minutes before cutting and serving.

VARIATIONS

• Marinate the chicken with chopped fresh herbs, grated lemon zest, and crushed coriander seeds in addition to salt and pepper.

• When using a sauce, brush it on the chicken 10 minutes before it is done. If it is put on earlier, the sauce will burn.

• Cook smaller pieces of chicken in the same manner; they will take less time to cook.

Grilled Duck Breast

Three duck breasts will usually serve four people. To prepare the breasts, turn them skin side down and trim away the tenderloin, the long, easily detached muscle that runs almost the length of each breast. (The tenderloins can be cooked separately.) Cut away any skin that is protruding around the edges. Turn the breasts over and use a sharp knife to score the skin and fat in a diamond crosshatch pattern. This cross-hatching allows the skin to render more of its fat as the breast cooks. Season the breasts generously with salt and fresh-ground black pepper. For extra flavor, sprinkle with herbs and spices.

Take the breasts out of the refrigerator 15 minutes before you are ready to grill. Prepare a medium to medium-hot fire with coals that are gray and no longer glowing red. (If the coals are too hot, the breasts will burn; if they are not hot enough, the fat will not render and the skin will get neither crisp nor golden brown.) Grill the breasts skin side down for 10 minutes, or until the skin is nicely browned. You will need to stand guard to be sure the coals do not flame up from dripping fat. If they do, move the breasts away from the flames or they will burn. Turn the breasts and cook for another 3 or 4 minutes. The duck should be cooked medium rare. When overcooked, duck becomes quite dry. Let the breasts rest for 5 to 10 minutes before slicing to allow the juices to stabilize. Slice fairly thin, pour any accumulated juices over them, and serve.

Braised Duck Legs with Leeks and Green Olives

4 SERVINGS

This especially satisfying one-pan dish is delicious served with soft polenta, mashed potatoes, or shell beans. Good choices for the green olives are unpitted Lucques or Picholines.

Trim the excess fat from:

4 duck legs
   (drumsticks and thighs, attached)

Several hours ahead or the night before, season with:

Salt
Fresh-ground black pepper

Cover and refrigerate.

Preheat the oven to 425°F.

In an ovenproof skillet just large enough to hold the duck legs comfortably, heat:

2 tablespoons olive oil

Add:

2 leeks, white and pale green parts
   only, washed and coarsely chopped
1 carrot, peeled and coarsely chopped

Cook over medium heat for 3 minutes. Stir in:

Salt
6 thyme sprigs, leaves only
6 parsley sprigs, leaves only
1 bay leaf
1 cup green olives

Cook for 3 more minutes. Place the duck legs in the skillet, skin side down. Add to the skillet:

½ cup white wine
1½ cups chicken broth

with:

1 strip of lemon zest

The liquid should be about 1 inch deep; add more liquid if needed. Raise the heat, bring to a simmer, and immediately put the skillet in the oven. After 30 minutes, take the pan from the oven and turn the legs skin side up. If necessary, pour off and reserve some of the liquid so that all the duck skin is exposed. Turn the oven down to 325°F and continue cooking for 1 to 1½ hours more. The duck is done when the skin is browned and the tip of a knife slips easily in and out of the meat.

Set the duck legs aside and pour the braising juices and vegetables into a small bowl. Allow the liquid to settle, then skim off and discard the fat. The duck legs will render a surprising amount of fat. Taste for salt and correct the seasoning if needed. If it's too thin, reduce the braising liquid to concentrate it. Pour the liquid and vegetables back into the skillet with the duck legs on top. Just before serving, return to a simmer and reheat for a few minutes.

VARIATIONS

• Pitted olives can be substituted, but use fewer, about ½ cup, and don't add them to the braise until the last 15 minutes of cooking.

• Substitute dry sherry for half the wine.

• Substitute dried fruit such as prunes or figs for the olives. Use red wine instead of white and add a piece of bacon or pancetta to the braise. Omit the lemon zest.

• Substitute chicken legs for the duck legs. Reduce the cooking time by 30 minutes.

Roast Duck

4 SERVINGS

Remove any fat from the cavity of:

1 duck (3 to 4 pounds)

Make small piercing incisions all over the skin of the legs and breast with the tip of a small sharp knife or skewer, so that as much fat as possible will be rendered during roasting. Season the duck well, inside and out, the day before if possible, with:

Salt

Fresh-ground black pepper

Take the duck out of the refrigerator an hour before roasting. Preheat the oven to 400°F. Put the duck in a roasting pan, breast side up. Roast for 20 minutes, turn the duck over onto its breast, and roast for another 20 minutes. Carefully take the pan out of the oven, remove the duck from the pan, and pour out all the fat. Put the duck back in the pan, breast side up, and roast for a final 20 minutes, or until done. The meat right next to the bone should still be pink. Let the duck rest for 10 minutes before serving. Carve as you would a chicken.

Roast Turkey

Turkeys in the 12- to 18-pound range are easier to handle than larger birds and will feed 8 to 12 people, allowing for some leftovers.

Season the bird generously with salt and pepper, inside and out, at least a day ahead, preferably two or three. Turkeys can also be made tastier by being submerged in a seasoned saltwater brine for a day or two, but I no longer bother with brining, especially since more flavorful heritage breeds of turkey have become available again. Flavor the turkey with herbs, if you like: stuff the cavity with herb branches, rub the skin with chopped herb leaves, or work sprigs under the skin of the breast and thighs.

Make sure the turkey is at room temperature when it goes into the oven, and rub it first with softened butter, both outside and under the skin. If you stuff it, do so at the last minute, with freshly made stuffing, also at room temperature. Fill the cavity loosely so the bird will cook evenly. Extra stuffing can be cooked separately in an ovenproof dish.

Put the bird in a heavy roasting pan, breast up, preferably on a rack or cushioned by a bed of herb branches, in a preheated 400°F oven. Figure roughly 12 minutes per pound for a 15-pound unstuffed turkey (less for a bigger one). If the turkey is stuffed, allow about 5 minutes more per pound.

After about one third of the total cooking time lower the heat to 350°F and turn the turkey over. Roast it breast down for the middle third, and turn it back breast up for the final third. Baste it once or twice while it roasts after the final turn. Check for doneness at the leg joint as you would a chicken. Cook it to a temperature of no more than 160°F at its thickest points, at the fattest part of its breast and deep in its inner thigh. Take it out of the oven and let it rest for at least 20 minutes before you carve it (its internal temperature will continue to climb). The pan juices make wonderful gravy (see page 226).

Meat

Braised Short Ribs

4 SERVINGS

Braising short ribs on the bone makes one of the most succulent meat dishes there is.

Season, a day in advance, if possible:
> **3½ pounds grass-fed beef short ribs,
> cut into 2-inch pieces**

with:
> **Salt**
> **Fresh-ground black pepper**

Cover and refrigerate until an hour before cooking. Preheat the oven to 450°F. Place the short ribs in a roasting pan in a single layer, bone side down. Roast for about 25 to 30 minutes to brown the meat and render some of the fat. Remove from the oven, pour off the fat, and set the pan of ribs aside.

While the short ribs are roasting, cook the vegetables. Heat in a large skillet:
> **1 tablespoon olive oil**

Add:
> **2 small onions, peeled and quartered**
> **2 carrots,**
> **peeled and cut into large pieces**
> **1 celery stalk, peeled and quartered**
> **6 garlic cloves,**
> **peeled and coarsely chopped**
> **6 thyme sprigs**
> **4 parsley sprigs**
> **1 bay leaf**

Cook over medium heat, stirring occasionally, for 10 minutes. Add, and cook for 5 minutes longer:
> **3 tomatoes, cored and quartered**

Pour in and bring to a simmer:
> **¾ cup red wine**
> **2 cups chicken or beef broth**

Remove the short ribs from the roasting pan and pour the contents of the skillet into the pan. Place the short ribs on top of the vegetables, bone side up. Cover tightly with a lid or foil. Put the pan back in the hot oven. After about 20 minutes, when the liquid just begins to bubble, lower the heat to 325°F, and loosen the lid or foil to vent some of the heat so the liquid doesn't boil. Continue braising the short ribs until the meat is very tender and begins to fall off the bones, about another 1 to 1½ hours. Lift the ribs out of the braising liquid and set aside. Strain the liquid, pressing down with the back of a spoon on the aromatic vegetables to extract all the juices. Discard the vegetables. Allow the braising liquid to settle and skim off the fat. Taste the liquid; if it has reduced too much or is a little salty you may need to add a splash of water. Reheat the short ribs in the braising liquid just before serving.

VARIATIONS

◆ Add a slice of bacon or pancetta to the aromatic vegetables while they are cooking.

◆ Add a few dried porcini mushrooms and sauté with the aromatic vegetables.

◆ In summer, reheat the short ribs on the grill. Serve with the hot braising liquid on the side.

◆ Leftover short ribs, shredded and simmered with their braising liquid and more aromatic vegetables (onions, carrots, celery, and tomato, chopped and cooked), makes a fine sauce for pasta or polenta.

◆ For an excellent ravioli filling, finely chop the meat of leftover short ribs and mix with cooked, chopped onions, carrots, and celery; softened butter; and chopped herbs such as parsley and marjoram.

◆ Cook oxtail the same way. The total cooking time may be longer.

◆ Sprinkle with Gremolata (page 231) just before serving.

Italian Meatballs

4 SERVINGS

I like to make these meatballs about the size of Ping-Pong balls and toss them with tomato sauce and spaghetti. Sometimes I make them a bit smaller, roll them while still hot in grated Parmesan cheese, and serve them as an hors d'oeuvre.

Season:

1 pound ground grass-fed beef
¾ pound ground pork shoulder

with:

Salt
Fresh-ground black pepper

In a small bowl, combine:

1 cup torn-up pieces of day-old
   country-style bread, crusts removed
½ cup milk

Set aside to soften. Grate, using the large-holed side of a box grater:

1 small yellow onion, peeled

This will make a sort of rough purée that will add moisture and flavor to the meatballs. Squeeze most of the milk out of the bread and put the bread in a large mixing bowl with the seasoned meat and the grated onion. Add:

1 tablespoon olive oil
2 garlic cloves, peeled and pounded to
   a paste with a pinch of salt
1 tablespoon chopped fresh oregano
   (or 1 teaspoon dried, crumbled)
1 tablespoon chopped parsley
A pinch of cayenne pepper
1 egg, lightly beaten
¼ cup grated Parmesan cheese
Salt
Fresh-ground black pepper

Combine the ingredients with your hands, gently but thoroughly. Overworking the mixture makes the meatballs tough. Fry a little meatball in a small skillet and taste. Adjust the seasonings as needed. If it seems dry, add a little milk. The mixture will be soft. Gently form the mixture into meatballs, either by hand or with a small ice-cream scoop. Bake the meatballs on a rimmed baking sheet in a 450°F oven until just cooked through, about 6 minutes. Or fry them in a little oil in a cast-iron pan, turning them occasionally for even browning.

VARIATIONS

◆ Substitute ground turkey or chicken for the beef.

◆ Add other chopped herbs such as mint, marjoram, sage, or thyme.

◆ Add 2 garlic cloves, pounded to a purée, and 2 to 3 tablespoons red or white wine.

◆ Add pine nuts and currants to the mixture and serve with polenta and Baked Sliced Onions (page 314).

◆ Substitute ground lamb for some or all of the meats. Add some ground cumin and coriander. Omit the oregano and cheese. Brown the meatballs, then braise them in lamb or chicken broth until tender, about 30 minutes. Sprinkle with cilantro, and serve with couscous.

◆ Substitute cold, cooked rice or potato for the bread.

Hamburgers

4 SERVINGS

I like ground chuck from grass-fed, pasture-raised beef for hamburgers because of its flavor and its ratio of fat to lean meat.

Mix together:

1¾ pounds ground grass-fed chuck
Salt
Fresh-ground black pepper
2 garlic cloves, chopped fine

Shape the meat into 4 patties, packing the meat well. For even cooking, smooth the edges of each patty and make a depression in the center to compensate for the swelling that will occur as the meat cooks. For medium-rare hamburgers, grill for 9 minutes over medium-hot coals, turning once or twice. Toast on one side:

8 slices of bread
    (levain or focaccia are good choices)

Serve the hamburgers on the toasted bread with grilled onions, some leaves of arugula or lettuce, and your favorite condiments.

VARIATION

⬧ Chop about 2 teaspoons herbs and add to the meat. Lovage is particularly good.

Roast Beef

A beef roast can be a simple cross-rib shoulder roast or a luxurious whole tenderloin. The same technique is followed, regardless of the cut. The most important steps to remember are: season the roast ahead of time, allow plenty of time for it to come to room temperature before roasting, and allow it to rest after it comes out of the oven. All these steps improve the flavor and texture of the meat and help it cook more evenly.

Before you season the meat, trim off most of the excess fat, leaving a ¼-inch-thick layer. Season with salt and fresh-ground black pepper. A small roast of 2 to 3 pounds can be seasoned the day before, but it is even better seasoned 2 days in advance. A larger roast is best seasoned 2 to 3 days in advance.

It is not crucial to tie a roast, but it will help it cook more evenly. Have your butcher do this, or use cotton twine and tie a loop around the meat—snugly, but not tightly—with a simple slip knot every 3 inches or so.

To bring to room temperature, take small roasts out of the refrigerator an hour before cooking; larger roasts, 2 to 3 hours before.

I cook small roasts at 400°F and larger roasts of 5 pounds or more at 375°F. Figure on roughly 15 minutes per pound, and start checking the internal temperature early. Take the meat out of the oven when it is a little rarer than you want it to be; the temperature will continue to rise as it rests. Take the temperature in more than one place, aiming for the thickest parts. The temperature to go by is the lowest one registered. Allowing the roast to rest permits the internal temperature to stabilize and the juices to settle. I suggest a rest of at least 20 minutes for a small roast and 30 minutes or more for a larger one. To keep the roast warm, you can make a loose tent over it with a piece of foil, but don't seal the edges or the heat will be trapped and the meat will keep cooking.

The internal temperatures I follow are:

120°F for rare

125°F for medium rare

135°F for medium

145°F for medium well

155°F for well done

Beef Pot Roast

4 SERVINGS

Season, at least several hours ahead or the night before:

3 pounds grass-fed beef chuck roast

with:

Salt

Fresh-ground black pepper

Cover and refrigerate until an hour before cooking. Heat a Dutch oven or other heavy deep pot until hot. Pour in:

2 tablespoons olive oil

Quickly, carefully place the chuck roast in the pot, tilting it a little to spread the oil around the meat. Brown the roast for 3 to 4 minutes on each side. Add:

1 tablespoon butter

Turn the roast, sprinkling on all sides as you turn it:

1 tablespoon flour

Brown for another 3 minutes on each side, then add to the pot:

1 onion,
  peeled and cut into large pieces
1 leek, trimmed,
  washed, and cut into pieces
1 carrot, peeled and cut into pieces
2 celery stalks,
  washed and cut into pieces
3 garlic cloves, halved

4 thyme sprigs
1 parsley sprig
1 bay leaf

Pour in:

½ cup red wine
Water or broth

Add enough water to come almost to the top of the meat. Bring to a simmer, stirring occasionally, and skim thoroughly. Cover, adjust the heat to maintain a slow simmer, and cook until the meat is very tender, about 2½ hours.

While the pot roast is simmering, cook separately, in salted boiling water, until very tender:

3 carrots, peeled and cut into pieces
3 celery stalks, cut into pieces
4 medium yellow potatoes,
  peeled and cut into pieces

When the pot roast is cooked, take it out of the liquid and keep it warm while you strain the cooking liquid, pressing down with the back of a spoon to extract all the juices from the vegetables left in the strainer. Discard the vegetables. Allow the liquid to settle and skim well. Return the liquid to the pot and bring back to a simmer. Slice the roast, put it back in the pot, and add the separately cooked vegetables. Bring to a simmer, and serve hot.

VARIATIONS

◆ Add a thick slice of pancetta to the pot for richer flavor.

◆ Substitute or add other vegetables to be served with the pot roast. In spring, for example, peas, turnips, and parsnips; in summer, fresh shell beans and whole peeled tomatoes.

◆ Serve with Salsa Verde (page 45), with grated horseradish flavored with a little white wine vinegar, or with mustard.

Long-Cooked Lamb Shoulder

4 SERVINGS

Lamb shoulder, because it is a cut of meat with lots of connective tissue, cooks to a very succulent, tender roast. You might have to ask your butcher for a whole, bone-in roast.

Season, the night before if possible:
> **Bone-in lamb shoulder roast
>   (3 to 4 pounds)**

with:
> **Salt
> Fresh-ground black pepper**

In a heavy earthenware dish or roasting pan that just accommodates the roast, combine:
> **4 medium tomatoes or one 14.5-ounce
>   can organic whole peeled tomatoes,
>   cored and coarsely chopped
> 2 medium onions,
>   peeled and coarsely chopped
> 2 carrots, peeled and coarsely chopped
> 5 garlic cloves
> 3 savory branches
> 3 thyme branches
> 7 black peppercorns
> 1 chile pepper**

Put the shoulder roast on top and pour in:
> **2 cups chicken broth or water
> ¾ cup white wine**

Cook uncovered in a 375°F oven for about 2½ hours. Check the level of liquid every once in a while and add more broth or water if it gets too low. After 1½ hours, turn the shoulder over and cook for another 30 minutes. Turn once more and cook for 20 minutes, or until golden. The meat should be soft and tender, almost falling off the bones; if not, continue cooking, turning the roast every 20 minutes. When done, remove the lamb from the pan and pour the vegetables and liquid into a bowl. Skim off all the fat and discard. Pass the vegetables through a food mill and return to the cooking liquid. Taste for seasoning and adjust as necessary. The sauce can be thinned with broth or water, if necessary. Cut or pull the meat off the bones and cut into large pieces. Reheat the meat in the sauce and serve.

VARIATIONS
* If you've cooked the shoulder ahead of time, another way to reheat the meat is to put it on the grill over a medium-hot fire, which makes the outside crispy. Slice and serve with crispy potatoes and a salad.
* Make a lamb stew instead of a roast using 3 pounds lamb shoulder cut into 2-inch pieces. Brown the meat in olive oil over medium-high heat, and add it to the pan with the vegetables. Add the liquids, cover, and cook at 325°F until tender, about 2½ hours.

Braised Lamb Shanks

4 SERVINGS

The shank is the best part of the lamb to braise. It is a meaty cut from the foreleg. A shank is a generous serving; braise them whole or ask your butcher to cut them in half lengthwise. Gremolata, a mixture of parsley, garlic, and lemon zest, adds a final bright fresh garnish to the long-cooked braise.

Trim any excess fat from:
> **4 lamb shanks**

Season liberally, the day before if possible, with:
> **Salt
> Fresh-ground black pepper**

Into a heavy-bottomed pan over medium-high heat, pour:
> **Olive oil**

Use enough to generously cover the bottom of the pan. Add the shanks and brown them well on all sides. This will take a good 12 minutes or so. When the shanks are brown, remove them from the pan, pour out most of the fat, and add:

> **2 onions,**
> > **peeled and cut into large pieces**
> **2 carrots,**
> > **peeled and cut into large pieces**
> **1 head of garlic, cut in half**
> **1 small dried chile pepper**
> **4 black peppercorns**
> **1 rosemary sprig**
> **1 bay leaf**

Cook for a few minutes, stirring now and then, until the vegetables soften. Add:

> **¾ cup white wine**
> **2 medium tomatoes or half of a**
> > **14.5-ounce can of organic whole**
> > **tomatoes, cored and chopped**

Turn up the heat to reduce the wine and scrape up any brown bits from the bottom of the pan. When the wine has reduced by half, put the shanks back in the pan and pour in:

> **2 cups chicken broth**

The liquid should come about halfway up the sides of the shanks. Bring to a boil and immediately turn down the heat, cover, and cook for 2½ to 3 hours at a bare simmer, on the stovetop or in a 325°F oven. When braising in the oven, remove the cover for the last 20 minutes of cooking to brown the meat a little. The lamb should be meltingly tender and falling off the bones. Take out the lamb shanks. Skim off all the fat. Pass the sauce through a food mill. If it is very thick, thin it with a bit of chicken broth. Taste and adjust the seasoning as needed. Return the shanks to the sauce.

Prepare
Gremolata (page 231)
Warm the sauce and shanks and serve sprinkled with gremolata.

Grilled Lamb Loin Chops

4 SERVINGS

Season:
> **8 lamb loin chops cut 1½ inches thick**
with:
> **Salt**
> **Fresh-ground black pepper**

Prepare a medium-hot bed of coals. Brush and clean the grill. Brush the chops with oil and put them on the grill. Cook for 3 minutes and rotate 45 degrees if desired, for grill marks. Turn the chops after 6 minutes and cook until medium rare, about another 4 minutes. Let rest for 4 minutes before serving.

VARIATIONS
• To grill lamb rack chops, count 3 per person, and season as above, but cook over a hot fire for only about 3 minutes on each side.
• Grill pork chops over medium coals. One-inch-thick pork chops will take about 10 to 12 minutes to cook.

Grilled Pork Spare Ribs

4 SERVINGS

You can make your own mild chile powder for this recipe by lightly toasting and grinding whole dried sweet chiles such as Anaheim or ancho.

Season, the night before, if possible:
> **2 slabs pork spare ribs
> (about 3 pounds)**

with:
> **Salt**
> **Fresh-ground black pepper**

Mix together:
> **2 teaspoons coriander seeds,
> toasted and ground**
> **1 teaspoon fennel seeds,
> toasted and ground**
> **3 teaspoons mild chile powder**
> **2 teaspoons sweet paprika**

Pat the spice mixture onto both sides of the meat. Refrigerate. Bring the ribs to room temperature before cooking. Prepare a wood or charcoal fire. Drizzle the ribs with:
> **Olive oil**

When the fire is medium-hot, put the meat on the grill and cover loosely with foil. The ribs should cook slowly. If they grill too quickly, the meat will toughen and the spices can burn and become bitter. Turn each slab of ribs every 10 minutes or so until they are well browned and cooked through, about 1 hour. Tend the fire to maintain a steady temperature. Cut between the bones to separate the ribs and serve.

VARIATIONS

• Roast the ribs on a baking sheet in a 375°F oven for 1 hour, turning every 10 minutes.
• Replace the chile powder and paprika with dried chile flakes and add whole fresh thyme leaves, rosemary, and sage to the mixture.

Simple Homemade Sausage

MAKES 1 POUND

Sausage is quite easy to make. This recipe is for sausage meat that won't be stuffed into a casing. It is good for making patties and meatballs, and for stuffings and pasta sauces. In general, for sausage to have a good texture it should contain 25 to 30 percent fat. Much of this fat is rendered while the sausage cooks, but without it the meat will be dry and lack flavor. It follows that the best ground pork to use is ground from the shoulder, which has more fat than the leg or loin. When made with fresh meat, sausage will keep in the refrigerator for up to a week.

Using your hands, lightly mix together:
> **1 pound ground pork**
> **1 teaspoon salt**
> **¼ teaspoon fresh-ground black pepper**
> **2 teaspoons chopped fresh sage leaves or
> 1 teaspoon dried sage**
> **A pinch of freshly grated nutmeg**
> **A pinch of cayenne**

Mix well enough to distribute the seasonings evenly, but avoid mashing the meat. Make a small patty of meat, fry it in a small skillet, and taste. Adjust the seasoning as needed.

VARIATION

• To make fennel sausage, replace the sage, nutmeg, and cayenne with 2 teaspoons fennel seeds, toasted and lightly pounded; 2 garlic cloves, pounded to a purée; 3 tablespoons red wine; and if you like, 2 teaspoons chopped parsley and ½ teaspoon dried chile flakes.

Roast Pork Loin

4 SERVINGS

Roast pork, with its tender interior and crusty juicy exterior, is superb eating. Pork loin can be roasted boneless or as a standing rib roast. When requesting a bone-in roast, ask your butcher to cut it from the rib end and to remove the chine (or spinal) bone. A bone-in roast can be carved into thick chops with rib bones attached or it can be completely boned after roasting and sliced thin. In that case, cut apart the bones and serve them along with the meat.

Season, the day before if possible:

1 bone-in 4-rib pork loin, or
    1 boned 2½-pound pork loin

with:

Salt
Fresh-ground black pepper

If the roast has its bones, use a sharp knife to partly separate the meat from the ribs, stopping about 1 inch before the end of the bones. Season the roast liberally all over. Take the roast out of the refrigerator 1 hour before cooking. Tie it snugly in a few places with cotton string to promote even roasting.

Preheat the oven to 375°F. Place the roast in a roasting pan, fat side up, and cook until the internal temperature registers 130°F, about 1 hour and 15 minutes; start checking the temperature after 45 minutes. When the roast is done, let it rest for 20 minutes before carving. Pour off some of the fat from the roasting pan, then deglaze the pan with some wine and broth or water, scraping up all the brown bits on the bottom of the pan. Add the juices released from the roast while resting and reheat. When ready to serve, cut the strings from the roast, slice, and serve with the roasting juices.

VARIATIONS

• After separating the bones from the meat, season generously with a mixture of herbs (such as sage, fennel, or rosemary), garlic, salt, and pepper; tie the roast with cotton string; and spread more of the herb mixture over the exterior.
• While the meat is coming to room temperature, slice a lemon very thin and line up the slices between the rib bones and the meat before tying the roast. If the roast is boneless, arrange the slices underneath the roast.
• Roast a leg of pork the same way.

Carnitas

4 SERVINGS

Carnitas is the traditional crispy pork filling for little tacos that are eaten with chiles, cheese, and all sorts of salsas. It is simply stewed until tender and then browned in its own fat.

Cut into 1-inch cubes:

1½ pounds boneless pork shoulder

Place the meat in a wide heavy-bottomed pan in a single layer. Add water to just cover the meat.

Stir in:

½ teaspoon salt
2 teaspoons fresh lime juice

Bring to a simmer, cover the pan, and cook gently until tender, about 45 minutes. Take off the lid, turn up the heat, and allow the liquid to boil away. When the meat begins to sizzle, turn down the heat, and fry gently until golden. Remove the meat from the pan and allow the excess fat to drain off. Taste for salt and add more if needed.

Desserts

(CONTINUED)

Winter Fruit Compote

8 SERVINGS

Almost any combination of dried fruits can be refreshed this way and turned into a dessert to be served alongside a slice of cake, or with a little crème fraîche. Fresh winter citrus fruits also make beautiful winter compotes when soaked in syrup flavored with their zest.

In a medium-size saucepan, combine:
½ cup golden raisins
¼ cup Zante currants
¼ cup dried cherries
½ cup dried apricots, diced
½ cup dried apples, diced
1¾ cups fresh orange juice
3 strips of orange zest
¼ cup brown sugar
Split in half lengthwise:
One 1-inch piece of vanilla bean
Use the tip of a sharp knife to scrape the black seeds from the inside of the bean directly into the saucepan; then add the bean, along with:
1 star anise (optional)
Cook over medium heat until the dried fruits have plumped and the juice has slightly thickened, about 3 to 5 minutes. Let cool slightly, then discard the vanilla bean, orange zest, and star anise, if using.

VARIATIONS
◆ Add sliced poached pears or quince to the cooled fruit.
◆ The compote makes a memorable tart filling. Strain off the liquid and use the fruit to make a galette (see Fruit Tarts, page 178). Reduce the liquid and use it to glaze the galette after baking. Serve with crème fraîche, whipped cream, or ice cream.

Summer Fruit Compote

4 SERVINGS

This is only one example of the many summer fruit compotes that turn combinations of fruit into delectable desserts. All the fruits of summer—plums, peaches, apricots, nectarines, cherries, figs—can be cut up and soaked together in their own juices with a little sugar and lemon juice. Summer fruit compotes are delicious by themselves; on pancakes or waffles; with almond cake or angel food cake or a plate of cookies; or with ice cream, whipped cream, or sherbet.

Hull and slice:
1 cup (½ pint) strawberries
Add:
½ cup blueberries
½ cup blackberries
½ cup raspberries
Add, to taste:
Juice of 1 lemon
2 to 3 tablespoons sugar
Mix together gently. Cover and let the fruit soak together for at least 10 to 15 minutes.

Poached Kumquats

MAKES ABOUT 4 CUPS

I usually poach more kumquats than I need for a particular dessert; they keep well in their poaching liquid in the refrigerator for 2 weeks or more. They are lovely combined with sliced fresh blood oranges or with other poached fruits, especially prunes (poach the kumquats, lift them out when they're done, and poach the prunes in the same syrup, combining them when the prunes are done and the syrup has cooled a bit).

Wash and trim off the ends of:
1 pound kumquats
Slice them crosswise into ⅛- to ¼-inch pinwheels, removing the seeds as you go. Combine in a small saucepan:
2 cups water
1 cup sugar
One 1-inch piece of vanilla bean,
split lengthwise, seeds scraped into
the pan
Bring to a boil, stirring to dissolve the sugar. Adjust the heat to a low simmer and add the sliced kumquats. Let them cook gently until translucent and tender, about 12 to 15 minutes. Remove from the heat and let them cool in the poaching syrup.

Strawberries in Orange Juice

4 SERVINGS

This is an utterly simple dessert that is a refreshing finish to any meal. Be sure to use bright red ripe berries.

Wash and hull:
1½ pints sweet ripe strawberries
Cut the berries in half or in quarters if they are large.

Stir together:
1½ cups fresh orange juice
(from 3 large oranges)
3 tablespoons sugar, or to taste
Pour the juice over the berries and let them soak for at least 30 minutes. Serve cold.

VARIATIONS
• Substitute a fruity red wine for the orange juice and add a squeeze of lemon juice.
• Add the segments of 1 or 2 oranges to the sliced strawberries.

Strawberry Shortcake

6 SERVINGS

Hull and slice:
4 cups strawberries
(about two 1-pint baskets)
Stir in:
¼ cup sugar
Purée one quarter of the strawberry mixture. Stir the purée back into the sliced strawberries and let sit for 15 minutes.
Combine in a bowl:
1 cup heavy cream
½ teaspoon vanilla extract
1 tablespoon sugar, or to taste
Whip together, until the cream just holds a soft shape. Slice in half:
6 baked 2-inch Cream Biscuits
(page 275)
Place the biscuit bottoms on serving plates. Over each biscuit, spoon strawberries and a dollop of the flavored whipped cream. Top with the other biscuit half and dust with:
Powdered sugar (optional)
Serve immediately.

VARIATION
• For the strawberries, substitute any berries in season, in any combination.

Baked Peaches

4 SERVINGS

Nectarines and apricots are also delicious baked this way.

Preheat the oven to 400°F.
Cut in half:

4 large ripe peaches

Remove the pits and place the peach halves cut side up in a 9- by 13-inch shallow earthenware baking dish.
In a small bowl, whisk together:

5 tablespoons apricot jam

2 tablespoons honey

1 cup water

1 tablespoon lemon zest

2 teaspoons fresh lemon juice

Spoon the mixture over the peach halves and sprinkle each half with:

½ teaspoon sugar

Bake for 30 to 45 minutes, until the peaches are tender. Very ripe peaches will cook faster. Check several times during baking, basting them with their juices each time you do. Serve warm, with ice cream. Drizzle the juices over the top for a delicious sauce.

VARIATION

◆ Substitute ½ cup Sauternes (or other sweet wine) for half the water. Omit the honey.

Tarte Tatin

8 SERVINGS

This is one of the most delicious tarts there is. The apples caramelize on the bottom of the pan, the pastry bakes crisp and brown on top of the fruit, and the whole tart is flipped upside down, revealing the dark caramel-drenched apples.

On a lightly floured surface, roll out to an 11-inch circle:

9 to 10 ounces Tart and Pie Dough (page 174) or puff pastry

Brush off any excess flour, transfer the dough circle to a parchment-paper-lined baking sheet, and refrigerate until needed.
Quarter, peel, and core:

3 to 4 pounds apples (Granny Smith, Golden Delicious, or another variety that holds its shape when cooked)

Don't worry about the peeled apples discoloring. Any browning will be invisible because of caramelization.
Preheat the oven to 400°F. Put a 9-inch cast-iron skillet over medium-high heat. Add:

2 tablespoons butter

6 tablespoons sugar

Swirl the pan, or stir with a wooden spoon or heat-proof spatula to caramelize the mixture evenly. Cook until the caramel is dark brown and bubbly, but don't let it burn. Remove the pan from the heat when the caramel is a deep amber brown color. It will continue to cook and brown off the heat; return the pan to the heat to darken the caramel if necessary. The success of the tart depends on deep caramel flavor.

While the pan is cooling, cut the apple quarters in half lengthwise. Arrange the apple slices in a ring around the outside edge of the pan, rounded sides down, with the narrower tips towards the center. Make another ring of apples inside the first ring. Fit two more rings of apples, rounded sides up, between the apple quarters that form the rings in the pan. Cut smaller pieces of apple to fill any gaps; the apples will shrink as they cook. Press down lightly on the apples to make sure they fit. Place the pastry circle on over the apples. When it has softened slightly, tuck the edges of the pastry between the fruit and the edge of the pan. Cut 3 or 4 small slashes in the top of the pastry to allow steam to escape while baking. Bake in the middle level of the oven for 35 to 40 minutes or until the pastry is well browned. The contents of the pan should shift slightly when the pan is shaken gently. Remove from the oven and cool on a rack for a minute or two. Place a serving plate larger than the pan upside down on top of the pan. Lift the two together, holding the plate tightly on top of the pan, and flip them over quickly. Give the pan a gentle twist and lift it off. If any fruit has stuck to the pan, remove it with a spatula and put it back in place on the tart.

Serve warm with crème fraîche or vanilla ice cream or whipped cream.

Lemon Curd Tart

MAKES ONE 9-INCH TART

To make a lemon curd tart, fill a prebaked 9-inch Sweet Tart Dough shell (page 183) with 2 cups Lemon Curd (page 199). Smooth out the curd and bake in a preheated 375°F oven for 15 to 20 minutes or until the curd is set.

Blueberry Pie

MAKES ONE 9-INCH PIE

Soften at room temperature:

Two 10-ounce disks Tart and Pie Dough (page 174)

Roll one of the disks of dough into a 12-inch round. Line a 9-inch tart or pie pan with the dough. Trim the edges leaving a ½-inch-long overhang. Roll the other disk of dough into a 12-inch round. Place on a parchment-paper-lined baking sheet. Refrigerate the lined pie pan and the round of dough while preparing the fruit.

Position a rack in the lower third of the oven. Preheat the oven to 400°F.

In a medium bowl, stir together:

6 cups blueberries
¾ cup sugar
4 tablespoons quick-cooking tapioca, pulverized in a mortar
2 teaspoons grated lemon zest
1 tablespoon fresh lemon juice
¼ teaspoon salt

Let stand for 10 minutes. Pour the mixture into the prepared pie shell.

Cut into small cubes and sprinkle over the berries:

2 tablespoons unsalted butter

Cover the pie with the top crust. Fold the edge of the top crust under the edge of the bottom crust. Pinch the crusts together, crimping all around. In a small bowl beat:

1 egg

Lightly brush the top crust with the beaten egg. Cut 4 small steam vents in the top. Place the pie on a baking sheet and bake for 15 minutes. Turn the oven down to 350°F and bake until the pie is golden and thick juices are bubbling through the steam vents, another 45 minutes or so. If the edges are browning too quickly, cover them with a ring of foil. Let the pie cool completely on a rack before cutting.

VARIATIONS

◆ You can substitute blackberries, black raspberries, huckleberries, olallieberries, or any combination of berries.

◆ For apple pie, toss together 3 pounds apples (such as Golden Delicious, Sierra Beauty, or Gravenstein, cored and cut in ½-inch pieces) with ¼ to ½ cup sugar and, if you like, 2 teaspoons brandy or Calvados or ¼ teaspoon cinnamon. Fill and finish as above.

Pumpkin Pie

MAKES ONE 9-INCH PIE

It's easy to make your own pumpkin or squash purée and it makes the best-tasting pie. However, most pumpkins are for carving, not eating, and their flesh is too watery and flavorless to make a good purée. Look for sweet pumpkin varieties (for example, Sugar Pie, Long Pie, or Cinderella) or use butternut squash. To make a purée, see page 324.

Soften at room temperature:

One 10-ounce disk Tart and Pie Dough (page 174)

Roll out the dough into a 12-inch circle.

Line a 9-inch pie pan with the pastry. Refrigerate for at least 1 hour. Preheat the oven to 375°F. Prick the bottom all over with a fork. Line the shell with a piece of foil or parchment paper and fill with a layer of dried beans reserved for this purpose (or other pie weights). Bake in a 375°F oven for 15 minutes, or until lightly golden around the edge. Take the tart out of the oven; remove the foil and the weights. Return to the oven and cook for another 5 to 7 minutes, until the tart is an even light golden brown.

Set aside to cool.

In a small saucepan whisk together:

¼ cup cream

2 teaspoons flour

Heat the mixture over low heat until it comes to a boil and thickens. Slowly whisk in:

¾ cup cream

Continue whisking until the mixture returns to a boil. Remove from the heat. In a medium bowl whisk together:

15 ounces (1½ cups) pumpkin purée

3 eggs

In another bowl combine:

¼ cup brown sugar

1 tablespoon granulated sugar

1 teaspoon ground cinnamon

¼ teaspoon ground cloves

¼ teaspoon ground ginger

½ teaspoon salt

A pinch of fresh-ground black pepper

Stir the sugar and spice mixture and the thickened cream into the pumpkin mixture. Whisk in:

1½ teaspoons brandy (optional)

Pour into the prebaked pie shell and bake for 45 to 50 minutes, until the center is almost set. If the edges are browning too quickly, fit a ring of foil around the rim. Let cool completely on a rack before cutting.

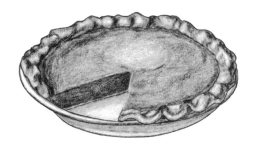

Cranberry Upside-Down Cake

MAKES ONE 8-INCH ROUND OR SQUARE CAKE

This cake is very versatile and can be made with apples, pears, peaches, plums, or any full-flavored, slightly acidic fruit. Arrange the sliced fruit as you would for a Tarte Tatin (page 366).

Preheat the oven to 350°F.

Measure into an 8-inch cast-iron skillet or heavy-duty cake pan:

4 tablespoons (½ stick) unsalted butter
¾ cup brown sugar

Cook over medium heat, stirring constantly, until the butter melts and starts to bubble. Remove from the heat and allow to cool. Heat together in a small saucepan:

2¾ cups fresh cranberries
¼ cup fresh orange juice

Cook until the cranberries just start to pop. Remove from the heat and pour evenly over the cooled caramel.

Separate:

2 eggs, at room temperature

Measure:

½ cup whole milk,
at room temperature

Measure and stir together:

1½ cups unbleached all-purpose flour
2 teaspoons baking powder
¼ teaspoon salt

In another bowl or in a stand mixer, beat to lighten:

8 tablespoons (1 stick) unsalted butter, softened

Add:

1 cup granulated sugar

Cream until light and fluffy. Beat in the 2 yolks, one at a time. Stir in:

1 teaspoon vanilla extract

When well mixed, add the flour mixture alternately with the milk, starting and ending with one third of the flour. Stir just until the flour is incorporated. Beat the egg whites until they hold soft peaks. Fold one third of the egg whites into the batter and then gently fold in the rest. Pour the batter over the cranberries in the pan and smooth the top with a spatula. Bake for 30 to 35 minutes or until the top is golden brown and the cake pulls away from the sides of the pan. Remove from the oven and allow the cake to cool for 15 minutes. Run a knife around the edge of the pan and invert the cake onto a serving plate.

Almond Cake

MAKES ONE 9-INCH ROUND CAKE

Preheat the oven to 325°F.

Butter a 9- by 3-inch cake pan and line the bottom with parchment paper. Butter the paper and dust the pan with flour, shaking out the excess.

Sift together:

1 cup cake flour
1½ teaspoons baking powder
¼ teaspoon salt

Mix together:

7 ounces almond paste
1¼ cups sugar

Stir until the almond paste is in very small pieces. Or, more easily, pulverize together in a food processor or stand mixer.

By hand or with a stand mixer, beat to lighten:

½ pound plus 4 tablespoons (2½ sticks) unsalted butter, softened

Add the almond paste and sugar mixture to the butter and cream together until light and fluffy, then beat in:

1 teaspoon vanilla extract
Beat in, one at a time:
6 eggs, at room temperature
Scrape down the sides of the bowl repeatedly to ensure that all the ingredients are thoroughly incorporated. Gradually add the flour mixture, mixing until just combined. Pour the batter into the prepared cake pan and bake for 1 hour and 15 minutes or until a toothpick inserted into the center comes out clean. Remove from the oven and let cool. Turn the cake out of the pan and remove the parchment paper. Serve the cake plain or with sliced fruit and whipped cream.

VARIATIONS
◆ For a sheet cake, prepare a half-sheet pan as above, pour in the batter, smooth the top, and bake for about 40 minutes. Or, bake in two 9-inch cake pans for a two-layer cake.
◆ For 24 individual mini-cakes, bake in muffin tins that are buttered, lined on the bottom with small parchment circles, and floured as above. Fill each cup two-thirds full and bake for about 30 minutes. Or use cupcake liners to make cupcakes.
◆ To dress up this cake, spread it with a thin layer of apricot or raspberry jam. Sprinkle it with toasted sliced almonds and dust with powdered sugar.

Chocolate Cake
MAKES ONE 9-INCH ROUND CAKE

This is a moist and versatile cake that stores well. It can be made in any format from cupcakes to a multitiered wedding cake.

Preheat the oven to 350°F.

Butter a cake pan and line the bottom with parchment paper. Butter the paper and dust the pan with flour or cocoa, shaking out the excess.
Put in a heat-proof bowl:
4 ounces unsweetened chocolate, coarsely chopped
Set the bowl over a pan of simmering water. (The water should not touch the bowl.) Turn off the heat. Stir the chocolate from time to time until completely melted and smooth. Remove the bowl from over the pan.
Sift together:
2 cups cake flour
2 teaspoons baking soda
½ teaspoon salt
6 tablespoons cocoa powder
In a large bowl, beat until creamy, by hand or in a stand mixer:
8 tablespoons (1 stick) butter, softened
Add and cream until light and fluffy:
2½ cups brown sugar
2 teaspoons vanilla extract
Beat in, one at a time:
3 eggs, at room temperature
When fully incorporated, stir in the melted chocolate. Add half the dry ingredients to this mixture and combine, then stir in:
½ cup buttermilk, at room temperature
Stir in the rest of the dry ingredients. Gradually pour in, mixing until just incorporated:
1¼ cups boiling water

Pour the batter into the prepared pan and bake for 45 minutes or until a toothpick inserted into the center comes out clean. Place the pan on a wire rack and allow the cake to cool completely. Run a knife around the edge of the pan to loosen the cake. Remove the cake from the pan and peel off the parchment paper. If not using the same day, store the fully cooled cake in the pan, tightly covered.

VARIATIONS

• For a sheet cake, prepare a half-sheet pan as above. Pour in the batter, smooth the top, and bake for about 20 minutes. Or, bake in two 9-inch cake pans for a two-layer cake.

• For 24 individual cupcakes, bake for about 30 minutes.

Chocolate Pavé

MAKES ONE 9- BY 13-INCH CAKE

Pavé is the French word for "paving stone." Chocolate pavés are very rich, smooth, and dense. Chocolate cakes like this are often called flourless cakes, because they are completely gluten-free.

Preheat the oven to 350°F.

Butter a 9- by 13-inch baking dish and line the bottom with parchment paper. Butter the paper and dust the pan with flour or cocoa powder, shaking out the excess.

Set a medium heat-proof bowl over (but not touching) simmering water and add:

3½ ounces unsweetened chocolate, coarsely chopped

4 ounces semisweet chocolate, coarsely chopped

15 tablespoons (2 sticks minus 1 tablespoon) unsalted butter

Heat until melted and smooth, stirring often. Set aside to cool.
Separate:

6 eggs, at room temperature

Whisk the 6 yolks with:

½ cup sugar

Continue to whisk until the mixture forms a ribbon when the whisk is lifted from the bowl and all the sugar has dissolved, about 10 minutes. Fold the yolk mixture into the melted chocolate.

In a separate bowl, whisk the 6 egg whites until foamy. Gradually add:

½ cup sugar

¼ teaspoon salt

Continue to whisk until the mixture looks glossy and holds a soft shape.

Fold the whites into the chocolate mixture in three parts. Fold only until there are no visible streaks of white.

Pour the batter into the prepared baking dish, smooth the top, and bake for 35 to 40 minutes. As the cake cooks it will develop cracks on the top; this is normal. The cake is done when the sides are set and the center is still slightly soft. Let the cake cool completely. Invert the cake onto a baking sheet, remove the parchment paper, and then invert onto a serving platter. Dust the top with:

Sifted powdered sugar

VARIATION

• Decorate the top of the cake with melted chocolate or Chocolate Sauce (page 386). Dip the tines of a fork into the chocolate and dribble it in thin lines over the top of the cake.

Angel Food Cake

10 SERVINGS

Tall, airy angel food cake is lovely just plain, but I usually serve it with Summer Fruit Compote (page 364) and whipped cream. Day-old angel food cake is delicious sliced thin and toasted.

Preheat the oven to 350°F.
Sift together:

> **1 cup cake flour**
> **¾ cup sugar**
> **½ teaspoon salt**

In a medium bowl or in a stand mixer with the whip attachment, whisk until frothy:

> **1½ cups egg whites (about 12 egg whites), at room temperature**

Whisk in:

> **1 tablespoon water**
> **1 tablespoon fresh lemon juice**
> **1 teaspoon cream of tartar**

Keep whisking until the foam is very soft, holds a slight shape, and has increased 4 to 5 times in volume.
Whisk in:

> **¾ cup sugar**

Continue whisking until the mixture forms glossy, soft peaks. The mixture should not be stiff or dry. Transfer to a large bowl. Sift a fine layer of the dry ingredients over the whites and fold them in with a rubber spatula, gently and quickly. Continue sifting and folding until all the dry ingredients are incorporated.

Pour the batter into an ungreased 10- by 4-inch tube pan with a removable bottom. Smooth the top. Bake for 40 to 45 minutes. When done the cake should spring back when touched gently. Invert the pan to keep the cake from sticking or deflating. (If the cake pan has legs, turn it over onto them; otherwise invert the tube pan onto the neck of a large bottle.) Cool completely. To remove the cake from the pan, run a knife around the inside of the pan and around the center tube. Gently push up the bottom, using the knife to help guide the cake out, if necessary. Use a sharp serrated knife to cut the cake, dipping the knife into water between cuts to help keep the cake from sticking.

VARIATIONS

• Add ¼ teaspoon orange flower water or rose water to perfume the cake lightly.
• For a lemon- or orange-flavored cake, add the finely grated zest of 1 lemon or 1 orange.

Flan

6 TO 8 SERVINGS

Pour into a small heavy pot:

> **¼ cup water**

Sprinkle over in an even layer:

> **¾ cup sugar**

Measure and have ready another:

> **¼ cup water**

Cook the sugar and water over medium-high heat until the sugar caramelizes. Do not stir, but swirl the pan gently if the caramel is cooking unevenly. Let the sugar caramelize to a rich golden brown color. Remove from the heat. The caramel will continue to cook and color off the heat. When the caramel is a dark golden brown color, step back from the pot and pour in the measured water. The caramel will bubble up and spatter. Stir the caramelized sugar and water together with a wooden spoon. Immediately pour the caramel into a 9-inch round glass or ceramic ovenproof dish to cool and harden. Combine in a heavy saucepan:

> **2¾ cups milk**
> **¼ cup cream**

Warm until steaming over medium heat, but do not boil. Add:

¾ cup sugar

2 teaspoons vanilla extract

Remove from the heat, stir to dissolve the sugar, and let cool until lukewarm.

Whisk together:

3 egg yolks

3 eggs

Whisk the eggs into the cooled cream mixture.

When ready to bake, preheat the oven to 350°F. Pour the custard mixture into the prepared dish. Place the dish inside a larger ovenproof pan and fill with warm water to a depth halfway up the side of the dish. Cover the larger pan with foil, place in the oven, and bake for 55 minutes to 1 hour or until the custard is just set around the sides, but still jiggly in the center. Take the flan out of the water bath and let it cool. Run a knife around the flan to release it. Cover with a serving platter large enough to hold the flan and retain the caramel sauce. Quickly invert the custard onto the dish. Tap the bottom of the baking pan and gently lift it off. Serve the flan in slices with its sauce spooned on top.

VARIATIONS

◆ To make individual flans, divide the caramel and custard among 8 individual ramekins or ovenproof custard cups. Bake in a water bath for 35 to 40 minutes or until just set.

◆ Omit the vanilla and heat the milk with 1 cinnamon stick and 1 tablespoon orange zest. When the milk has cooled, strain it though a fine-mesh strainer.

Panna Cotta

8 SERVINGS

Brush eight 4-ounce ramekins lightly with:

Almond oil or a flavorless vegetable oil

Chill the ramekins until ready to use.

Measure into a small bowl:

3 tablespoons water

Sprinkle over:

One .25-ounce package gelatin

Set aside until the gelatin has softened.

Combine in a heavy saucepan:

3 cups heavy cream

1 cup milk

¼ cup sugar

3 strips of lemon zest

Split in half lengthwise:

½ vanilla bean

Scrape the seeds into the cream mixture and add the bean. Heat just to a simmer; do not boil. Remove from the heat. Pour 1 cup of the hot cream over the gelatin and stir to dissolve. Pour the gelatin mixture back into the cream mixture and let it cool until just warm to the touch, about 110°F. Remove the vanilla bean and squeeze all the seeds and liquid from it back into the cream mixture. Pour into the ramekins. Cover and chill for at least 6 hours.

To serve, run a small knife around the inside of each ramekin. Turn each ramekin over onto a small serving plate, shake gently, and lift off the ramekin. Serve with fresh berries or strawberries or with a fruit compote or sauce.

Vanilla Bean Ice Cream

MAKES 1 QUART

A vanilla custard makes a perfectly delicious ice cream and can be flavored in more ways than you can imagine.

Separate:
   6 eggs
Whisk the yolks just enough to break them up. Pour into a heavy-bottomed pot:
   1½ cups half-and-half
   ⅔ cup sugar
   A pinch of salt
Split in half lengthwise:
   ½ vanilla bean
Scrape the seeds into the pot with the half-and-half and sugar, then add the bean. Warm over medium heat until steaming, but do not allow to boil. Stir to dissolve the sugar. Whisk a little of the hot half-and-half into the egg yolks to temper them, then whisk the warmed yolks back into the hot half-and-half. Cook over medium heat, stirring constantly, until the mixture thickens and coats the back of a spoon (170°F). Remove from the heat and strain into a bowl. Retrieve the vanilla bean from the strainer and squeeze all the seeds and liquid from it back into the custard. Stir in:
   1½ cups heavy cream
Cover the custard and chill thoroughly.

   Freeze the chilled custard in an ice-cream machine according to the manufacturer's instructions. Transfer the frozen ice cream into a clean dry container, cover, and store in the freezer for several hours to firm up before serving.

VARIATIONS

⋆ Once the ice cream is frozen, but before you store it in the freezer to form up, fold in 1 cup chopped chocolate, chopped toasted nuts, chopped candied nuts, or chopped candied citrus peel—or any combination.

⋆ Chocolate ice cream: Melt 5 ounces semisweet chocolate and 1 ounce unsweetened chocolate, coarsely chopped, with 2 tablespoons butter. Gradually whisk in the warm custard mixture, stir in the heavy cream, chill, and freeze as above.

⋆ Coffee ice cream: Omit the vanilla and add to the half-and-half ¾ cup coffee beans with the sugar. When warm, turn off the heat and steep for 15 minutes. Strain, reheat, and proceed with the recipe.

⋆ Ginger ice cream: Omit the vanilla. Peel a 3-inch piece of ginger and slice thin. Add to the half-and-half and sugar. When warm, turn off the heat and let steep for 15 minutes. Strain, reheat, and proceed with the recipe. If you like, fold ¼ cup chopped candied ginger into the frozen ice cream.

⋆ Cinnamon ice cream: Omit the vanilla and add 2 cinnamon sticks, slightly crushed, to the half-and-half and sugar. When warm, turn off the heat and steep for 25 minutes, or so. Strain when the flavor is to your taste, reheat, and proceed with the recipe.

⋆ Mint-chocolate ice cream: Omit the vanilla and add 1 cup lightly packed fresh spearmint leaves to the half-and-half and sugar. When warm, turn off the heat and steep for about 10 minutes. Taste now and then, and strain when the flavor is to your taste. Reheat and proceed with the recipe. If you like, stir in 1 cup grated bittersweet chocolate.

⋆ Caramel ice cream: Caramelize the sugar with ¼ cup water. When dark brown, remove from the heat, pour in another ¼ cup water, stir to dissolve the caramel, add to the half-and-half, and proceed with the recipe.

⋆ Liqueur-flavored ice cream: Omit the vanilla bean and add ¼ cup dark rum, Cognac, Calvados, or other liqueur with the cream.

Pear Sherbet

MAKES ABOUT 1 QUART

Choose ripe, flavorful pears—juicy, but not soft or mushy. The flesh of the pear should just give to gentle pressure near the stem end. Comice and Bartlett are almost always good, but try others available in your area; Warren and Kiefer are two that I like.

Working with one pear at a time, quarter, core, and peel:

6 to 8 ripe pears (about 3 pounds)

As each pear is prepared, cut the quarters into rough slices, about ½ inch thick. Put the slices in a stainless-steel or other nonreactive bowl. Immediately squeeze into the bowl through a fine strainer:

1 teaspoon fresh lemon juice

Add:

1 tablespoon sugar

Toss the fruit to coat with the sugar and lemon juice. This prevents the fruit from browning as you work. Continue with the rest of the pears, tossing them in the lemon juice and sugar as you go. When all the pears are done, add:

⅓ cup sugar

1 egg white

Purée the pear mixture in a food processor or blender until smooth. Taste and correct the seasoning with lemon juice or sugar. You should be able to taste both sweet and tart. Freeze right away in an ice-cream maker according to the manufacturer's instructions. Any delay before freezing will allow the mixture to turn brown.

VARIATIONS

• Add a teaspoon or two of Armagnac, Cognac, or Poire William to the mixture before freezing; don't add more than that or the sherbet will not freeze properly.

Lemon Sherbet

MAKES 1½ QUARTS

Combine in a medium-size saucepan:

1 cup fresh lemon juice

2 cups water

1¼ cups sugar

Heat just until the sugar has dissolved. Remove from the heat and add:

¾ cup milk

Transfer the mixture to a bowl, cover, and place in the refrigerator until completely cool. Freeze in an ice-cream maker following the manufacturer's instructions. Transfer the frozen sherbet into a clean dry container, cover, and store in the freezer for several hours to firm up before serving.

VARIATIONS

• Add 2 strips of lemon zest when dissolving the sugar. Remove before freezing.

• Use Meyer lemons and reduce the sugar to 1 cup.

Frozen Peach Pops

MAKES 6 POPS

Peel, pit, and cut into pieces:

5 medium peaches (about 2½ cups)

Purée in a blender or food processor until smooth. Add:

½ cup white grape juice

Pour the puréed fruit into frozen pop molds or paper cups (with a wooden stick). Leave ½ inch of space at the top to allow the mixture to expand when freezing. Freeze for at least 4 hours or overnight. Gently pull the frozen pop out of the mold. Run the mold under hot water for a few seconds if necessary.

VARIATIONS

• Substitute 2½ cups (about 2 pints) blueberries, strawberries, nectarines or plums for the peaches.

Vanilla Custard or Pots de Crème

4 SERVINGS

Whisk until just mixed in a medium bowl:

4 egg yolks

Measure and pour into a medium bowl:

¾ cup heavy cream

Combine in a small pot:

¾ cup half-and-half

¼ cup sugar

One 2-inch piece of vanilla bean, split lengthwise and seeds scraped into the pan with the bean

Warm just until steaming over medium heat. Stir occasionally to dissolve the sugar. When warm, whisk into the egg yolks. Strain this mixture into the cold cream and mix well. Remove the vanilla bean from the strainer and squeeze all the seeds and liquid from it back into the custard mix. The mixture can be refrigerated for up to 2 days.

When ready to bake, preheat the oven to 350°F. Pour the mixture into a 2½-cup custard mold, or into 4 custard cups. Place the mold or cups into a large, deep pan and pour in hot water until it reaches about halfway up the sides. Cover the top of the pan with foil and seal tightly. Bake until the sides of the custards are set but the center is still soft when jiggled, about 50 minutes for the large mold and 25 to 30 minutes for the smaller cups. Remove from the water bath and let cool. Serve warm or cool in the refrigerator.

VARIATIONS

• Top the cooled custards with a few tablespoons of raspberry purée.

• Stir 2 tablespoons dry Marsala, sherry, or a liqueur into the custard mixture.

• Melt 3 ounces bittersweet chocolate and ½ ounce unsweetened chocolate over hot water. Stir the melted chocolate into the hot half-and-half. Stir in the cream and whisk in the egg yolks. Add ½ teaspoon brandy or Cognac, if desired.

• For crème brûlée, cool the custards and sprinkle 1 tablespoon white sugar evenly over the top of each custard. With a small handheld propane torch, pass the flame over the sugar to caramelize evenly. Heat until the sugar turns a dark amber brown. Alternatively, caramelize the sugar under a broiler but keep a sharp eye on the custards—they burn easily. Let cool to harden and serve.

Pastry Cream

MAKES ABOUT 1 CUP

Pastry cream can be used as a base for soufflés or in baked tart shells as a sweet layer of custard beneath a topping of raw fruits such as orange sections or raspberries. It is also the classic filling for éclairs, plain or flavored or blended with whipped cream.

In a small saucepan, heat until steaming but not boiling:

1 cup milk

While the milk heats, beat until thick in a small bowl:

3 egg yolks

½ cup sugar

Add and beat until smooth:

3 tablespoons flour

Continue beating while slowly adding the hot milk. Pour the mixture into the saucepan and place over medium heat. Continue beating until the mixture thickens and comes to a simmer. Stir with a wooden spoon or heat-proof spatula for 2 or 3 minutes more, carefully scraping the sides and bottom of the pan to prevent scorching.

Remove from the heat and add:

1 tablespoon butter

A pinch of salt

½ teaspoon vanilla extract

Stir until the butter is melted and the pastry cream is smooth. Transfer to a small bowl, place plastic wrap right on the surface of the pastry cream to prevent a skin from forming, and chill thoroughly before using.

Apricot Soufflé

6 SERVINGS

Homemade apricot jam is the secret to this easy soufflé. Plum jam and citrus marmalades are also good choices for soufflés.

Generously butter a 1-quart soufflé or gratin dish and coat with a thin layer of sugar. Preheat the oven to 425°F and position an oven rack in the center of the oven. In a medium bowl combine:

½ cup Pastry Cream (opposite)

6 tablespoons Apricot Jam (page 385)

A few drops of almond extract

Mix well and set aside. In a large copper or stainless-steel bowl, combine:

6 egg whites, at room temperature

A pinch of salt

Whisk until soft peaks form. Add:

2 teaspoons cornstarch

Beat a few more seconds, then sprinkle on:

⅓ cup sugar

Continue to beat the whites for a few more seconds. Quickly but gently fold the egg whites into the apricot mixture until just blended. Pour the soufflé mixture into the prepared dish. Place the dish in the middle of the oven and bake for 20 to 25 minutes, until it is puffed and browned. Serve immediately with heavy cream or Vanilla Pouring Custard (page 198), if you like.

Grand Marnier Soufflé

6 SERVINGS

Homemade candied orange or tangerine peel (page 382) makes this soufflé special.

Earlier in the day, or the day before, prepare:

Pastry Cream (opposite)

In a small bowl combine:

2 tablespoons finely chopped candied orange or tangerine peel

½ cup Grand Marnier liqueur

Cover tightly and set aside to soak for several hours or overnight.

When ready to make the soufflé, generously butter a 1-quart soufflé or gratin dish (or six 4-ounce ramekins) and dust with a fine layer of sugar.

Preheat the oven to 425°F. Position the top rack in the middle of the oven. In a medium bowl, mix together the Grand Marnier mixture and:

½ cup Pastry Cream

In a large copper or stainless-steel bowl, mix together:

6 egg whites, at room temperature

A pinch of salt

Whisk until soft peaks form. Add:

2 teaspoons cornstarch

Beat a few more seconds, then sprinkle on:

⅓ cup sugar

Beat until soft peaks form. Quickly but gently fold the egg whites into the pastry cream mixture until just blended. Pour the soufflé mixture into the prepared dish. Place the dish in the middle of the oven and bake until the soufflé is puffed and browned, about 25 minutes (7 to 8 minutes for ramekins). Serve immediately with heavy cream or Vanilla Pouring Custard (page 198), if you like.

Buckwheat Crêpes

MAKES ABOUT 4 CUPS BATTER,
ENOUGH FOR 30 CRÊPES

At one time, my fondness for crêpes almost led me to open a crêperie. Friends prevailed and I opened a restaurant instead, but crêpes are still one of my favorite desserts—especially made with buckwheat flour. The batter is best made a day in advance.

Warm in a small saucepan:

> **2 cups milk**
> **¼ teaspoon salt**
> **½ teaspoon sugar**
> **4 tablespoons (½ stick) butter**

When the butter has melted, remove from the heat and let cool. Measure into a bowl and stir together:

> **1 cup unbleached all-purpose flour**
> **¼ cup buckwheat flour**

Make a well in the flour and stir in:

> **1 tablespoon vegetable oil**
> **3 eggs**

Stir until the batter is stiff and free of lumps. Add the milk mixture, bit by bit, whisking until smooth after each addition. If the batter is lumpy, pour through a strainer. Whisk in:

> **½ cup beer**

Cover and refrigerate overnight. Take the batter out of the refrigerator 1 hour before frying the crêpes.

Heat a crêpe pan (a 6-inch steel pan with shallow sloping sides) over medium heat. Moisten a folded paper towel with oil and grease the hot pan lightly. Using a small ladle or large spoon, pour in about 2 tablespoons batter. Tilt and rotate the pan to cover it evenly with the batter. Cook until brown, about a minute or two, and with the aid of a butter knife, lift up an edge and use your fingers to grasp it and flip it over. The crêpe will be very thin and hard to turn with a spatula; using your hands is really the best way and with a little practice, it's easy to do. Cook briefly on the other side, no more than a minute, and turn the crêpe out onto a plate. (As with pancakes, consider the first crêpe or two a test.) Serve the crêpes right away, hot from the pan, or continue to cook crêpes, stacking them one atop the next. The crêpes can sit at room temperature for several hours and be reheated before serving. Spread them with flavored butter; fold them into triangles, like little handkerchiefs, on a baking sheet; sprinkle with sugar; and reheat them in a hot oven for a few minutes. Or reheat them in a frying pan (folded or not). Cooked crêpes (and any unused batter) can be covered and stored in the refrigerator for 2 days.

VARIATIONS

⁜ Buckwheat crêpes are very good with a compound butter made with citrus juice and zest and sugar. Or spread them with fruit preserves or marmalade.

⁜ Drizzle buttered crêpes with warm honey.

⁜ Crêpes can also be taken in a savory direction, with grated Gruyère cheese and ham, for example.

Buckwheat Crêpes with Tangerine Butter and Poached Kumquats

4 SERVINGS

Prepare and cook:

12 Buckwheat Crêpes (opposite)

Stack the crêpes as they are cooked. Don't refrigerate them if you are using them within a few hours.

Prepare:

Poached kumquats (page 365)

Prepare the tangerine butter. Remove, with a fine grater, the zest from:

1 tangerine

Cut the fruit in half and squeeze the juice into a measuring cup.

In a small bowl mix together:

4 tablespoons (½ stick) butter, softened

2 tablespoons sugar

Beat until soft and creamy and then, with a fork, stir in the zest and half of the tangerine juice. When mixed stir in:

2 tablespoons Grand Marnier or Cointreau

This will take a while, but keep stirring until the liquid is incorporated. If possible add a bit more of the tangerine juice. The butter will appear lumpy; this is not a problem.

Remove a crêpe from the stack and, with the pale side up, spread a spoonful of butter over half of the crêpe. Fold the crêpe in two over the butter, and then in half again to make a triangle. Repeat with the rest of the crêpes. Lay them out in a buttered baking dish in slightly overlapping rows. If desired, sprinkle them lightly with more liqueur. Right before serving, bake the crêpes in a preheated 350°F oven for 5 to 8 minutes to warm through. While the crêpes are heating in the oven, warm the poached kumquats. Serve the crêpes hot from the oven and top each serving with a few spoonfuls of poached kumquats and their syrup.

VARIATIONS

◆ Serve the crêpes with the segments of 3 tangerines, raw with their juice, instead of the poached kumquats.

◆ Instead of the tangerine, use an orange or a blood orange to make the butter. Use only 1 teaspoon of its zest and start with about one third of its juice.

◆ Serve with vanilla ice cream or tangerine sherbet.

Oatmeal Currant Cookies

MAKES 3 DOZEN COOKIES

What makes these cookies crisp is the mixing together of baking soda and boiling water before adding them to the batter.

Preheat the oven to 375°F.
Put into a small saucepan:

½ cup currants
¼ cup water

Warm over medium heat until the currants are plumped and the water is absorbed.

Measure into a blender and process until ground:

1½ cups (6 ounces) rolled oats

Transfer to a bowl and stir in:

½ cup flour
½ teaspoon salt
½ teaspoon ground cinnamon

In another bowl, cream together until light and fluffy:

8 tablespoons (1 stick) unsalted butter
6 tablespoons granulated sugar
6 tablespoons dark brown sugar

In a small bowl mix together:

1 teaspoon baking soda
1 teaspoon boiling water

Stir this baking soda mixture into the butter mixture, then beat in:

1 egg
1 teaspoon vanilla extract

Stir in the dry ingredients and the currants.

Scoop the dough into 1-inch balls and put them on parchment-paper-lined baking sheets about 2 inches apart. Bake for 8 to 10 minutes. Rotate the baking sheets in the oven halfway through baking. When done they should be golden brown around the edges and soft in the center.

Chocolate Crackle Cookies

MAKES ABOUT 3 DOZEN COOKIES

Chop together very fine, or pulverize in a food processor:

1 cup almonds, toasted
2 tablespoons sugar

Put them in a bowl, and sift over:

½ cup flour
½ teaspoon baking powder

Mix together.

Melt in a heat-proof bowl over simmering water:

8 ounces bittersweet chocolate, coarsely chopped
3 tablespoons butter

Stir in:

1½ tablespoons brandy

Set the mixture aside off the heat. Whisk together:

2 eggs, at room temperature
¼ cup sugar

Continue whisking until the mixture forms a ribbon, about 5 to 7 minutes. Stir in the melted chocolate and the almond and flour mixture. Chill the dough in the refrigerator for 1 to 2 hours or until firm.

Before baking, preheat the oven to 325°F.
Fill a small bowl with:

Granulated sugar

Fill another small bowl with:

Sifted powdered sugar

Roll the cookie dough into 1-inch balls. Roll a few at a time in the granulated sugar to coat them, then roll them in the powdered sugar. Set them on parchment-lined baking sheets 1 inch apart. Bake for 12 to 15 minutes. Midway through baking, rotate the baking sheets for even baking. When the cookies are done they will have cracks in their white shells and they will be firm on the edges, but still soft in the center. Do not overbake.

Butter Cookies

MAKES ABOUT 4 DOZEN COOKIES

This is a classic cookie to serve with a bowl of sliced fruit or a poached fruit compote (see page 364). The dough can be formed into logs of different shapes—round, square, oval— before chilling and slicing; or roll it out and cut with cookie cutters.

Cream together until light and fluffy:

> **1 cup (2 sticks) unsalted butter, softened**
> **⅔ cup sugar**

Beat in:

> **1 teaspoon vanilla extract**
> **½ teaspoon salt**
> **1 teaspoon lemon zest (optional)**
> **1 egg, at room temperature**
> **2 teaspoons milk**

Add gradually, stirring until just incorporated:

> **2¼ cups unbleached all-purpose flour**

Divide the dough into thirds and shape each portion into a log with a diameter of about 1½ inches. Shape the logs into ovals, squares, or rectangles for different-shaped cookies. Wrap the logs in plastic wrap and chill until firm, about 2 hours. The logs can be frozen for up to 2 months. Unwrap the logs and slice cookies about ¼ inch thick. If you like, slice only as many cookies as you need and return the log to the freezer for later.

For rolled cookies that can be shaped with cookie cutters, divide the dough in half. Roll each half between two pieces of parchment paper until the dough is uniformly ¼ inch thick. Transfer to a baking sheet and refrigerate for 20 to 30 minutes or until the dough is firm. Gently peel away the top layer of parchment and turn the dough over onto a fresh layer of parchment paper. Then gently peel away the second layer of parchment. Cut the dough into shapes with a knife or a cookie cutter.

Preheat the oven to 350°F. Transfer the cookies with a spatula onto lined baking sheets, spacing them 2 inches apart. Bake for about 10 minutes, or until golden. If you like, decorate the baked cookies with frosting.

VARIATIONS

◆ For spiced cookies, add 1 teaspoon ground cinnamon and ¼ teaspoon ground ginger along with the flour.
◆ Sprinkle the cookies with granulated sugar or ground almonds before baking.

Cat's-Tongue Cookies

MAKES 3 DOZEN COOKIES

These are very thin, crisp, fragile cookies that complement soft desserts such as sherbets, ice creams, and fruit compotes.

Preheat the oven to 325°F.
Cream until light and fluffy:

> **4 tablespoons (½ stick) butter, softened**
> **⅓ cup sugar**

Beat in one at a time, mixing well after each addition:

> **2 egg whites, at room temperature**

Stir in:

> **¼ teaspoon vanilla extract**

And then mix in until just incorporated:

> **½ cup minus 1 tablespoon flour**
> **¼ teaspoon salt**

Scoop the batter into a pastry bag fitted with a small round tip. Line baking sheets with parchment paper or, even better, nonstick silicone sheets. Pipe 2-inch-long straight lines of batter 1 inch apart. Bake for 7 to 10 minutes or until golden brown, rotating the baking sheets halfway through for even baking. Gently remove the cookies while still warm by running a small offset spatula underneath each one. When cool, store in an airtight container.

VARIATION

◆ Instead of piping the batter, use a spoon or offset spatula to spread the batter very thin in the shape of cats' tongues—or other shapes.

Chocolate Truffles

MAKES ABOUT 30 TRUFFLES

Sift into a small bowl and set aside:

½ cup cocoa

Melt together in a medium heat-proof bowl set over simmering water:

½ pound bittersweet chocolate
10 tablespoons (1¼ sticks) unsalted butter

Stir in:

6 tablespoons heavy cream
1 to 2 tablespoons brandy (optional)

Refrigerate the mixture until very firm (this will take a few hours). Using a melon-baller or a small spoon, scoop ½-inch balls onto a parchment-lined baking sheet. Roll the balls between your palms to smooth them and then drop them, a few at a time, into the sifted cocoa. Roll them in the cocoa to coat and place on a parchment-lined tray. Put in the refrigerator until firm. Truffles may be stored in the refrigerator for up to 2 weeks. For best flavor, bring truffles to room temperature before serving.

VARIATIONS

◆ Use different liqueurs, such as Cognac, pear eau-de-vie, or grappa, for different flavors.
◆ Roll the truffles in powdered sugar or ground toasted nuts instead of cocoa.

Candied Citrus Peel

This is a delicious way to use the peels of citrus after they've been juiced. Candied peel, either plain or dipped in chocolate, makes a zesty ending for a meal. Candy only unsprayed, organic citrus fruit.

Cut 2 grapefruits, 8 lemons or tangerines, or 4 medium oranges in half. Juice them; drink the juice or save it for another purpose. Put the juiced halves in a saucepan and cover with cold water by an inch or so. Bring to a boil over medium heat. Lower the heat and simmer until the peel is very tender when tested with the point of a paring knife. Start checking after 10 minutes. Let the peel cool until it can be handled easily. With a spoon, scrape out the pulp and as much of the white part of the rind as possible. Cut the peel into long strips, about ⅛ to ¼ inch wide. Put the strips of peel in a heavy saucepan. Add:

4 cups sugar
2 cups water

Cook over medium heat, stirring the mixture often, until the sugar is dissolved and the syrup is simmering. (If there is not enough syrup to completely submerge the strips of peel, add additional sugar and water in the same two-to-one proportions.) Maintain the heat so the syrup simmers slowly. Cook until the peel looks translucent and the syrup is thick and bubbling. Turn up the heat and cook the syrup to the thread stage (the syrup will form a thread when it is dropped from the spoon), 230°F measured with a candy thermometer. Remove the pan from the heat and cool for 5 minutes.

Set a wire rack over a baking sheet and carefully scoop out the strips of peel with a small, flat strainer or slotted spoon. Spread the strips evenly on the cooling rack and let them dry overnight. The next day toss the strips of candied peel with granulated sugar in a large mixing bowl, separating any strips that stick together. Store in an airtight container in the refrigerator. Candied peel will keep for months. Save the syrup to flavor drinks or thin with water and use it to poach dried fruits.

Apple Jellies

MAKES ABOUT SIXTY-FOUR 1-INCH PIECES

Jellies, also known as fruit paste or *pâte de fruit*, are beautiful bite-size confections with intense fruit flavor. Fruits such as apples, quince, and plums are slowly cooked with sugar to a concentrated purée, then cooled in a mold or pan until set and firm. The jellies can be cut into all sorts of shapes, rolled in sugar, and served as candies. Without a sugar coating, fruit paste is a delicious accompaniment to cheese.

Lightly rub an 8- by 8-inch baking dish with flavorless vegetable oil. Line with parchment paper and lightly oil the parchment.
In a large heavy-bottomed pot, combine:

>**8 medium apples (about 3 pounds), washed, quartered, and cored**
>
>**1 cup water**

Cover and cook over medium heat until the apples are soft, about 20 minutes.

Pass the mixture through a food mill or sieve. Return the purée to the pot and stir in:

>**1½ cups sugar**
>
>**Juice of 1 lemon**

Simmer over low heat, stirring often, for about 1 hour. As the mixture cooks and reduces, it starts to thicken and bubble. Scrape the bottom of the pan thoroughly while stirring to keep the purée from sticking and burning. Wear an oven mitt to avoid being scorched by any spatters. The purée is done when it holds a mounded shape. To be sure, breifly chill a small amount on a plate in the freezer. It should appear and feel jelled.

Spread the mixture evenly into the prepared dish. Cool for several hours or overnight. When cooled completely, invert onto a parchment-lined baking sheet. Remove the top layer of parchment paper. Leave to dry, uncovered, overnight. The paste should be firm enough to cut. If not, put the paste in a 150°F oven for an hour or more until firm. Let cool completely before cutting. The paste can be stored whole, wrapped tightly in plastic. Or trim the edges and cut into 1-inch pieces before wrapping. Store at room temperature or refrigerated for up to a year.

VARIATIONS

◆ Before serving, toss the pieces in granulated sugar to coat.

◆ Quince paste and plum paste can be made in the same manner. Wash quinces well and rub off their fuzz before cutting and coring. Increase the water to 3 cups and the sugar to 2 cups. Don't add the lemon juice until the purée has finished cooking.

Candied Nuts

MAKES 3½ CUPS

Serve these nuts as candy, use them to garnish a cake, or fold into homemade ice cream.

Preheat the oven to 325°F.
In a medium bowl whisk until frothy:
>**1 egg white**

Add:
>**¾ cup brown sugar**
>**1 tablespoon ground cinnamon**
>**½ teaspoon ground ginger**
>**A pinch of ground cloves**
>**A pinch of cayenne pepper**
>**¼ teaspoon salt**
>**2 teaspoons vanilla extract**

Stir until combined, then add:
>**3½ cups (about 1 pound) pecan or**
>**walnut halves or whole almonds**

Mix together until all the nuts are coated. Pour onto a lightly oiled baking sheet. Bake for 30 minutes. Turn the nuts from time to time with a large offset spatula until all the nuts are coated and dry. Let cool before serving. Store in an airtight container.

Raspberry Syrup

MAKES ABOUT 2½ CUPS

Try this syrup mixed with sparkling water to make fruit sodas, or add to lemonade with a sprig of mint to make pink raspberry lemonade. For an aperitif, pour a little into a glass and add white wine, Champagne, or spirits.

Combine in a medium heavy-bottomed saucepan:
>**1 pint (2 cups) raspberries**
>**1 cup water**
>**2 tablespoons sugar**

Cook over medium heat, stirring constantly, until the berries begin to break down and release their juices, about 4 minutes. Add:
>**1½ cups cold water**
>**½ teaspoon fresh lemon juice**

Bring to a boil, then immediately turn down to a simmer and skim off any foam that bubbles to the top. Cook for 15 minutes. Strain the mixture through a cheesecloth-lined strainer, pressing on the fruit to squeeze out all the juices. Return the liquid to the pan and add:
>**1½ cups sugar**

Stir until the sugar dissolves. Bring to a boil and cook for 2 minutes. Remove from the heat and let cool. Store in a tightly sealed container in the refrigerator for up to 3 weeks.

VARIATION
◆ Use other berries instead—cranberries, blackberries, or olallieberries, for example.

Apricot Jam

MAKES 4 CUPS

Jam making doesn't always have to be a big production. I sometimes make small amounts and keep it in the refrigerator instead of canning it for unrefrigerated storage. Apricot jam is especially versatile as a glaze for an apple tart or almond cake, or as the base for a soufflé.

Put a small plate in the freezer for testing the jam later. Pit and cut up into ½-inch pieces:

2½ pounds ripe apricots (about 6 cups)

If you like, to give a bitter almond flavor to the jam, crack open apricot pits with a hammer and remove 4 kernels; set aside. Put the apricot chunks in a medium heavy-bottomed nonreactive pot, and stir in:

3¾ cups sugar

Bring the apricots and sugar to a boil, lower the heat to medium, and boil steadily, stirring often, for 20 to 25 minutes, skimming off any foam that rises to the top. As the liquid thickens and the fruit becomes soft and translucent, start testing for consistency by putting a spoonful of jam on the chilled plate to cool down quickly. When the jam is the thickness you want, stir in:

Juice of 1 lemon

Allow the jam to cool, put in a container with an apricot pit in each one, and store in the refrigerator for up to a year.

VARIATION

◆ For long storage, prepare four 8-ounce canning jars and self-sealing lids according to the manufacturer's instructions. When the jam is cooked, put an apricot kernel into each hot sterilized jar, and carefully ladle in the jam, allowing at least ¼ inch of headspace. Follow the manufacturer's instructions for sealing the jars.

Caramel Sauce

MAKES ABOUT 1 CUP

Serve warm caramel sauce with ice cream or stir it (at room temperature) into just-made ice cream before putting it in the freezer to firm up. It is lovely drizzled over poached pears.

Measure and set aside:

¾ cup heavy cream

Put in a medium heavy-bottomed saucepan:

1 cup sugar

Carefully pour in:

6 tablespoons water

Cook over medium heat, without stirring, until the sugar starts to caramelize. Swirl the pan gently if the sugar is browning unevenly. When the caramel is uniformly golden brown, remove from the heat. Stand back from the pan and add ¼ cup of the measured cream. Stir slowly with a wooden spoon, until combined. Add the rest of the cream and:

½ teaspoon vanilla extract
A pinch of salt

Let cool and strain if necessary. Serve warm or let cool and store in the refrigerator for up to 2 weeks. Reheat gently over simmering water before serving.

VARIATION

◆ For coffee caramel sauce, with the second addition of cream stir in 3 tablespoons brewed espresso and, if you want, 1 tablespoon coffee-flavored liqueur.

Simple Frosting

MAKES ABOUT 2 CUPS

This is a basic frosting good for cupcakes and decorated cookies. This makes enough frosting for one 9-inch cake or 24 cupcakes.

Beat until light and fluffy:

> **12 tablespoons (1½ sticks) unsalted butter, softened**

Beat in:

> **1⅓ cups powdered sugar, sifted**

Continue beating until light and fluffy. Add:

> **1 teaspoon vanilla extract**
> **½ teaspoon fresh lemon juice**

Beat until smooth.

VARIATION

◆ Flavor the frosting with 2 ounces melted, but not warm, bittersweet chocolate, or with ½ teaspoon lemon, orange, or tangerine zest.

Chocolate Sauce

MAKES ABOUT 2 CUPS

In a medium heavy-bottomed saucepan, warm together:

> **½ cup heavy cream**
> **½ cup milk**
> **¼ cup sugar**
> **2 tablespoons unsalted butter**

Stir to dissolve the sugar. When the butter is melted, add:

> **½ pound bittersweet chocolate, chopped**
> **1 teaspoon vanilla extract**

Turn off the heat. Let the mixture stand for a few minutes and then whisk until smooth. Serve warm. This sauce can be covered and stored in the refrigerator for up to 2 weeks. Reheat over simmering water.

VARIATION

◆ For a thick chocolate glaze to use as a simple frosting, warm ½ cup cream, turn off the heat, add 4 ounces chopped semisweet chocolate, let sit, and whisk together when the chocolate is melted. This will thicken as it cools. While still soft, pour or spread over cakes or cupcakes.

Whipped Cream

MAKES ABOUT 2 CUPS

In a cold stainless-steel bowl, whisk together:

1 cup cold heavy cream
1 tablespoon sugar, or to taste
½ teaspoon vanilla extract

Keep whisking until the cream just holds a soft shape.

VARIATIONS

• Add ⅛ teaspoon orange flower water.
• Instead of using vanilla extract, split a 1-inch piece of vanilla bean and scrape its seeds into the cream.
• Stir in about 1 tablespoon rum, Cognac, Calvados, or another strong-flavored liqueur.

Tisane

Tisane is a fresh tea, an infusion of fragrant herbs, or flowers and spices, in boiling water. It is a soothing and refreshing finish to a meal, is complementary to most desserts, and offers a mild alternative to coffee. Tisane can be made from such flavorings as lemon verbena, mint, lemon thyme, lemon balm, hyssop, chamomile, citrus rind, and ginger—alone or in combination. The one I make most often is a combination of mint and lemon verbena. It is very beautiful made in a glass teapot so you can see the brilliant green leaves. Rinse several branches of fresh herbs, put them in a teapot (or saucepan), and pour boiling water over them. Let the tisane steep for several minutes and serve. I like to use small clear tea glasses, as they do in Morocco, so the lovely pale green color is visible.

Resources

THESE DAYS you can find almost anything you want by searching on the Internet. A great deal of free information about food, much of it reliable, is accessible instantaneously. You can research such subjects as organic farming and sustainable seafood; you can find local farmers' markets, CSA (community-supported agriculture) farms, community gardens, and recycling centers; and you can easily locate such material as video demonstrations of cooking techniques, archives of recipes, and innumerable online communities and blogs devoted to various aspects of food. Furthermore, you can read reviews of, compare prices for, and make purchases of heritage seeds, organic olive oil, dried beans, spices, knives and cookware, and on and on.

Don't forget, however, that the benefits of shopping locally at farmers' markets include learning about the agriculture of your own locality directly from the farmer—not to mention participating in a real community rather than a virtual one. And rather than rely exclusively on e-commerce for nonlocal products, whenever possible shop at nearby stores and groceries where you can taste things and learn about them at firsthand, before you buy. This is particularly helpful when buying such staples as cheese, wine, and olive oil.

Nor can the Internet ever be a substitute for your own library of cookbooks and other books about food. The number of books about food that I love is too long to list, but I would like to recommend a few authors that have inspired me with their passion for the traditions and beauty of simple food and fresh ingredients. Richard Olney and Elizabeth David are the two twentieth-century cooks most responsible for fine-tuning my food sensibilities. The following are my favorites, but all their other cookbooks are well worth reading, too. Olney was also the chief editorial consultant for the production in the late 1970s and early 1980s of a worthwhile twenty-eight-volume Time-Life series of illustrated cookbooks called *The Good Cook*.

> *Simple French Food*, by Richard Olney
> *Elizabeth David Classics*, by Elizabeth David
> *French Provincial Cooking*, by Elizabeth David
> *Honey from a Weed*, by Patience Gray

And for reference:

> *The Oxford Companion to Food*, by Alan Davidson
> *On Food and Cooking: The Science and Lore of the Kitchen*,
>   by Harold McGee

The Oxford Companion is not only an up-to-date, comprehensive, and reliable compendium of knowledge; it is also genuinely companionable:

relaxed, pleasant, witty, and beautifully written. McGee's brilliant book provides an expansive and convincing treatment of current scientific knowledge about the many everyday mysteries of cooking and eating, on every level from the historical to the molecular. He has an interesting Web site:

www.curiouscook.com

Paul Johnson has been fishmonger for Chez Panisse for over thirty years, educating all of us about fish, what really fresh fish is, and sustainable fisheries. He has lots of good information and links on his Web site:

www.webseafood.com.

I am involved in a few organizations I would encourage anyone interested in preserving traditional food values to investigate:

Slow Food International: www.slowfood.com

Slow Food USA: www.slowfoodusa.org

Chez Panisse Foundation: www.chezpanissefoundation.org

Seeds of Change: www.seedsofchange.com

Glossary

Aromatic vegetables, vegetables that can withstand long cooking and add deep sweet flavor to soups, broths, stuffings, stews, and braises; most commonly considered to be onions, carrots, and celery, but fennel and leeks are used this way as well.

Blanch, to immerse briefly in boiling water.

Boil, to heat to the boiling point; to be in boiling water, which for water at sea level is 212°F (100°C).

Bouquet garni, aromatic herbs or plants tied together into a little bundle, used to flavor stews and sauces, and removed before serving.

Braise, to cook slowly with a small amount of liquid in a closed pan.

Brown, as applies to meat and vegetables, to cook the surface until brown in color.

Caramelize, strictly speaking, means to cook sugar until it liquefies and browns. The more sugar cooks, the browner it gets, and the more pronounced the distinctive strong flavor of burnt sugar. Foods in general are said to caramelize when they have browning reactions as they are being grilled, or roasted in the oven, or passed under the direct flame of a broiler or a propane torch.

Chiffonade, to slice leafy herbs, lettuces, or greens crosswise into very thin strips or ribbons.

Clarified butter, butter that has had all of the milk solids and water removed; also called drawn butter. Clarified butter has a high smoking temperature and is good for sautéing and frying.

Court bouillon, a briefly cooked vegetable stock flavored with white wine, primarily used for poaching fish.

Cream, to beat butter and sugar together until lightened and aerated.

Crème fraîche, heavy cream that has been cultured and thickened with a live enzyme like the one found in buttermilk. Crème fraîche has a wonderful rich, tangy flavor and is very useful in cooking because it will not separate when boiled.

Deglaze, to add liquid to a pan to dissolve the flavorful residue left in the pan after browning or roasting meat or vegetables.

Dice, to cut into even cubes.

Dock, in baking, to prick rolled-out dough to keep air bubbles from forming while the pastry is cooking.

Double boiler, a saucepan with a detachable upper compartment heated by boiling water in the lower one, used to protect foods from direct heat.

Dredge, to coat lightly with flour or sugar.

Drizzle, to slowly pour a very thin stream of liquid in a random pattern over the surface of food.

Fillet, to bone a fish by removing its fleshy sides from its rib cage. Also, a fleshy boneless piece of meat or a boned side of a fish.

Fold, to gently incorporate a heavier mixture or ingredient into a lighter and airier one, such as whipped egg whites, without stirring or beating, mixing the two together by cutting down into the center and lifting with a rubber spatula or other tool while rotating the bowl.

Gratin, a dish that has been browned in the oven or under the broiler and formed a thin crunchy crust on top.

Julienne, to cut vegetables or other foods into long, thin matchsticks.

Macerate, to tenderize and flavor a food by soaking it in a liquid.

Mandoline, a utensil, for slicing vegetables, made of a flat frame with adjustable cutting blades.

Marinate, to flavor fish, meat, or other foods in a marinade (a mixture of oil, herbs, spices, aromatic vegetables, and vinegar or wine) prior to cooking.

Mince, to cut food into very small, uniform pieces.

Mirepoix, a French term for a mixture of chopped onions, carrots, and celery (usually about twice as much onion as carrot and celery) used as an aromatic base for numerous stews, soups, and sauces.

Mise en place, a French term that means the setup in which ingredients have been measured, prepared, and laid out in advance, so that they are ready and within reach when you actually start the cooking process.

Poach, to cook gently submerged in simmering liquid.

Purée, to grind, press, or strain to the consistency of a soft paste or thick liquid.

Reduce, to boil down and concentrate.

Sauté, to rapidly cook food in a small amount of fat in a shallow pan by keeping it moving over high heat.

Season, to enhance the flavors of food by adding salt, pepper, herbs, or spices.

Shred, to pull or tear apart into shreds something fibrous (such as a cooked chicken breast or a braised pork shoulder), or to cut cabbage and other leafy vegetables into thin shred-like strips.

Simmer, to cook food gently in water or other liquid that is heated to the point at which bubbles are just breaking on the surface, not to a full, rolling boil.

Soffritto, an Italian term for a sautéed mixture of chopped aromatic vegetables cooked at the outset of a recipe that forms a foundation for many soups, sauces, and stews. See *mirepoix*.

Toss, to mix ingredients together lightly and gently.

Whip, to whisk rapidly into a froth.

Whisk, to stir or beat rapidly, with a light, sweeping, aerating motion. (A whisk is a handheld beater consisting of a bulbous cage of wires attached to a handle.)

Zest, the thin, colored, oily layer of peel on a citrus fruit, which can be removed in paper-thin strips with a swivel-bladed vegetable peeler (or in a tiny julienne using a hand tool called a zester) or grated off with a fine grater.

Index

Alice Waters was born on April 28, 1944, in Chatham, New Jersey. She graduated from the University of California at Berkeley in 1967 with a degree in French cultural studies before training at the International Montessori School in London. Her daughter, Fanny, was born in 1983.

Chez Panisse Restaurant opened in 1971, serving a single fixed-price menu that changed daily. The set menu format remains at the heart of Alice's philosophy of serving the most delicious organic products only when they are in season. Over the course of three decades, Chez Panisse has developed a network of local farmers and ranchers whose dedication to sustainable agriculture assures Chez Panisse a steady supply of pure and fresh ingredients.

The upstairs café at Chez Panisse opened in 1980 with an open kitchen, a wood-burning pizza oven, and an à la carte menu. Café Fanny, a stand-up café that serves breakfast and lunch, was opened a few miles away in 1984.

In 1996, in celebration of the restaurant's twenty-fifth anniversary, Alice created the Chez Panisse Foundation. The Edible Schoolyard at Berkeley's Martin Luther King Jr. Middle School is the foundation's primary beneficiary. More information is available on the foundation's website, www.chezpanissefoundation.org.